Teaching for Commitment

Teaching for Commitment

Liberal Education, Indoctrination, and Christian Nurture

ELMER JOHN THIESSEN

McGill-Queen's University Press
Montreal & Kingston • London • Buffalo

Gracewing. • Leominster

© McGill-Queen's University Press 1993
ISBN 0-7735-0998-4 (cloth)
ISBN 0-7735-1162-8 (paper)

Legal deposit fourth quarter 1993
Bibliothéque national du Québec

Printed in the United States on acid-free paper

This book has been published with the help of grants from the
Canadian Federation for the Humanities, using funds provided by the
Social Sciences and Humanities Research Council of Canada, and
from Medicine Hat College.

Published in the United Kingdom by
Gracewing,
2 Southern Avenue
Leominster
Herefordshire HR6 OQF
ISBN 0 85244 248 3

British Library Cataloguing in Publication Data
A catalogue for this record is available from the British Library

---

CANADIAN CATALOGUING IN PUBLICATION DATA

Thiessen, Elmer John, 1942-
    Teaching for commitment : liberal education,
    indoctrination and Christian nurture
    Includes bibliographical references and index.
    ISBN 0-7735-0998-4 (bound)
    ISBN 0-7735-1162-8 (pbk)
    1. Christian education—Philosophy.
    2. Education, Humanistic—Philosophy.   I. Title.
    LC109.T48   1993   268'.01   C93-090265-3

Various parts of the arguments in this book draw on my previously
published articles. Chapters 3 and 4 draw extensively from articles
appearing in the *Journal of Philosophy of Education,* and the *Canadian
Journal of Educational Thought.* Earlier versions of certain parts of the
author's argument have also appeared in *Spectrum, The Christian
Librarian, Ethics in Education,* and *Salt: Journal of the Religious Studies
and Moral Education Council,* published by the Religious and Moral
Education Council of The Alberta Teachers' Association.

In several chapters the author draws on arguments previously
published in *Interchange*: Thiessen, E.J. 1984. "Indoctrination and
Religious Education." *Interchange* 15(3):27-43; Thiessen, E.J. 1989.
"R.S. Peters on Liberal Education – A Reconstruction." *Interchange*
20(4):1-8. Copyright to articles published by *Interchange* is held by the
Journal. Reprinted by permission of Kluwer Academic Publishers.

The author is grateful to the editors of all these journals for
permission to draw on the previously published material.

To
Magdalene,
who has shared the challenge of nurturing our children in the Christian faith,

and
Audrey, Andrew and Gregory,
who, in their own unique ways, have chosen to give creative expression to the Christian faith in which they were nurtured.

Contents

Preface

Religious nurture or a confessional approach to religious education, such as occurs in the home, in the church, and in religiously based schools and colleges, is receiving a lot of bad press these days. Opposition to such religious instruction is very often expressed by labelling it "religious indoctrination." The central purpose of this book is to defend religious nurture and instruction against this frequent charge of indoctrination. In doing so, I will question the prevailing ideal of liberal education which underlies the charge of religious indoctrination. My purpose is also a constructive one: to formulate the outlines of a new ideal of liberal education, which will in turn lead to a new definition of indoctrination.

Although I will illustrate my arguments primarily by referring to initiation into the Christian religion, much of what I have to say could apply equally to the initiation of individuals into other religious traditions. It should also be noted that in defending the central thesis of this book, I am addressing both the critics of Christian (or religious) nurture and Christians (or adherents to other religious traditions) who often find themselves subject to the charge of indoctrination by those critics.

My first serious study of religious indoctrination was done in relation to my doctoral program at the University of Waterloo. My dissertation, completed in 1980, dealt with the problem of indoctrination and religion, but from the rather narrow approach of conceptual analysis. I concluded that there was a lot of confusion in the concept of indoctrination. The charge of indoctrination was incoherent, even empty.

Over the years, I have become increasingly unhappy with my first response to the charge of religious indoctrination. My dissatisfaction is due, in part, to the approach I had taken—the focus of which was conceptual analysis. Yes, I still agree that there are problems with the concept of indoctrination that is used in making the charge. But this way of doing philosophy is no longer in fashion. Philosophers have come to realize that the clarification of language, while important, is not enough. We need to deal with the substantive issues involved in moral questions. We need to uncover the assumptions embedded in language. We need to focus on the confusion inherent in our values, not just the confusions inherent in our concepts.

I have gradually come to realize that there are problems with the values underlying the commonly held ideal of liberal education—the context out of which charges of indoctrination are made. This book grows out of an increasing dissatisfaction with what I will call the Enlightenment ideal of liberal education. My purpose is not only to answer the charge of indoctrination which is based on this Enlightenment ideal of liberal education, but also to propose a reconstruction of this ideal, a post-liberal ideal of liberal education.

Frederick Buechner, lecturing at Harvard, suggested that "all theology, like all fiction, is at its heart autobiography" (1982, 1). The same can surely also be said about philosophy. Although every attempt will be made to write as objectively as possible, in the best of philosophical tradition, the reader should perhaps be forewarned that this book also represents the culmination of a lifelong personal struggle on the part of the writer. My roots are Christian; I was raised in a Mennonite home and grew up in several small prairie towns in southern Saskatchewan, in the heart of what is sometimes known as the Canadian Bible Belt. Yet, most of my formal education, including all of my university study, occurred in a "secular" context, in the best of a liberal education tradition. This book therefore represents a personal and at times painful attempt to achieve a harmony between the faith of Athens and the faith of Jerusalem.

I should note that some quoted sources use masculine nouns and pronouns to refer to both sexes. This is not in keeping with current usage, but I have left the quotes as they are for a number of reasons. I believe it is important to preserve the original quotations. Not to do so would be counter to a central thrust of my book: that traditions need to be respected for what they were. Growth is possible only from within a specific tradition. Therefore, we need to acknowledge the past to which we are indebted, and hope, at least on a few matters, to do better than our forebearers.

I am grateful to Medicine Hat College for granting me a sabbatical leave in 1978-9, at the University of Waterloo, when I wrote my doctoral dissertation, a first exploration of the topic of this book. Work continued during a second sabbatical leave in 1985-6, which was spent at Oxford University. Medicine Hat College and the Social Sciences and Humanities Research Council of Canada provided financial support and release from teaching duties during 1989-90, during which time the book was completed. I am also grateful to Medicine Hat College for an additional publication grant.

The research grant from the Social Sciences and Humanities Research Council of Canada also made possible a return visit to England in April and May 1990, enabling me to benefit from the expertise of many individuals. In addition to providing valuable insights and criticisms of my ideas, Jeff Astley, Trevor Cooling, and Terry McLaughlin kindly arranged sessions where I could deliver papers based on my work. I am also thankful to Richard Allen, David Attfield, Leslie Francis, Mark Halstead, John Hull, Ieaun Lloyd, Richard Russell, Nicola Slee, and Adrian Thatcher, who all gave of their precious time to listen to my ideas and to make criticisms and suggestions.

I am indebted to various Canadian and American friends and colleagues for their encouragement, advice, criticisms, and suggestions. Brian Hendley first challenged me to explore this topic and graciously put up with my first explorations. Harold Coward, Evelina Orteza-y-Miranda, Ron Neufeldt, Hugo Meynell, Terence Penelhum, all from the University of Calgary, have been so kind as to treat me as a colleague whenever I have felt the need to overcome the philosophical isolation that comes from teaching in a one-person philosophy department at Medicine Hat College. William Hare, Terence Penelhum, and Roy Wilson each commented on earlier drafts of a chapter. Bob Anderson, Gary Colwell, Jay Newman, and Ralph Page provided further valuable input and encouragement. My thanks also to John Franklin, who suggested the title of this book. Several anonymous readers provided many valuable comments on earlier drafts of the manuscript. I am indebted to both the Canadian Federation for the Humanities and McGill-Queen's University Press for their assistance and co-operation at each stage of the publication process. A special thanks to Peter Blaney for his faith in the project and for his constant encouragement. I also wish to thank Joy Chandler for her able assistance in the final stages of the writing process.

I especially want to thank my editor, Frances Rooney, who taught me more about writing style and proper English than I care to admit.

My family deserves special mention. I would like to express my thanks to my wife and children for putting up with a husband and father who, during the year in which most of this was written, was even more absent-mindedly absorbed in his own thoughts than is usually the case.

Things fall apart; the centre cannot hold;
Mere anarchy is loosed upon the world ...
The best lack all conviction, while the worst
Are full of passionate intensity.
                W.B. Yeats, *The Second Coming*

Therefore every teacher ... is like the owner of a house
who brings out of his storeroom new treasures as well as
old.   Matthew 13:52

Introduction

One of the central objections against religious instruction as it occurs in the home, in the church, and in church-related schools and colleges is that such instruction often, and even necessarily, involves indoctrination. For example, Robin Barrow and Ronald Woods, in their popular introductory text in the philosophy of education, open the topic of indoctrination with a description of a paradigm case, a Catholic school in which all the teachers are committed Catholics, where all the children come from Catholic homes and have parents who want them to be brought up as Catholics, and where the entire school is committed to nurturing children into the Catholic faith (1988, 70). But indoctrination is generally understood to be the very antithesis of liberal education in that it violates the principles of rationality, critical openness, freedom, and respect for persons. Indoctrination is therefore considered to be a highly immoral activity. My central purpose is to defend religious nurture and instruction against the frequently recurring charge of indoctrination.

It needs to be stressed that by "religious instruction" I mean the initiation of a person into a particular religious tradition – such as the Christian tradition. Indeed, I will illustrate my arguments primarily by referring to initiation into the Christian religion, because that is the religion with which I am most familiar. A description of Christian nurture will be provided in chapter 1. It should be noted, though, that most of what I have to say could be applied equally to the initiation of individuals into other religious traditions. The thesis of this book then is that initiation into the Christian tradition – also sometimes referred to as Christian nurture or catechesis or a confessional approach to religious instruction – should not automatically be labelled "indoctrination" where this term is understood in its pejorative sense as something immoral and to be avoided. I need to stress that I am only arguing that we should be much more cautious in making the charge of indoctrination with regard to Christian nurture. I want to establish that indoctrination is not inevitable or even as probable as is often assumed by liberals who attack the confessional approach to religious education.

A second aim of this book will be of primary interest to those readers who are Christians (or adherents to other religious traditions). While I agree that the charge of religious indoctrination is an important one which Christians need to take seriously, there is a danger that it can be taken too seriously, particularly if it is to a large extent unwarranted, as I hope to show in this book. I believe the charge has, in fact, been taken so seriously by some Christian educators that the fear of indoctrination has caused them to water down Christian nurture to such an extent that it fails in one of its primary functions – initiating individuals into the Christian tradition. This emphasis will no doubt be worrisome to those steeped in the liberal education tradition, so perhaps even they will want to examine those parts of the book where I challenge Christian parents and teachers not to be afraid to initiate children into the Christian tradition.

All this is not to say that indoctrination never occurs in Christian homes and schools. It can and sometimes does. But before we can legitimately make the charge of indoctrination we need to redefine the concept of indoctrination as it is traditionally understood. We also need to "deconstruct" and reconstruct the Enlightenment ideal of liberal education from which the charge arises. In particular, I will argue that liberal education needs to be more sensitive to the traditions in which a child has been nurtured. The ideals of autonomy, rationality, and critical openness also need to be modified so as to become more realistic and philosophically defensible. This need for realism in our educational ideals will in fact be a theme that runs throughout the book as I attempt to redefine these ideals in terms of "normal autonomy," "normal rationality," and "normal critical openness."

A third central aim of the book, therefore, involves both a reformulation of the ideal of liberal education and a redefinition of the concept of indoctrination. My reconstructions will seek to do justice to some themes found in an array of contemporary writings in philosophy which go by a variety of names: post-modernism; critical theory; hermeneutical philosophy; communitarian critiques of liberalism, conservativism, anti-foundationalism, the new sociology of knowledge and the new philosophy of science. However, although I will at times draw from some of this literature, my reconstruction of the ideal of liberal education will not be based on a systematic analysis of these writings. Instead, it will grow out of a careful critique of traditional understandings of indoctrination and liberal education.

A fourth but more secondary objective of this book concerns the practice of religious nurture. We can learn much from an examination of the charge of indoctrination that would help to develop a constructive approach to religious education that is specifically Christian. A reconstruction of the ideal of liberal education will lead to some practical suggestions as to how Christian parents and teachers should go about nurturing their children and students in the Christian faith.

Although I focus primarily on the charge of indoctrination as it relates to Christian nurture, the conclusions from an analysis of this problem will also have profound implications for education generally. It should be obvious that a reconstruction of the ideal of liberal education and a redefinition of the concept of indoctrination will necessitate a rethinking of what occurs in our "secular" public schools, which are often characterized as liberal institutions providing a liberal education. Such rethinking would seem to be called for given that many people feel our state-maintained system of public education is in disarray. My final purpose is to apply the ideal of liberal education and the concept of indoctrination to a state-maintained system of public education.

The charge of religious indoctrination raises a broad spectrum of concerns and issues. It crosses the boundaries of religion, philosophy, epistemology, ethics, and education. Although much has been written about indoctrination in the last twenty-five to thirty years, the treatment of the charge of indoctrination has unfortunately been rather narrow in focus. It has largely been the concern of educational philosophers writing for educational philosophers, most of whom belong to the analytic tradition of educational philosophy in which the primary concern is conceptual analysis, for example, clarifying the concept of indoctrination. Although part of my concern will be to evaluate critically the commonly held views concerning the meaning of "indoctrination," I wish to move beyond the sometimes narrow and seemingly futile preoccupation with conceptual clarification which has been typical of most of the rather extensive writing about indoctrination in the recent past.

I also wish to broaden the focus of the debate by drawing on the more recent research, in the various disciplines, which relates in some way to the issues and concerns surrounding the problem of indoctrination. Such a broadening of focus carries with it the risk of being judged superficial, but I am willing to run this risk. I am well aware that there is much additional literature in the related fields that bears on the concerns being discussed, but is not referred to in my discussion. However, I trust that I will draw on the other disciplines sufficiently to establish the claim that the charge of indoctrination against Christian nurture is to a large extent unwarranted.

In broadening the focus of the debate concerning indoctrination, I further hope that this discussion will be of interest not only to educational philosophers but also to specialists and students in fields such as philosophy and religious studies. Given the very practical nature of the problem being discussed, I hope that this book will also be read by those who are in any way involved in religious education, be they professional educators, pastors, educational administrators in churches, Sunday School teachers, or knowledgeable parents. I am particularly concerned that philosopher and non-philosopher alike understand what I have written. The danger of this approach is that neither type of reader will be entirely satisfied, but I am willing to run this risk: what is at stake here is of crucial importance to everyone, not only professional philosophers. It is therefore important that the arguments be presented in such a way that both the philosopher and lay reader can benefit. Every attempt has been made to keep the use of technical language to a minimum.

Chapter 1 explores the different forms of the charge of religious indoctrination and the alternative approaches to religious education that have been proposed as ways to avoid indoctrination. One way to answer the charge of religious indoctrination is to challenge the ideal of liberal education itself, which, it is argued in chapter 2, is the context out of which concern for indoctrination arises. My approach, however, is not to reject this ideal entirely, since I believe that Christian educators can and should accept it, though it needs to be qualified in some important respects.

Chapters 3 to 6 centre around four criteria thought to be essential to the concept of indoctrination – content, methods, intention, and consequences – and the important questions these criteria raise: (a) Is indoctrination necessarily limited to doctrines such as occur in religion? Are religious beliefs or doctrines more susceptible to indoctrination than scientific beliefs? (b) Is it wrong to initiate a child into a particular religious faith? Are the methods used to do this necessarily objectionable? (c) Are the intentions of religious parents or teachers suspect? (d) Is a closed mind more commonly a result of religious teaching than of scientific teaching? How open-minded should and can we be? The central thrust of these four chapters will be to show that there are problems with the way in which indoctrination is generally understood, and that we should therefore be extremely cautious in making the charge of indoctrination.

Chapter 7 is devoted to a frequently ignored aspect of the problem of indoctrination having to do with the sociological, political, and institutional dimensions of education. The argument centres on a recent important sociological study of a fundamentalist Christian school by Peshkin (1986), who describes the school as a "total institution" which indoctrinates. I will argue that Peshkin's conclusion is unwarranted because it is based on criteria that are problematic in that they fail to distinguish total institutions from liberal institutions.

Chapters 8 and 9 attempt to draw some conclusions from all this. I argue that the problems associated with the traditional charge of indoctrination call for a reconstruction of the ideal of liberal education – the context out of which the charge arises. This reconstructed notion of liberal education then leads to a new definition of indoctrination. The final chapter applies these reconstructed definitions of liberal education and indoctrination to Christian nurture. I try to show how Christian nurture can avoid indoctrination, satisfy the ideal of liberal education, and still boldly initiate a child into the Christian tradition.

1 The Charge of Religious Indoctrination

"Indoctrination" is a word which, by and large, has strongly pejorative overtones. It was not always so. In tracing the evolution of the concept of indoctrination, Gatchel notes that, until a little over half a century ago, the term "indoctrination" was no more offensive in educational circles than the term "education" (1972, 9). In fact, most dictionaries today still define indoctrination as a neutral term, as something akin to teaching and education. But the ways in which words are used can and do change over the years. Indoctrination is one word whose meaning has been so radically altered in the last half a century that it is now usually used as a derogatory term, as something incompatible with true education. In chapter 2 I will place this negative use of the term in a broader context, but for now it is sufficient to note that, when talking about the charge of religious indoctrination, we use the term "indoctrination" in its pejorative sense.

Much has been written about indoctrination since it acquired its negative overtones. Indeed, this notion has perhaps attracted more attention from educators and educational philosophers than any other, and has engendered a body of literature of its own (I will say more about this literature later in the chapter). The reason for all this attention is not hard to find. The charge of indoctrination seems to get to the heart of what we want to avoid in providing true education.

The charge of indoctrination surfaces again and again in discussions about education. While this book focuses on the charge of religious indoctrination, it is important to note that this is not the only context in which the charge is made. Public schooling and even university education have come under recent attack. The very titles of books are suggestive: *Illiberal Education: The Politics of Race and Sex on Campus* (D'Souza 1991); *The Closing of the American Mind* (Bloom 1987); *Compelling Belief: The Culture of American Schooling* (Arons 1983). D'Souza, in his carefully documented analysis of the agenda of political correctness on American university campuses, repeatedly uses the term indoctrination to draw attention to the new world-view consolidating itself at our universities (1991, 92, 155, 224, 227). Not only in the United States but also in Great Britain, the charge of indoctrination surfaces repeatedly in expressions of concern about a national curriculum (Roques 1989) or about leftist political programs subverting true education in the schools (Scruton, Ellis-Jones, et al. 1985).

The charge of indoctrination probably comes up most frequently in the context of religious instruction. One writer, commenting on a provincial study of religious education in Canada, sums up public attitudes in this way: "The public discussion of religious education in Ontario has continually been stalked by the ghost of 'religious indoctrination' " (Fernhout 1979, 20). This modern ghost is not limited in its appearances to a province or a country, but would seem to have international manifestations. In an important sociological analysis of a fundamentalist Christian school in Illinois, Alan Peshkin concludes that "as a total institution Bethany Baptist Academy logically indoctrinates its students" (1986, 284). A British writer introduces an article on indoctrination with an anecdote concerning advice given him by the headmaster of a secondary modern school after a disastrous lesson on sex which the writer had given to a class of fourteen-year-old boys early in his teaching career. "I've always said so, and I'll say it again, lad: you can teach anything you like in school, as long as you keep off just three things: religion, sex and politics" (J.P. White 1972a, 117). Why this advice? Here again, the ghost of indoctrination would seem to be making its appearance. More recently, another British writer expressed his regret at the potential resistance to rethinking an aspect of religious education in British schools because "the ghost of confessionalism may haunt so powerfully" (Copley 1990, 6). Confessionalism, as will be seen later, is often thought to be synonymous with indoctrination in modern thinking about religious education.

The central purpose of this book is to prove that the modern ghost of religious indoctrination is indeed ghost-like, largely a phantom of our liberal minds. But before proceeding with this daring enterprise,

I shall elucidate this charge that is so frequently made against religious instruction. This will be done, first, through some historical and then some philosophical observations and examples.

SOME HISTORICAL OBSERVATIONS AND EXAMPLES

A study of the history of education in Canada, the United States, Great Britain, and other western countries reveals a curious paradox. While all levels of education in these countries were initiated mainly by Christian churches, this child of church endeavour has, in the main, rejected its Christian parentage. The historic link between church and school, which once was accepted as normal and rational in practice, if not in theory, is increasingly being called into question. While education and religion were once considered to be inextricably intertwined, many people are now calling for their complete separation. Whereas the purpose of education was once understood to include initiation into the Christian faith, this is now viewed as archaic and a misuse of education. In fact, it is a commonly held position that the very idea of "religious education" in the old-fashioned sense of Christian nurture is a contradiction in terms.

Remnants of the past harmony between Christian religion and state education persist. A number of schools and even university buildings are still adorned with a biblical text over their main entrance. Over the door of Emerson Hall at Harvard, for example, are the words of Psalm 8:4: "What is man that thou art mindful of him?" In Canada, Bible readings, prayers, the singing of religious songs, and the observance of religious festivals still occur in some public schools. The long-standing close relation between religion and education in Britain has just recently been reaffirmed in what one writer has described as "the most obscure and complicated piece of religious education legislation in the history of this country" (Hull 1989, 119). The 1988 Education Reform Act requires that maintained schools in England and Wales ensure both that the daily act of worship "shall be wholly or mainly of a broadly Christian character" and that local syllabi of religious education "shall reflect the fact that the religious traditions in Great Britain are in the main Christian" (Her Majesty's Government 1988, 5-6).

For many people, however, these remnants of a partnership between church and state in education seem antiquated in the context of a secular society committed to secular education, and even these remnants are fast disappearing in the face of increasing scrutiny and criticism. Even in Britain, with its long tradition of an established state church, there is growing opposition to the traditional link between the Christian religion and education. John Hull, for example, expresses concern that Christianity is thrust "into a position of embarrassing prominence" in the 1988 Education Reform Act. He goes to great lengths to interpret (or reinterpret) the Christianizing clauses of the Act to incorporate the multi-faith approach to religious education that he has done so much to promote in Britain, calling those who oppose his interpretation "tribalistic" (1989, 119, 125). (The Education Reform Act was preceded by the influential report *Education for All*, more commonly referred to as the Swann Report [1985], which recommends a nondenominational and undogmatic approach to religious education that helps students to understand and appreciate the diversity of religious faiths. The report further urges the Department of Education to review the partnership between church and state as defined in the long-standing 1944 Education Act in light of the fact that Britain is today a multi-racial and multi-religious society.)

The disappearance of the traditional link between the Christian religion and public education is perhaps most pronounced in the United States where the First Amendment's "wall of separation" between church and state has been invoked to exclude any remnants of religion in schools. The culmination of this process is seen in the 1963 landmark Supreme Court case Abington Township v. Schempp, which removed compulsory prayer, Bible reading, and other religious ceremonies from the schools.

In Canada, the Charter of Rights and Freedoms adopted in 1982 has led to several precedent-setting decisions concerning religious education in state-maintained schools. On 23 September 1988, the Ontario Court of Appeal decision in Zylberberg et al. v. Sudbury Board of Education struck down a law which had compelled Ontario schools to hold daily religious exercises consisting of reading the Scriptures and repeating the Lord's Prayer. Then, on 30 January 1990, the Ontario Court of Appeal struck down a long-standing regulation requiring that religious education (i.e., Christian education) be included in Ontario public school curricula (Corporation of Canadian Civil Liberties Assoc. et al. v. Ontario et al.).

Historically, Quebec has had a "dual confessional" school system, one for Catholics and one for Protestants (Blair 1986, 21-6; Gourlay 1990). The province retains the dual confessional system, much of the responsibility for which shifted to the Ministry of Education (after its creation in 1964). "No longer did the bishops control Catholic education," writes a Catholic commentator (Gourlay 1990, 23). This may be somewhat of an overstatement since Protestant and Catholic committees were still retained and given power to make regulations, though with regard to confessional issues only. There is much ferment concerning education in Quebec today; many people are pressing for nondenominational, nonconfessional schools.

Why then is this traditional link between church and state in education being called into question in most western countries? There are, no doubt, many factors, such as the growing secularization of society and the growing acceptance of the ideal of the separation of church and state. There are two specific objections to state-supported Christian education which are, in my opinion, not always clearly differentiated. The first is based on the democratic principle of the freedom of religion: it is surely wrong to initiate all children in our schools into a particular religious tradition when many of them come from other religious backgrounds. I have no quarrel with this argument. In fact, given our present system of state-supported public education (a system which might itself be in need of challenge), I am quite in sympathy with those who object to various Christian observances such as the reciting of the Lord's Prayer as these are surely an affront to the fact of religious pluralism.

It is quite another matter, however, to object on specifically educational grounds to the initiation of children into a particular religious tradition. This is at the heart of the second objection to Christian nurture in our schools and is usually expressed by the charge of indoctrination. While this charge may not always be explicit, it is nonetheless at the root of much of the rejection of the traditional partnership between church and state in education as found in most Western societies. It is explicitly made, for example, in an essay providing historical and philosophical background to a recent report of the Commission on Private Schools in Ontario (Shapiro 1985). Here Mark Holmes identifies, as one of several approaches to the provision of education, the classical/Judaeo-Christian position, or the "traditionalist" view of education in which state education is given the mandate to foster cultural continuity via the transmission of Judaeo-Christian values (1985, 118-19). He points out that Ontario's Education Act still gives expression to this traditionalist approach when it speaks of the teacher's duty to "inculcate by precept and example respect for religion and the principles of Judaeo-Christian morality," although this section of the Education Act has fallen into disuse. It is to Holmes's credit that he clearly distinguishes the two basic criticisms of a traditionalist view of state education which I have already identified. First, he argues, "It becomes increasingly inappropriate ... to impose a single traditional, cultural hegemony" on a society characterized by cultural pluralism. A second criticism against traditionalism is that "it is ultimately dependent on indoctrination" (Holmes 1985, 119).[1]

Here it might be helpful to focus more specifically on developments in approaches to religious education in our schools (see Blair 1986; Hull 1984, ch. 3). I would like to identify three broadly distinguishable approaches to religious education as found in the history of state-supported schools in western countries. In the past, religious education was overtly Christian. Its aim was to nurture children in the Christian faith. Today we use the words "Christian nurture" or "confessional" to describe this approach, and many people, particularly in North America, have reacted to it by advocating that no religion at all be taught in our schools. Though perhaps never entirely put into practice, this approach has been, and for many people still is, the ideal. A third approach has emerged in the last fifteen years, perhaps in part due to the realization that religion is not dead or even dying. A more significant factor, no doubt, is the growing awareness of the pluralistic nature of western societies. Thus it is felt that while liberal education cannot include the teaching *of* religion, it should include the teaching *about* religion(s), justified not on theological but on educational grounds. This shift is particularly evident in Great Britain where the compulsory religious education courses in schools have clearly moved away from fostering Christian faith toward an open, descriptive, critical, enquiring study of world religions.[2] Examination of the rationale behind this transformation frequently reveals implicit if not explicit criticisms of the older confessional approach as indoctrinatory.

John Hull, though himself a Christian and sympathetic to Christian nurture, has been a leading exponent of the multi-faith approach to religious education in British schools. Hull has been particularly concerned to show that this new approach is compatible with Christian convictions and can even be justified from a Christian point of view. However, despite his sympathies with the Christian religion and with Christian nurture in certain contexts, Hull seems unable or unwilling to avoid painting the traditional nurturing approach in a negative light. For example, one of the reasons he gives for his embarrassment over the christianizing clauses in the 1988 Education Reform Act is that they are not "easily compatible with educational principles" (1989, 119). The rest of Hull's writings make it clear that he is here concerned about satisfying the principles of a liberal education, one of which is the avoidance of indoctrination.[3]

Hull is very explicit in giving, as another reason for his preference of a multi-faith approach to religious education, the fact of religious pluralism in British society (1984, ch. 4; 1989, 119), and with this I heartily concur. However, I believe Hull shares the confusion mentioned earlier in that he allows this legitimate rationale for the new approach to religious education to colour his evaluation of Christian nurture from an educational/epistemological point of view, and thereby to cast it in a negative light, tending to associate it with indoctrination.

Others are much more explicit in defending the teaching-*about*-religion approach as a way to avoid indoctrination (which they view as inevitably associated with the older, traditional, confessional approach to religious education). The historic ruling of the Ontario Court of Appeal referred to earlier specifically argues against the traditional approach to religious education on the grounds that the Canadian Charter of Rights and Freedoms does not "permit the indoctrination of school children in the Christian faith." The Court, however, hastened to add that it was not prohibiting "education about religion" (Corporation of Canadian Civil Liberties Assoc. et al. v. Ontario 1990, para. 18, 70).

The new directions in contemporary religious education in Canada, Great Britain, and elsewhere have had a curious effect on the discussion of indoctrination. Very little has been recently said and written about indoctrination, especially in Great Britain where there has traditionally been much concern about this topic. In fact, the impression is frequently given that religious indoctrination is a dead issue. I suggest that this is partly because it is felt that the new approach to religious education is really immune to the charge of indoctrination and that the old indoctrinatory approach to religious education is a relic of the past which has been left far behind. Hull, for example, in commenting on the *Birmingham Agreed Syllabus Of Religious Instruction* published in 1975 – a syllabus which clearly abandons the explicitly christianizing intentions of the older religious education in favour of a study of world religions – points out that it would not occur to any reader of this syllabus "that it could ever be accused of being slanted in the direction of religious indoctrination" (1984, 106-7). Hull is no doubt a little too optimistic, as there are a few writers who maintain that even the teaching-about-religion approach is susceptible to indoctrination.[4]

Hull is probably right in implying that such objections to the study *about* religion(s) in schools are few and far between and hence that concern about religious indoctrination has all but vanished. We must be very careful, however, not to be misled by this silence. While many people might feel that the danger of religious indoctrination has been largely overcome by adopting a new approach to religious education, the question of whether the older approach of

Christian nurture should have been rejected in favour of the new on the grounds that the former was susceptible to indoctrination remains. Perhaps the switch from Christian nurture to teaching about religion was unnecessary. Here we must be careful not to reject the Christian nurture approach simply on the basis of the objection that it fails to take into account religious pluralism. Even if we grant the validity of this argument, as I have already done, we must remember that there are ways to accommodate this objection. We could, for example, replace a state system of education with a system of educational pluralism in which each school would be committed to religious nurture (i.e., Christian nurture, Hindu nurture, secular nurture, etc.). Once we entertain this possibility, we will see that the issue of religious indoctrination has not really gone away, as many people would no doubt object to such an alternative by resurrecting the charge of religious indoctrination. In fact the educational scene, particularly in North America, is being altered fairly significantly with the growth of independent religious schools; a consideration of this phenomenon highlights another aspect of my historical treatment of the charge of religious indoctrination.

The disappearance of the traditional partnership between church and state in education and the emergence of a secular ideal of education has not gone without resistance from the Christian community, particularly in North America. While some Christians are calling for a return to the past partnership, others are recognizing that this is not possible, and perhaps not even desirable in the light of the pluralistic nature of North American society. Instead, they are supporting the idea of educational pluralism which would allow for Christian schools in which Christian nurture can again be an integral part of education. In the last decade there have been such dramatic increases, both in the number of Christian day schools and in total enrolment in these schools in Canada and the United States, that they are being viewed as a serious threat to the educational establishment.[5] Thus church schools and Christian education are increasingly coming under attack and the criticisms are various.

One important criticism which surfaced in two recent government reports, one in Great Britain and the other in Canada, is that independent religious schools and the kind of religious education that goes on in these schools encourage attitudes of intolerance and foster divisiveness in society.[6] Another criticism that is increasingly coming to the fore challenges the rights of parents to bring up their children within a particular religious tradition.[7] Paul H. Hirst expresses a more frequently raised objection to Christian education when he argues against the very possibility of a distinctively Chris-

tian curriculum or even a distinctively Christian approach to education generally (1972). "Christian education" for Hirst is a contradiction in terms.[8] These criticisms, though important, will be dealt with
in this book only by way of passing comment. Instead, I wish to focus on one other criticism – perhaps the most persistent and the
most damning criticism of Christian schools – that children attending these schools often, and even invariably, are indoctrinated.

This criticism is implicitly expressed in the colourful titles of recent
books published on Christian schools: *God's Choice: The Total World of
a Fundamentalist Christian School* (Peshkin 1986); *Keeping Them out of
the Hands of Satan: Evangelical Schooling in America* (Rose 1988). Indeed, as we have already seen, Peshkin, in his fine sociological
study of Bethany Baptist Academy, charges the school with indoctrination because it is a total institution (284).

John Hull, who, as I have already noted, claims to be sympathetic
to Christian nurture, nonetheless comes down very hard on Christian schools, suggesting that only those parents who belong to a
sect, not a church, want their own Christian schools to provide nurture *instead* of education (1984, 40). Hull also warns against the dangers in the proliferation of religiously related schools in which education is conducted along "sectarian lines," and he goes on to make
the observation that church aided schools "might find it increasingly
embarrassing that they are offering something which in the vast majority of schools would not be thought educationally valid" (Hull
1984, 48).

Others who are less sympathetic to Christianity are much more
blunt. For example, Antony Flew, well-known British philosopher
and agnostic, argues that "certainly in Britain and surely in the
United States of America also, the most widespread and the most
successful programme of indoctrination is that of the schools which
maintain their separate and independent existence precisely in order
to inculcate belief in the doctrines of the Roman Catholic Church"
(1972b, 106). The report of the Commission on Private Schools in
Ontario charges some private schools with "extreme narrowness
ideologically," and then rather grudgingly concedes that "while it
remains, at least in many ways, an open question as to whether or
not the religious education offered in private schools constitutes indoctrination," other practices are clearly held by public school sup-
porters to be discriminatory (Shapiro 1985, 8, 24).

One other development should be noted. Most objectors to Christian nurture in church-related schools are quite ready to allow for
Christian nurture in the church or in the home, invoking as justification the familiar private/public distinction of liberalism. For

example, Paul Hirst, while objecting strenuously to Christian nurture in schools, nevertheless seeks to protect the church and the family as private institutions which a rational society must allow to exist alongside public and secular schools committed to true education (1974b, 89-90). The Swann Report in Great Britain similarly accepts the confessional approach to religious education as "perfectly proper" within the community of faith (Swann 1985, 474). This is a curious position because, if Christian nurture really involves indoctrination, which Hirst and the Swann Report suggest in various places, then surely they should also object to it in the church and the home.[9] The charge of indoctrination has moral connotations in that it is felt to be immoral to restrict the development of children in terms of their autonomy and rationality. But moral concerns are by their very nature universalizable, and hence those who associate Christian nurture with indoctrination should be concerned about indoctrination wherever it occurs. The hesitation in objecting to Christian nurture in the church and the home points, I suggest, to the problematic nature not only of the private/public distinction of liberalism but also of the charge of religious indoctrination itself, a problem which will be dealt with in later chapters.

Some recent writers recognize this inconsistency and are beginning to challenge the right of parents to bring up their children in their own particular religious faith. Thus, whereas in the past the primary focus of the concern about indoctrination was on teachers and schools, we are now witnessing increasing concern about parents as indoctrinators. For example, John White challenges the alleged right of parents to bring a child up in their own religion: "If the parent has an obligation to bring up his child as a morally autonomous person, he cannot at the same time have the right to indoctrinate him with any beliefs whatsoever, since some beliefs may contradict those on which his educational endeavors should be based. It is hard to see, for instance, how a desire for one's child's moral autonomy is compatible with the attempt to make him into a good Christian, Muslim or Orthodox Jew" (J.P. White 1982, 166). More recently Callan has argued as follows: "Parents who rear their children within a particular religion incur a significant risk of indoctrinating them" (1985, 117; cf. Gardner 1988, 1991). Here some philosophers are questioning the right of parents to bring up their children within a religious tradition and are challenging this right, which has been largely taken for granted in liberal democratic states, on the basis of concern about indoctrination.

It should finally be noted that the charge of indoctrination is not only made by those opposed to religion. It also occurs among those who are committed to religion in one form or another. Many Christians are concerned about the use of "mind control" or indoctrination on the part of various religious sects such as the Unification Church of Reverend Moon.[10] Efforts at deprogramming children who have been indoctrinated in these ways have been widely discussed and raise further concerns about using indoctrinative methods to overcome indoctrination. But it is not only religious sects which Christians view with suspicion. Individuals within a particular Christian tradition sometimes charge each other with indoctrination.[11]

This review of some historical examples of the charge of religious indoctrination has moved from the very broad to the very specific. We have found concern expressed about state systems of education being too closely aligned with fostering a particular religious faith. But this concern is also extended to church-related schools and more recently even to parents seeking to raise their children within a particular religious tradition. In all of these, the concern about indoctrination seems to centre around such items as narrowness, bias, the lack of openness, and the failure to cultivate rational critical abilities that are thought to be essential to a child's growth towards autonomy. I will provide additional historical background to the charge of indoctrination in chapter 2 when I review the history of liberal education.

SOME PHILOSOPHICAL OBSERVATIONS AND EXAMPLES

Religious indoctrination has received considerable attention from philosophers in the last twenty-five to thirty years, except perhaps for the most recent past, as was observed in the previous section. That discussion occurs within a more general discussion of the concept of indoctrination which has attracted more attention from contemporary analytic philosophers of education than nearly any other educational concept. In fact, the topic of indoctrination is one of the few areas of educational philosophy which has developed a body of literature of its own. This attention is well deserved, as the distinction between true education and indoctrination is one of the most important educational distinctions to make.

In order to understand this philosophical interest in religious indoctrination, we need to review some developments in the philosophy of education and in philosophy generally. I.A. Snook introduces his important anthology, *Concepts of Indoctrination*, by referring to a leading philosopher, who a few years earlier described philosophy of education as "a subject struggling to be born" (1972a, 1). Since problems of education have been the concern of philosophers since the time of Plato, Snook suggests that it might be better to talk of a *re-birth* of philosophy of education. There are two reasons why it might be appropriate to talk about a re-birth of philosophy of education. First is the general revival of interest in philosophy of education in the last twenty-five to thirty years. In North America, interest was intense in the early 1900s when John Dewey dominated the philosophical and educational scene. For Dewey, philosophy and educational theory were essentially equivalent, and thus, in the early part of this century, philosophers thought it an important part of their job to concern themselves with problems of education.[12] But with the emergence of new philosophical movements and the decline of pragmatic philosophy after Dewey's death, interest in the philosophy of education also seemed to wane until the revival of interest in the 1960s.

Second, there was a fundamental change in the way philosophy of education was conceived and practised. Traditionally, the discipline made "global" pronouncements about education and the aims of education – pronouncements which were derived from certain conceptions about the nature of man and reality. But in the middle of this century, there was what is often referred to as a "revolution in philosophy," inspired in the main by the work of Ludwig Wittgenstein (1889-1951). Philosophers became unwilling to make pronouncements based on speculations about the nature of humankind and reality, but saw their work as limited to second order activities of linguistic or conceptual analysis. It was largely due to the work of a "pure" philosopher, R.S. Peters, that this new approach to philosophy was applied to educational problems and concepts, and the philosophy of education was reborn in this second sense. Although there had been a few earlier scattered attempts to do analytic philosophy of education, it was only after Peters assumed the chair of Professor of the Philosophy of Education at the University of London Institute of Education, in the fall of 1963, that the movement gained momentum and developed a body of literature of its own.

As an aside, it should be noted that since the heyday of analytic philosophy of education in the 1960s and 1970s there has been a growing interest in returning to the more traditional way of doing philosophy, though obviously the concern for greater clarity in language remains. Indeed, in his later writings, Peters himself calls for a return to a more constructive, integrative approach to doing philosophy of education (1977, 129).

Much of the philosophical writing concerning indoctrination belongs to the earlier analytic period of the philosophy of education, having its roots in Peters's analysis of the concept of education. Two early essays attempting to analyze the concept of indoctrination were written by Wilson (1964) and Hare (1964) and were collected in the often-reprinted anthology, *Aims in Education: The Philosophic Approach* (Hollins 1964). The 1960s and 1970s saw a plethora of articles on indoctrination, many of which were collected in Snook's anthology, *Concepts of Indoctrination: Philosophical Essays* (1972a). Snook himself wrote an accompanying monograph entitled *Indoctrination and Education* (1972b). A good summary of these analytical discussions of the concept of indoctrination is found in Barrow and Woods (1988, ch. 5). The literature written during this period will serve as the springboard for much of my discussion of the relation between indoctrination and religion.

After the 1970s, interest in indoctrination waned for a time. There are several reasons for this declining interest. Many philosophers no doubt believed that the last word had been said on the topic. There was also the feeling that the concept of indoctrination had been "analyzed to death" (Laura 1983, 43). The return to a more traditional approach to doing the philosophy of education also provides a partial explanation. I would suggest as a final reason the historical developments in the area of religious education. As I pointed out in the previous section, religious education in our schools has shifted largely to non-confessional approaches such as the teaching *about* religion(s). The topic of religious indoctrination is therefore felt to be a dead issue because the new approaches to religious education are thought to be immune to indoctrination. But perhaps we were too quick to label the older approach to religious education "indoctrination." Perhaps as Laura has reminded us, we have become complacent too quickly "by assuming that we have answers to questions that we have not yet begun to ask" (Laura 1983, 43). With Laura, I believe there "is still much work to be done, if the ghost of the indoctrination issue is to be laid to rest" (43).

As Leahy observes in a recent essay on indoctrination and religious education (1990), there has been a revival of the discussion of the problem of indoctrination in the latter part of the 1980s.[13] This resurgence of interest attests to the importance of the topic and also suggests that there may still be some stones to uncover on the issue. While a few of those essays are still preoccupied with defining indoctrination using the tools of conceptual analysis, most break away from this way of doing philosophy and deal with the substantive issues that are raised in the distinction between education and indoctrination. Some place the discussion within a broader context, drawing on developments in epistemology and the philosophy of science. There would also seem to be a greater willingness to focus more on applying philosophical insights to educational practice. As will be explained in more detail later in this chapter, the approach in this book aligns more closely with some of the recent writings on indoctrination.

I would like now to examine more carefully some analytical treatments of the concept of indoctrination written in the 1960s & 1970s. The purpose of educational philosophy in its analytic mode is to analyze various educational concepts as they arise in ordinary language – concepts such as "education," "teaching," "school," and "indoctrination." This task is frequently described in terms of mapping the logical geography of these concepts, to borrow a description first given by Ryle (see Flew 1972a, 72). The aim of conceptual analysis is to discover what principle or principles govern the use of a word. This is often described in terms of finding the logically necessary and sufficient conditions for the applicability of a certain word. Thus, with regard to "indoctrination," the aim of philosophers is to find certain characteristics such that if and only if these characteristics are present would we say that a teacher or parent is indoctrinating. One technique sometimes used by philosophers to help them in conceptual analysis involves the identification or construction of paradigm cases – examples of the use of a word that are so clear and unproblematic that they can then be used to exhibit part of the meaning of the word being analyzed.

Frequent references to paradigm cases of indoctrination appear in analytical philosophical treatments of this topic. For many, such as Antony Flew, "the outstanding paradigm case of indoctrination" is "the enormous and generally effective effort made in our own two countries [i.e., Britain and the United States of America] by a particular highly traditional Christian Church [i.e., the Roman Catholic Church], which seeks to fix in the minds of children an unshakable conviction of the truth of its specific distinctive doctrines" (1972b, 114). John Wilson, in an early essay that initiated the analytical discussion of indoctrination, suggests the following as obvious model cases: "Brainwashing people to believe in Communism, teaching Christianity by the threat of torture or damnation, forcing people by early training to accept social roles as those described in Huxley's *Brave New World*" (1964, 26). Kai Nielsen, well-known Canadian philosopher and agnostic, has argued more recently that, even if we cannot give a clear analysis of the criteria of indoctrination, we still know what indoctrination means because we can point to "unequivocal instances of religious indoctrination" such as the following:

"The kind of moral majority radical fundamentalism so loved – or apparently so loved – by Reagan and Moslem fundamentalists involves clear cases of belief systems that extensively engage in religious indoctrination. Much that occurs on Christian television stations in the United States and on Iran Television (if the accounts I have read are to be trusted) are paradigmatic instances of religious indoctrination" (Nielsen 1984, 70).

Barrow and Woods, in a popular introductory text on the philosophy of education, describe what for many is considered to be the paradigm of all paradigm cases of indoctrination (1988). I quote the full description of this paradigm because I will be referring to it frequently in the chapters that follow.

Imagine a Catholic school in which all the teachers are committed Catholics and where all the children come from Catholic homes and have parents who want them to be brought up as Catholics. Imagine also that the teachers are determined to try to bring up the children as devout Catholics. They deliberately attempt to inculcate in their pupils an unshakable commitment to the truth of Catholicism and of the various claims or propositions associated with it. They thus bring up the pupils to believe in the unquestionable truth of such propositions as "The Pope is infallible," "One should not use artificial birth-control methods" and "God (defined in terms of the Catholic conception of God) exists." They bring them up to believe in these and similar propositions in such a way that the pupils come to regard those who do not accept them as true propositions as being simply mistaken or in error, and in such a way that no reasoning put forward that might cast doubt upon their assurance that Catholicism and the propositions related to it are incorrigible truths can cause them to reconsider their assumptions. They are, let us assume, drilled by their teachers in answers that explain away any possible doubts about or objections to the claims of Catholicism. The techniques used by the teachers to evoke this commitment to Catholicism may be many and various: some of the propositions presented may be put forward with rational explanation, but others will be cultivated by means of the example set by the teachers, the use of praise and blame or the withholding of approval by the teachers, or simply the use of their authority to reinforce their insistence on the undeniable truth of the Catholic view of the world and man's place in it. (Barrow & Woods 1988, 70)

Barrow and Woods conclude: "It is difficult to conceive of anyone seriously doubting that these teachers are indoctrinating" (1988, 70). On the contrary, I for one do have some serious doubts about this necessarily being a case of indoctrination, and I am sure that I am not alone in this. These doubts raise, of course, a key problem about the use of paradigms as a technique for conceptual analysis, and I will have more to say about this shortly.

Since paradigms are used by philosophers to exhibit various strands of meaning of a word, I turn now to four different strands commonly thought to be essential to the concept of indoctrination. In each case I want to consider how this essential feature of indoctrination has been used to criticize religious instruction.

The first, and perhaps most widely accepted criterion of "indoctrination" is that of content. It is generally assumed that indoctrination is limited to certain kinds of belief, specifically doctrines or ideologies. We have already seen that it is religious doctrines that are singled out as susceptible to indoctrination in the paradigms considered earlier. Clearly there is an etymological connection between the words "indoctrination" and "doctrine" and thus many have assumed that "indoctrination" is conceptually linked to doctrines. R.S. Peters, for example, in his analysis of educational processes, argues that "indoctrination cannot be ruled out as a process of education on the same ground as conditioning can. The reason is that, whatever else 'indoctrination' may mean, it obviously has something to do with doctrines, which are a species of beliefs" (1966, 41). Flew puts it bluntly, "No doctrines, no indoctrination" (1972b, 114). Kazepides reminds us that "the original and proper home of doctrines is religion" (1989, 393). It follows then that indoctrination can only occur with regard to doctrines such as occur in religion, politics, and morality. Further, since it is widely assumed that science does not contain doctrines, many philosophers and educators hold that the teaching of science is immune to indoctrination (see Kazepides 1987).

Several other aspects of this association between indoctrination and doctrines will only be mentioned here, as they will be analyzed more carefully later. Some writers, while denying a logically necessary connection between "indoctrination" and "doctrines," nevertheless maintain that there is a strong contingent connection. In other words, indoctrination is thought to be much more likely to occur in areas such as religion or politics than in other subject areas. Closely related is the claim of many philosophers, educators, and lay people that, when teaching religious doctrines, there is a very high probability that one is indoctrinating. Others make the even stronger claim that teaching religious beliefs necessarily involves indoctrination, although what is meant here is that certain approaches to teaching certain religious beliefs necessarily involve indoctrination. Snook, for example, argues that with regard to doubtful religious propositions, "teaching for belief in them [i.e., Christian nurture] is always indoctrination" (1972b, 74; cf. Flew, 1972b, 113).

Discussion about the content of indoctrination inevitably raises questions about the way in which this content is taught and this leads to the second major criterion of "indoctrination" – the methods criterion. John Wilson shows how these two criteria are related. "It is not surprising that the word 'indoctrination' implies that the beliefs are usually of a certain kind, namely, those that might properly be called *doctrines*: for these are the kinds of beliefs to induce which, because of our ignorance of how to use rational methods of teaching, non-rational methods have commonly been used instead – par excellence in the case of political, moral, and religious beliefs" (Wilson 1972b, 19). Chapter 4 includes a careful review of the various teaching methods that have been associated with indoctrination. Here it is sufficient to note that the various descriptions of those methods can be, and often are, summed up in the expression "a nonrational teaching method," and it is because religion is thought to be nonrational or even irrational that religious teaching is frequently associated with indoctrination.

A third criterion of indoctrination which seems to have gained increasing acceptance among philosophers of education is the intention criterion. Most recently, Callan has defined "indoctrination" in terms of "the intentional inculcation of unshakable beliefs" (1985, 113). I.A. Snook, a leading proponent, defines "indoctrination" in terms of teaching with the intention that pupils believe a proposition regardless of the evidence (1972b, 47). Snook applies his intention criterion to the area of religious beliefs and sums up his position concerning the relation between religion and indoctrination thus:

1 Indoctrination is the teaching of any subject matter with the intention that it be believed regardless of the evidence.
2 Indoctrination, so defined, is morally reprehensible.
3 Religious propositions are meant to be true, but the evidence for all of them is inconclusive and some of them are false. (That we cannot identify which ones are false does not affect the argument.)
4 If the parent or teacher teaches with the intention of being believed, he or she indoctrinates.
5 It is difficult to see what else the teacher of religion could intend.
6 Indoctrination is inevitable if religion is taught.

7 The teaching of religion is an immoral activity. (Snook 1972b, 75-6)

R.M. Hare shifts the focus slightly in an earlier discussion of the intention criterion of indoctrination. For Hare, "indoctrination only begins when we are trying to stop the growth in our children of the capacity to think for themselves" (1964, 52). In other words, indoctrination is being defined in terms of the intention to stop growth toward autonomy. This is again thought to create problems for Christian nurture because many would concur with J.P. White that any attempts to make a child into a good Christian are incompatible with a desire for one's child's autonomy (1982, 166; See full quote on p. 17).

Implicit in the intention criterion is reference to the fourth and final criterion of indoctrination, the consequences criterion. If teaching results in pupils believing something regardless of the evidence, or in having unshakable beliefs, then this is taken by many to be a sign that indoctrination has occurred. William Hare, for example, maintains that indoctrination "involves coming to hold beliefs in a closed-minded fashion" (1985, 21). Closed-mindedness is often linked with the inability to critically reflect on one's beliefs, and hence an indoctrinatory outcome is often contrasted with the ideal of "critical openness." Again religion is singled out as "a prime (perhaps *the* prime) example" of those domains where "people are prone to hold their views tenaciously regardless of evidence or argument" (Snook 1972b, 74). The frequency of closed minds in religion is therefore taken to be an indication of the prevalence of indoctrination in this area of religion. Paul Hirst, for example, argues that church-related schools are "not even in principle" committed to developing minds characterized by critical openness (1985, 14-15).

Contemporary attitudes towards religious and Christian instruction stand in sharp contrast to those of the past. In fact, the history of education in most western countries can be described as one continuous process of disenfranchisement of the Christian connection with education. This divorce of Christianity and education has not at all been arrived at in an amicable fashion. Charges and countercharges have been and continue to be made. Central among the charges levelled against traditional Christian education is that of indoctrination.

What is it possible to conclude from this survey of past developments and discussions of education and indoctrination? Not all or every kind of religious teaching is ruled indoctrinatory. Various methods, such as an objective and comparative study of religions, a phenomenological approach to studying religion, a personal development approach to the study of religion(s), and teaching the philosophy of religion, would generally be thought to be exempt from the charge of indoctrination. It is not teaching *about* religion or learning from religions but the teaching *of* a specific religion that is often viewed as indoctrinatory. And it is the confessional approach to religious education that is labelled indoctrination. It is Christian nurture as it occurs in the home, the church and in church-related schools that is found to be objectionable. Or, more generally, it is teaching for commitment that is thought to involve indoctrination.

Various aspects of Christian nurture (or the teaching *of* any other specific religion) are viewed as indoctrinatory. Very often the intention behind Christian teaching is criticized. Concern is expressed about seeking to persuade or to convince someone to accept certain religious claims as true. At other times, the focus is on the results of Christian nurture. Indoctrination is associated with teaching which results in a blind conviction held apart from any consideration of evidence or openness to critical re-evaluation. People object as well to the nonrational teaching methods that seem to be an inescapable ingredient in the teaching *of* religion or in Christian nurture. The aim of this book is to defend Christian nurture and the teaching *of* religion against the frequent charge of indoctrination.

DEFINITION OF CHRISTIAN NURTURE

In today's philosophical climate, it is still thought to be important to define the key terms used in a treatise, and thus I might be criticized for not having begun this work by providing a careful definition of "Christian nurture." My approach has instead been an inductive one. I have begun with an examination of expressions of the charge of indoctrination as applied to religion, charges which often include implicit and explicit descriptions of Christian nurture. The description by Barrow and Woods of a paradigm case of indoctrination in a Catholic school captures the essential features of Christian nurture. In my survey of the charges of indoctrination, I have, of course, also appealed to our common understanding of terms like "Christian nurture," or a "confessional approach to Christian education."

In tracing the etymology of the term, we learn from the *Oxford English Dictionary* that nurture meant "to feed or nourish; to support and bring up to maturity; to rear," and also, "to bring up, train, educate." Etymology and normal usage suggest a species of formative education, with a focus on what we refer to today as socialization or enculturation. I will have more to say on these terms shortly. In a study commissioned by the British Council of Churches and later published under the title *The Child in the Church and Understanding Christian Nurture*, nurture is simply described "as the process of learning and growing which intends to deepen Christian faith" (1984, 46). The report stresses the fact that the Christian life is one of continual growth, a claim that is so well captured in the statement found in the New Testament: "Grow in the grace and in the knowledge of our Lord and Saviour Jesus Christ" (2 Peter 3:18; British Council of Churches, 19).

Obviously, Christian nurture can take various forms, and later chapters will distinguish between those that are educationally acceptable and those that are not. Nevertheless, both kinds of nurture must still share some essential features by virtue of which we call them "Christian nurture." Drawing on M. Oakeshott's (1972) and R.S. Peters's (1966, ch. 2) descriptions of education as initiation, Christian nurture can be defined as the initiation of a person (a child or an adult) into a Christian heritage, an inheritance of Christian sentiments, beliefs, imaginings, understandings, and activities (see also British Council of Churches 1984, 27).

One possible synonym for Christian nurture is "catechesis," an ancient Christian word which came to be used almost exclusively by Roman Catholics, though Protestant educationalists have begun to use the term more recently. Etymologically, catechesis refers to the activity of re-echoing or retelling the story of the Christian faith. Some recent writers such as Westerhoff (1976, 1983) have expanded the meaning to include the whole process of Christian becoming, or what might be better named Christian socialization or enculturation (Groome 1980, 26-8; 115-21). (The term "socialization" tends to be viewed very negatively by some philosophers [e.g., Kazepides 1982], and therefore I prefer the term "initiation" which is perhaps more neutral in its overtones.) However, catechesis as the telling of the story of the Christian faith is certainly part of the meaning of Christian nurture. Other connotative baggage of the sociological school of religious education theory should not be attached to my use of the term catechesis.

Hirst correctly highlights two features of Christian nurture when he suggests that "the aim is from the stance of faith, the development of faith" (1981, 89). A better word for faith today might be commitment. Christian nurture clearly operates from the stance of commitment and seeks the development of commitment. Christian nurture takes as its starting point the affirmation of Christian truth, hence the use of the term "confessional" to describe this approach to religious education. Christian nurture further clearly seeks to foster belief as well as commitment, hence the title of this book, *Teaching for Commitment*.

There is one other way in which Christian nurture might be characterized, and this way will help to elucidate the central thrust of this book. Groome prefers the term "Christian religious education" to "Christian nurture'" because his term includes the word "education," thereby enabling him to draw on "the science of education" to empower the activity (1980, 27). But despite the fact that Oakeshott and Peters seem to have no problems linking "initiation" and "education," it would be premature to describe Christian nurture as education, since that is precisely what is at issue in the debate concerning the charge of indoctrination as it is applied to Christian nurture. Indoctrination is generally understood to be the very antithesis of education. Hence, those who claim that Christian nurture involves indoctrination are saying that Christian nurture is incompatible with education. Hirst, for example, draws a sharp distinction between education and catechesis, suggesting that they differ in "their aims, in the forms of response that are sought, the states of mind they seek," as well as in "the methods of and the materials of teaching" (1981, 92). We see here a reference to each of the four criteria that have traditionally been used to distinguish education from indoctrination, and Hirst, in fact, claims that Christian nurture "is likely to favour the procedures of exposition, instruction, catechesis and indoctrination" (1985, 7).

Another paper which reflects the changing scene of religious education in Britain describes the confessional approach to religious education as a "dogmatic approach" that "begins with the assumption that the aim of religious education is intellectual and cultic indoctrination" (Schools Council Project 1971). But are Hirst and the writers of the working paper correct in making this generalization? This brings us to the heart of the questions to be addressed in this book. Is Christian nurture compatible with education? Does Christian nurture necessarily involve indoctrination? Or does Christian nurture very likely involve indoctrination? The relation between Christian nurture and education must therefore, at this point, be left as an open question.

Here it should be noted that the charge of religious indoctrination focuses mainly, if not exclusively, on one aspect of religion – the belief component. This is so because there would seem to be agreement that indoctrination always has to do with the shaping of beliefs (Page 1980, 28). Indoctrination is therefore contrasted with conditioning which has to do with behaviour, and with brainwashing which has to with psychological manipulation (see Wilson 1972b,

17). There may be some difficulties in sharply separating beliefs from behaviour and psychological make-up, as will be argued later in this book. Here it is simply necessary to recognize that indoctrination is largely understood as having to do with the teaching of beliefs; hence, the charge of religious indoctrination concerns the teaching of religious beliefs. There are clearly other dimensions common to religions. Ninian Smart has identified six: doctrine, myth, ethics, ritual, experience, and social aspects (1968, 15-18). Given the specific focus of the charge of indoctrination, we are primarily concerned with doctrine and myth and only incidentally with the remaining aspects insofar as the belief component of a religion informs them. The charge of religious indoctrination therefore concerns objectionable ways in which religious beliefs are taught.

Finally, something needs to be said about the word "Christian" in "Christian nurture." Obviously Christianity is not all of one piece. There are liberal and conservative traditions within Christianity. The charge of indoctrination is generally made against the more conservative Christian traditions – Roman Catholic and Protestant evangelical schools are often singled out as guilty (see Flew 1972b, 114; Barrow & Woods 1988, 70; Peshkin 1986). Although these two Christian traditions can be, and often are, quite different, they can, and often do, have much in common, especially in terms of doctrines. Since, as already has been shown, the charges of indoctrination focus on the belief component of religion, it is this shared doctrinal base of Roman Catholicism and evangelicalism that would account for these two Christian traditions bearing the brunt of indoctrinatory charges. I will therefore attempt to answer the charge of indoctrination from within the context of a fairly conservative interpretation of Christian doctrine.

Christian nurture, therefore, is grounded in a very specific commitment. It involves the initiation of children or adults into the Christian world-view with its particular beliefs, values, and sentiments. Its content includes all the essential components of the Christian tradition. The processes or methods of Christian nurture reflect the character of Jesus Christ. The goal of Christian nurture is to develop Christian commitment. Christian nurture is often deliberate, but much of it, especially with young children, occurs unconsciously. Children simply share in the Christian way of life as practised by their parents, for example (see Deuteronomy 11:18-19). But it must not be thought that Christian nurture is limited to the teaching of children. Whatever a person's age, Christian nurture includes "any and every ... learning experience that gives rise to the adoption or deepening of a person's Christian beliefs, attitudes, values or dispositions to act and experience 'in a Christian way' " (Astley & Day 1992, 17; cf. Nichols 1992). This raises the central question of this book: Does Christian nurture involve indoctrination?

APPROACH TO BE TAKEN

How then to proceed to answer the charge of religious indoctrination? It might be thought that, in keeping with the long-standing approach to doing philosophy, the first task should be to critically evaluate past analyses of the concept of indoctrination, showing how they have failed to provide the necessary and sufficient conditions governing the use of the term "indoctrination." This approach, which I have attempted elsewhere (Thiessen 1980), will not be taken in this book for a number of reasons. Philosophers are increasingly recognizing the problematic nature of conceptual analysis as it has traditionally been practised. Language is simply not so precise as this approach demands. Thus many philosophers have cautioned against fitting conceptual analysis into a logically tight straight jacket (see Hirst & Peters 1970, 4-5; Snook 1972b, 36-7).

Another problem with a preoccupation with conceptual analysis is that it tends to focus on the descriptive rather than the normative components of concepts. "It is time we stopped hiding evaluative disputes under the cloak of conceptual analysis" (Dunlop 1976, 42). We need to pay much more attention to the normative aspect of a concept such as indoctrination and to questions of justification that are necessarily involved when we criticize someone for indoctrinating.

One of the problems with conceptual analysis is its ahistorical nature. But language is embedded in our history, terms need to be understood within in their cultural and political contexts (see Bowers 1987, viii; Neiman 1989), and it is necessary to examine the context out of which concern for indoctrination arises (this will be addressed in the next chapter).

Laura also complains that past conceptual debate on indoctrination has suffered from lack of breadth of vision in failing to take into account the epistemological assumptions built into the pejorative use of the term (1983, 43). Like Laura, I want to set the problem of indoctrination in the context of critical theory and a more adequate epistemology.

As well, there is always the danger of arbitrariness in philosophical attempts to analyze a concept. There is in fact a long-standing debate in contemporary philosophy about whether conceptual analysis does, as Wittgenstein put it, merely describe actual usage and leave everything as it is. It would seem as though philosophers invariably also go on to revise, to reconstruct, and to straighten out our concepts, and here again an element of arbitrariness enters in. It might further be the case that the distinctions of ordinary language themselves are arbitrary. For example, while in ordinary usage, "indoctrination" might be understood to be necessarily restricted to doctrines such as occur in religion, the question surely needs to be raised about whether this restriction is justified. Are there perhaps some prejudices implicit in ordinary language? Hirst and Peters have correctly warned us that ordinary language "should never be treated as a repository of unquestionable wisdom" (1970, 8). It is because of the pervasiveness of the problem of arbitrariness that I reject a strictly analytical approach to the central question raised in this book about the relation between indoctrination and Christian nurture. Ordinary language, proposed analyses of "indoctrination," and the selection of paradigms of indoctrination all run the danger of resolving the central question of this book in an arbitrary fashion and hence they must themselves be subjected to critical scrutiny.

There is also the danger of becoming so preoccupied with conceptual analysis as to lose sight of the real problems to be addressed. Language is a tool; and while it is important to have good tools, it is equally important to *use* our tools. Conceptual analysis, with its emphasis on clarifying or sharpening concepts, has been compared to sharpening an axe. And while it is clearly important to sharpen an axe, there is surely something wrong if we never get to use the axe for what it is intended because we are so preoccupied with sharpening it. Similarly, it is important to get beyond conceptual clarification to the resolving of problems that are described by language.

A comparison might help us to understand the difficulties in the conceptual analysis approach to resolving the relation between indoctrination and Christian nurture. If a city has a law forbidding the use of wheeled vehicles in a park and the question subsequently arises as to whether skateboards can be used in the park, it would be foolish to spend a lot of time trying to define "wheeled vehicles" in order to determine whether skateboards are wheeled vehicles. What is required here is that we face directly the question of whether we want skateboards in the park, giving reasons, of course, for this particular decision.

Similarly, it would be a mistake to attempt to define "indoctrination" in the hope that this will help us to decide whether Christian nurture falls under the concept of indoctrination. Because this concept, with that of "wheeled vehicle," is loose at the edges, we are always in danger of settling this question by arbitrary definition. Instead, we would be much better advised to examine directly whether the methods, content, aims, and consequences of Christian nurture are educationally and morally acceptable. These four criteria which philosophers have identified in their attempts to define "indoctrination" will be used in this book as signposts to direct the discussion, and in this they serve a useful function. My aim, however, is not primarily to explore the question of whether "indoctrination" can be defined in terms of one or more of these criteria, but rather to consider whether Christian nurture satisfies the moral and educational requirements that can be usefully identified in terms of each of these criteria.

Before turning to this, however, it is necessary to examine the context out of which concern about indoctrination arises. What are the presuppositions underlying the charge of indoctrination? What concept of education is presupposed by those making the charge? These questions will be answered in the following chapter by looking at the ideal of liberal education.

2 Liberal Education: The Context of the Charge of Indoctrination

In order to respond to the charge of religious indoctrination, it is important first to clarify the context out of which this charge arises.[1] Clearly, indoctrination is related in some way to education and teaching. It has already been suggested in chapter 1 that the term "indoctrination" is used today primarily as a derogatory term. Indoctrination is generally viewed as the opposite of true education or good teaching. But just what kind of education or teaching is indoctrination being contrasted with? I will argue in this chapter that when indoctrination is viewed as the opposite of true education or good teaching it is being contrasted with liberal education. The ideal of liberal education is the context out of which indoctrination acquires its pejorative overtones.

What is the ideal of liberal education? And why does this ideal give rise to concern about indoctrination? I wish to answer these questions using two approaches. Later in this chapter I will examine in some detail a characterization of liberal education as given by R.S. Peters, who is generally recognized as the father of the modern analytic approach to the philosophy of education. A focus on Peters's analysis of the concept of education is justified because, as noted in chapter 1, much of the philosophical literature on religious indoctrination was written during Peters's time and was in fact based on his characterization of liberal education.

One of the problems with this analytical approach to discussing liberal education and indoctrination is that it is largely ahistorical. But concepts do not float in mid-air. To understand them we need to look at their historical, cultural, and political contexts. This then leads to the second of the two approaches being taken in this chapter to clarify the ideal of liberal education and the concerns about indoctrination that have arisen from it. Obviously a history of liberal education is a topic in its own right. I can at most make some general observations, drawing on the work of others who have dealt with this question in greater detail.

HISTORY OF LIBERAL EDUCATION

Bruce Kimball (1986), in his recent and careful study of the history of the idea of liberal education, argues that there is not just one idea of liberal education but many differing conceptions, all of which are built on two central notions. The first is an oratorical conception of liberal education, elements of which can be traced to the Greeks. However, according to Kimball, this conception only became normative in Roman times and under the influence of such Roman orators as Cicero and Quintilian (33, 206). Critical of the speculation and the endless pursuit of truth as demonstrated in the philosophical tradition of Socrates and Plato, the orators stressed the need to pass traditions on to the uninitiated, to express the truth for all to hear and judge (33, 35). The curriculum of the oratorical ideal of liberal education came to be known as the *septem artes liberales*. The seven liberal arts included the *trivium* (grammar, logic, and rhetoric) and the *quadrivium* (arithmetic, geometry, astronomy, and music). The purpose of this liberal arts curriculum was to train citizen-orators to lead society from a base of the virtues found in the great classical texts (37-8; 228). This helps us to understand the etymological roots of the work "liberal," used with regard to education. In Roman antiquity, *liberalis* denoted "of or relating to free men ... Thus, *liberalis* characterized the *liber*, the free citizen who was 'gentlemanly ... magnanimous, noble, ... munificent, generous,' as well as the 'studies, education, arts, professions' in which the free citizen participated" (13).

One important feature of the oratorical ideal of liberal education is its "dogmatist epistemology," a "belief that truth can be known and expressed" (38). This leads to the view that the aim of education is to teach students virtues already known, rather than to teach students how to search for the virtues (37-8). This oratorical tradition was adapted to Christian aims during the middle ages and persisted in Renaissance humanism and the Reformation, according to Kimball (ch. 4).

The long history of the oratorical ideal of liberal education provides, I would suggest, a partial explanation of the long-standing positive overtones of the term "indoctrination." Raywid (1980) and Gatchel (1972), in their explorations of the history of indoctrination, point out that the terms "indoctrination" and "education" were roughly synonymous until well into the present century. The *New England Dictionary* of 1901 defines indoctrination simply as "instruction, formal teaching" (Raywid 1980, 2). If the focus of liberal education in the oratorical tradition is to convey truth already achieved, then one can appreciate why the term "indoctrination" was freely used to describe the process of liberal education.

The philosophical conception of liberal education, according to Kimball, has its roots in Socrates, with his uncompromising, never-ending search for truth (1986, 116). With the rise of experimental science and the dawning of the Enlightenment in the seventeenth and eighteenth centuries, there was a renewal of philosophical activity leading to the development of the more recent ideal of liberal education – what Kimball calls the "liberal-free ideal" of liberal education (115). The "folk hero" of Renaissance thinkers was Socrates, the free-thinker and critic (116). The word "liberal" underwent significant transformation from the sixteenth to the eighteenth centuries. Whereas earlier "liberal" was applied to the activities of gentlemen who were free by virtue of having leisure, in line with the historical tradition of *liberalis*, the word later took on the positive connotation of "free from narrow prejudice, open-minded" (115).

Kimball identifies seven characteristics of the modern liberal-free ideal of liberal education (1986, 119-22, 228). The foremost characteristic is an emphasis on freedom, especially freedom from tradition and a priori strictures and standards. There is also an emphasis on rationality, critical skepticism, tolerance, and egalitarianism. Another powerful idea within this ideal of liberal education is its ethic of individualism as distinct from "the obligations of citizenship found in the *artes liberales* ideal" (122). Finally, there is a concern for growth. Not truth, but the search for truth is viewed as desirable. "Hence, Gotthold Lessing, a prominent German writer of the Enlightenment, maintained that if God were to offer him the truth with one hand and the search for truth with the other, he would choose the latter" (122).

Kimball maintains that what has happened to liberal education in the nineteenth and twentieth centuries is a series of "accommodations" to these earlier ideals, though tensions between these two ideals persist. It would seem that the liberal-free ideal of liberal education is by far the predominant ideal in modern and contemporary educational thought and practice.[2] In 1944, John Dewey, for example, noted, "Nothing is more striking in recent discussions of liberal education than the widespread and seemingly spontaneous use of *liberating* as a synonym for *liberal*" (Kimball 1986, 158). This emphasis clearly continues to the present day. Kimball also points to the rising status of the liberal-free, or what I will refer to as the Enlightenment ideal of liberal education (218).

Kimball also calls attention to the widespread use of language about "liberation," "liberalism," and "freeing" in connection with the more recent ideal of liberal education (1986, 213). This suggests a close relation between the emergence of this ideal of liberal education and both the emergence of liberal education theory and the rise of liberalism. While recognizing the difficulties inherent in defining liberalism, there would seem to be some justification for linking it with the Enlightenment ideal of liberal education. Kimball points to the historical parallels as providing justification for the linkage. Many of the thinkers associated with the formation of liberalism defended the liberal/free ideal of liberal education. Too, there seems to be a parallel in the basic values that define liberalism and underlie liberal educational theory and the modern/contemporary ideal of liberal education (255-9). Although, as Kimball notes, there have been further developments in liberalism which would seem to call into question the plausibility of interpreting the liberal-free ideal of liberal education as an extension of the movement of "liberalism," the originating parallels are nonetheless significant. In what follows, I will therefore assume a close relation between a liberal theory of education, the Enlightenment ideal of liberal education, and liberalism. Obviously much more could be said about the complex relations among these concepts, but as Aristotle warned long ago, we should look for only so much precision as the subject allows and needs.

The central liberal values include freedom, autonomy, individualism, equality, a suspicion of authority and tradition, toleration, critical rationality, science, and a belief in progress (Kimball 1986, 256; Bowers 1987, 17, 19-31). More generally, these same values are central to defining the modern world view or modernity (Toulmin 1990). Here the interesting question arises as to why these values have come to shape the modern world view, including the contemporary ideal of liberal education. Or, to use the sub-title of Toulmin's fascinating reinterpretation of the Renaissance, What was the hidden agenda of modernity (1990)?

Toulmin, in his study of the origins of modernity, argues that the seventeenth-century philosophers' "Quest for Certainty" was in fact "a timely response to a specific historical challenge – the political, social and theological chaos embodied in the Thirty Years' War" (1990, 70). It was within this context of a crisis-ridden, war-torn Europe that intellectuals rejected religious authority and tradition, which were blamed for the problems of society, and searched instead for a solid foundation upon which to base society so it could become a "cosmopolis," a society which was as rationally ordered as the Newtonian view of nature (Toulmin 1990, 67-9).

It is within this context that the ideal of liberal education came to be reshaped in accordance with the agenda of modernity and modern liberalism. Following Descartes's methodology of doubt, the Enlightenment ideal of liberal education emphasized the importance of subjecting our inherited systems of belief to doubt, to try to start with a clean slate, and to search for truth apart from tradition and authority. The oral, the particular, the local, and the timely were all viewed with suspicion (Toulmin 1990, 30-5). The aim of liberal education is to help children move "beyond the present and the particular," to use the title of a fairly recent book attempting to give us a theory of liberal education (Bailey 1984).

Indoctrination, on the other hand, gradually came to be associated with keeping children locked within the present and the particular, within a particular tradition, and subject to authority. Gatchel, in tracing the evolution of concepts of indoctrination, points out that it was within the context of the progressive education movement in the United States that education came to be closely associated with social democracy and that the term "indoctrination" acquired its pejorative overtones (Gatchel 1972, 10). It was communist and fascist schools that indoctrinated. Schools within a democracy were committed to liberal education. Raywid similarly reminds us that John Dewey, as early as 1915, accused traditional education or authoritarian education of engendering attitudes of "obedience," "docility," "submission," and "passivity" (Raywid 1980, 3). This same suspicion with traditionalist education is reflected in writers like Hirst and Peters whom I will consider later.

Why is there concern about indoctrination? Liberal education frees. Indoctrination enslaves. Liberal education is democratic. Indoctrination is authoritarian. Liberal education is rational. Indoctrination justifies by tradition. Liberal education fosters tolerance. Indoctrination promotes bigotry because it dares to teach exclusive claims to truth. Liberal education respects the worth of each individual. With indoctrination, individuality is undermined by community standards and beliefs. Liberal education is progressive, open, and scientific. Indoctrination keeps children enslaved to myth, superstition, and false consciousness.

And what about religious education? With the emergence of the Enlightenment ideal of liberal education, religious education came under increasing suspicion. In part this was due to the anti-religious bias of the Enlightenment. The fundamental idea behind liberal education now was to free individuals – to free them from ignorance, superstition, prejudice, and narrow dogmatism – in other words, to free them from religion. The idea of liberty inherent in the Enlightenment ideal of liberal education entailed that such education could not be made subservient to religious goals. Eventually, liberal education came to be seen as incompatible with an education based on a religious commitment, the goal of which was the fostering of religious commitment. The very idea of a Christian liberal education came to be seen as a contradiction in terms (Hirst 1972). An education subordinated to religious ends came to be associated with indoctrination (Marples 1978; Schools Council Project 1971, 21).

PETERS'S CONCEPT OF LIBERAL EDUCATION

Analytic philosophers of education, by and large, would not be too bothered about the historical context of concern about indoctrination. Indeed, their "decontextualized" approach to doing philosophy of education is very much in keeping with the spirit of modernity. It is useful, however, to examine the concept of liberal education from an analytical perspective.

Clarity has always been an aim of the analytic approach to philosophy, and thus by examining the writings of analytic philosophers of education, we might come to a better understanding of the specific ideal of liberal education which provides the context for much of the contemporary concern about indoctrination. Also, given that there are varying interpretations of the ideal of liberal education, it is good to provide a detailed description of one such interpretation, one which has given rise to present discussions about religious indoctrination.

R.S. Peters began his work in the philosophy of education by trying to define the concept of education. In describing his initial attempts, he informs us that he "was unable to unearth any previous explicit attempt to demarcate the concept of 'education' " (1967, 1). It should be noted that Peters is talking here about *the* concept of education as if there were only one concept of education. Various objections to his analysis of *the* concept of education eventually led Peters to revise his earlier interpretation of his work and to admit that there really are two different concepts of education – an older, undifferentiated concept which refers in a very general way to the bringing up or rearing of children, and a more recent, more specific concept which is necessarily related to certain normative, cognitive, and procedural criteria, about which I will say more later (Peters 1972). Peters informs us that this more specific concept of education only emerged in the nineteenth century, together with the ideal of an educated person, and he admits that it was the analysis of this more recent and specific concept of education that had been his concern from the beginning.

It further becomes apparent that this more recent, more specific concept of education is really the concept of liberal education. Initially, Peters maintained that it was not his intention to equate his concept of education with that of "liberal education" (1965, 101). A little later, however, he admits that the two are "almost indistinguishable" (1966, 43). After analyzing the demand for a liberal education, and after reviewing the criteria implicit in his central cases of education, Peters concludes: "Indeed the analysis of 'liberal education' has served as an effective and concentrated summary of these basic criteria" (1966, 45). Thus, Peters is in effect equating the two. We must therefore not be misled by the omission of the qualifier "liberal" from Peters's analysis of the concept of education. In fact, he is throughout concerned with analyzing the criteria implicit in the specific concept of liberal education. Here it is important to keep in mind Kimball's historical review of the idea of liberal education. Peters is clearly analyzing what Kimball refers to as the liberal-free ideal of liberal education which emerged in the nineteenth century. In other words, Peters is providing us with an analysis of the Enlightenment ideal of liberal education.

What has all this got to do with indoctrination? Peters at first gives the impression that indoctrination is incompatible with education generally or with any concept of education. After distinguishing between an older and a more recent concept of education, he is forced to concede that indoctrination would be quite compatible with the older, undifferentiated concept of education which indiscriminately marks out a vast range of activities associated with child-rearing and does not have certain value criteria attached to it. However, indoctrination does become a concern if we are talking about the more recent concept of liberal education.

This helps to explain a point that has already been made several times when it was noted that "indoctrination" has not always been a term with pejorative overtones. Even today, we use the term "indoctrination" in a non-pejorative sense, but when this is done we are placing it in the context of the undifferentiated concept of education identified by Peters. If, however, we use the term "education" to refer to the specific concept of liberal education, then and only then is indoctrination incompatible with education. Hence, concern about indoctrination arises out of the context of an acceptance of the Enlightenment ideal of liberal education. An examination of this ideal, together with its underlying values and assumptions, should therefore help to understand the charge of indoctrination as it is made against Christian nurture.

I turn now to a consideration of several strands in Peters's treatment of the ideal of liberal education.

Criteria of Liberal Education

In several of his writings, Peters identifies three sets of criteria implicit in the notion of liberal education – the normative, cognitive, and procedural criteria (Peters 1965, 87-111; 1966, ch. 1; 1967, 1-23; unless otherwise indicated, all quotations in this section are from these three essays). I will briefly consider each criterion.

The first criterion of 'liberal education' is the normative or value criterion. According to Peters, the normative or desirability condition of education governs both the matter and the manner of education. "Education" implies that "something worthwhile is being or has been intentionally transmitted in a morally acceptable manner."

There are several cognitive aspects of liberal education. (1) The educated person must have some body of knowledge. (2) This knowledge must not be merely a collection of disjointed facts. There must also be "some understanding of principles for the organization of facts." (3) This knowledge and understanding will extend to all the "forms of thought and awareness." (4) There must also be an understanding and caring for the internal standards of appraisal that belong to each form of thought and awareness. There must be concern for "cogency, simplicity, and elegance." Commitment to these standards only comes as a result of being "on the inside of a form of thought." (5) Neither knowledge nor understanding can be inert in the sense of being merely memorized, or a result of mindless drill, "for 'education' implies that a man's outlook be transformed by what he knows." (6) This transformation includes caring "about the valuable things involved" in such knowledge and understanding. Educated people must not value these merely for utilitarian or vocational reasons, but they should delight in such things for their own sake. (7) Finally, a certain "wholeness," "breadth," or "cognitive perspective" characterizes the educated person, in contrast to someone who has been merely trained in a narrow specialty.

The third set of criteria governing "liberal education" involves the processes of education. "Education," for Peters, does not refer to just one particular type of activity but refers to many types of activities or processes such as "training, instruction, learning by experience, teaching, and so on." However, governing all these processes are fundamental principles of liberty and respect for persons. We have already seen that the normative criterion applies also to the manner of education. What is taught must be transmitted in a morally acceptable manner. But the criteria of educational processes are also governed by the cognitive criterion. Teaching which is educative not only involves getting students to acquire knowledge, skills, and modes of conduct, "but to acquire them in a manner which involves understanding and an evaluation of the rationale underlying them." Education therefore rules out some procedures of transmission such as conditioning and brainwashing "on the grounds that they lack wittingness and voluntariness on the part of the learner." Peters also identifies indoctrination as incompatible with education.

It is now possible to understand better the context out of which concern about indoctrination arises – the Enlightenment ideal of liberal education. Those who advocate this position rule out indoctrination because it violates the normative, the cognitive, and the procedural criteria which govern the concept of liberal education.

Unfortunately, Peters nowhere gives us a detailed analysis of his concept of indoctrination. However, he does describe it sufficiently for us to understand what he takes it to mean: a process which involves lack of respect for the learner and "is intended to produce a state of mind ... in which an individual has either no grasp of the rationale underlying his beliefs or a type of foundation which encourages no criticism or evaluation of beliefs (e.g., an appeal to authority)" (1966, 42). Peters gives us a succinct description of indoctrination in a later essay: "For 'indoctrination' involves the passing on of fixed beliefs in a way which discourages questions about their validity" (1973b, 138). In another passage, Peters seems to suggest that indoctrination need not be restricted to "processes of teaching and learning which deliberately seek to achieve forms of unthinking behavioral response." It also includes central teaching and learning processes "which do intentionally promote thought, criticism and considered action, but deliberately seek for some purpose to restrict the cognitive framework within which these occur" (Hirst & Peters 1970, 85). Peters further suggests that teaching which, while not seeking to prevent the achievement of understanding, does not encourage it, also involves indoctrination (Hirst & Peters 1970, 85). He finally describes indoctrination as involving "authoritarian education" which discourages independence of mind and the development of autonomy on the part of the student (Peters 1977, 79-84).

There are, in Peters's scattered descriptions of indoctrination, explicit or at least implicit references to all four criteria considered essential to the concept of indoctrination by various philosophers: methods, content, intent, and consequences. It would seem that the dominant emphasis in Peters's description has to do with the method of transmission. Indoctrinatory methods display a lack of respect for the learner, are authoritarian, fail to enhance rational and critical thought, involve biases, and so forth. Peters also argues that indoctrination "obviously has something to do with doctrines" (1966, 41). Implicit in this statement is the suggestion that doctrines somehow fail to satisfy the cognitive criteria, and perhaps also the normative criterion, in that the content is not "worthwhile." Peters is clearly also introducing the intention and consequences criteria when he describes indoctrination as a process in which a teacher intends to produce a closed state of mind.

Liberal Education as Initiation

I turn now to the second strand of Peters's treatment of liberal education. After his analysis of the three criteria of liberal education, Peters goes on to provide "a more positive" and "synthetic" account of the nature of education, a very different account of liberal education inspired no doubt by Michael Oakeshott (Peters 1965, 102-10; 1966, ch. 2; unless otherwise indicated, all quotations in this section are from these two essays). Peters was very sympathetic to Oakeshott's description of education as initiation into the conversation of civilization (Oakeshott 1962, 199). In fact, Peters's inaugural lecture at the London Institute of Education was entitled "Education as Initiation." In that talk he characterized education as involving the development of the mind. But, according to Peters, this development of the mind is not a product of individual experience as the empiricists held. Instead, it is "the product of the initiation of an individual into public traditions enshrined in the language, concepts, beliefs, and rules of a society." Peters also criticizes Kant and Piaget for not recognizing "the extent to which the development of the mind is the product of initiation into public traditions enshrined in a public language." A "social dimension of the development of mind" makes it appropriate to compare education to a process of initiation. Peters even suggests that all education (i.e., liberal education), in so far as it involves initiation into public traditions, can be regarded as a form of socialization.

Included in these "public traditions" are "the more specific modes of thought and awareness such as science, history, mathematics, religion and aesthetic awareness, etc.," each of which is characterized by a "content or 'body of knowledge' and by public procedures by means of which this content has been accumulated, criticized, or revised.[3] Each has its own family of concepts peculiar to it and its own distinctive methods of validation." These "forms of knowledge" are viewed as "a public inheritance" parents and teachers are inviting the child to share and into which he or she is again "initiated." The process is picturesquely described as a transformation of children who are like "the barbarian outside the gates. The problem is to get them inside the citadel of civilization."

Peters is very explicit in his defence of the appropriateness of the term "initiation" to describe liberal education. The term is general enough to cover a wide range of activities such as training, instruction, and teaching, all of which can be part of education. Peters also argues that the comparison of initiation and education is consistent with his earlier analysis of the various criteria governing the concept of education. He states for example, that "initiation," "even when connected with various ceremonies and rites suggests an avenue of access to a body of belief, perhaps to mysteries that are not revealed to the young." Thus the comparison of education to initiation is consistent with the second group of criteria of "education" involving knowledge and understanding. "Initiation" also presupposes that the initiate has freely chosen to be initiated and thus the requirements of "wittingness and voluntariness" in education are satisfied. Initiation, however, does not necessarily satisfy the normative criterion of education, as one can be initiated into things "that are not worthwhile such as gambling or devil worship." The concept of education is therefore a little narrower than initiation. Peters still maintains, however, that liberal education must be seen as a process of initiation (1965, 102; 1966, 54-5).

It is fairly evident that Peters's description of education as initiation captures the heart of the oratorical ideal of liberal education as outlined by Kimball (1986). Earlier in this chapter I noted that Kimball considers the oratorical and philosophical ideals of liberal education to be in constant tension. This same tension appears in Peters's analysis of the various strands of liberal education, where there is a decided break in his treatment of the three criteria of liberal education and his positive account of liberal education as initiation. A similar tension also exists between Peters's description of liberal education as initiation and as liberation, to be considered in the next section. The relation between these two strands is never clearly defined, I believe. This relation will play an important part in my reconstruction of the ideal of liberal education in chapter 8.

Liberal Education as Liberation

Another strand in Peters's treatment of the ideal of liberal education occurs in two later essays: "Ambiguities in Liberal Education and the Problem of its Content" and "Dilemmas in Liberal Education" (1977, chs. 3, 4). In each of these, Peters considers three interpretations of liberal education: liberal education as the pursuit of knowledge for its own sake, liberal education as all-round development, and liberal education as non-authoritarian education or the development of the free human being. In doing so, he uses historical analysis to show how our contemporary understanding of liberal education is rooted in past conceptions of this ideal. This goes somewhat contrary to Kimball (1986) who, as noted earlier, stresses the variety of meanings "liberal education" has taken on in its history.

Peters suggests that the unifying idea behind liberal education is "that of the unimpeded and unconstrained development of the mind" (1977, 46). Liberal education liberalizes. The Latin for liberal is *libere*, which means "to free." Peters examines the expression of this theme of liberation in each of the three historical interpretations of liberal education which he identifies. A review of Peters's analysis will demonstrate what these interpretations have contributed to our understanding of indoctrination, especially as applied to Christian nurture.

The Greeks introduced the ideal of liberal education. It evolved as a reaction to education which was utilitarian in orientation and in which knowledge was pursued for some practical end. The central idea in the Greek notion of liberal education was that knowledge should be pursued for its own sake. This notion was of course based on certain assumptions about human nature, society, and reality (Hirst 1974a, ch. 3). It assumed that reason belonged to the essence of man and that therefore the chief end of humankind was the development of reason. The distinction between liberal and practical education was also based upon a distinction of classes in Greek society in which slaves and tradesmen required only a practical education and in which the leisure class could devote itself to the development of the mind. A metaphysical theory is also at the root of the distinction between liberal and practical education: physical and practical concerns have a lower status in the hierarchy of being than immaterial and intellectual ones.

This ideal of liberal education as the pursuit of knowledge for its own sake was carried over to the middle ages and was used to justify theology as the queen of the sciences. It was strongly upheld by nineteenth-century thinkers such as Matthew Arnold and Cardinal Newman at a time when there was a rapid development of technology (Peters 1977, 47). This view of liberal education is still with us today. I have already noted under the cognitive criteria of Peters's analysis of the commonly accepted meaning of liberal education that the educated person must not value knowledge and understanding merely for utilitarian or vocational reasons but should delight in such things for their own sake. One of the problems of the contemporary discussion of this aspect of liberal education is that of justifying the pursuit of knowledge for its own sake. Peters and Hirst, for example, are very careful to point out that their ideal of liberal education is not dependent on the old Greek doctrines of the function of humankind and the nature of reality (Hirst 1974a, ch. 3; Peters 1966, 153; 1977, 76). They have therefore appealed to a so-called "transcendental" argument, though White (1982, ch. 2), for one, challenges this kind of justification and questions whether this ideal can in fact be supported without a web of metaphysical beliefs, as was the case with the Greek ideal.[4]

It is interesting to note that during the Renaissance the theological adaptation of this ideal of liberal education in the middle ages was called into question because of its alignment with the Church and its nearly exclusive association with the preparation of the clergy. Such practical concerns were thought to undermine the idea of knowledge for its own sake and thus liberal education came to be identified with humanistic studies – a knowledge of the literature and language of Greece and Rome. We see here an expression of the same kind of concern that surrounds the charge of religious indoctrination in which education becomes aligned with an ulterior motive – that of producing good Christians – and hence is viewed as suspect. This problem will be explored further in chapter 5.

The central theme of liberalizing or freedom is captured in this interpretation of liberal education as liberation from practical utilitarian ends which are thought to act as constraints or limitations on the mind's development (Peters 1977, 49). The mind is therefore freed to function according to its true nature, to pursue knowledge and truth, and thereby to find fulfilment and satisfaction.

Peters identifies a second major interpretation of the nineteenth-century ideal of liberal education – the notion of educated "as characterizing the all-round development of a person morally, intellectually and spiritually" (Peters 1972, 9; 1977, 47, 68). The central idea here is all-round development. Today we use the term "general education" to highlight this aspect of liberal education.

Again, the Greeks expressed this aspect of liberal education in what came to be known as the *septem artes liberales* – an introduction to all the forms of knowledge as they were then conceived, as Paul Hirst has observed (1974a, 30-2). This emphasis was surely also an essential component of liberal education in the middle ages when it was stressed that all-round development should include spiritual development, and during which time a study of Holy Scripture was incorporated into the curriculum. During the Renaissance, theology lost its status as the queen of the sciences, and the content of liberal education shifted to the humanities: the philosophy, literature, history, and art of ancient Greece and Rome. The rise of the natural sciences in the eighteenth century led to an expansion of the content of liberal education to include a study of science. More recently, some knowledge of the social sciences has been added to the scope of general education.

The nineteenth-century demand for liberal education must therefore be seen as a renewal of a long-standing emphasis on general education made more urgent now, of course, by the growing specialization and compartmentalization of knowledge and the rapid development of technology and technical training. It was, as Peters notes, as a form of protest against these forces that nineteenth-century thinkers such as Matthew Arnold and Cardinal Newman called for liberal education with all-round development instead of narrow training and specialized schooling.

This ideal of liberal education as all-round development is still very much with us today, though it is now generally described in terms of general education. A significant though subtle change, however, should be noted. Whereas in the middle ages and for some nineteenth-century thinkers all-round development included the development of a person morally, intellectually, and *spiritually*, the third component seems to have evaporated into thin air in modern times. In Peters one finds a subtle shift in emphasis from "all-round development" to "all-round understanding" (1972, 11). I will say more about this later when I explore the secularization of the notion of liberal education. For now it is sufficient to note how this subtle shift expresses itself in contemporary approaches to religious education.

How then is the unifying idea of liberation and freedom expressed in this interpretation of liberal education as general education? The emphasis here is on the mind being freed from a narrow perspective. The aim is to move the child "beyond the present and the particular," a phrase which has been used as the title of a book attempting to develop a theory of liberal education (Bailey 1984). The hope is that as the mind is freed to pursue the full range of truth in all areas it will find fulfilment, freeing the individual from ignorance and prejudice and helping him or her to make intelligent choices in the light of broadened horizons.

How concern about religious indoctrination arises becomes clear here. A religious upbringing is thought to be narrow and confining. It keeps the child within the present and the particular and thus does not allow for choice on the basis of exposure to the full range of religious and non-religious options. It is precisely the narrowness of Christian nurture, its concern merely to transmit a given set of beliefs, and its failure to openly, rationally, and critically explore other ways to interpret experience that leads Paul Hirst, for example, to describe Christian nurture as primitive and indoctrinative (1985, 6-7, 16).

Whereas the previous interpretation of liberal education focuses on the content of education, the third interpretation focuses on methods, aims, and consequences. The central aim of liberal education in this interpretation is the development of autonomy – "the independence of mind of the 'free-man' " (Peters 1977, 79). What is to be avoided is an education that results in unthinking conformity to popular opinion, blind acceptance of authority, dogmatism, and a closed mind. Thus close attention must be paid to methods of education, avoiding authoritarian instruction, stimulating rational thought, and encouraging critical reflection.

This ideal again can be traced back to Greek times when "the assumption was that movement towards the natural end of rationality was self-originated, the development of a potentiality immanent in any individual" (Peters 1977, 62). For Plato, the properly educated person was one whose mind was not swayed by mere popular opinion, and whose body was not controlled by mere passions, but in whom reason was firmly in control of both beliefs and behaviour. Immanual Kant, however, is probably most responsible for the modern emphasis on autonomy. For Kant, the ideal is a society in which each individual is autonomous and voluntarily submits to a moral law that originates from himself.

The theme of liberation and freedom is perhaps most clear in this interpretation of liberal education. The aim of liberal education is the development of free individuals who can think for themselves. The context of teaching is carefully monitored so as to be free from dogmatism and authoritarianism. The result of a liberal education is individuals whose minds are free to reason and to evaluate critically the beliefs of others as well as their own.

This interpretation also shows, perhaps most clearly, how concern about indoctrination arises. Indoctrination does not aim for individual autonomy. Instead, teaching methods are used which have "a general tendency to discourage us to be curious or critical" (Peters 1977, 82). Indoctrination results in blind and dogmatic acceptance of authority and public opinion. And again Christian nurture is thought to be guilty of indoctrination because it suffers on all these counts. Critics maintain that Christian nurture does not aim for autonomy; it discourages critical thinking about one's Christian commitment; it relies on authority and results in a dogmatic and closed mind.

Liberal Education as Secular Education

Another dimension of liberal education I would like to highlight is only implicitly dealt with by Peters. I want to argue that liberal education has acquired a secular meaning in modern times and that we need to take this into account in coming to a full understanding of the context of the charge of religious indoctrination. I have already hinted at this in my treatment of general education where it was noted that in medieval Europe the study of Holy Scripture was viewed as an essential element of liberal education. In fact, the Christian religion was viewed as the foundation of liberal education. Then starting with the Renaissance and continuing with the rise of the natural sciences in the eighteenth century, theology and religion were gradually pushed into the background.

I am referring here to the process of secularization in western society about which much has been written. Secularization has been interpreted in a number of ways but its central thrust is a reference to the gradual erosion of the influence of religious ideas and institutions on all aspects of society, culture, and thought (Guinness 1983, ch. 3; Hirst 1974b, ch. 1). It needs to be stressed that secularization is a process that affects our institutions, our culture, and our thinking, though largely in an unconscious way. We do not choose this modern mentality. Rather, it rubs off on us as we live in our secular cities. "Secularization" needs to be distinguished from "secularism," which is a philosophy and which some people consciously adopt. The process of secularization can obviously enhance the spread of secularism as a philosophy, and this makes it difficult to always separate these two concepts, but I believe it is still important to make a distinction. It should also be noted that a basic assumption underlying the Enlightenment ideal of liberal education is that this process of secularization is a positive process, a key ingredient in the progressive evolution of societies towards modernity (Berger 1977).

There was a time, as was noted in chapter 1, when education in the western world was thoroughly imbued with a Christian orientation. Over time, however, and given the secularization of society, education – and more specifically liberal education – discarded its Christian foundations and orientation. The sciences, morality, art, history, and social and political thought are now considered autonomous areas which can function independent of any religious considerations. Paul Hirst, for example, makes this point repeatedly (1974b, chs. 1, 5; 1981; 1985). In a chapter entitled "The Secularization of Education," Hirst attempts to give an account of "a secularized concept of autonomous education" and concludes with the observation that a rational society will necessarily have its "thoroughly secular schools" (1974b, 85, 90).

Hirst goes on to apply this secularized account of autonomous education to religious education. Interestingly he advocates a kind of "secular religious education" (1974b, 89) which, on the surface, sounds contradictory. But for Hirst, a secular approach to religious education involves an objective study of religion which is autonomous in the sense that it does not itself rest on any particular religious commitments. We see here the basis of the "teaching about religion" approach that is so predominant in our schools today. John Hull too argues for "an open, secular, critical view of religious education," and he does this in the light of the secularization of society and the need for a secular education (1984, 206, 40, 260, 263; cf. 1987).

That this secular approach to religious education is thought to be immune to the charge of indoctrination because of its objective, rational, and modern approach is all too frequently forgotten. It seems to me that the acceptance of various aspects of modernity – such as secularization – as positive features of the contemporary world is a fundamental assumption of much of the criticism of Christian nurture as indoctrinative. Both Hirst and Hull describe the process of secularization as needing to be accepted, not critiqued, and it is for this reason that old-fashioned approaches to religious education involving nurture and initiation into the Christian faith are viewed negatively and even described as "primitive" and "simple" (Hirst 1974b, 80; Hull 1987). Peter Berger, in his assessment of the widespread acceptance of secularization as a positive feature of modern society, challenges the common liberal assumption that the search for identity and meaning in one's ethnic, cultural, and religious heritage is part of the primal, primitive, and pre-rational past out of which we are evolving (1974, esp. 14, 199, 210). A critical assessment of this assumption appears in later chapters. Here I simply want to underscore the fact that this assumption underlies the modern conception of liberal education. Liberal education has acquired a secular meaning.

Liberal Education and Schools

A final aspect of liberal education needs to be taken into account. For most people, liberal education is closely linked with public schooling or with state-supported education. Paul Hirst, for example, in his analysis of the implications of secularization for education, links the previous point regarding secular liberal education with the need for secular institutions that provide liberal education. "Just as in intellectual affairs religious thought has been displaced by the growth of autonomous, secular areas of thought, so in society religious institutions have been displaced by the growth of autonomous, secular institutions" (Hirst 1974b, 5). Thus Hirst argues again and again for "thoroughly secular schools" financed by a secular society as the context in which secular liberal education should take place (1974b, 88-90; 1981, 1985).

Similarly R.S. Peters argues that "with the coming of industrialism ... and the increasing demand for knowledge and skill consequent on it, 'education' became increasingly associated with 'schooling' and with the sort of training and instruction that went on in special institutions" (1972, 8-9). This large-scale change, Peters informs us, culminated in the development of compulsory schooling for all. Peters describes schools as having a double function: their essence is liberal education, but they also have a subsidiary role in performing certain instrumental functions concerned with satisfying the interests of the state and of individual children (1966, 74, 167). Peters further admits that the ideal of a liberally educated person "has very much taken root" in educational circles today, and that "it is natural, therefore, for those working in educational institutions to conceive of what they are doing as being connected with the development of such a person" (1972, 9). Thus, when Hirst and Peters discuss liberal education, they are not just talking about liberal education but rather about liberal education within the context of the school, and I believe this reflects the meaning ordinarily attached to this term today. The notion of liberal education is really loaded with some additional baggage belonging to such notions as "schooling," "formal education," "compulsory education," and "state education."

This can be further verified by examining the way in which liberalism as a social/political theory is related to the Enlightenment ideal of liberal education. Penny Enslin explores this relationship when she distinguishes between various forms of liberalism, one of which – liberal-socialism – maintains that the state must accept responsibility for the welfare of its citizens, including education (1984). I would suggest that it is this strand of liberal thinking that underlies and is an integral part of our modern concept of liberal education. Peters, while recognizing the seeming incompatibility of state-enforced compulsory education and the principle of freedom inherent in liberalism, nevertheless justifies this by arguing that the state has a responsibility to provide all children with the necessary background and knowledge to be able to make autonomous choices later in life (1977, 80).

If therefore we want to understand the context out of which concern for indoctrination arises, we must also take into account the institutional and the liberal-socialistic overtones implicit in today's ideal of liberal education. It is because of the liberal-socialistic assumptions underlying Hirst's view of secular and state-supported liberal education that he views the education that occurs in church-related schools and homes with a good deal of suspicion. Religion is relegated to the private sphere and as such has no place in public institutions except, of course, in so far as it is studied from an objective and secular point of view.

It is also very important to keep in mind that, just as liberal education is today associated with institutions (schools supported by the state), so indoctrination should be seen as having institutional meaning. This is often overlooked in discussions concerning indoctrination which frequently assume that it is individual persons who indoctrinate. On closer inspection, however, it will be found that it is not just an individual, but a teacher *in a school* who is charged with indoctrination. In other words, there is an institutional context in which the individual is operating. Hence the paradigm of indoctrination discussed in chapter 1: Roman Catholic teachers in Roman Catholic schools supported by the Roman Catholic Church. It is for this reason that I will devote an entire chapter to the often overlooked topic of institutional indoctrination.

The primary thrust of this chapter has been to locate the context out of which concern for indoctrination arises. The charge of indoctrination does not simply emerge out of thin air. It is based on certain assumptions and values. I have argued that we can only fully understand the charge of religious indoctrination if we understand the assumptions and values underlying the ideal of liberal education. Indoctrination is today understood to be the antithesis of the very specific concept of liberal education, the Enlightenment ideal of liberal education. I have tried to highlight some of the essential features of liberal education by philosophical and historical analysis. I turn now to some possible implications of the above analysis for providing an answer to the charge of religious indoctrination.

ONE POSSIBLE REPLY TO THE CHARGE OF RELIGIOUS INDOCTRINATION

One possible response to the charge of religious indoctrination is to my mind often overlooked. If the charge of indoctrination has its roots in the specific context of liberal education, then one way in which to answer the charge of religious indoctrination is simply to reject the ideal of liberal education out of which the charge arises. The critic who makes the charge of religious indoctrination does so on the basis of certain assumptions and values which, as I have argued, are implicit in the ideal of liberal education. The Christian parent or teacher can therefore respond by simply rejecting the assumptions and values inherent in the critic's charge, surely a respectable answer to the charge as long as it is done in a responsible manner. The ideal of liberal education is certainly not a self-evident ideal and thus there is nothing to stop a Christian parent or teacher from saying, "I simply disagree with your ideal of liberal education. I have a different theory of education."

Some rationale can indeed be given in support of this position. Peters himself has admitted that there are certain "ambiguities" or "dilemmas" inherent in the ideal of liberal education (1977, chs. 3, 4). A problem emerges when we focus on the theme of liberation or freedom central to liberal education. Peters draws our attention to the well-known "paradox of freedom" (1977, 68). Freedom and autonomy can never be absolute because individuals need to submit themselves to the necessary constraints of law, justice, and the welfare and interests of others. The ideal of general education is also difficult to achieve because of the need for specialization. As well, there is the problem of making a clear-cut distinction between knowledge for its own sake and practical knowledge. The ideal of autonomy is especially problematic because education necessarily involves being told things by others, being initiated into public traditions, and being influenced by example (1977, 62). There is also a problem with compulsory schooling which clearly conflicts with the liberal ideal of freedom (1977, 80). These ambiguities and dilemmas could be seen as justification for rejecting the ideal of liberal education entirely.

It can further be argued that the assumptions and values underlying the ideal of liberal education are not self-evidently correct. In fact, there clearly are difficulties in justifying the ideal of liberal education – witness the arguments and the objections to these arguments in recent discussions of this matter – some philosophers offering a "transcendental" justification, others objecting to it, and still others admitting that there are difficulties in justifying various aspects of the ideal of liberal education without assuming certain religious and metaphysical doctrines which are in turn problematic (Bailey 1984, ch. 4; Hirst 1974a, ch. 3; Peters 1966, ch. 5; J.P. White 1982, ch. 2).

While there have always been some people who have criticized the values inherent in liberalism and the theory of liberal education, there seem to be renewed criticisms today. Some, those for example from a Marxist perspective, most Westerners would tend to dismiss, perhaps too quickly (see, for example, Harris 1979; M. Matthews 1980). However, other important recent critiques of liberalism are written by scholars who must otherwise be acknowledged as quite sympathetic with western democratic values (for example, the communitarian critics of liberalism such as Hauerwas 1983; MacIntyre [1981]1984; and Sandel 1982). Still other writers critique these theories from the perspective of philosophical hermeneutics, critical theory, philosophical historiography, or what is sometimes simply referred to as postmodernism (Baynes, Bohman, et al. 1987; Stout 1981; Toulmin 1990).

Some writers go so far as to say that the intellectual scaffolding of modernity is systematically being dismantled (Toulmin 1990, ch. 4). Others maintain that liberalism is crumbling and in disarray, and that we are entering a post-modern and post-liberal era (Bowers 1987, ch. 1).

Given that there are problems inherent in the ideal of liberal education itself, that there are problems in justifying the ideal of liberal education, and that there are many scholars who, while in other respects rational and intelligent, reject this ideal, we cannot simply dismiss too quickly those who reply to the charge of religious indoctrination by rejecting outright the liberal context from which this charge arises. I believe that this is one possible response to the charge of religious indoctrination and I believe that it deserves to be taken seriously, *but this is not the approach taken in this book*. Instead, I am interested in answering the charge from a liberal point of view, though it is most important to note that I will be making some significant qualifications to these liberal assumptions and values and to the ideal of liberal education described in this chapter. My qualified liberal starting point is based on a conviction that we need to seek a reconciliation between the insights of "modern" and "post-modern" thought (see Toulmin 1990, ch. 5). My approach is very much in keeping with that found in C.A. Bowers's study, *Elements of a Post-Liberal Theory of Education* (1987). We need to revitalize the ideal of liberal education, building on the strengths of liberalism, drawing on the correctives of conservatism, and thereby developing a more adequate notion of liberal education (Bowers 1987, 111-12). My approach can also be seen as restoring a needed balance between the oratorical and philosophical ideals of liberal education as referred to earlier and as suggested by Kimball (1986, 239-41).

The purpose of this chapter is therefore not only to understand the context out of which the charge of indoctrination arises, but also the context out of which the *reply* to the charge of religious indoctrination will be made. I agree (in part) with the basic assumptions and values underlying liberalism and liberal education as traditionally understood and as outlined by R.S. Peters. I accept the value of knowledge and understanding. I agree that teaching must respect the freedom and integrity of the student. I believe that autonomy is a legitimate goal of education. I accept the importance of rationality and critical openness. I agree that the state has an interest in the education of its citizens. I would hasten to add, however, that all this does not say very much because these statements cry out for clarification and, as I have already stated, I will want to make some important qualifications with regard to each of them.

Here it is necessary to return to Peters's own identification of ambiguities and dilemmas inherent in the ideal of liberal education. His later essays conclude by frankly admitting that he has not resolved these same ambiguities and dilemmas. Instead, he confesses that his analysis points to "the necessity for much more thought" in resolving them, particularly in trying to distinguish liberal from illiberal teaching procedures (1977, 84-5, 66-7). Peters's frank confession concerning the need for more clarity in distinguishing liberal education from non-liberal education is significant and needs to be taken seriously, and can be seen as the starting point for my approach in this book. While broadly accepting the ideal of liberal education, together with its underlying values and assumptions, I want to subject all of this to critical scrutiny, not with a view to discarding the ideal, but rather with a view to moving toward a more defensible and carefully defined ideal. I will argue that much of the thrust of the charge of indoctrination against Christian nurture is rooted in what Peters identifies as the ambiguities and dilemmas in liberal education.

I will be particularly concerned to define more carefully the distinction between liberal and non-liberal education, with a view to overcoming the ambiguities and dilemmas identified by Peters. More specifically, I will argue that the ideals of autonomy, rationality, and critical openness need to be modified so as to become more realistic and philosophically defensible. A more realistic version of these ideals will be identified by qualifying each with the preface "normal" – hence, normal autonomy, normal rationality, and normal critical openness. Overcoming the ambiguities and dilemmas inherent in the traditional ideal of liberal education and introducing the necessary qualifications to make this ideal more philosophically defensible should remove much of the sting of the charge of indoctrination against Christian nurture.

For those of my readers who adhere to the Christian faith, let me add that I believe that my starting point is consistent with a fairly orthodox interpretation of Christianity. Here we need to keep in mind that the ideal of liberal education has its Christian moorings as well. It is John Henry Cardinal Newman, former Protestant turned Catholic, who is generally acknowledged as providing us with a classical exposition of the theory of liberal education. Ryken, in "Puritan Piety and the Liberated Mind," notes that Luther believed that "you parents cannot prepare a more dependable treasure for your children than an education in the liberal arts" (1980, 26). It was this Christian ideal of the liberally educated mind that first inspired the establishment of schools in western societies as has already been noted in chapter 1. Similar observations could be made about liberalism generally. A biography of G.K. Chesterton illustrates this well. A.S. Dale describes, as one "fascinatingly original aspect" of Chesterton's conversion, how he discovered that the roots of his liberalism were in fact orthodox credal Christianity. Chesterton found the classic principles of liberalism "so intertwined in his thinking about Christianity that he himself seemed not to know where one began and the other ended" (Dale 1982, 103).

I would therefore suggest that the underlying principles of liberal education, when properly qualified, are compatible with a fairly orthodox version of Christianity. What is being assumed here is the possibility of some shared convictions and beliefs between Christians and non-Christians. This is quite in keeping with long-standing Christian doctrines such as the Roman Catholic doctrine of Natural Law or Natural Reason and the Protestant doctrine of Common

Grace (see Hirst 1981, 88-9; Van Til 1974). Some common ground exists between Christians and non-Christians and I believe that the essential aspects of the theories of liberal education and liberalism are among them. More will be said about this when dealing with specific components of liberal education.

This is not at all to suggest that there might not be some Christians who would strongly disagree with the above claims about the compatibility of orthodox Christianity and the ideals of liberal education and liberalism. Anti-liberal forces have always existed in the Christian church, but I would suggest that these do not belong to mainstream Christian thought. To establish this claim is of course a topic in its own right and cannot be explored here. Nor should I be understood to suggest that there are not some secular writers who would strongly disagree with my suggestions that the principles of liberalism and liberal education are compatible with the Christian tradition. Clearly some people might reject outright the possibility of such compatibility while others do allow for some degree of compatibility in certain areas.

This question of the compatibility between Christian and non-Christian thought about education calls for further exploration because it relates to one important problem which is often overlooked in the debate concerning religious indoctrination: the danger that those who make the charge win their case in an arbitrary fashion. We need to recognize the possibility of so defining liberal education and Christian nurture that they are incompatible and hence Christian nurture is labelled as indoctrinatory. For example, if the ideal of autonomy in liberal education is defined so as to rule out any acceptance of outside authority (as sometimes occurs in the literature), then of course a problem arises with regard to orthodox Christian beliefs and education in which believers are called to acknowledge the authority of God and in some way submit to him. A strict and strong sense of autonomy is clearly incompatible with Christian faith. I would suggest, however, that to appeal to such a strict and strong sense of autonomy and then to use this definition of autonomy as a basis of labelling Christian nurture as indoctrinatory is somewhat arbitrary because this notion of autonomy is itself problematic as will be shown later. Those who charge religious indoctrination must therefore be very careful not to win their case by definition, a danger recognized by a few writers (e.g., White 1972a, 125).

This chapter has been primarily concerned with exploring the context of the charge of indoctrination against Christian nurture. An exploration of the ideal of liberal education has also served as a rough outline of the context from which an attempt will be made to respond to this charge in the chapters that follow. I agree in general with the basic values that underlie the contemporary ideal of liberal education, though this ideal may need reconstruction in order to overcome some ambiguities and dilemmas inherent in the ideal, problems that even its staunchest advocates have recognized.

This chapter should also serve to explain why the charge of indoctrination against Christian nurture merits the attention it is being given in this book. The ideal of liberal education is an important one and it gives expression to some fundamental values shared by most of us, Christian and non-Christian alike. Peters is also surely correct in suggesting that the ideal of liberal education is intimately related to our ideal of what it means to become a whole person. Indoctrination, however, is generally understood to be the very antithesis of liberal education. It therefore follows that the notion of indoctrination is very important for educationalists, most of whom feel that it should be avoided at all costs. Since contemporary philosophers of education have paid so much attention to the concept of indoctrination, it is important to achieve a clear understanding of that which violates the principles of the ideal of liberal education.

Moreover, if Christian nurture necessarily involves indoctrination, as is claimed by some, either it must be condemned or the charge against it refuted. Much of this book is devoted to refuting the charge that Christian nurture necessarily involves indoctrination. Even if the charge against Christian nurture is the more modest claim that such nurture often involves indoctrination or that there is a high probability of indoctrination in nurture – which is perhaps the more common way of expressing the charge – it needs to be taken very seriously. One approach that could and will be taken is to show that the probability of indoctrination is not so great as is often thought. But given that there is still some danger of indoctrination in Christian nurture, we need to become clear about where and how it occurs, so that it can be avoided. This too will be investigated.

The next four chapters explore four common ways in which the charge of indoctrination has been made against Christian nurture. They are based on criteria that have been traditionally thought of as defining the concept of indoctrination: content, methods, intention, and consequences. Each criterion will be related to a key ingredient of the ideal of liberal education: content to the scientific ideal, methods to the ideal of rationality, intention to the ideal of autonomy, and consequences to the ideal of critical openness. In each case, I want to show that there are problems in our understanding of the criterion of indoctrination and its associated ideal and that the charge of indoctrination against Christian nurture is therefore less strong than it is generally thought to be. In these chapters I am particularly concerned to show that Christian nurture does not necessarily involve indoctrination, that it is possible for Christian nurture to satisfy the ideals of liberal education.

3 Content of Indoctrination and the Scientific Ideal

Indoctrination is usually associated with a certain kind of content. One writer goes so far as to make content, and only content, the necessary and sufficient criterion for determining whether a person is indoctrinated (Kazepides 1987, 233). Most others make the more modest claim that content is one of several necessary conditions of indoctrination. What is generally assumed here is that indoctrination is in some way related to a certain kind of belief – namely doctrines, sometimes also identified as ideologies or world-views.[1] R.S. Peters, for example, argues that "whatever else "indoctrination" means, it obviously has something to do with doctrines" (1966, 41).

Doctrines or ideologies are generally thought to be found primarily in such areas as religion, politics, and perhaps also morality. Hence, indoctrination is seen as in some way specially related to religious beliefs, political ideologies, and moral convictions: "The original and proper home of doctrines is religion," and hence "the paradigm cases of indoctrination are to be found in religious communities and institutions" (Kazepides 1987, 234, 230). Christian nurture, therefore, since it involves the teaching of doctrines, is a prime suspect for indoctrination.

Kazepides further argues that science contains no doctrines and that it therefore follows that indoctrination cannot occur in science (1987, 229). Barrow and Woods concur: "The very nature of scientific activity precludes the possibility of indoctrination in science" (1988, 76). While others might allow for the possibility of indoctrination in science, there is general agreement that science epitomizes that which is ideal in a liberal education. It is in science that one finds rationality, critical openness, logical rigour, objectivity, and procedures by which to test competing claims. Paul Hirst, for example, along with Peters, identifies the content of a liberal education in terms of several "forms of knowledge," each of which is distinguishable in terms of certain central concepts, a distinctive logical structure, and unique criteria with which to test statements against experience (Hirst, 1974a, ch. 3). Science has no trouble qualifying as a publicly accepted form of knowledge, and it would seem that it is the measuring stick for other components in a liberal education. It is because there are questions about religion's being a publicly accepted form of knowledge that Hirst has some doubts as to whether teaching for commitment in the area of religion is appropriate for a liberal education and that he tends to associate the teaching of religion with indoctrination (1974a, 180-8; 1985, 7).

This relation between indoctrination and doctrines has been defined in several not always clearly distinguished ways. It is first frequently suggested that indoctrination is necessarily limited to doctrines. Many philosophers point to an etymological connection between "indoctrination" and "doctrines" which would suggest that "indoctrination" is conceptually linked to "doctrines." Antony Flew, for example, bluntly states, "No doctrines, no indoctrination" (1972b, 114). This is how philosophers generally describe the content criterion of indoctrination: doctrines are a logically necessary condition of indoctrination.

Second, some writers, while denying that "indoctrination" is necessarily restricted to "doctrines," would nevertheless concede that there is a strong contingent connection between the two. What is being suggested here is that indoctrination is very likely to occur in doctrinal areas such as religion, though it is not necessarily limited to these areas.

The third possible relation between indoctrination and doctrines relates closely to the second. It is widely maintained that when teaching doctrines, there is a high probability that one is indoctrinating. Antony Flew, for example, argues not only that indoctrination is limited to doctrines but also that the teaching of doctrines very probably involves indoctrination (1972a, 73-7; 1972b, 113-14). Even the philosophers who reject the first relation suggesting that doctrinal content is a logically necessary condition of indoctrination nevertheless still want to maintain that there is a strong contingent connection between indoctrination and doctrines. J.P. White and Snook, for example, reject the content criterion of indoctrination but still argue that the teaching of religious doctrine most often involves indoctrination (White 1972a, 129; Snook 1972b, 56-7, 68, 74-5).

White and Snook along with other writers sometimes seem to be making the even stronger claim that the teaching of religious doctrines necessarily involves indoctrination. Here it is necessary to be careful to distinguish teaching *of* religion from teaching *about* religion. We have already seen that many people consider that various approaches such as a comparative study of religions or a philosophical study of religion escape religious indoctrination. It is only the teaching of religion, teaching for commitment, religious nurture, that is singled out in making the indoctrinative charge, and a few writers make the very strong claim that Christian nurture, for one, necessarily involves indoctrination. White comes very close to suggesting this when he states, "If rational conviction is here impossible, it is difficult to see how one could teach religion (qua religion) without indoctrinating" (1972a, 129). Snook too seems to make such a strong claim as applied to the teaching of at least some religious statements: "Indoctrination is inevitable if religion is taught" (1972b, 75). Here then is a fourth possible relation between indoctrination and religious doctrines. For some, the teaching of religious doctrines necessarily entails indoctrination.

This chapter focuses on the claim that indoctrination is conceptually related to doctrinal content. The bulk of the chapter attempts to show that indoctrination is not necessarily limited to religious doctrines. I also want to show that Christian nurture is not necessarily incompatible with the scientific ideal implicit in liberal education. Much of the argument used to establish the above objectives will also serve to weaken the other claims concerning relations of probability between indoctrination and the teaching of religious doctrine. A full consideration of these other relations appears in chapter 8 since they can only be adequately dealt with after treating the remaining criteria of indoctrination.

"DOCTRINES"

Before it is possible to evaluate whether or not indoctrination is limited to the doctrinal sphere, it is essential to become clear about the meaning of the notion "doctrine."

It is surprising that, despite the widespread acceptance of the content criterion of "indoctrination" which limits indoctrination to doctrines, very little attention has been focused specifically on the concept "doctrine" presupposed by this criterion. Snook, among

others, points to this neglect and then goes on to give as his "principal argument" against the content criterion that the concept "doctrine" is itself extremely vague (1972b, 32). But surely this in itself
cannot be used as an argument against the content criterion of "indoctrination." If a concept is vague, then the philosopher's assign-
ment becomes to sharpen the concept so as to eliminate vagueness.

I therefore propose to examine some of the vague descriptions of
doctrines as found in the literature on indoctrination. I will focus primarily on the following authors who make the content criterion primary in their analyses of "indoctrination," and who therefore have
more to say about doctrines than most other writers: Kazepides
(1987, 1989), Spiecker (1987), Wilson (1964, 1972a, 1972b), Flew
(1972a, 1972b), and Gregory and Woods (1972).

Logical Status of Doctrinal Beliefs

Frequent reference is made, in describing the content criterion of
"indoctrination," to the "logical status" of those beliefs which are
subject to indoctrination. This phrase is useful in grouping one set of
characteristics thought to be essential to "doctrines." For Wilson,
the essential aspect of the logical status of doctrinal beliefs is that
they are uncertain (1964). Kazepides claims that doctrines "are outside the rational tradition" (1987, 235). For Flew, the essential characteristic of a doctrine is that it involves beliefs which are "either
false or not known to be true" (1972a, 70-1; 1972b, 112-13). Gregory
and Woods agree with Flew, except that they do not wish to include
false beliefs or "manifest untruths" as doctrine (1972, 171). These
characterizations are, however, highly ambiguous, and thus we
need to unpack the various meanings implicit in these descriptions
of the logical status of doctrines.

False beliefs. Flew suggests that doctrines may involve false beliefs.
He interprets Wilson as also defining doctrines in terms of "the actual falsehood" of beliefs involved (Flew 1972a, 68-9). Wilson in
places describes beliefs subject to indoctrination as "irrational," and
at times seems to equate these with false beliefs (1964, 35-6, 38;
1972a, 103).

Beliefs with insufficient or no evidence. The frequent descriptions of
doctrines as "not known to be true" are, unfortunately, both vague
and ambiguous. "Not known to be true" can be interpreted in several ways. To say that a doctrine involves a belief not known to be
true may mean that there is no evidence for the belief or at least not

sufficient evidence. Although these two notions are different, I believe they can be conveniently grouped together. Wilson describes these beliefs as uncertain in the sense "that we have no logical right to be sure," there is "no publicly accepted evidence for them" (1964, 27, 28). Flew contrasts beliefs which can "on the best possible evidence, reasonably be said to be known; and those at the opposite extreme for which, whether or not they happen to be true, there is no evidence at all" (1972b, 107). It is the latter which are subject to indoctrination for Flew.

Beliefs with ambiguous evidence. Another interpretation of the phrase "not known to be true or false" is alluded to most clearly by Gregory and Woods. "Doctrines provide, as it were, room for manoeuvre in debate. There is something to be said in support, and something to be said against" (Gregory & Woods 1972, 172). The "uncertainty" that Wilson and Flew talk about could be attributed to the ambiguity of evidence. Thus, Flew also describes doctrines as involving "debatable issues" (1972b, 108).

Unfalsifiable beliefs. Another important characteristic frequently associated with doctrines is that they cannot be verified or falsified. Kazepides states that "doctrines are in principle unfalsifiable beliefs about the existence of beings, states of affairs or relationships" (1987, 235). When Wilson talks about a deeper level of uncertainty characteristic of doctrines such as religious, political, and moral beliefs, in contrast to scientific beliefs, he is suggesting that "we do not know what sort of evidence to look for ... We cannot even be sure that any question of truth, falsehood, or evidence arises at all" with doctrinal beliefs (Wilson 1964, 29-30). Wilson seems to be alluding to the positivist principle of verification or falsification by which metaphysical, moral, and religious beliefs are classified as factually meaningless because there are no criteria by which to settle questions of truth or falsehood.

Flew can also be interpreted as alluding to this when he describes indoctrination as "teaching as known the sort of thing which really is not or *cannot be known*" (1972a, 78; emphasis mine). This would certainly be in line with other of Flew's essays on religion in which he uses the positivist principle of falsification to show that religious language is factually meaningless (see Flew 1972b, 116, note 34).

Snook and White both interpret Gregory and Woods as also defining doctrines as unverifiable (Snook 1972b, 33; White 1972b, 192-3). It would appear that Gregory and Woods do have this interpretation in mind when they characterize an example of a "pure doctrine," such as religion, in the following way: "[It] is a logical nonsense to talk, in the sphere of religion, of the setting up of hypotheses and of the subsequent attempt to confirm or disconfirm them experimentally" (1972, 173, cf. 168).

Beliefs held obstinately. The question of verification or falsification is often confused with what I want to argue is a quite different notion of "obstinacy." Verification or falsification has to do with the logical status of the beliefs involved. But sometimes it is not the beliefs themselves but a certain psychological fact about persons holding these beliefs that makes it impossible to prove these beliefs false to the believer. Thus, doctrines are sometimes described as beliefs which cannot be proven false because *believers* in these doctrines hold onto them in an obstinate manner. Spiecker has recently highlighted this aspect of doctrines when he maintains that "people who subscribe to certain doctrines screen these propositions from criticism" (1987, 262).

I believe both Gregory and Woods and Flew have confused the two different notions of obstinacy and verification/falsification. Gregory and Woods, for example, describe doctrines thus: "From the standpoint of the believer they have the status of universal, unfalsifiable truths" (1972, 168). Here we have references to both the status of the beliefs themselves and to the believer. Gregory and Woods clearly move to the notion of obstinacy when they stress that it is *people* "who elevate these doctrines to the status of incorrigible truths, who passionately believe in their essential truth," or who hold them as "absolutely and incorrigibly true" (1972, 177, 167-8).

Flew also seems to refer to this psychological characteristic of the way in which people hold on to doctrinal beliefs regardless of the counter-evidence. He criticizes the traditional Christian Church "which seeks to fix in the minds of children an unshakable conviction of the truth of its specific doctrines" (1972b, 114; see also 1972a, 76). Thus, associated with doctrines is that they are held with unshakable conviction. Strictly speaking, this feature of obstinacy should not be considered under the heading "logical status of beliefs" at all as it involves a psychological description of the believer. I treat it here because it is so often associated with the issue of falsification which does involve the question of the logical status of religious beliefs.

Beliefs lacking public agreement. The final interpretation of doctrines as beliefs "not known to be true or false" involves the lack of public agreement concerning these beliefs. Wilson's description of religious, political, and moral beliefs as "uncertain" clearly turns also on the fact that there is no "publicly accepted evidence" for them (1964, 28). Even the characterization of these beliefs as involving a deeper level of uncertainty about whether or not there are any truth criteria involves the problem of lack of agreement. We are agreed, Wilson states, on how to answer scientific questions, but we are not agreed on how to answer metaphysical and moral questions. "These are complex matters, about which philosophers are still not in agreement" (Wilson 1964, 29, 30).

Flew's description of doctrines as "debatable issues" includes the connotation that these are issues over which there is public disagreement (1972b, 108). Flew chides Wilson for not sufficiently taking into account the fact of "disagreements about what, or what sort of (thing) is or is not known" (Flew 1972a, 78). There is also an implicit reference to public disagreement in Gregory and Woods' statement, "Doctrines provide, as it were, room for manoeuvre in debate" (1972, 172).

Scope of Doctrinal Beliefs

Another important set of characteristics frequently associated with doctrines has to do with their scope, two aspects of which need to be dealt with.

Systems of beliefs. "Doctrines are not isolated beliefs but form a system of interrelated beliefs that constitutes the foundation of a particular world view, defines human nature, and determines man's 'proper' place in the world," according to Kazepides (1987, 235). Gregory and Woods make passing references to "systems of belief" as another sense of "doctrine" (1972, 182, 175-6). "The indoctrinator's conclusions form part of a constellation," according to Scruton Ellis-Jones et al. (1985, 22). This would concur with one meaning assigned to "doctrine" in the *Oxford English Dictionary*: "A body or system of principles or tenets; a doctrinal or theoretical system."

We have already seen how Flew holds that a doctrine is necessarily a belief which is either false or at least not known to be true. But this is not sufficient because, as he himself admits, there are many such beliefs which are not classified as doctrines. In order to be classified as doctrines, beliefs must satisfy another condition. They must be "somehow tied up with something wider and more ideological" (Flew 1972a, 71). What Flew means by this is not entirely clear. Part of the meaning seems to be that doctrines involve a wider system of beliefs. But there seems to be more to it than this.

Wide scope and generality. I believe that the real focus of Flew's description of doctrines as "somehow tied up with something wider and more ideological" has to do with the wide ranging implications of a doctrinal belief. This is the point stressed by Gregory and Woods. In contrast to other beliefs, doctrines "have a scope and generality that others do not" (Gregory and Woods 1972, 168; cf. 174, 185). Often they entail a complete world-view or a comprehensive philosophy of life. This broad scope may be due to the fact that doctrines involve a complete system of beliefs. But a single statement, involving a fundamental presupposition of a system of beliefs, can itself have a broad scope. Thus Flew seems to allow for doctrines which are individual statements (e.g., 1972b, 114).

Momentous Character of Doctrinal Beliefs

A final set of characteristics of doctrines, stressed by Gregory and Woods, involve various aspects of the momentousness of these beliefs.

Importance of beliefs. Doctrines such as those in religion and politics involve beliefs that are "of great moment to mankind involving as they do considerations relating to man's place in the universe and the ways in which societies may best be organized" (Gregory & Woods 1972, 166; cf. 168). The importance of these beliefs derives in part from their scope, as considered in the previous section. This description is no doubt somewhat vague. However, Gregory and Woods are trying to do justice to the fact that generally we would not call unimportant details "doctrines."

Self-involving beliefs. Gregory and Woods argue that because doctrines are matters of great moment to mankind, "acceptance of the doctrinal system or ideology is no mere academic matter – there is commitment to act in particular ways, to profess and act out a particular value and way of life" (1972, 166; cf. 177-8). Doctrinal beliefs are "intimately related to action and purposive activity in a way in which many other beliefs are not" (Gregory & Woods, 1972, 168). Doctrines have "an overriding prescriptive function," according to Kazepides (1987, 235; cf. Spiecker, 1987, 262).

Wilson also alludes to this feature of doctrines. He suggests that political and moral beliefs are "closer to the heart of the individual than other beliefs and skills" (Wilson 1964, 27). Commenting on the content criterion of "indoctrination," he argues that "it is not merely contingent that those areas which involve free commitment – preeminently morality, politics, and religion – offer model cases for indoctrination" (Wilson 1964, 103).

Beliefs promoted with evangelistic zeal. There is also a certain evangelistic zeal which seems to characterize those holding doctrinal beliefs (Scruton, Ellis-Jones, et al. 1985, 24). Gregory and Woods trace this zeal to the fact that those holding them consider such beliefs to be of momentous concern to mankind. The importance of doctrinal beliefs "leads to a strong urge to convince others, the waverers, the unbelievers, of their essential truth" (Gregory & Woods, 1972, 168; cf. 177-8). This feature is also related to a previous point concerning the actions and attitudes implied by a doctrinal belief. It would seem that doctrines necessarily entail commitment to evangelism or the persuasion of others to accept these beliefs.

Beliefs backed by a group or institution. A final aspect of doctrinal beliefs involves their social or institutional character. This feature is again related to the previous points. It is because of the importance of these beliefs and the need to engage in evangelism that a group or an institution promotes them. Kazepides similarly argues that doctrines "presuppose the existence of *authorities* or *institutions* which have the power to uphold them when they are challenged by critics, the heretics, or the faithless and to punish the enemies" (1987, 235). Thus Gregory and Woods and Flew make frequent reference to the Roman Catholic Church or the Communist Party as providing the context out of which doctrines arise (Flew, 1972a, 75-6, 79; 1972b, 106, 109; Gregory & Woods, 1972, 166, 187-8).

DOCTRINES, RELIGION, AND SCIENCE

We are now in a position to evaluate the above characterizations of doctrines as found in the literature on the concept of indoctrination. Before dealing with the major criticism, I wish to make a few preliminary comments about past descriptions of doctrines.

The very necessity for such a detailed analysis of the past descriptions of doctrines implies a criticism. Given the long-standing and general acceptance of the content criterion, and given the fact that there exists a considerable body of literature dealing with the concept of indoctrination, one would expect that the concept "doctrine" would have been clarified. One would further expect philosophers steeped in the analytic tradition not to describe doctrines in vague and ambiguous phrases such as "not known to be true." Snook is therefore in part justified in objecting to past descriptions of the content criterion of "indoctrination" because of the extreme vagueness of the concept of doctrines (1972b, 32).

Second, some of the characteristics identified above contradict each other. For example, if it is maintained that doctrines cannot be verified or falsified, then it cannot also be maintained that doctrines involve those beliefs that are false. To identify a doctrine as false is to admit the possibility of evidence or counter-evidence. But this is precisely what is denied when it is claimed that doctrines cannot be verified or falsified. Further, to talk of "no evidence" or "lack of sufficient evidence" presupposes that it does make sense to talk of evidence or the lack of it. But to affirm at the same time that doctrines cannot be verified or falsified is to reject the very possibility of talk of evidence, and is therefore again to contradict oneself.

Third, there is a problem involving the "logical status" of doctrinal beliefs. If doctrines are defined as false beliefs or as beliefs with no evidence, insufficient evidence, or even ambiguous evidence, a fundamental question arises of who assigns status to the beliefs. There are obviously differences of opinion about whether a belief is false or lacks evidence, and this is problematic for people who wish to define doctrines in terms of these criteria. Although some writers touch on this problem, I do not think it is adequately dealt with or resolved.

My major criticism concerning past descriptions is that the characteristics assigned to doctrines do not clearly and unproblematically distinguish paradigm cases of doctrine from paradigm cases of non-doctrine. There is general agreement among those defending the content criterion of "indoctrination" that religious beliefs are a paradigm of doctrine, and scientific beliefs are a paradigm of non-doctrine. If, therefore, it can be established with some degree of plausibility that the characteristics dealt with in the previous section are present in scientific beliefs, or absent in religious beliefs, then I will have undermined the basic thrust of the content criterion of "indoctrination," since the whole point of this criterion is to distinguish doctrinal from non-doctrinal beliefs and to limit indoctrination to the former. I will put my detailed argument into broader perspective later in the chapter.

Logical Status of Doctrinal Beliefs

The first three descriptions of doctrines falling under the logical status of beliefs can be conveniently dealt with as a group. If doctrines are defined in terms of any or all of these criteria, then it should be obvious that science too contains doctrines. A review of the history of science would reveal many cases in which false beliefs were adhered to and promulgated. Similar considerations also suggest that science sometimes accepts beliefs based on insufficient evidence and even on no evidence at all.

It can further be argued that there are certain presuppositions or first principles underlying science that various authors have recognized as not being susceptible to proof or evidence. The problem of presuppositions and their status is also related to the problem of verification/falsification (see below).

Finally, science contains beliefs for which the evidence is ambiguous. Progress in science rests in part on noting anomalies, a process which really involves a recognition of ambiguity in evidence. Various authors have pointed out that no theory ever fits all the relevant observations (Feyerabend 1975, ch. 5). If so, it follows that some observations always seem to mitigate against any particular scientific theory. Thus, the acceptance of a scientific theory always takes place in the context of some ambiguity of evidence.

We have seen that another feature often attributed to doctrines involves their having the status of not being falsifiable or verifiable. It is quite understandable that Wilson, Flew, Gregory and Woods, and others would choose the verification/falsification principle as a means of distinguishing doctrine from non-doctrine. One of the main objectives of positivism, which introduced this principle, was to distinguish science from metaphysics and theology, and to rule out the latter as factually meaningless.

It would seem, however, that the choice of this principle to distinguish doctrine from non-doctrine is an unhappy one because it was precisely in its attempts to distinguish science from non-science (or nonsense) that positivism encountered most of its difficulties. The verification/falsification principle was revised again and again largely because each version was found, on close examination, to be inadequate in distinguishing science from metaphysics and theology. Malcolm Diamond, in a review of the developments of the positivist movement, comments on the tenacity and even the partisanship that became more and more evident as the positivists pursued their objective: "There was, after all, something prejudicial and dogmatic about the tortuous efforts of the positivists to achieve a version of the verifiability principle with the right combination of permissiveness ('science-in') and restrictiveness ('metaphysics-out')" (Diamond 1975, 38).

There appears to be general consensus that the positivists have failed to distinguish science from non-science on the basis of the principle of verification/falsification. Patricia Smart, for example, points to the "notorious" difficulties of the criterion of verifiability or falsifiability, because a "criterion which is stringent enough to exclude metaphysics also excludes propositions of science and a criterion which includes scientific statements also includes metaphysics" (1973, 41). Smart concludes that any attempt to define "doctrines" on the basis of the positivist principle of verification or falsification will only serve to establish that science too contains doctrines (41-2). Various writers such as Ronald S. Laura (1978, 1981) and John F. Miller (1975) have examined the logical status of presuppositions, first-order principles, or epistemic primitives in science, and have argued that they are not verifiable or falsifiable. Thus again it would seem that doctrines cannot be distinguished from non-doctrines on the basis of the verification/falsification principle.

I next consider obstinacy as a defining feature of "doctrines." In my earlier discussion of obstinacy I noted that obstinacy really has to do with believers, not beliefs. Unfortunately, the psychological problem of obstinacy in persons is often confused with the problem of a belief having the logical status of failing to satisfy the principle of verification/falsification. Hence, my treatment of the problem of obstinacy here. It must be admitted that religious doctrines are often held in an unshakable manner. But religious believers do sometimes become agnostics and atheists. Evolution and change exist within religious thought. Alistair McKinnon correctly observes that anyone who has seriously studied the history of any living religion will have to acknowledge that there is real development and change in the beliefs of a religious tradition (1970, 66-7). This is evident not only in early Christianity and the well-known Church Councils where basic Christian doctrines were debated, but also in contemporary theological debates which clearly show evolution of thought in such areas as ecclesiology and hermeneutics. Thus this feature of obstinacy does not invariably accompany so-called doctrines.

It can further be shown that holding beliefs in an obstinate manner is frequently present in paradigm cases of non-doctrine. A survey of the history of science and other recognized disciplines would reveal many examples of theories stubbornly held onto despite evidence against them. In fact Flew himself, in another context, gives one such example.[2]

Thomas Kuhn's analysis of the structure of scientific revolutions provides additional support for the claim that the holding of beliefs in an obstinate manner might also characterize scientists. Obstinacy occurs both in "normal science" where the majority of scientists conduct research under the guidance of a paradigm whose presuppositions and techniques are seldom, if ever, critically examined, and in "extraordinary science" where there is debate among proponents of competing paradigms, but where no trans-paradigmatic grounds exist for evaluating them. This leads the writers of one essay, interestingly, to express concern about the implication that this would make paradigm adoption "closer to a religious than an intellectual endeavour" (Fennell & Liverette 1979, 118).

Finally, some research, referred to by T.F. Green (1972), suggests that obstinacy applies to the holding of beliefs in any areas of thought. Thus, it would seem that obstinacy also cannot be used uniquely to describe religious doctrines.

The final aspect of the logical status of doctrinal beliefs concerns the question of whether doctrines can be defined in terms of beliefs about which there is public disagreement. This is a very common description with an initial plausibility about it. There does seem to be a tendency to label as doctrinal those areas where debate and disagreement abound. But this description of doctrines is also not without its problems.

How is "public" to be defined in the expression "public agreement?" Is a belief identified as a doctrine as long as fewer than 100 percent of the public agree on it? Or is it only the "experts" who are consulted? If so, what is an expert? And what if the experts disagree with "established opinion"? Does this make it a doctrine? If public agreement is strictly defined as unanimous agreement by all the public, then all beliefs are doctrines, as there is no belief that is not disputed by someone. Under this interpretation of "public agreement," science also contains doctrines, as the history of science reveals countless examples of disagreement, not only by the public at large, but also within the scientific community.[3]

If, on the other hand, "public agreement" is defined more loosely so as not to require 100 percent agreement by either the public or the "experts," then it turns out that religion is no longer doctrinal in nature. Religious beliefs are most often held by a community of people, often by a large community, which even includes many who would otherwise be considered quite rational. There is, therefore, "public agreement" in religion and, according to this definition, religion should not be defined as involving doctrines.

Taking into account the position of William James in *Varieties of Religious Experience* (1902), that there are some common elements in all religions, including a nucleus of beliefs, I suggest that far too much is made of both the diversity of religious beliefs and the agreement concerning scientific beliefs. The notion of public agreement, therefore, does not distinguish paradigm cases of doctrine from non-doctrinal ones.

Scope of Doctrinal Beliefs

It has been suggested that doctrines are broad in scope, primarily in the sense that they are tied to a wider system of beliefs. It should be obvious that this feature will not serve to distinguish paradigm cases of doctrine from those that are non-doctrinal because the sciences also involve broad systems of belief (Snook 1972b, 33). Gregory and Woods admit that theories in science function as part of "a very complex theoretical system" (1972, 172). Various philosophers have come to see that it is precisely because science too is characterized by "elaborate systematic conceptual structures" that difficulties arise concerning verification (Miller 1975, 380; Quine & Ullian 1978, ch. 2).

It is also evident that doctrines cannot refer only to "systems of belief" (White 1972a; 1972b). We do talk of individual statements as doctrines. We not only speak of "Catholic doctrine" but also of individual doctrines within Catholicism, such as the doctrine of the future life, the doctrine of the infallibility of the pope. Gregory and Woods give some examples of single propositions which are called doctrines (1972, 172, 178). If it is argued that an individual statement is a doctrine only if it is tied to a wider doctrinal system of beliefs, as Flew intimates (1972a, 71), then all statements qualify, since all statements evolve in some way from a wider system of beliefs.

If we instead interpret the broad scope of doctrines in terms of the wide-ranging implication of these beliefs, then science again contains doctrines. Surely the principle of causality and determinism is just as broad in scope and generality as many religious claims. In fact many people extend this scientific principle to all domains, including that of religion. The same could be said for other first-order principles, theories, and laws of science, all of which have wide-ranging implications. Broadness of scope, however interpreted, will not therefore distinguish science from the paradigm cases of doctrine.

The Momentous Character of Doctrinal Beliefs

This leads to the final group of criteria, in which doctrines are described in various ways as momentous beliefs.

Doctrines are "of great moment to mankind," or "of momentous concern to mankind." But according to this, there are many doctrines in science as well. Surely the discovery of nuclear fission is of great moment or of momentous concern to mankind. Surely Darwin's evolutionary theory has been and still is of momentous concern to mankind, not only from a scientific point of view, but also in terms of the ethical, epistemological, and political theories it has inspired.

Doctrinal beliefs are "intimately related to action and purposive activity" (Gregory & Woods 1972, 168). They entail commitment to act in accordance with the values inherent in them. There is an initial plausibility to this since the paradigm cases of doctrines – religion, politics, and morality – all are intimately related to actions and commitment. On the other hand, when one asserts or accepts a scientific theory or observation report, it seems that one can do so without committing oneself to future conduct or without expressing any personal attitude for or against what is asserted.

Before critically evaluating this feature of doctrines, we must take note of an ambiguity in the expression "an intimate tie-up of doctrine and action" (Gregory & Woods 1972, 167). This expression can first be taken to mean that belief in a doctrine necessarily entails a "commitment to act in particular ways." Doctrines simply cannot be accepted as "a mere academic matter" (Gregory & Woods 1972, 166). To believe is to be committed to certain actions or attitudes. Thus some writers have suggested that it is impossible to acknowledge the doctrines of God's existence and then not respond to him in worship or obedience.

But "an intimate tie-up of doctrine and action" can also be interpreted to mean that doctrines are unique in that they entail certain "action-beliefs." Here we are not asking, as in the first interpretation, whether doctrines necessarily entail actual commitment. Rather, we are asked whether certain beliefs have as their entailments other beliefs about behaviour, and this quite apart from the question of whether the believer will actually act upon these beliefs. Gregory and Woods argue, for example, that Catholic doctrine entails that the believer "is expected to live his life in the sight of God and to strive at all times to see that the quality of that life measures up to the Divine law" (1972, 167).

There are problems, however, with both interpretations. Surely it is possible for someone to believe that God exists and yet fail to respond in worship or obedience. This may be due to hypocrisy, irrationality, or the willful refusal to respond in a way that might normally be deemed appropriate. Roger Trigg states, "It does not seem self-contradictory to imagine someone accepting fully that there is a

God and repudiating Him completely. This is presumably the position the Devil holds in Christian theology" (1973, 41).[4] This first interpretation of a connection between doctrine and commitment or action is thus itself an implausible one. We need not ask whether science can be characterized in this way since there are difficulties characterizing any beliefs, including religious and political beliefs, as entailing commitment and personal response to action.

Do all doctrines entail "action-beliefs"? Gregory and Woods seem to be unaware of the force of a counter-example they themselves raise. They admit that it is "difficult to see what differences to one's daily life, acceptance or rejection of [Berkeley's metaphysical doctrine] would make" (Gregory & Woods 1972, 167). Even in the paradigm cases of doctrinal domains, I believe it is possible to identify some beliefs that do not entail action-beliefs. For example, what implications follow from the claims that God is eternal spirit or Jesus was crucified?

A further difficult question can be raised as to whether "entailment" should be interpreted in a logical sense in the above relation. Surely religious doctrines involving factual claims in some sense have implications for what ought to be done by the believer who accepts them. But if entailment is interpreted loosely, then science too contains doctrines because many, if not most, scientific statements "entail" some action-beliefs. An understanding of the law of gravity "implies" that one should not jump off a high bridge. "H_2SO_4 is an acid" makes chemistry instructors warn students to be careful not to spill any on their hands or clothes. Our "technological society" and its way of approaching life is surely an "implication" of the acceptance of the scientific method and the beliefs associated with it.

Doctrines are promoted with evangelistic zeal (Gregory & Woods, 1972, 168). It must be admitted that the holding of religious and political doctrines is often associated with a "strong urge to convince others." But is this *necessarily* the case? The zeal of a few radicals must not blind us to the fact that many believers in religious or political doctrines hold their beliefs very dispassionately, with little or no attempt to persuade others of what they believe. It is a contingent matter whether doctrines are kept to oneself, shared with others on certain occasions, or whether the convincing of others becomes an all-consuming passion.

Evangelistic zeal is also present at times in those who hold scientific beliefs. Many people would give as an example the perpetration of evolutionary theory in schools, print, and the media. They might admit that this does not seem exactly like religious evangelism, but this is only because evolutionary theory is part of established opinion. Were it a minority view, recourse would have to be taken by making special attempts to convince others: special rallies, paid broadcasts, and so forth. As it is, these special efforts are unnecessary since those who accept evolutionary theory have the entire educational system at their disposal. Malcolm Muggeridge speaks to this issue in a more general sense: "The dogmatism of science has become a new orthodoxy, disseminated by the Media and a State educational system with a thoroughness and subtlety far exceeding anything of the kind achieved by the Inquisition" (1975, 25).

Doctrines are supported by a group of people or an institution. It should be obvious that this feature also will not distinguish paradigm cases of doctrine and non-doctrine. Lest the above quote from Muggeridge be dismissed as obscurantist, I refer to John Dewey, whose writings have perhaps done more to shape North American education than those of any other writer. Dewey is very clear in advocating that schools promote science and the use of the scientific method ([1916]1966, ch. 17). Thus the institution of public education or schools backs and promotes not only science generally but also specific scientific beliefs. It is simply naïve to assume that only religious or political beliefs are backed by institutions. I will say more about institutional indoctrination in Chapter 7.

This concludes a rather detailed evaluation of various features that have been attributed to doctrines in past analyses of "indoctrination." Athough I have attempted to show that some of the proposed criteria need not apply to the paradigm cases of religious or political doctrine, I was primarily concerned to show that all the proposed criteria are present, to some degree, in the paradigm example of non-doctrine: science. The common assumption that religion and science can be distinguished in terms of possessing or not possessing doctrines is therefore problematic.

It might be objected that there are other criteria which past descriptions of doctrines have somehow overlooked. For example, is it not an obvious difference between scientific and religious beliefs that the one refers to the supernatural while the other does not? I would suggest that there are good reasons that this has not been proposed as a distinguishing feature of doctrines. First, there is some question as to whether all religions do make reference to the supernatural. Guthrie warns against applying this "western folk category" cross-culturally since some cultures simply do not think in terms of a "natural-supernatural" distinction. Guthrie further suggests that there may even be some supernatural elements within science (1980, 184-5). Perhaps scientists are merely suppressing the metaphysical assumptions underlying the scientific enterprise (Laura & Leahy 1980, 260). Finally, it would be inadvisable to define "doctrine" in terms of the supernatural because it is generally believed that indoctrination is not only limited to religious beliefs. Political beliefs are also susceptible to indoctrination and these obviously do not have to refer to the supernatural.

There may be other possible criteria of doctrines, but until they are proposed, I believe we must conclude that there are problems with defining doctrines in such a way as to make religion doctrinal and science non-doctrinal.

The conclusion arrived at from a detailed critique of various proposed descriptions of doctrines can be further substantiated by an appeal to ordinary usage. We do talk about doctrines in areas other than religion or politics. The *Oxford English Dictionary* assigns three meanings to "doctrine":

1 The action of teaching or instruction; instruction; a piece of instruction, a lesson, precept.
2 That which is taught. a. In the most general sense: instruction, teaching; a body of instruction or teaching ... b. That which is taught or laid down as true concerning a particular subject or department of knowledge, as religion, politics, science, etc.; a belief, theoretical opinion; a dogma, tenet.
3 A body or system of principles or tenets; a doctrinal or theoretical system; a theory; a science, or department of knowledge.

None of these meanings restricts doctrines to religion or politics. In fact, the last two meanings specifically refer to science as an example of a doctrine.

This is further substantiated by an examination of actual usage of the term "doctrine." J.S. Mill, for example, writes about "the detailed doctrines of science" ([1861]1957, ch. 1). White refers to a paper by C. Ormell in which he talks of doctrines in mathematics such as "the doctrine of Logical Sequence" (White 1972b, 190). Gregory and Woods give some examples of talk about doctrines in the sciences, but dismiss them as unusual usages (1972, 172-4). The fact remains that these are examples of the term "doctrines" being used in the sciences, and many more such examples could be provided. Thus, an examination of current actual usage further substantiates the conclusion that any attempt to limit doctrines to areas such as religion or politics is simply due to arbitrary decision.

Kazepides (1987, 1989) has strenuously objected to the position that doctrines exist in science. Drawing on Wittgenstein, he concedes that a great number of propositions provide the "river-bed," the "axis," the "scaffolding," the "hinges," and the "unmoving foundations" of all our thinking, including science (1987, 237). Examples include the basic propositions of logic, some pseudo-empirical propositions (e.g., "Physical objects exist," "Objects continue in existence when not perceived"), and some empirical propositions about which we "can hardly be mistaken" (e.g., "I have two hands," "I am a human being"). But Kazepides argues that these river-bed propositions of science are radically different from doctrines such as occur in religion: (a) River-bed propositions are the foundations of rationality, whereas religious doctrines are not; (b) One cannot doubt, modify, or abandon river-bed propositions, while there are alternatives to religious doctrines; (c) River-bed propositions are acquired or inherited without thinking, investigation, or justification, while religious doctrines are learned; (d) River-bed propositions enable us to think, while religious doctrines act as "stoppers" that control, limit, and channel thought and disallow alternative beliefs (Kazepides 1987, 238-9).

There are many problems with Kazepides's argument. His list of supposedly non-doctrinal river-bed propositions in science is very selective. Many other fundamental propositions of science, as I argued above, share the features of doctrines. Even Kazepides' river-bed propositions are doctrine-like, as he admits – they are non-rational, unfalsifiable, wide ranging, and important. Kazepides further forgets that arguments can be and have been presented showing that belief in God is foundational to rationality and hence should also be treated as a river-bed proposition.[5] The history of philosophy further reveals that his river-bed propositions have been doubted and alternatives entertained. Berkeley, for example, doubted that physical objects exist and he proposed an alternative metaphysics which interestingly made God the foundation of all science. Given that alternatives are possible, it will be found that Kazepides's river-bed propositions also act as stoppers that control, limit, and channel thought. And who is to say that river-bed propositions are not learned or religious doctrines are not acquired or inherited? Indeed, as Peters has argued in his description of education as initiation, all our thinking is initially acquired or inherited (1966, ch. 2).

I therefore conclude that Kazepides's argument is unsuccessful and that the overall thesis of this section stands: doctrines as traditionally understood, even by Kazepides, exist in science as they do in religion.

INDOCTRINATION AND DOCTRINES

Now to turn to the questions that prompted inquiry into past descriptions of doctrines. Is indoctrination limited to doctrines? Can the absence of doctrine serve as a criterion of a form of knowledge acceptable to a liberal education? Are doctrines more susceptible to indoctrination than other areas of knowledge and belief? Does the teaching of doctrines necessarily entail indoctrination?

It is generally assumed that doctrines are to be found only in religion, politics, and morality, and that the danger of indoctrination exists only in these areas. I have argued, however, that "doctrines" as described by Kazepides, Wilson, Flew, Spiecker, and Gregory and Woods are also found in what is usually taken to be a paradigm of non-doctrine: science. It therefore follows that even if "indoctrination" is seen as limited to "doctrines," and if the latter term is understood as it has been in the past, this still does not entail that indoctrination is restricted only to the areas of religious, political, and moral beliefs.

It further follows that the absence of doctrines cannot serve as a criterion of a form of knowledge acceptable to a liberal education. Earlier in this chapter I pointed out that it is generally assumed that science is a form of knowledge and that indeed science epitomizes that which is ideal in a liberal education. But I have argued that doctrines, however defined, are also found in science. Hence the presence or absence of doctrines can be used neither to distinguish what is or what is not a form of knowledge nor to distinguish what should or should not belong to a liberal education.

This conclusion can be substantiated in another way. I tentatively suggest the following as a more coherent account of the notion of a doctrine, based in part on past descriptions of this notion but avoiding the problems of past accounts. "Doctrines" refer to the central beliefs of any belief system, variously identified as first-order principles, primary beliefs, presuppositions, epistemic primitives.[6] As such, doctrines are broad in scope, of critical importance, and not directly verifiable or falsifiable, though they can be indirectly verified or falsified as part of an entire belief system. I would further tentatively suggest that doctrines so defined are an essential part of all forms of knowledge. Hence a liberal education will invariably involve the teaching of some doctrines. The teaching of doctrines should therefore not automatically be associated with indoctrination.

Thus far we have been assuming that there is a conceptual link between "indoctrination" and "doctrines." I have shown that even if this is assumed, it does not have the usually intended effect of limiting indoctrination to religious, political, and moral beliefs. Another way to undermine this limitation of indoctrination to certain areas of belief which are considered suspect is to show that the assumption of a conceptual link between "indoctrination" and "doctrines" is itself problematic. This is the strategy of J.P. White, who argues both for a weaker claim, that "indoctrination" should not be understood as being limited to doctrines at all, and for a stronger claim (about which he is a little less confident), that indoctrinated beliefs could be of any kind whatever (1972a; 1972b). White contends that appeal to linguistic usage is ambiguous because we do talk about indoctrination in all areas and with regard to all beliefs, as even dictionaries confirm. He further maintains that we can conceive of a teacher trying to indoctrinate true propositions or very specific propositions. We should also recognize the possibility of there being ways to implant unshakable beliefs other than by teaching doctrines or even beliefs. "What of those schools where in a hundred and one different ways some teachers try to get their pupils to see themselves as future hewers of wood and drawers of water?" (White 1972a, 123). Surely this is indoctrination even if it does not involve the overt teaching of beliefs, let alone doctrines. Finally there is the problem of arbitrariness. We should perhaps be most concerned about indoctrination precisely in those areas which we think are immune to indoctrination: "it is a complacency-puncturing recommendation" (White 1972b, 195).

I agree fully with White that we should not limit indoctrination to doctrines and that indoctrination can occur with respect to all beliefs. Green has similarly argued that the distinction between education and indoctrination has nothing to do with the contents of beliefs, as it is perfectly possible to indoctrinate (i.e., foster a non-evidential style of belief) people into the truth (Green 1972, 33-4). This argument will be further substantiated after we examine the misconceptions concerning science which underlie the sharp distinction between doctrines and non-doctrines.

This should not be taken to mean that indoctrination is likely to occur with all beliefs. I suggest that indoctrination is indeed more likely to occur with regard to doctrines understood in terms of non-falsifiable, first-order principles and presuppositions of broad scope and importance: it is simply easier to indoctrinate doctrines. It is very difficult to indoctrinate observational statements or beliefs that are obviously true or false.

For this reason we generally use the word "indoctrination" in connection with the teaching of doctrines (Gregory & Woods 1972, 181; White 1972a, 123). But this is a contingent, not a conceptual matter. We seldom talk of indoctrinating a "scientific fact" because that would be most difficult to bring about. But it is conceivable, and even possible, as White demonstrates (1972b, 200-1.).

It is important, however, not to misunderstand the claim that indoctrination is most likely to occur with regard to doctrines. I have argued that however doctrines are defined, they are to be found in science as well as religion. Thus the suggestion that doctrines are more susceptible to indoctrination *does not mean* that indoctrination is more probable in the area of religion, as is generally assumed. Indoctrination may be just as common in science as in religion because there are doctrines in both areas. In fact, some writers argue that indoctrination is very common in science. Paul Feyerabend, for example, agrees entirely with Malcolm Muggeridge when he expresses concern that scientific "facts" are taught in our schools in the very same manner in which religious "facts" were taught only a century ago. Little attention is paid to wakening the critical faculties in pupils. "At the universities the situation is even worse, for indoctrination is here carried out in a much more systematic manner" (Feyerabend, 1988, 36). Feyerabend's and Muggeridge's suspicions highlight an earlier suggestion of mine that we should be especially concerned about indoctrination in those areas generally thought to be immune to this charge. This is, however, not the place to pursue the question of the probability of indoctrination in science – or in religion, for that matter. As mentioned earlier, questions about the probability of indoctrination in religion will be considered in chapter 8.

It should finally be noted that my arguments attempting to refute the limitation of indoctrination to doctrines, especially religious doctrines, also serve to undermine the position that the teaching of religious doctrines necessarily involves indoctrination. Clearly, if science and religion are less different than is generally assumed, and if despite the presence of presuppositions and the problem of uncertainty regarding various claims in science we nevertheless hesitate to make the charge of indoctrination with regard to scientific teaching, then surely it is quite unreasonable to suggest that the teaching of religious doctrines necessarily entails indoctrination. If indoctrination is not inevitable when teaching scientific doctrines, then it is not inevitable when teaching religious ones, because science and re-

ligion share many features. Obviously there may be other considerations, and so a full refutation of this position appears in chapter 8.

CHRISTIAN NURTURE, INDOCTRINATION AND THE IDEAL OF NORMAL SCIENCE

Thus far my argument has been based on a rather detailed analysis
of the concept "doctrine." I now wish briefly to place this argument
into a broader perspective.

As Ian Barbour has noted, many people today still see science and
religion as *"strongly contrasting enterprises* which have essentially
nothing to do with each other" (1971, 1). However, many writers,
including anthropologists, philosophers, and scientists, argue that
religion and science are similar in aims, methods, and criteria by
which to evaluate the fulfilment of these aims. Stewart Guthrie, in
an important article on this topic, argues this position and reviews
the writers who also argue for similarity between science and religion (1980). The issue is by no means settled, but this fact in itself
suggests that the distinction between paradigm cases of doctrine
and non-doctrine is at least problematic.

I would further suggest that the contrast between doctrinal and
non-doctrinal areas of belief rests on a caricature of religion and an
illegitimate idealization of science, together with misconceptions of
each. I wish to outline, very briefly, some of the key problems in the
conception of science underlying discussions of indoctrination, thus
pointing the way to a more realistic and philosophically defensible
account of science which I will call "normal science," not to be confused with Kuhn's notion of normal science, though my account will
incorporate some features of Kuhn's interpretation of the history of
science.

Various writers have identified one of the central problems in the
current debate concerning the meaning of indoctrination as the failure to take into account recent discussions in epistemology and the
philosophy of science. Laura and Leahy, for example, express surprise about the persistence of a naïve realist epistemology in the
philosophy of education, "given its virtual abandonment among
philosophers of science over the last 20 years" (1989, 255; cf. Page
1980, 37, 118). Ratzsch points out that the dominant view of science
from the seventeenth century until the mid-twentieth century,
which still persists in some circles (e.g., philosophy of education),
was characterized by three central notions: empiricality, objectivity,
and rationality. According to this conception of science, empirical
data impress themselves upon the observer through the senses (em-

piricality); the observer, without any prior assumptions, presuppositions, or theories, collects the data for examination (objectivity); and the observer then draws conclusions from the data in a rigorously logical fashion (rationality) (Ratzsch 1986, ch. 2).

This conception of science, however, has increasingly come under attack since the 1960s, largely as a result of the work of Thomas Kuhn and the publication of his ground-breaking work, *The Structure of Scientific Revolutions* ([1962]1970). Since Kuhn, it is generally acknowledged that observation is theory laden and that the doctrine of "immaculate perception" which underlies the traditional conception of science is fundamentally flawed (Leahy 1990, 140). It is also generally acknowledged that the scientist brings a host of convictions, commitments, assumptions, and values to his or her task, and that the process of thought in science is not rigorously logical but rests in imaginative leaps, with several theories often being proposed to account for the same data. Empirical accuracy is therefore only one of the criteria used to evaluate alternative theories. Others include consistency, breadth, simplicity, aesthetic elegance, and fruitfulness (Guthrie 1980, 192, 196; Miller 1975, 360; Ratzsch 1986, 70-1). It is now generally recognized that individual scientific claims can only be adequately assessed as part of a broader theory and as part of a whole process of investigation which changes over time (Page 1980, 37; Quine & Ullian 1978, 22). All of these features are essential to what I call "normal science."

In the traditional conception of science, the scientific enterprise is often characterized as completely autonomous, carried on by independent researchers who are themselves autonomous. But as Polanyi ([1946]1964), among others, has shown, the scientific enterprise is very much dependent on the existence of a scientific community governed to a large extent by tradition and authority. Authority in science, exemplified in the necessary apprenticing of pupils to masters, can be seen as a "modern version of the Apostolic Succession," according to Polanyi. Indeed, "normal" science is very much an institution, or a set of institutions (Polanyi [1946]1964, 44, 47).

Finally, a more down-to-earth or "normal" conception of science recognizes its own limits. It acknowledges that the foundational presuppositions of science cannot themselves be justified by science, and hence there must be some other sort of grounds for accepting at least some beliefs (Ratzsch 1986, 97-9). It also recognizes that there may be more to reality than empirical reality. To deny the possibility of a non-empirical dimension to reality on the basis of science, which is by its very nature restricted to gathering data by empirical means, is to beg the question. Sir Arthur Eddington illustrates this logical error by describing an an ichthyologist who, in exploring the life of the ocean, casts a particular net into the water and gets a fishy assortment which he then analyses. The net is very effective in catching this particular group of fish, but it would be fallacious for this ichthyologist to conclude that there are no other fish in the ocean. Similarly, the scientific method is splendidly adapted to catching empirical fish, but it would be foolish to conclude that there are no non-empirical fish in reality (Eddington, [1939]1958, 16). Normal science acknowledges the limitations of its scientific net. It recognizes that there are legitimate and important questions about the ultimate purpose of our existence or of the universe which science simply cannot address on its own.

Clearly with this conception of "normal science" the stark contrast between science and religion breaks down, and I will have more to say on this shortly. It should be noted here that this "new philosophy of science" (Siegel 1988, 91-2) is not without its critics. By putting humans and human subjectivity at the centre of science, Kuhn has been criticized especially for opening the door to complete subjectivity, relativism, and historicism. But though some philosophers have taken Kuhn's position to such an extreme, I do not believe it necessary to do so, and I further suggest that this represents a distortion of Kuhn's own position, since he himself stresses that a degree of objectivity, rationality, and empiricality is still possible and important in science (Kuhn 1977, 320-39). However, we must never forget that science is "a decidedly human pursuit," and should be seen "as no more ruggedly and rigidly objective and logical than the humans who do it" (Ratzsch 1988, 54-5).

The contrast between doctrines and non-doctrines rests on a distorted view not only of science but also of religion. Both Hirst (1974b) and Kazepides (1987, 1989) draw extensively on Wittgenstein's interpretation of religion as a unique "form of life" or "language game." Religion here is understood as essentially expressive and non-cognitive, and hence non-scientific. But this is only one interpretation of religion. C.G. Prado (1980), for example, has argued that it makes religion "inherently unstable." Non-credal religion is above criticism because it is beyond elucidation and hence it offers only an illusion of faith. Further, a non-cognitive understanding of religion is fundamentally at odds with an orthodox interpretation of Christianity, the framework within which the problem of indoctrination is being treated in this book. Orthodox Christianity is credal in nature, and claims to make affirmations about the nature of reality that can be rationally defended, thereby running the risk of being refuted.

Given a credal and cognitive understanding of religion, and given a more contemporary and philosophically defensible conception of science, we are better able to see why the distinction between doctrines and non-doctrines breaks down. Both science and religion involve theoretical attempts to understand the world we live in. Both are trying to make sense of empirical reality, though the focus may be on different aspects of reality. The theorizing in both science and religion must begin with central beliefs which are variously identified as "first order principles," "primary beliefs," "presuppositions," "epistemic primitives," or "doctrines." Both science and religion are very much human enterprises, and while both are shot through with elements of subjectivity, neither is entirely subjective. Both search for objective truth. Both are subject to verification involving a variety of criteria such as applicability to empirical data, coherence, simplicity, and explanatory power. Science like religion, in its attempt to explain empirical reality, seems to make reference to a hidden structure of reality, though there is some debate among philosophers of science as to the ontological status of this underlying structure of nature. This has led writers such as Quine to suggest that there is very little difference between the theoretical entities posited by science and the gods posited by religion (Quine [1953]1961, 20-46).[7]

Much more could and should be said about these similarities between science and religion, but my purpose is primarily to place the detailed argumentation of the previous section into a broader perspective. Past attempts to distinguish between doctrines and non-doctrines are rooted in misconceptions of both science and religion. We should now be in a better position to appreciate why indoctrination is possible both in religion and science. If theorizing in both areas is very much a human enterprise, then the dangers of extreme subjectivity and hence indoctrination exist in both. Indeed, if all thinking rests on "epistemic primitives" (i.e., doctrines), and if indoctrination is defined in terms of the failure to provide students with a critical awareness of the dependence of thinking on these epistemological assumptions, then, according to Leahy, "the danger of indoctrinating students is at least as great, if not greater, in the secular subjects (e.g., science) where such dependence is invariably taken for granted, than in religious education where it is not" (1990, 143). This assessment of the relative probability of indoctrination in science and religion is, of course, somewhat premature since it depends on a certain view of indoctrination. However, it does illustrate the primary thrust of this chapter – showing that indoctrination is not necessarily limited to religious doctrine, and that it is indeed possible in such seemingly sacred areas as science.

So far I have been talking about religion and science generally. I wish to add just a few comments about the compatibility of Christian nurture and the scientific ideal inherent in liberal education. Much has been written about this and it would be futile to attempt to do justice to the question here. But a few comments are in order. It is appropriate, for example, to remind those who want to establish a necessary link between indoctrination and religious doctrines that historically there is a close connection between Christianity and the rise of modern science, as various authors have pointed out.[8] Orthodox Christianity is further firmly rooted in the empirical. "In the beginning was the Word, and the Word was with God, and the Word was God ... The Word became flesh and lived for a while among us" (John 1:1,14). Another description of this event at the heart of Christianity again has a very empirical ring to it: "That which was from the beginning, which we have heard, which we have seen with our eyes, which we have looked at and our hands have touched – this we proclaim concerning the Word of life" (John 1:1). And Paul similarly picks up this empirical dimension of orthodox Christianity, nearly sounding as though he is responding to the modern falsification challenge: "And if Christ has not been raised, our preaching is useless and so is your faith" (1 Corinthians 15:14).

Of course many religious sceptics would concur with Malcolm Diamond, who labels the approach to theology in orthodox Christianity as "utterly naïve" (Diamond & Litzenburg 1975, 45). This kind of comment can be quickly dismissed as it suffers from the fallacy of *ad hominem* argument. It simply will not do to label theologians who take seriously the historicity of the Christian scriptures as "naïve." Nor will it do to assume that those who are embarrassed by the miraculous elements of the Bible should be called "sophisticated theologians" (43). Interestingly, Diamond is forced to admit that orthodox Christians are not vulnerable to the scientifically oriented verificationist critique of Christianity (44), and there have been very sophisticated defenses of orthodox Christianity against such a critique.[9]

Christianity is very supportive of the scientific enterprise, and, as Ratzsch, among others, points out, "Many of the best-known scientists historically have been Christians" (1986, 119). I would suggest that incompatibility only arises when the limits of science are not recognised, or when science becomes "scientism," a religion which by definition excludes God.

Finally, orthodox Christianity shares with science the principle of fallibility. "For we know in part and we prophesy in part," Paul reminds us (1 Cor. 13:9). Here I am of course parting company with those segments of Christianity, both Catholic and Protestant, which explicitly or implicitly make claims to infallibility. Critical reflection and openness are also encouraged in orthodox Christianity as they are in science (Acts 17:11; Hull 1984, ch. 18; British Council of Churches 1984, ch. 9). More will be said on critical openness in chapter 6.

These all-too-brief comments must suffice to show that orthodox Christianity is indeed compatible with science, if understood in terms of what I have called "normal science." We can therefore tentatively conclude that it is possible for Christian nurture to satisfy the scientific ideal inherent in liberal education. I say tentative because there are other aspects of the scientific ideal such as rationality, autonomy, and critical openness which will be dealt with in later chapters. Here I have focused primarily on those aspects of science related to the notion of doctrines. The central thrust of this chapter is to show that indoctrination is not necessarily limited to religion by virtue of its suspicious-looking doctrines. Doctrines, however defined, also exist in science. Further, if indoctrination is not inevitable in science, then neither is it inevitable in religion because both religion and science are doctrinal in nature. Barrow and Woods are therefore fundamentally mistaken in highlighting the content of teaching in what they take to be a paradigm of indoctrination – a Catholic school teaching Catholic doctrine (1988, 72). Teaching doctrine is not necessarily indoctrination.

This chapter has focused on attempts to define indoctrination in terms of content. Some philosophers, Kazepides for one (1987, 223), have even suggested that indoctrination can be defined in terms of content alone. But this is surely absurd, as it should be rather obvious that content cannot indoctrinate on its own. Somebody has to be teaching this content. Implicit in attempts to define indoctrination in terms of content is always something other than content – for example, the methods of teaching.

The next chapter considers teaching methods as a way of defining "indoctrination." Because of the close interrelation between content and methods, some of the arguments of this chapter will be fleshed out in greater detail in the next.

4 Methods of Indoctrination and the Ideal of Rationality

Most philosophers closely associate the content and methods criteria of "indoctrination." In other words, discussions about the content of indoctrination are most often linked with concern about the way this content is taught. Alan Peshkin, for example, in his study of Bethany Baptist Academy (BBA), links doctrine with methods when he argues that BBA indoctrinates its students, "refusing to treat issues to which doctrine applies as matters for discussion" (1986, 284). Christian nurture is here being charged with indoctrination both because of *what* is taught and *how* it is taught. Another interesting example is provided by Kazepides, who, though he tries to define indoctrination in terms of content alone, is forced to make reference to methods. "The indoctrinator, because he is inculcating doctrines, must resort to some educationally questionable methods such as failing to provide relevant evidence and arguments or misapplying them, misusing his authority, etc." (Kazepides 1987, 233). Here we see some typical concerns about the teaching methods involved in Christian nurture – concerns which lead some people to conclude that Christian nurture necessarily or very probably entails indoctrination.

John Wilson also clearly links content and methods. "It is not surprising that the word 'indoctrination' implies that the beliefs are usually of a certain kind, namely, those that might properly be called *doctrines*; for these are the kinds of beliefs to induce which, because of our ignorance of how to use rational methods of teaching, non-rational methods have commonly been used instead – par excellence in the case of political, moral and religious beliefs" (Wilson 1972b, 19). Flew agrees with Wilson on the necessity of combining the content and methods criteria in coming to a proper understanding of the meaning of indoctrination. It is precisely the uncertainty of religious beliefs that makes it difficult for anyone to teach them in a non-indoctrinatory manner, according to Flew (1972a, 86-7; 1972b, 112-13). We have seen that J.P. White similarly ties indoctrinatory teaching methods and religious content. "If rational conviction is here impossible, it is difficult to see how one could teach religion (qua religion) without indoctrinating" (White 1972a, 129).

Of all the criteria, the methods criterion, it seems, is the most plausible candidate for demarcating the concept of indoctrination. Thus it is somewhat puzzling to find that very few, if any, philosophers have attempted to analyze the concept of indoctrination in terms of the methods criterion alone. There is, however, widespread agreement that methods must be one essential component in defining "indoctrination." In fact, of the four criteria usually proposed as essential, the methods criterion is probably the one most agreed upon as a necessary condition of "indoctrination." It can further be shown that even people who object to the methods criterion and propose other criteria (such as intention) nevertheless implicitly refer to it in their own proposed analysis of "indoctrination."[1] It is therefore necessary to pay careful attention to teaching methods associated with indoctrination.

INDOCTRINATORY TEACHING METHODS

It is surprising that, despite the widespread acceptance of the methods criterion, very little attention has focused on defining the precise methods deemed to be indoctrinatory. I therefore wish to begin this chapter with a fairly exhaustive list of various teaching methods frequently associated with indoctrination. Here it should be noted that I am not using the term "teaching methods" in the way writers in curriculum and instruction might use the term to refer to practical ways of using resources in order to help students learn curriculum content. Philosophical concern about teaching methods is instead about the way in which content is selected and taught. I will classify these indoctrinatory teaching methods under certain broad categories, acknowledging that some degree of arbitrariness is inevitable in any attempt at classification. After listing the indoctrinatory teaching methods, I will attempt to isolate certain features that emerge as central to the methods criterion of indoctrination.

Non-evidential Teaching

Green describes indoctrination as teaching which creates a "non-evidential style of belief" (1972, 35, 37). Such teaching can be characterized in various ways. (a) It can involve teaching which simply fails to give reasons, evidence or arguments for the beliefs taught. With indoctrination, according to Hull, "reasons are concealed and reason is bypassed" (1984, 178). (b) Closely related is a preoccupation with *what* is taught rather than *how* it is taught. Green suggests that "when, in teaching, we are concerned simply to lead another person to a correct answer, but are not correspondingly concerned that they arrive at that answer on the basis of good reasons, then we are indoctrinating" (1972, 37). (c) Some writers consider the preoccupation with learning correct answers via mindless drill, recitation, and rote memorization to be indoctrinatory (Passmore, 1967, 193-4). (d) A final method of non-evidential teaching involves attempts to persuade the subject "by force of the indoctrinator's personality, by emotional appeal, or by use of a variety of rhetorical devices," rather than by reasons, evidence, and proof (Benson 1977, 336).

Misuse of Evidence

Whereas the previous classification of indoctrination involves complete disregard for reasons and evidence for beliefs, the feature I now wish to consider, while it does not entirely disregard reasons and evidence does involve misuse of them. There are several ways in which this misuse is described. (a) Indoctrinatory methods are sometimes associated with deliberate falsification of evidence. (b) A feature more frequently associated with indoctrination involves the use of "rationalizations" in contrast to genuine reasons and arguments (Wilson 1972b, 19, 21). (c) Making use of reasons for a "foregone" or "predetermined" conclusion is another expression closely related to the above, which is sometimes used to identify indoctrinatory methods (Green 1972, 38; Scruton, Ellis-Jones, et al. 1985, 16). Here reasons are given or sought, not in an open-ended search for truth, but as a means of defence for beliefs one accepts or as a weapon against beliefs one opposes. (d) Indoctrination is often associated with "a one-sided or biased presentation of a debatable issue" or with the suppression of counter-evidence (Moore 1972, 93). (e) But the misuse of evidence is not limited to controversial issues. It can equally arise with established forms of knowledge. Thus Crittenden describes indoctrination in terms of using any pedagogical method which is "inconsistent with the requirements of the general nature of inquiry" or which "violates the criteria of inquiry" of the forms of knowledge involved (1972, 139-40, 146, 148-9). (f) Finally, misuse of evidence can also occur when there is a violation of the logical status of the beliefs taught. Flew, for example, expresses concern about teaching beliefs which are false, or at least not known to be true, *as if* they were true (1972a, 75-6, 78, 85-6). More generally, indoctrinatory methods involve the inculcation of a higher degree of certainty and conviction than evidence warrants.

Perversion of Teacher-Pupil Relationships

The misuse of authority is frequently identified as involving indoctrinatory teaching methods (Flew 1972a, 86; Moore 1972). But it is difficult to define precisely what methods involve a misuse of authority because the teaching process by its very nature involves an authority type of situation. Thus, as Peters notes, there is a need to distinguish between a proper use and a misuse of authority. He describes the teacher-pupil relationship as one in which "the teacher has to learn to be in authority and to be an authority without being authoritarian." It is only the latter which is associated with indoctrination (1973a, 47-8, 54-5).

Indoctrinatory methods are also described as violating the autonomy of the student (Peters 1973a, 155; cf. 1966, 35, 42). Indoctrination is "an assault on the person of the hearer," according to Hull (1984, 178). But similar difficulties arise here. Autonomy, like authority, is very much a matter of degree. What degree of autonomy must be allowed in order to avoid indoctrination? This might be difficult to define, but there is nonetheless agreement that, at some point, the teacher can fail to respect the autonomy of the student, and this is indoctrination.

Peters (1966, 261-2), Benson (1977, 336-7), and others sometimes identify doctrinaire and dogmatic teaching as indoctrination. Benson describes dogmatic presentation as involving "the promotion of the misleading impression that p is true simply because the indoctrinator says it is or because p is so obvious and certain as to require no defense." Here we see that dogmatic teaching is closely related to the non-evidential teaching already discussed.

Indoctrination is also frequently associated with the refusal to let students think for themselves. Crittenden, for example, contrasts indoctrination with educative pedagogical methods which allow the learner "to examine the evidence voluntarily, to raise questions and objections and so on" (1972, 139). Closely related to the failure to let pupils question and think for themselves is the failure to allow for discussion, which is also sometimes seen as an indoctrinatory method (Benson 1977, 337).

Reward and punishment in teaching can be a method of indoctrination. Green gives an illustration in which, over a period of time, a student is rewarded for giving a correct answer and punished in some way for a wrong answer to a certain question (1972, 35). In this way, "he may learn to respond correctly and without hesitation," but the belief is held, not on the basis of evidence, but simply in expectation of reward or punishment (cf. Benson 1977, 343).

Intellectual Virtues

Indoctrination is also sometimes described in terms of a failure to cultivate a group of qualities which, since Aristotle, have often been referred to as the "intellectual virtues," or "rational emotions." Intellectual virtues, according to Spiecker, include "demands for evidence and the search for grounds for beliefs, impartiality, consistency, being unprejudiced, cautiousness, and the courage to reconsider one's opinion" (1987, 263). Rational emotions refer to such "motivating emotions" as "veracity or truthfulness, integrity, carefulness and preference for accuracy" (Spiecker 1987, 263; cf. Crittenden, 1972, 141, 146, 148-9).

Spiecker (1987) and Passmore (1967) see the cultivation of these intellectual virtues and rational emotions as essential to teaching a child to be critical. Teaching methods which discourage the development of "a critical spirit" are frequently identified as indoctrinatory (Benson 1977, 339; Moore 1972, 98).

Common Features

Having completed the survey of specific teaching methods which are commonly identified as indoctrinatory, it is now possible to identify certain features common to all or most of them. Benson gives a most helpful summary statement, which he unfortunately does not follow up in his own analysis: "Throughout the literature touching on the methods of indoctrination, two logically distinct themes are sounded again and again, albeit in diverse terms: the indoctrinator manipulates the subject matter and/or the indoctrinator manipulates his subjects" (Benson 1977, 333).

Teaching methods are first called indoctrinatory because they involve manipulating the subject matter, either by failing to provide reasons, evidence, or justification of beliefs taught, or by misusing the evidence in some way. A second major emphasis running through the examples of methods of indoctrination involves the manipulation of the subject, that is, the student, thus endangering the freedom and autonomy of the individual being taught. Some philosophers have attempted to describe indoctrinatory methods as being in some way non-volitional, thereby raising the issue of the misuse of authority by the teacher.

These themes are captured in the frequent expression used to describe methods of indoctrination: inculcating beliefs by the use of "a non-rational method" (Benson 1977, 334; Snook 1972b, 22; Spiecker 1987, 262). Teaching methods can be non-rational or irrational by manipulating the subject matter, either by failing to provide evidence or by misusing evidence in some way. Further, teaching methods can be non-rational in that beliefs are acquired by the student, not on the basis of reason or argument, but by virtue of other influences involving some kind of manipulation of the student.

UNAVOIDABILITY OF INDOCTRINATION

Having examined various non-rational teaching methods typically associated with indoctrination, I now wish to deal with a central problem that emerges if indoctrination is defined in this way. Indoctrination, it must be stressed, is generally understood to be incompatible with education and is viewed as a strongly pejorative term by those who, like Peters, are concerned about liberal education. It will be argued that, given the commonly accepted meanings attributed to liberal education and indoctrination, a problem arises in that liberal education would seem to involve indoctrination. This problem arises particularly with respect to the initiation component of liberal education. Here it might be well for the reader to review Peters's description of liberal education as initiation into the forms of knowledge (see chapter 2).

In treating this problem, I am in fact opening for examination one of the central problems of defining the concept of indoctrination, a problem touched on again and again but seldom faced squarely. Later I will consider ways in which it has been skirted. But first I will examine how this problem arises by considering such aspects of education as the authoritative nature of the initiation process, the force of tradition, the way in which children learn by imitation and identification, and finally some aspects of learning to be rational. I will argue that in all these areas, the use of indoctrinative teaching methods is inevitable. I will also argue that attempts to escape the problem of the unavoidability of indoctrination have been unsuccessful. Thus there would seem to be a real problem in defining "indoctrination" in terms of non-rational teaching methods. This problem will be placed into a broader perspective later in this chapter, where it will be suggested that we need to revise the notion of rationality implicit in attempts to define indoctrination via non-rational teaching methods.

It might be objected that my entire argument is irrelevant because discussions of indoctrination should be concerned with advanced rather than early education. However, it is precisely at the initial stages that it is most critical to distinguish between acceptable (educative) and non-acceptable (indoctrinative) methods of teaching. Snook has correctly observed that, although a small child may teach his or her parent, or a student a professor, we would not say that the child or a student indoctrinated either of these people (1972b, 48-9, 101-2). Indoctrination occurs in situations in which there is some degree of authority control, and thus it is primarily with children and the early stages of education that we should be most concerned about indoctrination.

In discussing "autonomy," Dearden pointedly remarks that philosophers "may have been too apt to overlook or ignore the fact that men have childhoods" (1975, 6). It seems to me that a fundamental problem of all past analyses of indoctrination is that they tend to discuss it only in terms of features of adult learning. Surely the problem of indoctrination has to do primarily with children, as Snook correctly observes. But it is precisely here that we find that initiation involves indoctrination.

A fundamental consideration has to do with the authoritative nature of the initiation process. The parent, the teacher, or society, not the child, determines the inheritance into which the child is initiated. The child is simply not given a choice. But if, as we have seen, indoctrination is understood as involving the violation of the autonomy of the individual or the manipulation of the subject, then the initiation process necessarily involves indoctrination.

Here it should be noted that Peters, in his description of initiation, fails to do justice to the coercive dimension of most typical initiation rites and ceremonies. In chapter 2 I mentioned Peters's claim that initiation presupposes free choice by the initiate (1966, 54). But surely there are some real problems in describing paradigm cases of initiation as entirely voluntary. In typical *rites de passage* it is precisely the initiation process which transforms immature adolescents into responsible adults. The young adolescents do not choose to belong to their particular tribe. Nor do they choose to be initiated into the particular customs they will have to adopt after initiation. Much more needs to be done by way of analysis of initiation rites and the concept of coercion, but I would suggest that it can be safely concluded that initiation is generally not entirely free of coercion.

White in bringing to the fore the problem of the status of the child, suggests that "we are right to make him unfree now so as to give him as much autonomy as possible later on" (1973a, 22). White here recognizes that we are forcing a curriculum on children. But given a definition of indoctrination in terms of the use of coercion, it follows that indoctrination is unavoidable in the process of initiating children into public traditions.

Of course Peters (1973a, 47-8, 54-5), White (1973, 22-3), and others want to argue that this does not involve indoctrination because the teaching situation need not be authoritarian, and it will eventually lead to an autonomous state.[2] But Peters's distinction between being in authority and being authoritarian is meaningless in the case of children, and to point to future results of having children taught by someone in authority is to sidestep the issue at stake. What is being argued is that the process of initiating children into certain public traditions is non-rational, as described earlier in this chapter. Children are not given a choice of whether they want to be initiated or into which tradition they are initiated. Of course this is quite justified because children are simply not in a position to choose. What this entails is that indoctrination, defined in terms of non-rational methods, is unavoidable. Thus I concur with Moore (1972, 97) when he proposes a modification to the older liberal theory of education, and suggests that "we frankly admit that learning necessarily begins with an authoritative and indoctrinative situation."[3] Later, however, I will argue that it is a mistake to call a child's early learning experiences indoctrination.

Tradition also is operative in initiation. The child is initiated into *public traditions*, Peters tells us. There are several things to note about these traditions. They are viewed as absolute in some sense by Peters, Hirst, and others. The barbarian is introduced to the "citadel of civilization," and it seems as though there is only one such citadel. Advocates of liberal education sometimes seem to forget that the public traditions into which they want to initiate children are the public traditions of western society only.[4] There are other traditions. Which traditions will children be initiated into? Young children will and can only be initiated into *our* traditions. But surely this must be seen as indoctrination if by "indoctrination" we mean "a one-sided or biased presentation of a debatable issue" (Moore 1972, 93).

There is also the danger that public traditions be viewed as fixed. Despite some recognition of the possibility of evolution and change with regard to our public traditions (Hirst, 1974a, 92-6, 139-40), Hirst and others fail to recognize that we can only transmit those public traditions which we at present consider to be true, which we risk viewing as final truth. Also, young children, being children, cannot understand the possibility of evolution and change in the public traditions they are taught. Initially the traditions are received and understood as fixed and absolute, and are accepted in an unquestioning manner. Barrow argues that children are incapable of grasping differences in the logical status of beliefs (1974, 54-5, 57). Various authors have recognized that it is only *after* children have been initiated into the public traditions that they can begin to evaluate them critically (Passmore 1967; Oakeshott 1967). But the focus here is on what happens *before* children reach the questioning stage, while they are in that stage of simple trust and unquestioning belief. Indeed, as Peters notes in referring to Piaget's research, it is doubtful whether most people ever emerge entirely from this stage of unquestioning belief in the public traditions they are taught. If so, then not merely with children, but even with adults, there is a component of the teaching/learning process that can only be described as non-rational and indoctrinative in nature (1977, 81).

Closer examination of *how* children are initiated into public traditions reveals further elements of the non-rational. Peters is well aware that initiation depends on mechanisms of imitation and identification; those who make the education process entirely child centred overlook the way in which "from time immemorial, most beliefs and forms of conduct have been learned by the human race, namely by picking them up from the example and instruction of more experienced people who rank as authorities or experts in a community" (Peters 1977, 83; cf. 1966, 60). But the processes of learning by example, imitation, or identification cannot themselves be described as rational processes. Here we must be careful to distinguish between *what* it is that is being imitated or identified with and the actual *mechanism* of imitation. I am not denying that the content being imitated might be intelligible and even rational. But the process of imitation itself is not one of reasoning and involves many of the features identified earlier as indoctrinatory. Imitation and identification clearly involve an authoritative, non-critical situation. These processes resemble closely the methods of drill, memorization, and learning to spout the correct answers, all methods which have been called indoctrinatory. It therefore follows that if indoctrination is defined in terms of non-rational teaching methods, then indoctrination is an inescapable ingredient in the initiation of individuals into the forms of knowledge.

A fundamental concern of Peters and others advocating initiation into the forms of knowledge is promoting rationality. I have already provided a negative description of rationality in the review of teaching methods commonly thought to be non-rational. This description concurs with various recent analyses of rationality. Snook, for example, describes rationality in terms of disciplined reflection, deliberation, thinking, either within the context of specific disciplines or as a general approach to problem solving (1973b). Barrow and Woods suggest that "the essence of rationality is the giving or holding of good or relevant reasons" with respect to one's beliefs or one's behaviour (1988, 84). It would further seem that the development of rationality involves the cultivation of a combination of skills, habits, attitudes, and even character (Snook 1973b, 154).

Several considerations, however, suggest that in the continuing process, as well as at the initial stages of the development of rationality, non-rational methods have to be used. One consideration has already been dealt with: children learn to be rational by imitating examples of rationality. But, as has already been argued, learning by imitation is essentially a non-rational process.

Further, rationality is connected with the cultivation of "intellectual virtues." But as Snook (1973b, 152-3) and others point out, the cultivation of these virtues entails acquiring certain habits and attitudes. Care and concern for evidence and the criteria of evidence must be fostered. Peters even talks about the cultivation of "love" for the citadel of civilization. But it should be evident that the cultivation of love, care, concern, and other attitudes is not entirely a rational process. In so far as the cultivation of intellectual virtues entails the acquiring of habits, it clearly entails the use of non-rational methods (Passmore 1967, 192-3).

A final consideration regarding the teaching of public traditions brings to the fore another aspect of rationality: that it is at least in part defined by the public traditions themselves. The criteria of rationality, critical thought, and judgment are inherent in the forms of knowledge. But if this is so, a problem arises in teaching others to be rational. If public traditions are the conditions of rationality, then inculcating these conditions cannot itself be rational because there are no criteria of rationality apart from those public traditions. It follows that initiation into rationality must itself be non-rational and hence indoctrinatory, if indoctrination is defined in terms on non-rational teaching methods.

Various writers have dealt with this and other aspects of the conditions of rationality and critical thought, and have recognized the problem of apparent indoctrination in the teaching of these conditions.[5] Green (1972), for example, specifically addresses the question of cultivating certain "enabling beliefs" such as "the belief that truth is powerful, attainable and to be treasured whenever identified" — beliefs which are the very foundation of rationality. These beliefs, Green says, "ought to enlist our most passionate loyalty, for they are the ones which enable us to hold all our beliefs in an evidential way." He admits that the development of rationality involves the cultivation of "passionate convictions" regarding the values of truth and reason. We must "seek closure of mind" regarding these enabling beliefs. But the cultivation of such convictions involves non-rational means according to Green's own definition of indoctrination. He is well aware of this and concedes that in this context indoctrination "has a perfectly good and important role to play in education." With admirable clarity, Green has drawn the only possible conclusion: that indoctrination is unavoidable in teaching children to be rational (1972, 41-5). Unfortunately, Green's candour and willingness to go where the argument leads is not shared by most philosophers dealing with this problem.

Passmore (1967, 192-211) and Oakeshott (1967, 156-76) also deal with the prerequisites of teaching pupils to be critical.[6] They concede that there is an "instructional component" in this process. Certain "arbitrary and inert" facts must be learned, and must be mostly "taken on trust." Language must be learned by drill. Rules must be learned which are arbitrary. The need for "building up a body of knowledge" involves the instilling of a "fixed body of beliefs." Passmore mainly wishes to establish and show how we can move beyond the instructional component to the cultivation of critical thought. But there remains, nevertheless, "a large instructional ingredient" inherent in the initiation process which bears striking resemblance to what he describes as indoctrination. Passmore finds it depressing that all subjects "tend towards an instructional state," yet he realizes that instruction is a necessary prelude to critical thought (Passmore 1967, 202). Here I want to stress primarily that these authors do admit that, in initiating students into rationality and critical thought, there is an identifiable component that involves the use of non-rational methods and which therefore must involve indoctrination. Of course Passmore and Oakeshott want to stress that we must move beyond the initiation stage, but there still remains an initiation stage which involves indoctrination.

I can only mention here some other recent discussions in educational literature which could help us to see the relation between initiation and indoctrination from a new perspective. Sociologists in particular have been exploring the relation between education and socialization.[7] As noted above, Peters (1965, 89) admits that education and the initiation into public traditions is a form of socialization, yet research shows that the process of socialization is essentially non-rational (Morgan 1974, 121-2; Peters 1966, 60). If therefore indoctrination is defined in terms of non-rational teaching methods, then education and the initiation into the forms of knowledge necessarily involve indoctrination.

Various writers reviewed by Barrow (1978, ch. 6) have also pointed out that there is an inescapable hidden curriculum in our schools. "The hidden curriculum, we are told, teaches kids to be docile ... transforms them into compulsive consumers ... propagates pernicious sexist and racist doctrines" (Gordon 1981, 4). But the beliefs and values implicit in the hidden curriculum are not taught by reasoned argument but are acquired with neither evidence and justification nor the opportunity to evaluate them critically – except of course in retrospect. Students acquire these values and give assent to these beliefs without being aware that they are doing so. The student is deprived of "the opportunity to withhold assent," which according to Benson (1977, 338, 342) is one form of indoctrinatory method. These and other aspects of the hidden curriculum clearly involve various non-rational methods we have already considered as examples of indoctrination. It therefore again follows that indoctrination is unavoidable in educating students in our schools.

This concludes a rather lengthy survey of various arguments showing that the use of non-rational methods in teaching is unavoidable. It is these considerations which have led to much of the confusion surrounding attempts at analyzing the concept of indoctrination. In the next section I wish to examine this confusion, hoping to lead eventually to a clearer understanding of the implications of the above argument.

RESPONSES TO THE UNAVOIDABILITY OF NON-RATIONAL TEACHING METHODS

This chapter began by examining teaching methods that have been commonly associated with indoctrination. It is important to keep in mind that both the concept of indoctrination and the indoctrinatory methods reviewed are generally understood to be pejorative or miseducative. In chapter 2, I examined Peters's description of liberal education as initiation into the forms of knowledge. Such initiation is seen to be a good thing – an ideal – since education is governed by a normative criterion. The major thrust of this chapter thus far has been to argue that indoctrination, as commonly understood in the pejorative sense, is unavoidable in the process of initiating individuals into the forms of knowledge. It follows that there is an inherent contradiction within the notion of liberal education advocated by Peters and accepted by most educational writers today.

Educational philosophers have not been entirely unaware that initiation entails indoctrination (see, for example, Crittenden 1972, 148; Flew 1972b, 108; Green 1972, 45; Moore 1972, 96-9). But this problem is, in my opinion, seldom faced squarely. Peters, for example, in some later essays, admits that there are certain "ambiguities" or "dilemmas" inherent in the notion of liberal education that still need to be resolved (1977, chs. 3, 4). One has to do with the seeming unavoidability of indoctrination, and Peters points to "the necessity for much more thought" on the problem of distinguishing liberal from illiberal teaching procedures (1977, 84). More often, however, Peters, along with other writers, tends to deny or escape this problem in a variety of ways. Their responses are inadequate.

Moore identifies three kinds of responses by liberals to the above arguments concerning the unavoidability of indoctrination. Some simply ignore the problem, others try to define it away, still others try to abolish teaching entirely (Moore 1972, 96). The first response can be quickly dismissed. We have already suggested that ignoring the problem will not do: this is to be philosophically dishonest. Nor is defining the problem away a solution. Some philosophers of education, for example, respond to the seeming inevitability of non-rational teaching methods by renaming this process "socialization," "cognitive socialization," or "incompetent teaching" (Flew 1972a, 70-1; Gatchel 1972, 16; Kazepides 1982, 163). But this is to engage in the questionable art of verbal gymnastics. If indoctrination is defined as the use of non-rational teaching methods, and if initiation into the forms of knowledge involves non-rational elements, then liberal education involves indoctrination and it will not do to try to circumvent the problem by introducing other words to describe the same thing.

The more extreme response, Moore tells us, is that of some progressive educators who "took the bull by the horns by advocating nearly total permissiveness in the earliest teaching situations, thus eliminating indoctrination in teaching by doing away with teaching" (1972, 96). In some respects, the deschoolers and the advocates of open education or free schools represent similar responses. But the fundamental problem with this kind of response is that teaching the young is as inescapable as is indoctrinating them. The choice is not one of whether or not to teach but rather of what and how we teach. Kathryn Morgan (1974) argues forcefully against the open educators who wish to reject socialization, but who in fact simply substitute one socialization pattern for another. Socialization or the teaching of children is inescapable; the unavoidability of non-rational teaching is thereby also inescapable.

Another major kind of response to the unavoidability of indoctrination is the appeal to additional criteria of indoctrination. Flew (1972b, 108) and Wilson (1964, 26, 34) explicitly introduce the content criterion of "indoctrination" as a way of avoiding the inevitability of indoctrinatory methods. I have already objected to the content criterion and will object to the intention criterion in chapter 5. Further, escaping the problem of the unavoidability of indoctrinatory methods by adding another criterion or two cannot help but seem somewhat arbitrary. Since I have argued in the previous chapter that science and religion share several non-rational features, the resulting use of non-rational methods in teaching science and religion lead to the conclusion that indoctrination is unavoidable in both areas. It is thus surely peremptory to introduce a content criterion of indoctrination so as to exclude science from the dangers of indoctrination when it shares the non-rational features of religion.

Hare introduces the intention criterion to escape the problem of the inevitability of non-rational teaching methods (1964, 49-50). But this approach again suffers from arbitrariness. A method such as non-evidential teaching is generally considered to be highly miseducative, but according to Hare it can be transformed into an acceptable teaching method simply by virtue of good intentions. Yet with religious instruction it is frequently argued that indoctrination occurs even though the religious teacher might avow good intentions. Philosophers should surely be wary of such capriciousness.

Another frequent response to the unavoidability of indoctrination is to introduce a non-pejorative kind of indoctrination (see, for example, Crittenden 1972, 139-40; Green 1972, 44-5; Moore 1972, 97; cf. Snook 1972b, 3-4, 24-5). It is certainly legitimate to use one word in two different senses as long as it is understood that we are dealing with two different concepts. (I suggest, however, that it would be less confusing to use a different word for "non-pejorative indoctrination.") But the fundamental problem with this response to the unavoidability of non-rational methods in initiating children into the forms of knowledge in a liberal education is that it is contradictory. The use of non-rational methods is generally seen as something to be avoided, as miseducative, and even immoral. Thus indoctrination, understood as a pejorative term, is often defined in terms of the use of non-rational methods. I have argued, however, that the use of non-rational methods is unavoidable and many writers are forced to concede that the use of such methods is both necessary and good. It is obvious that these two positions involve a contradiction: we must accept one or the other of them. Either (1) the use of non-rational methods is always wrong, in which case the methods criterion of indoctrination (pejorative sense), defined in terms of non-rational methods, is defensible or (2) the use of non-rational methods is not always wrong, in which case the methods criterion defined in those terms cannot serve as a *necessary condition* of indoctrination (pejorative sense). I have argued that non-rational methods are unavoidable, and thus their use is not always wrong. We must therefore give up the methods criterion of indoctrination (pejorative sense) as *commonly* understood.

This is not at all to suggest that we should give up the methods criterion of indoctrination entirely. I believe indoctrination must be defined, in part, in terms of a methods criterion, but, as Peter has suggested, much more careful analysis is required to distinguish liberal from illiberal ways of initiating individuals into the forms of knowledge. More specifically, much more attention needs to be given to the ideal of rationality implicit in the attempt to define indoctrination in terms of non-rational teaching methods. Before addressing this problem, I would like to look more specifically at a few of the non-rational teaching methods identified earlier.

NON-RATIONAL TEACHING METHODS RECONSIDERED

So far, I have dealt generally with non-rational teaching methods. I now wish to examine briefly some of the specific teaching methods which have been identified as non-rational and hence indoctrinatory. In so doing, I will raise objections to treating each of these methods as examples of indoctrination. I also want to highlight one other problem that surfaces repeatedly with the methods criterion of indoctrination: vagueness. While this problem is closely related to that of the unavoidability of non-rational methods in that it reinforces my earlier argument, it deserves separate treatment.

Snook underscores the problem of vagueness by asking the following question: "If a certain amount of the disfavoured method is allowable, what proportion is needed to make the teacher an indoctrinator?" (1972b, 23). As he points out, a certain amount of drill in teaching is generally thought to be quite acceptable. But how much? At what point does drill become classified as indoctrination? To define the precise point at which the use of drill becomes excessive and hence a non-rational indoctrinatory technique seems to involve an arbitrary decision. Snook concludes that there is an inherent vagueness in any attempt to define indoctrination in terms of non-rational teaching methods.

Peters identifies this problem as well, though in the context of a discussion of liberal education generally. He highlights certain "ambiguities" and "dilemmas" in liberal education which call for much more careful definition of teaching procedures "so as to distinguish those which are illiberal from those which are liberal" (1977, chs. 3, 4; 84-5). This distinction is indeed difficult to make and thus calls into question attempts to define indoctrination via non-rational teaching methods.

It is not possible here to deal with each of the non-rational teaching methods identified earlier. Space will only allow a consideration of one or two of the methods in each category.

Non-evidential teaching. Indoctrination is often defined in terms of a preoccupation with inculcating "correct beliefs" without a corresponding concern for providing reasons for these beliefs. But how preoccupied does one have to be with inculcating correct answers in order to be charged with indoctrination? How concerned does one have to be with providing reasons for beliefs? What is being overlooked here is that all teaching, in fact all communication, is to some degree preoccupied with conveying correct beliefs. And, as we have seen, all teaching fails to some extent to provide reasons for beliefs taught. The finiteness of the teacher and the pupil entail that not all beliefs can be taught evidentially. It is therefore very difficult to determine when teaching should be classified as indoctrinatory based on the above concerns.

Another category of non-evidential teaching involves attempts to persuade the subject "by force of the indoctrinator's personality, by emotional appeal, or by the use of a variety of rhetorical devices" (Benson 1977, 336). I would suggest, however, that all teaching contains elements of emotional appeal, rhetoric, and force of personality. Even the best-intentioned teacher, as Peters notes, often finds that students have been "inordinantly influenced" by his or her personality (1977, 83). When these elements dominate the teaching situation, it might be possible to say that indoctrination is occurring. But at what point are these normally legitimate elements misused? That is difficult if not impossible to define precisely, and thus reference to these elements will not help in defining precisely an indoctrinative situation.

Misuse of evidence. If indoctrination is described as the misuse of evidence, then the fundamental problem becomes one of identifying precisely when, or how, evidence has been misused. For example, misuse of evidence is sometimes associated with providing rationalizations rather than genuine reasons. But, as Smart points out, "It is not so easy to distinguish between reasons and rationalizations" (1973, 38).

The frequent objection to using reasons for establishing a predetermined conclusion is also problematic since all reasoning surely involves this process to some degree. It is in the nature of reasons and evidence to be *used*. All persons, and not just indoctrinated persons, use reason and argument either as a means of defence or as a weapon. Science, for example, operates on the basis of postulating a hypothesis which is then defended. Here too, reasons and arguments are used to establish certain predetermined conclusions and it is simply wrong to describe this as unique to the indoctrinator.

Indoctrination also cannot be described in terms of stilted, incomplete or one-sided arguments, because the finiteness of the teacher and the pupil entail that all teaching and learning of necesssity involves these ingredients to some degree.

Teacher-pupil relationships. I have already considered the problem of inescapable vagueness in describing indoctrination as a misuse of authority or as the failure to respect and promote the autonomy of the student. Some authority and some manipulation of the pupil seem unavoidable in the teaching/learning situation. The problem is in defining the precise point at which authority has been misused so as to involve excessive manipulation of the pupil.

This problem also plagues the specific description of indoctrination in terms of the use of reward and punishment. Peters and others have noted that authoritative devices such as praise and blame, rewards and punishment have to be used in educational institutions (1977, 82). Again the problem is one of defining the point at which an abuse of authority transforms these devices into an indoctrinative method.

To associate indoctrination with dogmatic teaching is also problematic because of vagueness, since all of us are dogmatic to a degree. Underlying most teaching, or even most attempts at communication, is the assumption that what is being communicated or taught is correct – surely a presumptuous assumption, given the fallibility of human opinion. William James, with a touch of satire, describes the "empiricists" who acknowledge that "we cannot infallibly know" in this way: "The greatest empiricists among us are only empiricists on reflection: when left to their instincts, they dogmatize like infallible popes" (James [1948]1968, 97).

Intellectual virtues. I have already dealt with some problems involved in describing indoctrination in terms of the failure to cultivate what many see as the key intellectual virtue, the critical spirit. Intellectual virtues refer to dispositions and here again it is difficult to determine the extent to which one is encouraging the development of these dispositions. Teachers and pupils alike can only achieve a degree of qualities such as intellectual honesty, courage in defending truth, consistency, and the avoidance of prejudice.[8] At what point do we make the charge of indoctrination? It is difficult, if not impossible to determine this.

Thus the problem of vagueness arises in many, if not all, the specific teaching methods often associated with indoctrination. Each of these methods, on closer examination, turns out to be problematic as an example of indoctrination. The difficulties encountered have also provided additional illustrations of the problem of the unavoidability of non-rational teaching methods. All these difficulties raise the question as to whether there is a more basic problem that needs to be addressed. Is there perhaps a problem with the ideal of rationality itself which underlies all attempts to define indoctrination in terms of non-rational teaching methods?

RATIONALITY

So far the notion of rationality in traditional accounts of the methods criterion of indoctrination has been treated as a given. I now want to argue that there are significant problems with the way in which philosophers of education have traditionally understood "rationality." An exploration of these problems will not only place the previous problems of the inevitability and vagueness of non-rational teaching methods into a broader context, but it will also serve to weaken further the charge of indoctrination as it has been made against Christian nurture.

Before critically examining the traditional notion of rationality, I will say just a few things about the importance of the ideal of rationality for education. This ideal does not come into play only in defining the methods criterion of indoctrination. Each of the proposed criteria of indoctrination can be seen to hinge on the problem of disregarding rationality: the teaching of doctrines which involve beliefs about which "rational conviction" is impossible, or about which there is no "publicly accepted evidence for them, evidence which any rational person would regard as sufficient"; teaching with the intent that pupils believe "regardless of the evidence"; teaching which results in a "closed mind," or in the holding of beliefs in a "non-rational" or "non-evidential" manner (Snook 1972b, 47; White 1972a, 129; Wilson 1964, 27-8). This leads Snook to suggest, in his introduction to *Concepts of Indoctrination*, that the concern of all the contributors to that anthology "is with the fostering of the child's rationality" (1972a, 3; see also Snook 1972b, 108). Since concern about indoctrination grows out of the ideal of liberal education, one would expect rationality also to figure significantly in discussions of this ideal. Indeed, central to Peters's concept of education (i.e., liberal education) is a concern about the development of the rational mind. This comes to the fore in a well-known collection of papers of which Peters is co-editor, *Education and the Development of Reason* (Dearden, Hirst, et al. 1972). And Hollins suggests that each of the contributors to his *Aims in Education* "puts forward as his chief aim of education the development of rationality in children" (1964, xii).

But exactly what is meant by "rationality"? I touched on this question in the discussion on initiation into rationality earlier in this chapter. Rationality is fundamentally concerned with providing reasons and evidence for beliefs held. Barrow and Woods express this traditional view of rationality just after describing the paradigm case of indoctrination referred to in chapter 2 (1988, ch. 6). There and in their analysis of indoctrination in terms of the traditional four criteria, concern for rationality comes up again and again. Barrow and Woods then suggest that "the essence of rationality is the giving or holding of good or relevant reasons" (Barrow & Woods 1988, 84).

Ralph Page highlights the fundamental problem with Barrow's and Woods' account of rationality, which he claims is very representative of much of the analytic work on indoctrination. "Missing from this account of rationality is just about every issue that has occupied epistemological debate for the last several decades" (Page 1980, 37). More recently, Laura and Leahy have similarly expressed concern about the outdated epistemology that underlies most of the writing being done on indoctrination (1989, 255). What is needed is a more comprehensive epistemological framework which, according to Laura, will alter our perception of both what indoctrination is and how it may be avoided (Laura 1983, 46).

In what follows, I will outline some of the central problems with the traditional account of rationality underlying past analyses of indoctrination. I suggest that there has been a general failure to take into account recent discussions about epistemology as found in the philosophy of science, philosophical hermeneutics, the sociology of knowledge, critical theory, postmodernism, Marxist and neo-Marxist critiques of liberal definitions of knowledge, and evolutionary and naturalistic epistemology. Rather than make extensive references to this vast literature, I will pick out some of the relevant central themes that run through it. In outlining my critique – and it needs to be stressed that this is merely an outline – I will, at the same time, be working toward an outline of some of the features that would characterize a more adequate account of rationality which I shall label "normal rationality," for want of a better term.

It is, first of all, important to distinguish between rationality and truth. In seeking to be rational, our aim is, of course, to arrive at the truth. But here is the rub. What is truth? And when can we be sure that we have arrived at the truth? Kierkegaard, quoting Lessing, has said, "If God held all truth concealed in his right hand, and in his left hand the persistent striving for truth, and while warning me against eternal error, should say: Choose! I should humbly bow before his left hand, and say: Father, give thy gift; the pure truth is for thee alone" ([1936]1967, 195). Rationality concerns the striving for truth, rather than truth itself. Past accounts of indoctrination, however, frequently confuse truth and rationality. This is evident, for example, in the tendency to associate rationality with a concept of knowledge typically defined by philosophers in terms of justified true belief (Green 1972, 34). Even when talking about evidence, there is a tendency to load this notion with the additional baggage of truth, at least implicitly. Thus Snook criticizes Green for using such problematic words as "adequate reasons," "clear account," "sound evidence" (Snook 1970, 92). The adjectives "adequate," "clear," and "sound" implicitly make reference to truth and hence are problematic. We need to acknowledge that it is possible to be rational without determining whether or not we have arrived at the truth. This is part of the meaning of normal rationality.

Normal rationality further recognizes the limitations inherent in any attempt to justify beliefs. Those attempting to define indoctrination in terms of a failure to promote rational justification of beliefs often seem to have in mind what Mavrodes calls the "proved-premise principle," that is, they claim that an argument is defective unless all of its premises are proved (Mavrodes 1970, 26). But as Mavrodes points out, no argument can satisfy this principle since it "demands the construction of an infinite series of arguments, each one of which embodies a proof of the premises of the succeeding argument" (27). Given that no finite human being can construct an infinite series of arguments, no argument can satisfy the proved-premise principle. All justification of beliefs faces this problem. Justification of beliefs necessarily begins by taking a number of things for granted. Providing evidence for beliefs necessarily presupposes that many things are accepted without evidence. Providing evidence for beliefs necessarily rests on what Laura calls "epistemic primitives" – the foundational elements of a belief system (1983, 54). Normal rationality is therefore more realistic in its demands for evidence and justification.

Ordinarily, of course, we have no problem starting to provide evidence and justification for the beliefs we hold. This is because, as members of a certain community or tradition, we agree on many things. This then becomes the starting point for any attempts at justifying our beliefs. The recognition of being part of a community or a tradition brings us to another fundamental problem with the traditional accounts of rationality underlying treatments of indoctrination – its individualism. Beliefs and moral principles are simply not "chosen by lonely, autonomous agents in an emotionally empty state of rational reflection" but by those "who have some feeling of what it is to be a person among other persons" (O'Hear 1982, 127-8). Hence tradition and authority play a very important part in rationality. R.T. Allen has recently given eloquent expression to this need in his critique of the individualism of modern rationalism characterized by "the conceit of being able to know and judge anything and everything by one's own 'criteria,' by one's own puny intellect, and of not needing to defer to anything or anyone which one cannot comprehend" (Allen 1987, 18). The result of such individualism, according to Allen, is cognitive and, ultimately, political anarchy. Instead, "as limited and fallible persons it befits us to be open to authority, to 'the general bank and capital of nations and ages,' to expert opinion, even and especially when we cannot hope to understand the matter in hand or the reasons and evidence for it" (Allen 1987, 19). Of course there are dangers here; and there is therefore a need to emphasize some of the ingredients, such as independent critical reflection, typically associated with liberal education. But this emphasis needs to be balanced by a proper regard for the limitations inherent in human nature which underscore the importance of tradition and authority.

Allen juxtaposes the problem of individualism with another problem inherent in the traditional account of rationality underlying treatments of indoctrination. "Rationalism always oscillates between an abstract Reason which is impersonal, formal, ahistorical and disembodied ... and the self-sufficiency of the individual's own reasoning powers which are identified with the former" (Allen 1987, 19). If any theme unites the various contemporary thinkers touching on questions of epistemology, it is that reason cannot be treated in abstraction. Epistemology has been typically defined as the study of the nature of knowledge. It is concerned with evaluating and establishing criteria for assessing knowledge claims. Or to use Hans Reichenbach's "celebrated" or "notorious" distinction, epistemology is concerned with the "context of justification" and this needs to be sharply distinguished from the "context of discovery" which involves an examination of the psychological, sociological, and historical determinants of knowledge claims (Reichenbach 1938).[9]

While this distinction is helpful as an abstraction, the many who use it fail to remember that it *is* an abstraction. The fundamental problem with epistemology as it is traditionally understood is that the question of justifying knowledge is approached from an idealized frame of reference – from the point of view of the ideally rational person, a consensus which grows out of "undistorted discourse" or "ideal speech situations" (cf. Habermas 1979), or a kind of rationality achieved by individuals divorced from their past, their emotions, their social context. But no human being is an ideally rational person. No speech situation is ideal and "absolutely free." Human beings cannot divorce themselves from their emotions, their pasts, and the societies in which they live.

Siegel, in his attempt to defend Reichenbach's distinction, raises an important and traditional objection to the above argument. He maintains that psychology (or sociology) is irrelevant to epistemology "because psychology cannot furnish good reason for taking any knowledge-claim to be true" (Siegel 1979, 60). But this argument begs the question by appealing to the notion of a "good reason" which is itself problematic. What is a good reason? In answering this question, we will invariably be forced to ask another. Who determines when a reason given for a claim is a good reason? Hence the appropriate title of MacIntyre's important volume, *Whose Justice? Which Rationality?* (1988). It is a person or a group of people (e.g., a community of scientists) who will establish the criteria for "good reasons." These questions can only be answered *practically* by referring to the psychology, sociology, or history of persons.[10]

This need not lead to a vicious kind of relativism (as is so often claimed) because the *ideal* of absolute truth still remains an essential part of human inquiry. It functions as a goal or as a regulative or heuristic principle.[11] William James captures this regulative function of absolute truth well when he describes the absolutely true as "that ideal vanishing point towards which we imagine that all our temporary truths will someday converge" ([1948]1968, 170). What is needed is an alternative theory of knowledge which does justice both to the ideal and the real, a theory of knowledge "which can account both for its normative character and for its being bound to the concrete historical and psychological situation of the thinker" (Kaufman 1960, 23).[12] The concept of normal rationality incorporates this balance.

Another problem with past accounts of indoctrination and the related ideals of liberal education and rationality is that they are generally based on a foundationalist approach to epistemology which is today by and large recognized to be inadequate, at least in its extreme forms. Foundationalism assumes that knowledge must be grounded on "basic facts" (or "basic linguistic rules") which we can know with absolute certainty and which we can approach with complete objectivity. Foundationalism also assumes that there is a "basic methodology" which allows us to draw conclusions in a formal manner (e.g., by deduction, induction, or by the method of critical doubt), and which will again guarantee certainty. But these assumptions are seen as problematic by many epistemologists and philosophers of science today (see Wolterstorff 1976, chs. 4-8). There are no basic facts because all observation is theory-laden. There are no unchanging formal rules because the distinction between fact and concept is itself problematic. There is no basic methodology because theorizing is an incredibly complex affair, involving the justification of whole belief systems rather than individual claims, and depending on a host of ingredients such as concepts, observations, presuppositions, past theorizing. Theorizing is also a process and therefore it is a mistake to focus on an argument or claim as it exists at a certain point in time or as it is allegedly supposed to exist for all time. The quest for absolute certainty is impossible and immodest, as was stressed by the oft-forgotten "second" component of the early Rennaisance – the sixteenth-century humanists, as well as by the New Testament writer, Paul (Toulmin 1990, 22-30; cf. 1 Corinthians 13:9, 12).

These problems in strong foundationalism have led some philosophers to reject it entirely. But they do so at the risk of falling prey to relativism. Others have sought to develop a more sophisticated version of foundationalism which overcomes the problems mentioned above and does justice to the insights of alternative approaches to epistemology.[13] Normal rationality is based on this more sophisticated version of a foundationalist epistemology which does justice to the complexity of justifying beliefs.

Jonas Soltis, in a book exploring the epistemological underpinnings of education, sums up the need for a new understanding of rationality and epistemology as follows:

I believe that as we approach the end of the century we are on the verge of formulating a view of knowledge, mind, and learning quite unlike the dominant view with which the century began. From a Cartesian view of mind, an associationist view of learning, and an objectivist-rationalist view of knowledge, I believe we are moving toward what might be called an "organic" view of mind, a "transactional" view of learning, a "personal-public-reasonableness" view of constructed knowledge, and an "embedded-in-human-action" view of knowledge in use. (Soltis 1979, 3-4; cf. Code 1987)

The major elements of my outline of some important elements of a reconstructed ideal of normal rationality are included in Soltis's prediction. Normal rationality recognizes that the justification of beliefs is an ongoing process conducted by human beings who have a psychology and a history and are part of a larger society with traditions. Normal rationality acknowledges that the desire to know is in part based on a practical desire to survive and a theoretical desire to know the truth. Both these desires can be realized only imperfectly. Normal rationality recognizes its limitations – we cannot go on justifying our beliefs forever. We need to start somewhere. Normal rationality, while very conscious of its subjectivity and fallibility, nevertheless seeks to be as objective *as is possible*, always being open to reassessing what is presently claimed to be the "truth," and always searching for more adequate expressions of truth.

I turn now to some implications of all this for religion and Christian nurture.

NORMAL RATIONALITY, RELIGION, AND CHRISTIAN NURTURE

Although much has been written about the question of the rationality of religion, here I can only outline some considerations that are particularly relevant to the discussion of indoctrination and teaching methods. The specific considerations can be seen as growing out of the central argument of the previous section. More generally, I would argue that challenges to the rationality of religion and Christian nurture are most often rooted in a notion of rationality that is itself problematic, as I have already argued. With a more defensible ideal of normal rationality, these challenges can be answered.

It should first be noted that the argument of the previous chapter can be seen as providing support for the rationality of religion since the ideal of science is closely related to the ideal of rationality. I argued there that, however rationality is defined – whether in terms of sufficient evidence, verification/falsification, or even public agreement – religion is similar to science in terms both of measuring up to these criteria or failing to measure up to them. It is important to acknowledge the impossibility of measuring up to the ideal of rationality, both in science and religion, because there are limits to our being fully rational: we are finite, all justification must take certain things for granted, we have to rely on authority, and so forth. If, despite these limitations, we deem scientific inquiry to be rational, then we must also classify religion as rational because science and religion are in fact very similar. The argument of the previous chapter would therefore suggest that the teaching of religion can be as rational or as irrational as the teaching of science.

Proceeding now to the argument of the previous section, one of the basic problems in most discussions about the rationality of religion is that we have too narrow a concept of rationality or proof. For example, religious believers are all too often called upon to give a tight deductive argument in support of their claim that God exists. But this demand rests on a strong foundationalist approach to epistemology which I rejected in the previous section. There is no "basic methodology" which will allow us to draw conclusions in a formal manner and which will guarantee certainty. Instead we need to do justice to the complexity of justification and allow for looser kinds of justification. With such lesser demands, religion can indeed be shown to be rational.

There is also a problem with the demand so often made of religious believers that they prove a single statement – for example, "God exists" – taken in isolation from all the rest of their beliefs. Quine and Ullian highlighted this point well in their popular introduction to epistemology, appropriately entitled *Web of Belief*, where they point out that no belief ever faces the tribunal of experience singly, even in science (Quine & Ullian 1978, 22; see also Quine [1953]1961, 42-6). Religion, like science, needs to be understood as a complex system in which many beliefs are closely interrelated to form a whole. Proving whole belief systems is, of course, much more complex than proving a single statement, but we need to face up to the complexity of the justification of beliefs. When this is done, it will be found that religion is, in this respect, as rational as science.

There is also much to learn from various writers who have encouraged us to look at alternative belief systems as different ways of interpreting reality (Hick 1966, Part II; Kierkegaard [1936]1967; Mitchell 1973). Assessment of belief systems then becomes one of finding the best interpretation of experience, and there are objective criteria for this though they will be less tight, rigid, and easily applied than most people would like. The following are some of the criteria that must be applied to assessing whole belief systems which provide the best interpretation of experience: simplicity, explanatory comprehensiveness, aesthetic elegance, internal consistency, and empirical accuracy (Quine 1970, Quine & Ullian 1978; Walsh 1963, ch. 11; Wolfe 1982, 50-5). As noted in the previous chapter, these are the same criteria used to evaluate scientific theories. The complexity of such assessment of belief systems makes it difficult to come to agreement on them, but it is still very much a rational process, both in science and in religion.

Assessment of whole belief systems is never a matter of simple deductive argumentation or even inductive argumentation. Instead, one appeals to a variety of considerations which, taken together, lead him or her to declare the one belief system true and the other false. One develops what Basil Mitchell calls a cumulative case in support of one's choice of a belief system (1973, ch. 3). Each consideration taken individually would be seen as inadequate, but when put together they add up to a substantial case. Again, the development of a cumulative case for a religious belief system is very much a rational enterprise, and the teaching of religion in this manner can only be described as a rational process.

William J. Abraham has called this approach to justifying religious belief "soft rationalism" – a term which he says is now beginning to find its way into the literature (1985, ch. 9). It should be obvious that "soft rationalism" is similar to what I have called "normal rationality." Other writers have similarly defended the rationality of religion. Kelly James Clark, for example, in a book with the teasing title *Return to Reason* (1990), after presenting a penetrating critique of the assumptions of Enlightenment evidentialism or foundationalism, develops a revised conception of rationality which he then uses to defend the rationality of religion (see also Clouser 1991; Plantinga 1979; Wolfe 1982; Wolterstorff 1976).

Much more could and should be said in support of this approach, but the preceding will have to suffice to support the general claim that religion is rational and that the teaching of religion need not therefore involve the use of non-rational teaching methods. Of course, sometimes religious teaching, like teaching in science or history, does not measure up to the ideal of normal rationality, and it is tempting to call this type of teaching indoctrination. But we must not be too hasty.

So far I have been considering the rationality of religion generally. Before moving on to a consideration of Christian nurture, I will comment briefly on the relation between Christianity and rationality. Here it must be stated at the outset that Christianity has often been considered anti-rational. Clearly there are interpretations which would make Christianity incompatible with the ideal of rationality. Clearly also there have been anti-intellectual forces within the Christian church. Richard Hofstadter, for example, in his classic study *Anti-Intellectualism in American life* (1963), devotes three chapters to documenting these anti-intellectual forces in early American Protestantism, particularly as found in evangelical revivalism.[14]

But we must be careful to avoid hasty generalizations. One of the problems with claims about the alleged incompatibility of Christianity and rationality is that such claims rest on a problematic definition of rationality. Christianity is, I believe, incompatible with the traditional concept of rationality, but I have already argued that this notion of rationality is philosophically indefensible. Here I just want to maintain the compatibility of Christianity with the ideal of normal rationality. Readers should also be reminded that this discussion is limited to orthodox Christianity. As I pointed out in the previous chapter, there have been many Christians who, following Wittgenstein, have interpreted their religion in a variety of non-cognitive ways. But such approaches do not belong to orthodox Christianity and hence are not my concern.

Even within orthodox Christianity, there are tensions between faith and reason. Paul, for example, seems to be advocating a kind of anti-rationalism when he speaks of the "foolishness" of the Christian gospel and the need to "destroy the wisdom of the wise" (1 Corinthians 1:18-31). However, as Gooch (1987) has shown, Paul is in no way condemning wisdom or rationality generally since he goes on to suggest that Christians do indeed "speak a message of wisdom among the mature" (1 Corinthians 2:6). Instead, he is condemning intellectual conceit, wisdom which fails to acknowledge its dependence on God and his revelation of truth. Paul himself was a master at debate and was constantly trying to provide a rational defence of his faith, even in the presence of philosophers (Acts 17:2, 17; 17:16-34; 18:4; 19:8). When Paul made his defence before Festus the Roman governor, his language is striking: "What I am saying is true and reasonable" (Acts 26:25). At the same time, however, he stressed the limitations of human knowledge – we only "know in part" – thus identifying with the ideal of normal rationality described above (1 Corinthians 13:9).

The Scriptures generally have a very high regard for the mind, culminating in the greatest commandment, "Love the Lord your God with all your heart and with all your soul and with all your mind" (Matthew 22:37). Wisdom and knowledge are repeatedly praised and spoken of as treasures (Proverbs 1, 2; 2 Peter 1:5-7; Philippians 1:9-10). Myths and "cleverly invented stories" are repeatedly condemned (2 Peter 1:16). It is passages such as these that lead Guinness, among others, to make this observation: "The Christian wholeheartedly supports genuine rationality ... Christianity is second to none in the place it gives to reason, but it is also second to none in keeping reason in its place" (1976, 253; see also Lovelace 1985, 184-193; Stott 1972).

I return now to the central question of this chapter: How do we respond to the charge that Christian nurture necessarily or very probably involves the use of indoctrinatory teaching methods? The last several pages have prepared the ground for another response to the charge under consideration: religion, including the Christian religion is rational, and hence rational teaching methods are possible in Christian nurture. Here it may be objected that I am moving too quickly: surely a defence of the rationality of religious content does not entail the rationality of teaching methods. I agree. But I am dealing here only with the *possibility* of rational teaching methods, and one of the common arguments against such a possibility is that religious content is non-rational or even irrational. As mentioned in the beginning of the chapter, there is a close connection between content and methods. J.P. White, for example, maintains: "If rational conviction is here impossible, it is difficult to see how one could teach religion (qua religion) without indoctrinating" (White 1972a, 129). Hirst similarly questions whether religion is an acceptable and rational "form of knowledge," and hence he tends to associate the teaching of religion, or the teaching for commitment in the area of religion, with indoctrination (Hirst 1974a, ch. 3, 180-8; 1985, 7). White and Hirst question the very possibility of rational teaching methods in religion because religious content is for them non-rational. I have argued, however, that such assessments of religion as non-rational are based on an inadequate epistemology. Religion is rational and therefore rational teaching methods are *possible*. It follows that charges of indoctrination which are based on the assumption that religion, including the Christian religion, is nonrational are problematic if not unfounded. A more adequate account of rationality will lead to fewer charges of indoctrination against Christian nurture.

I would be the first to admit that it is still possible to teach rational content via non-rational methods. There is a danger of exploiting non-rational teaching methods in Christian nurture. But even here, the danger is much less than critics commonly assume. If the arguments of the last two chapters are sound, there may be as much or as little danger of indoctrinating in religion as there is in science. But again, we must postpone a final conclusion on such assessments until we have considered all the criteria traditionally associated with indoctrination.

My critique of the traditional notion of rationality and my defence of a revised ideal of normal rationality further require revision of our understanding of non-rational teaching methods. Leahy, for example, is quite correct in objecting to the traditional formulation of the methods criterion by pointing out, "Logically, the prescription to provide reasons for content taught would permit an *ad infinitum* demand for such reasons from students" (1990, 139). This is not only impractical but impossible. What is needed is an account of both rationality and the methods criterion of indoctrination that is realistic in its demands for providing reasons for content being taught. More generally, it is necessary to be more careful in describing a "non-evidential style of belief" as failing to give reasons, evidence, or arguments for beliefs taught. Given the need to talk about entire belief systems, given the complexity of giving reasons, evidence, or arguments for entire belief systems, and given the limitations inherent in providing such reasons, evidence, and arguments, we will need to be much more cautious in labeling certain teaching methods as contributing to a non-evidential style of belief. Such qualifications will have the effect of further weakening the charge of indoctrination against Christian nurture.

Finally, the revised ideal of normal rationality helps to put the inevitability of non-rational teaching methods into proper perspective. We have seen that rationality is always the rationality of a particular person, and is shaped to a large extent by the particular culture into which he or she was born. Normal rationality recognizes the importance of authority and tradition in being rational. The ideal of normal rationality is therefore closely linked with the contingent conditions under which rationality is first developed. But when addressing the question of the development of rationality, another issue comes to the fore. Children need to be initiated into rationality, and such initiation is by its very nature non-rational. As noted earlier, children learn to be rational by imitation and identification, and these processes are non-rational. Such non-rational initiation should not therefore be condemned as indoctrinatory, given that the latter term is understood in its pejorative sense.

Much of the charge of indoctrination is unfairly applied against Christian nurture in that it focuses on the initiation phase of education which of necessity must be non-rational. All liberal education, while it aims at the development of rationality, must begin with non-rational teaching methods. Even as the child matures, learning to be rational proceeds largely on an apprenticeship model in which the master passes on the art of being rational to his or her apprentices. But as Allen notes, drawing on Polanyi, "The master of an art can pass on his mastery but only to apprentices who are able to follow his example and unconsciously pick up the rules of which even he is not explicitly aware. An apprentice is thus one 'who surrenders himself to that extent uncritically to the imitation of another'! While he is learning, he has to accept the master's judgments and pronouncements although he does not explicitly know the evidence for them" (Allen 1987, 18). Apprenticing to be rational proceeds in all areas by identification with and uncritical imitation of a master of rationality. This also applies to Christian nurture and it is simply unfair to single out the latter as guilty of indoctrination when non-rational teaching methods are an inescapable and necessary ingredient in teaching children to be rational.

In conclusion, I have argued that the charge that Christian nurture involves indoctrination because such nurture is based on non-rational teaching methods rests on a philosophically indefensible ideal of rationality. Once we adopt a more defensible ideal of normal rationality, much of the charge vanishes. It is of course still possible for Christian nurture (or scientific nurture) to fail to measure up to the ideal of normal rationality, and we may then want to make the charge of indoctrination. But before doing so, we need to examine other possible criteria of indoctrination. Perhaps they will provide further clues to a more adequate account of indoctrination.

5 Intentions of the Indoctrinator and the Ideal of Autonomy

Although there continues to be fundamental disagreement about the meaning of "indoctrination," if there is any hint of a move towards consensus, the favoured approach seems to define it in terms of intention.[1]

What is it that is suspect about the intentions of the parent or teacher as an indoctrinator? There are a variety of answers, though a common thread is apparent. McLaughlin (1984) provides a common description of indoctrination as the intentional inculcation of unshakable beliefs (cf. White 1972a, 119-20). Snook (1972b, 47) similarly argues that a person indoctrinates who intends that the pupil or pupils believe what is taught regardless of the evidence. Hare (1964) shifts the focus somewhat when he suggests that indoctrination only begins when we aim to stop the growth in our children of the capacity to think for themselves. The educator, according to Hare, is trying to turn children into adults while the indoctrinator is trying to make them into perpetual children. In other words, the indoctrinator intends to stop growth toward autonomy. McLaughlin interestingly also picks up this thrust in addition to his description of indoctrination mentioned earlier: indoctrination "constitutes an attempt to restrict in a substantial way the child's eventual ability to function autonomously" (1984, 78).[2]

Other aspects of indoctrinatory intentions could be identified. In fact, it will be shown that attempts to define indoctrination in terms of intentions are closely linked with the other criteria we have already considered or will consider in the next chapter. In order to avoid overlapping, then, the focus here will be on autonomy as an educational goal because it is this notion which captures the essence of what is of concern to those who want to define indoctrination in terms of intention. Further, the notion of autonomy incorporates many of the other concerns, as will be shown later.

THE ENLIGHTENMENT IDEAL OF AUTONOMY

I need first to clarify what is generally meant by the term "autonomy." The following ingredients would seem to be essential to the modern liberal notion of autonomy as found in various treatments of this concept in educational writings (Dearden 1972, 1975; Feinberg 1973; Peters 1973b), as well as in an important recent study of autonomy by Lawrence Haworth (1986).

Freedom. The autonomous person is free. Freedom is usually understood in terms of "the absence of constraints or restraints relevant to what we do or might want to do " (Dearden 1972, 450). There is some debate as to whether freedom is essential in defining autonomy. The sense in which prisoners can be autonomous in their thinking and attitudes, despite the obvious constraints of their situation, leads to the tendency of some philosophers to define autonomy only in terms of internal freedom. Yet there is another sense in which prisoners are not autonomous; they simply are not in charge of their own lives. Thus, some writers include freedom as essential to autonomy. Still others treat it as a pre-condition of autonomy. Clearly all agree that freedom is in some way closely interrelated with autonomy, so freedom shall be included as essential to the notion of autonomy.

Independence or authenticity. Autonomous people have a mind of their own and act according to it. They accept or make rules for themselves. They are capable of forming their own independent judgments. Their thoughts and actions are not governed by other people, by tradition, by authority, or by psychological problems.

Self-control. Autonomous people are not swamped by their own passions. They are able to order their wants, aims and ideals into an hierarchical structure and in relation to some life plan.

Rational reflection. Autonomous people think and deliberate about what they believe and do. They subject their actions and beliefs to reflection and criticism. They have the necessary knowledge to make intelligent decisions.

Competence. Autonomous people are agents and recognize themselves as agents whose projects define who they are. They have the abilities to see through to completion those plans and projects they set for themselves. They have the strength of will to carry out what they want to do. They possess the executive virtues of courage, integrity, and determination. Once judgments and decisions have been made in an independent, rational manner, there is a firmness with which autonomous people then adhere to these judgments and decisions.

People are obviously not born autonomous. Children, however, have a right to have their capacity for autonomy developed (Haworth 1986, 127). It is when parents or teachers intentionally fail to fulfil their duty to ensure development of children's capacity to live autonomously that they are frequently charged with indoctrination by liberal educators.

AUTONOMY AND CHRISTIAN NURTURE

How then do we apply this ideal of autonomy to the widespread concern about the intentions which prevail in the teaching of religion or in Christian nurture? Here it needs to be stressed again that I am not dealing with teaching *about* religion(s), an approach often described as the key to avoiding suspect indoctrinating intentions. The phenomenological approach to religious education, for example, is described as aiming for an open, critical, and rational understanding of various religions. The intent is to encourage personal autonomy in the religious realm of experience. With knowledge about the many religions and the ability to reflect critically on this knowledge, it is hoped that the child will eventually be able to make up her or his own mind concerning religious commitment, whether for or against (see Hirst 1981, 1985; Johns 1981; Slee 1989).

The intentions of the phenomenological approach to religious education are thought to differ radically from those of the confessional approach, sometimes also described in terms of catechesis. "Education and catechesis," Hirst tells us, "differ in their aims, in the forms of response that are sought, the states of mind they seek" (1981, 92).

In true religious education, according to Hirst, the educator seeks "from the stance of reason the development of reason in matters concerning religion," whereas in Christian catechesis "the aim is from the stance of faith, the development of faith" (Hirst 1981, 89) and it is this narrowness of intentions that leads Hirst to describe Christian catechesis or nurture as "inadequate," committed to goals that can only be described as "improper, even sub-human," and as likely to favour methods of indoctrination (1981, 92; 1985, 7, 10, 15).[3] John Hull similarly lauds the fact that "the Christianising period of religious education has largely come to an end," and has been replaced with a new approach to religious education "which seeks to foster a more critical and more autonomous individual" (1982, xiii).

Holley (1978) advocates a slightly different approach to an enlightened form of religious education which he sees as attempting to provoke an intellectual understanding of the spiritual dimension of personal life. But like Hirst, he contrasts this with the traditional approach to religious education in British schools whose purpose was conversion and edification in the Christian faith, a purpose which he describes as immoral and indoctrinatory. Holley maintains that we must beware "ecclesiastical hangovers" where there is a tendency to think of the task of religious education as identical to that of the evangelist (Holley 1978, 21). He feels that children should be seen as potential autonomous persons, and any tendency to think of them as being necessarily and inevitably members of one's own faith is immoral. Holley is sympathetic with a 1971 study of religious education in Britain, which rather bluntly describes the confessional or dogmatic approach to religious education as aiming at "intellectual and cultic indoctrination, which is contrary to the very spirit of liberal education (Holley 1978, 21; Schools Council Project 1971, 21, 27).

So far I have dealt generally with the apparent problematic nature of indoctrinatory intentions with regard to Christian nurture, contrasting these with the intentions behind the "teaching about" approach to religious education which is thought to facilitate growth toward autonomy. I will now identify briefly the main components of this general concern about the failure to promote growth toward autonomy in Christian nurture. There will necessarily be some overlapping in this outline, but it is nevertheless helpful to try to isolate the key elements of concern.

The ultimate intention behind Christian nurture is that children or students should become committed Christians. Barrow and Woods (1988, 70), for example, in their description of a paradigm case of indoctrination, highlight the intentions of Catholic teachers in Catholic schools who try to bring up children as devout Catholics. Many, like Holley, worry about the evangelistic aim of Christian nurture. Holley shows how this aim at conversion or edification in the Christian faith translates into a methodology: "To treat a child as if he were necessarily and ineffably going to be a member of one's own *congregatio fidelium* is surreptitiously to deny the possibility of deciding otherwise ... to deny his potential autonomy" (Holley 1978, 20). Clearly the hope of Christian parents or teachers is that their children will accept the faith in which they are being nurtured. Peshkin describes the teachers at Bethany Baptist Academy as agreeing that the important goal of their school is the salvation of each student, and once saved, they are to be induced "to put Christ first in their lives" (1986, 79). This contrasts sharply with what are often thought to be more honourable intentions in which the child is seen to have a "right to an open future" and in which any final choice the child makes with respect to religion would be entertained as equally welcome by the parent or the teacher.

Christian nurture, it is thought, does not aim at independence or authenticity. This concern about the ultimate intention behind Christian nurture relates to several aspects of the ideal of autonomy. The hope is that children will be bound by the religious tradition into which they were initiated. "Train up a child in the way he should go, and when he is old he will not depart from it" (Proverbs 22:6). Clearly the intention behind such an approach to child rearing is that the child will "necessarily and ineffably" become a member of one's own religious faith. Christian parents and teachers do not want their children to become autonomous adults who might independently reject the faith into which they were initiated: "The indoctrinator is *trying* to make them into perpetual children" (Hare 1964, 69).

Autonomy requires decision making based on knowledge. Because the intent behind Christian nurture is conversion or edification in the Christian faith, there is a tendency to ignore consideration of other religions or, if they are dealt with, to treat them from a biased perspective. Here we are of course dealing with *methods* of indoctrination, but intentions necessarily affect teaching methods. Dealing with other religions from a biased perspective or the failure to consider them at all makes it impossible for a child or student to make a decision concerning religion on the basis of evidence or knowledge. This is in part Snook's concern when he applies his definition of indoctrination to the teaching of religion (1972b, 73-6). He states that Christian parents or teachers are indoctrinating because they are teaching with the intention that the Christian beliefs being taught will be believed regardless of the evidence, that is, without a recognition of the variety of religious beliefs, the confusion that surrounds religion, or the dubious status of religious propositions (Snook 1972b, 74-5, 85-6, 96). It is this same restrictiveness which leads Peshkin (1986, 284-6) to describe Bethany Baptist Church and Academy as having indoctrinatory intentions.

Bethany fosters no Jeffersonian marketplace of contending ideas; none is intended. On the contrary, church and school consciously, unapologetically work to restrict their students' cognitive associations "in order to avoid contact with people, books and ideas, and social, religious, and political events that would threaten the validity of one's belief system." (Peshkin 1986, 190; cf. 9, 266)

Autonomous people must be able to reflect critically on their beliefs. But this would seem to be completely contrary to the aim of Christian nurture. Surely the intent here is appreciation and acceptance of the Christian faith, not critical reflection which might result in rejection. White points out that "many religious teachers openly avow that they want their pupils to have faith," a faith that is "rock-like" held with "intensity" and "passion" (1972, 128-9). These teachers surely are trying to get their pupils to hold "unshakable beliefs" or "fixed beliefs," beliefs which are immune to doubt and criticism. White observes that it is difficult to see how any religious teacher (i.e., Christian teacher) can deny having this intention (cf. Snook 1972b, 75, 94).

Christian nurture is frequently described as aiming at unconditional obedience to God. This is another very different concern about Christian nurture which is often related to indoctrinatory intentions. Peshkin, points out that Christian schools such as Bethany Baptist Academy (BBA) are founded on a notion of absolute truth, to which the only proper response is "absolute acceptance" and "unquestioning obedience" (1986, 14, 55, 254, 258-9). Obedience to authority, whether that be the authority of parents, teachers, the state, or ultimately God, is "extraordinarily important" at BBA (1986, 43). It is this commitment to absolute truth which "enslaves" and leads to "feeling a loss of autonomy" that makes Peskin describe BBA as "a total institution" which intends to indoctrinate its students (261, 247, 284).

INTENTIONS

I turn now to a response to the charge that the intentions of Christian teachers or parents are suspect in that they stifle a child's growth towards autonomy. This response can be divided conveniently into three sections. I will first say a few things about defining indoctrination in terms of intentions alone. Then I will examine the ideal of autonomy, and finally I will consider the problem of nurturing growth towards autonomy.

Were I to do philosophy in the strict analytic tradition, I would spend much time dealing with the question of whether reference to intentions is essential to defining the concept of indoctrination. Since, however, the focus of this book is to deal with substantive questions raised in the charge of religious indoctrination, I will only touch briefly on some of the problems in the intention criterion of indoctrination.[4] I will also limit my considerations to Snook's attempt to analyze "indoctrination" in terms of the intention criterion alone.

The first problem with defining indoctrination in terms of intention alone is that it is possible for teachers to intend to indoctrinate (in terms of the above definition), but for one reason or another fail to do so. Christian teachers, for example, may teach with the intention that their pupils all become committed Christians with unshakable convictions about the central truths of Christianity, but, because the teachers may not know how to bring this about, they may use methods that in fact produce a class of free thinkers. Just as some teachers intend to teach well but fail because of professional incompetence, so there may be some who intend to indoctrinate but fail because they do not know how to bring this about. Given this possibility, it follows that indoctrination cannot be defined in terms of intentions alone. Or to put it in philosophical terms, the intention criterion is not a sufficient condition of indoctrination.

Intention is also not a necessary condition of "indoctrination" because, given the usual meanings attached to the term, it is quite conceivable to have someone indoctrinate without intending to do so. Snook, in considering this objection, gives some examples: a Communist teacher in a Communist country, a Catholic teacher in a Catholic school, a racist teacher in a racist community (Snook 1972b, 51-2, 43). These teachers might all claim to have the best intentions. They might sincerely claim that they want their pupils to think for themselves, to evaluate what is taught, and to come to their own conclusions. But because these teachers have themselves been indoctrinated, or because they think there is nothing wrong with the evidence for the beliefs they teach, they describe their intentions as those of any good teacher: to promote in students growth toward autonomy.[5] Hence, reference to a teacher's intentions would seem to be unnecessary in defining "indoctrination."

Snook tries to get around this objection by making provisions for intentions to which the agent might not admit (1972b, 44). In other words, Snook maintains that, even though the avowed intention to indoctrinate is either denied or simply absent in the above examples, the real intention to indoctrinate is nevertheless present (cf. White 1972a, 122). Here we get into the thorny problem of defining "intentions" – a problem I do not want to pursue here, except to say that I do not believe that Snook's attempt to save his intention criterion by making the distinction between avowed intention and real intention is successful. In fact Snook himself admits as much (1973a) when he shifts the focus to the consequences of indoctrination and examines what it means to be an indoctrinated person or society. Here he concedes that, given a non-rational state of mind on the part of a pupil, and given that this was caused by the activity of a teacher, "it seems appropriate to say that the teacher indoctrinated him even though he neither desired nor foresaw this outcome", that is, even though he or she did not intend to indoctrinate (Snook 1973a, 59).

Finally, it should be obvious that "intention" alone is, in a sense, an empty concept. Reference to intention raises the further question of what it specifically is that one intends to do. With regard to indoctrination, the intention criterion will therefore need to be filled with such items as the intent to use certain teaching methods, or the intent to produce certain results. The intention criterion is therefore empty unless it is combined with a methods or consequences criterion.

I would suggest that, although Snook himself focuses on the intent aspect of his criterion, it is really the latter part of his definition that carries the weight of his analysis. Snook defines "indoctrination" as teaching with the intention that the pupil or pupils believe what is taught regardless of the evidence (1972b, 47). Implicit in this analysis is reference to both methods and consequences. Evaluation of the intention criterion therefore hinges on evaluation of these other criteria.

So far I have focused on problems related to defining the concept of indoctrination in terms of intentions alone. I have argued that indoctrination cannot be so defined. However, there surely is still some point to being concerned about the intentions of the Christian parent or teacher in teaching their children or students. It is therefore necessary to move on to the substantive question of whether the intentions behind Christian nurture are suspect. I suggested at the beginning of this chapter that a useful way to summarize the concerns of those who worry about the intentions of the indoctrinator is to describe the indoctrinator as intending to stop growth toward autonomy. The ideal of autonomy will therefore be the focus in the following section.

CRITIQUE OF THE ENLIGHTENMENT IDEAL OF AUTONOMY

I have already reviewed the key ingredients in the modern liberal ideal of autonomy about which so much has been written in educational literature. This emphasis is not surprising given the influence of liberalism in western cultures (for example, through the writings of such philosophers as Immanuel Kant and John Stuart Mill). Its pervasiveness today creates the danger that the ideal of autonomy is simply taken for granted, that it becomes a mere "hurrah" word (Halstead 1986, 34). But philosophers specialize in subjecting to critical evaluation that which is taken for granted. Even those who accept autonomy as an educational ideal would probably admit that it deserves critical scrutiny. Treatment will necessarily have to be limited to ways in which this ideal relates to Christian nurture. The approach will be first to analyze and evaluate the definition of autonomy as commonly understood since the Enlightenment. This examination will lead at the same time to a definition and defence of "normal autonomy." I will then examine the extent to which this more defensible ideal of normal autonomy is compatible with Christianity and Christian nurture.

One of the dangers of a term's becoming commonplace is that everybody assumes that it has a precise meaning shared by all who use it. If asked what autonomy means, most people (including most educators) would probably identify as its synonyms "independence" or "self-determination." But what does it mean to be independent or self-determining?

"Autonomy" and its synonyms might make sense when used in the context in which the Greeks first used these notions, to describe a free city state which was not under the rule of some conquering or imperial neighbour (Dearden 1972, 448). But what can the word mean when applied to persons? In that case, "autonomy" is in fact being used metaphorically (Halstead 1986, 34) and, as with all metaphors, the term is difficult to define.

"Autonomy" is both ambiguous and vague. Its ambiguity is evident from the fact that we talk about "moral autonomy," "personal autonomy," "institutional autonomy," and so forth. Ward distinguishes sixteen possible meanings of the term "autonomy" (1983). Though there would seem to be some overlapping in his analysis of these meanings, Ward's article does at least provide a much-needed corrective to the common assumption that the concept of "autonomy" is unambiguous (Halstead 1986, 34). Unfortunately, we are not always clear about the kind of autonomy being referred to in discussions of this educational ideal and there is a tendency to slide from one usage to another. The earlier analysis of autonomy in this chapter dealt with the notion of personal autonomy, although this is not always clearly distinguished from moral autonomy.

There is also an inherent vagueness in the ideal of autonomy.

There is simply no precise definition of how free, how independent, how self-controlled, how rational, or how competent a person has to be in order to be described as autonomous. Many writers, including Dearden (1972, 458, 461; 1975, 9), admit that autonomy is very much a matter of degree, but they fail to face up to the problems inherent in such an admission. This problem of vagueness is not resolved by suggesting that "autonomous" can conveniently be used as a short-hand for "autonomous to a relatively high degree, or in relatively important respects," as is sometimes done in educational writings (see, for example, Haydon 1983, 220). This simply begs the question. Just how high a degree of autonomy is required in students before it is possible to say that we have achieved the goal of fostering students' autonomy in education?

The expression "autonomous to a relatively high degree" illustrates a third fundamental problem with the typical modern concept of autonomy, its idealism. The expectation is that modern persons can indeed achieve a very high degree of autonomy. At times it is even implied that we can achieve absolute autonomy. Dearden, for example, suggests that Kant and Spinoza define autonomy in terms of some form of absolutely spontaneous activity (1975, 3-4). Allen argues that the modern ideal of autonomy ultimately presupposes the existentialist notion of absolute or radical freedom (1982, 201). He illustrates this by referring to Sartre, who describes the self as a self-defining and self-determining nothingness which faces no independent values and thus creates values by choosing them. But autonomy, when it is defined in absolute terms, is obviously deficient. It fails to recognize that choice always takes place in a certain context and is limited by that context and by a self which is in part determined by its heritage (Allen 1982, 201-2). The desire for absolute freedom, as Hegel saw in the French Revolution, is totally destructive. Dearden, a contemporary advocate of autonomy as an educational ideal, recognizes these and other problems and tries to disassociate himself from the notion of absolute autonomy (1972; 1975, 5-6), but he does so only at the cost of succumbing to vagueness.

Even where this extreme position of absolute autonomy is rejected, the concept of autonomy tends to be too idealistic. As Phillips notes, typical accounts of autonomy make the autonomous person "a rare – if not totally fictitious – person" (1975, 6). With a touch of satire, he further maintains that discussions about autonomy typically assume that all human beings can act "to a greater or lesser degree in the disciplined, rational, autonomous manner of a Cambridge don" (1975, 2). But most human beings are not Cambridge dons! There is an elitist element underlying much of the current discussion of autonomy, as Halstead has noted (1986, 38). Indeed, Kohlberg, among others, points out that very few people achieve what he describes as the autonomous level of moral thinking. What is needed is a more realistic account of autonomy (Rich & DeVitis 1985, 89; cf. Haworth 1980, 184).

Haworth, in his recent attempt to provide a more coherent and comprehensive account of autonomy, clearly confronts the issue that autonomy is very much a matter of degree (1986, 45, 83). He attempts to overcome the problem of vagueness by distinguishing between the minimal autonomy of a child and the normal autonomy of an adult. Because Haworth is particularly concerned with providing a "realistic ideal of full autonomy" (1986, 65) to counter the romantic notions of autonomy that abound, he emphasizes normal autonomy. Halstead makes essentially the same point by introducing the notion of "weak autonomy" (1986, 36). The juxtaposition of "weak" with "autonomy" is unfortunate; I prefer Haworth's "normal autonomy."

But exactly how autonomous are normally autonomous people? Haworth suggests that the answer to this question is ideologically driven (1986, ch. 12). Some people take a dim view of the degree of autonomy which is attainable by normal people. More common in our society, given the influence of economic theory, is the sanguine view in which economic man or woman is generally seen as highly autonomous. Unfortunately, here and elsewhere in Haworth's description of normal autonomy difficulty arises from his different answers to the question of the degree of autonomy achievable by ordinary human beings. Haworth further undermines his account of normal autonomy by still holding out an ideal of "unrestricted autonomy," "unlimited" self-control, independence, and critical competence, because in principle "there is no limit to the extent to which a person can become autonomous" (1986, 194). This comes back to the notion of absolute autonomy which has already been criticized.

Despite these weaknesses, Haworth has made an important contribution to the discussion of autonomy with his notion of "normal autonomy." One of the fundamental problems in the many critiques of Christian nurture in contemporary literature is their romanticized idea of the level of autonomy which is achievable by normal human beings.[6] I would suggest that once autonomy is defined in terms of "normal autonomy," the indoctrinative charge loses much of its sting.

In what follows, I will be pursuing the notion of normal autonomy, in some ways following up on Haworth's suggestions, while in other ways departing from his analysis. This exploration will be undertaken, however, in the context of identifying additional problems inherent in the commonly accepted Enlightenment ideal of autonomy. Both my critique of the modern ideal of autonomy and my defence of normal autonomy draw on themes found in communitarian critiques of liberalism, critical theory, post-modernist thinking, and recent work in sociology.

I have noted that the concept of autonomy presupposes a conception of the self as the subject of freedom, as an agent who can carry out projects. Allen maintains that the commonly accepted and unrealistic ideal of autonomy presupposes what Sartre made explicit, "that man is a self-defining and self-determining nothingness" (1982, 201). But as Allen, reflecting the thinking of many other current philosophers, points out, this conception is incoherent. "Human being is essentially finite, contingent and situated" (Allen 1972, 205). If we strip our conception of the governing self of its history, its situatedness, and of all the beliefs and values which it inherited, we are left with only "a bare impersonal Reason imprisoned in its own royal palace," and then the notion of autonomy itself becomes empty and incoherent (Feinberg 1973, 160). The human subject of autonomy must be given flesh and blood with historical roots, inherited tendencies, beliefs, and values. Other writers have similarly noted that self-determination requires self-knowledge and this in turn requires rootedness and filial bonds of various kinds (Page 1985, 109). When all this is seriously acknowledged, we will be more realistic about the level of autonomy that can be achieved by ordinary human beings. The ideal of normal autonomy acknowledges that to a large extent the self is always already defined by what it has inherited.

This entails the need to pay much more attention to the initiation phase of education, when children are given a whole stock of traditions, beliefs, and values which in turn serve to define who they are. It is precisely here that Christian parents are often accused of indoctrinating, but this accusation is misguided because initiation is a necessary part of forming a self. Liberal parents too, of necessity, initiate their children into a liberal tradition. All children are in part indebted for their sense of identity to the initiation process they were first exposed to. To describe these processes in a negative way as "primitive," "ghetto-istic," and contrary to the ideal of autonomy as do Hirst (1985, 7, 16) and others, is fundamentally mistaken and rests on an unrealistic notion of autonomy which fails to see that one's self-concept is always shaped to a large extent by one's past.

Accepting the givenness of the self further entails that we are never quite so independent and authentic as we like to think we are. Here again the commonly accepted ideal of autonomy is unrealistic. Joel Feinberg (1973, 162) provides an illustration of the dangers of setting our standards so high as to render authenticity an empty or unrealizable ideal. A friend and former colleague of his, a sensitive and gifted philosopher, informed Feinberg one day that after many years of teaching the philosophy of religion, he had come to believe in God. Given his background and profession, he had of course prepared a complex rationale for his important new conviction such that Feinberg could not doubt his authenticity. However, Feinberg did have some doubts about his colleague's authenticity when months later his friend announced that he had joined the local Methodist Church. This decision had been made without a careful investigation of the claims to truth of various denominations, let alone other religions. In fact, this friend and colleague had simply chosen to affiliate with the church of his parents and grandparents. Feinberg's reflective comments on this are significant:

I took this at the time as strong evidence of inauthenticity, of the acquisition of convictions and commitments in an "artificial" and "second-hand" way. But now I'm not so sure. Perhaps my standards of authenticity were pegged unrealistically high. My friend could not even consider becoming (say) a Buddhist or a Roman Catholic. These were, in James's phrase, absolutely dead options to him. After all, if one is a Burmese and finds God one becomes a Buddhist, and if one is Italian or Irish one becomes a Catholic. My friend was not shopping for a different nationality or ethnic identity; his own was too well fixed to be questioned. So he became a Methodist. Was he a "mere slave" to his time and place in this selection? I think not. We may all be, in some respects, irrevocably the "products of our culture," but that is no reason why the self that is such a product cannot be free to govern the self it is. (Feinberg 1973, 162)

Far too often the ideals of independence and authenticity are defined in the abstract and thus are set too high. The ideal of normal autonomy recognizes that people cannot completely transcend the culture of their time and place. To aim to do so in educating children is foolish.

Feinberg's illustration also touches on the rationality component of autonomy. I have noted that liberal educators aim for rational reflection and criticism based on a foundation of broad knowledge. But just how rational can we be? Again it is necessary to give up the ideal of "pure rationality" because our capacity to reason is finite.

Further, "autonomous Reason even of the authentic man will be at the service of some interests and ways of perceiving the world that are simply 'given' him by the *Zeitgeist* and his own special circumstance" (Feinberg 1973, 162). The liberal ideal of encouraging rational, autonomous choice, and the individual construction of beliefs, as O'Hear points out,

easily degenerates into a picture of the rational individual as an isolated Cartesian skeptic, reinventing the whole of knowledge and value for himself, and whose autonomous choosing is in the end weightless and flippant because of the impossibility of finding any criteria for his choices, which are not themselves chosen by him on the basis of yet further criteria he chooses, and so on and so on, until he finally just opts for something. Beliefs and choice, in any human sense, are impossible on this model, the reason being that in both cases, the autonomous subject is represented as an isolated ahistorical being outside human community and human history. (quoted in Halstead 1986, 51)

The choice and construction of beliefs is never the product of isolated, individual wills. Rather, as Halstead stresses, it is the "convictional community ... which objectivises and legitimates the public structure of beliefs and gives it internal coherence" (1986, 51). Rationality is necessarily imbedded within a tradition to some extent as was argued in the previous chapter. There would also seem to be growing recognition that tradition is much more complex than commonly assumed in the post-Enlightenment image that equates it with the "dead weight" of the past from which we must be emancipated (Bowers 1987, ch. 3; Shils 1981). There is, rather, a creative tension between tradition and emancipation.

It is significant that the tradition-bound nature of rationality is specifically acknowledged by Haworth (1986) as essential to his concept of normal autonomy. Borrowing the notion of "criticism internal to a tradition" from another writer, Haworth stresses in particular "the idea that the thinking that is to 'set us free' is simply a process of examining the basis of our values and beliefs from a perspective that takes for granted the other values and beliefs we acquired as a result of growing up within a determinate culture" (1986, 3-4).

Haworth is also recognizing here the limitations of critical reflection, another aspect of the rationality component of autonomy. Critical thinking, about which much is being written, is also necessarily tradition bound. Criticism always rests on some assumptions that are, for the time being, unquestioned, as even Dearden is forced to acknowledge (1972, 457). Critical reflection should, and in fact always does, occur within the context of a convictional community (Halstead 1986, 50). Normal autonomy is realistic with regard to the possibility of critical reflection.

Clearly, rationality and critical reflection need to go beyond the bounds of a tradition. Autonomous individuals are able to distance themselves to some degree from the confines of a tradition. But the important qualifier here is "to some degree." Here again it is necessary to be realistic about the extent to which this is possible for individuals who have achieved normal autonomy.

One final aspect of the rationality component of autonomy needs to be considered. The ideal of autonomy is often associated with being well informed, knowing all the options, and possessing the wherewithal for making knowledgeable decisions. J. P. White (1973) goes so far as to justify a compulsory curriculum on the grounds that it provides the necessary background for autonomous decision making later in life. The fundamental problem here is that it is impossible to be well informed about everything. There never was, nor ever will be, a truly Renaissance person! As far as the necessary background for religious autonomy goes, it is obvious that a child cannot be exposed to, let alone become well informed about all the religious (and non-religious options) of the world. Even with the phenomenological approach to religious education so much in vogue, an inordinate amount of selection occurs. Does this mean that the schools using this approach are not aiming for autonomy? Surely not. Selection and simplification are an inevitable and necessary part of all education as John Dewey taught us long ago ([1916]1966, 20). Again we need to be reminded that to be human is to be "necessarily situated in a contingent historical, cultural and social context, by which our existence and our choice are limited" (Allen 1982, 205). Normal autonomy also accepts the limitations that are a necessary part of human existence with respect to the requirement of being well informed. This of course does not mean that we are making a virtue out of keeping children ignorant. Clearly, expansion of horizons and growing awareness of options is essential to liberal education. But just how expansive or how well informed a child's training needs to be is a question that will not and need not be settled here. Our argument here is simply that normal autonomy requires only limited knowledge of options available.

I will not say more here about the rational component of autonomy since the ideal of rationality was considered in detail in the previous chapter. It should be noted, however, that normal autonomy obviously encompasses what was said in outlining a reconstructed ideal of normal rationality. Normal autonomy also includes what will be said about normal critical openness in the following chapter.

Another problem with the traditionally accepted liberal view of autonomy is best introduced by way of illustration. What does one say about individuals who have freely and "autonomously" chosen to submit themselves in some way to another? Examples include the Marxist who lives his life according to a code found in some Marxist text, the Christian who commits herself to being a follower of Jesus Christ, the young hockey player who imitates Wayne Gretzky in everything he does, the wife who chooses to submit herself to a traditional woman's role including submissiveness to her husband. Some people would argue that such individuals cannot be described as autonomous despite the earlier "autonomous" decision to be non-autonomous. Thalburg, for example, suggests that a woman who takes on a subsidiary and domestic role seems not to be "even faintly autonomous" in her behaviour and thinking and this must be due to some pernicious influence such as brainwashing or indoctrination. Interestingly, his solution is the "forcible 're-education,' or brainwashing" of adult women together with a new program of "conditioning" women from infancy so that they will come to value autonomy (1979, 27, 29 35-6).

Thalburg's analysis and solution raises a basic question. Are women who have been forcibly re-educated, or brainwashed, or systematically conditioned from infancy to value autonomy really autonomous? Surely the subsequent "choice" to value autonomy can no longer be described as having been made independently or authentically. We are here back again to the fundamental problem — the difficulty of describing what it really means to think and act on one's own when we are to a large extent shaped by our early upbringing. Thalburg recognizes the importance of socialization and its inevitability (1979, 33), but he fails to see the full implications of this for his analysis of autonomy. Neither liberated nor non-liberated women are as autonomous as they think they are, because their thinking is to a large extent determined by earlier socialization. Further, since "all forms of socialization are conventional and artificial," Thalburg (1979, 34) has undermined his basis for justifying the value of autonomy – a theme which I want to pick up in the next section.

There is one additional problem with the claim that those who choose in some way to be submissive to another person are not autonomous. Submission to others is in varying degrees inescapable. The graduate student submits to his supervisor, the vice-president submits to the president of the company, and the husband submits to his wife. Haworth (1986, 20-1, 218) and others make an important distinction between substantive and procedural dependence or independence. Substantive dependence describes actual relationships of subordination such as following another. There is no reference here to why it is that one conforms or follows. The explanation may be either that one feels insecure or threatened when one fails to conform or follow, or one may do so as an expression of independent convictions (given, of course, the qualifications that I have made above). Substantive dependence may or may not involve procedural dependence. Procedural dependence refers to the process involved in acquiring beliefs or adopting a life-style, a process in which one simply appeals to authority or tradition without thinking for oneself. Haworth gives the following example:

A cloistered nun, who devotes her life to Christ and whose days follow a set pattern has made herself substantively dependent. If the decision to enter cloistered life was a serious and personal one and if moreover it is renewed from time to time, her substantive dependence need not be taken as a sign that she lacks personal autonomy. (Haworth 1986, 20)

It is only a certain degree of procedural independence that is essential to defining personal autonomy. Inclusion of substantive independence in one's definition of autonomy creates a problem for all relationships and any notion of commitment to a person, a group or even to a goal (Haworth 1986, 218). Even Thalburg is forced to concede that autonomous persons can depend on others, trust them, and join them in co-operative ventures (1979, 36). All that is essential for normal autonomy is that these commitments and relationships be entered into with some degree of freedom and deliberation. In other words, normal autonomy requires only procedural independence, and even this only to a moderate degree, as has already been argued.

Several of the problems I have dealt with point to a final problem with the widely accepted ideal of autonomy. Autonomy as it is typically understood fails to take into account the value of community and its need for tradition. In fact, autonomy carried to the extreme destroys community (Allen 1982, 203-4). It destroys the communal bond of trust and acknowledgment of authority which is essential to providing security and the linking of one generation to the next. If autonomy is taken to be the ultimate value, you can only have a society of strangers, supposedly bound by a social contract. But, as has been argued so poignantly by Robert Bellah and his co-authors in *Habits of the Heart*, "We have never been, and are not, a collection of private individuals who, except for a conscious contract to create a minimal government, have nothing in common" (Bellah, Madsen, et al. 1985, 282). Even if we grant a contractual level of association, it becomes problematic in that it presupposes some prior sense of community bond or tacit emotional bonds, historical ties, and loyalties (Allen 1982, 204). We are reminded by some writers that "our word 'idiot,' derives from the Greek word for 'individual,' and that we should not forget the classical literature which counsels us to consider the community as prior to the individual" (Page 1985, 108).

Haworth (1986, ch. 12) acknowledges the problem and recognizes the need to integrate autonomy with community, although he still maintains that priority must be given to the value of autonomy. His argument regarding priority of values is I believe, unsuccessful,[7] and further assumes that we can only think in terms of autonomy having priority over community or vice versa. It is either/or. But surely another possibility is that each has equal value, though admittedly we also need moral requirements attached to each. What is important here is that normal autonomy will be understood to be limited in the sense that equal priority is given to community and its need for tradition and bonds of loyalty and trust. Independence must always be balanced by dependence as we by nature seek both autonomy and dependence, individuality and community.

JUSTIFICATION OF AUTONOMY

So far I have criticized various dimensions of the traditional idealized notion of autonomy. It is now time to look more broadly at the issue of justifying the ideal of autonomy. Here a problem comes to the fore when we consider Thalburg's (1979) call for a program of resocializing women so that they will come to value autonomy. But since all forms of socializing are conventional and arbitrary according to Thalburg, it would seem to follow that autonomy itself is an arbitrary value.[8]

This arbitrariness can be illustrated at an individual level. While many intelligent and sincere people accept the traditional ideal of autonomy, others reject this ideal and give reasons for doing so, as in the preceding pages. This arbitrariness can also be illustrated historically. The idea that autonomy is a possibility and indeed a good thing has come to us predominantly through the Enlightenment and the liberal revolt against the church (Page 1985, 107). Clearly this liberal emphasis on autonomy was not accepted prior to the Enlightenment and there would seem to be a growing rejection of this longstanding liberal tradition today (Bowers 1987, 55). This point is argued at length by MacIntyre who maintains that "modern liberalism, born of antagonism to all tradition, has transformed itself gradually into what is now clearly recognizable even by some of its adherents as one more tradition" (1988, 10).

Here it is important not to dismiss autonomy too quickly. I am only arguing that the defence of an extreme liberal version of autonomy as a value is arbitrary. One of the fundamental problems with justifications of autonomy has been that they fail to distinguish between an idealized liberal version of autonomy and normal autonomy. Once we limit ourselves to normal autonomy I believe it can be justified in a way that transcends arbitrariness. In fact, many of the arguments that fail when used to justify the traditional notion of autonomy do justify normal autonomy. There is, for example, a transcendental argument put forward by Dearden (1972, 459) among others. To question the value of normal autonomy presupposes a commitment to independent judgment, rational criticism, and so forth. Although Dearden is defending an extreme version of autonomy, he includes an interesting qualification in this same context: *"In a very minimal sense*, all human beings exercise autonomy" (Dearden 1972, 460; emphasis mine). In other words, it is normal autonomy which seems to be inescapable. Even the person who lives a life of substantive dependence will either have chosen this way of life or will from time to time reflect on this way of life, thus exhibiting procedural independence, and hence normal autonomy.

Although many writers who defend autonomy are cautious about appealing to human nature, their arguments invariably rely on such an appeal. Haworth argues that humans are distinguished from other creatures by their central tendency to grow, to become competent (1986, 124, 2). He lists a host of social scientists who support the thesis that growth toward minimal autonomy is natural, and the word "minimal" is important here (Haworth 1986, 56).[9] Thalburg, as we have seen, challenges this position that it is natural for people to become autonomous with his "malleability thesis" (1979, 30-1). Supported by an appeal to the research of the social sciences, he claims that we are naturally passive and dependent. But Thalburg commits the fallacy of thinking in terms of either/or. In describing human nature, we do not have to choose between a natural drive towards autonomy or a natural drive towards dependency. Human nature desires both dependency and autonomy, both community and individuality.[10] This is at the heart of the notion of normal autonomy being defended here.

Not only is it natural for human beings to desire growth towards normal autonomy, it is also a key to our happiness, our well-being, and our sense of dignity (Dearden 1972, 460-1; Haworth 1986, 123,

169-70, 183-4). Haworth (1986, ch. 10) goes to great lengths to show that autonomy is a more fundamental value than happiness, but he fails to take into account that just as happiness loses value in proportion as the happy individual loses autonomy, so autonomy loses value in proportion as the autonomous individual is not happy. Here again Haworth assumes that it is necessary to show that values must be prioritized, that there must be "the fundamental value" (1986, 184); but surely we can have several fundamental values. As Dearden points out, autonomy is clearly not the only thing that matters (1972, 461). We also need to value morality and truth, and to these I would add happiness, love, and community.

Much more could be said by way of justifying the value of normal autonomy but I am concerned with providing a broad outline of such a defence. What is perhaps more important for my purposes is whether the ideal of autonomy is compatible with Christian values. In the next section I wish to address this and other questions relating to Christian nurture and autonomy.

CHRISTIAN NURTURE AND THE IDEAL OF AUTONOMY

I am now in a position to address the central question of this chapter: Is Christian nurture indoctrinatory in the sense of failing to aim for and promote growth toward autonomy? Which in turn raises another question: Is autonomy a Christian value? It all depends on what is meant by autonomy. If autonomy is understood in its traditional strong and idealistic sense, then Christian nurture is incompatible with fostering autonomy. This is no surprise since, as Page reminds us, "The idea that self-determination is a possibility, much less a good thing, comes to us predominantly through the Enlightenment and Liberal revolts against the Church" (1985, 107). From a doctrinal perspective, the original sin consists of individual man and woman asserting their independence from the God who created them, placing their reason and will above God's. Emil Brunner sums it up well in his book *Man in Revolt*: "Sin is defiance, arrogance, the desire to be equal with God ... the assertion of human independence over against God ... the constitution of the autonomous reason, morality and culture" (1939, 129). Christianity is clearly incompatible with the strong liberal version of autonomy which dominates contemporary educational thought; however, we have found this traditional concept to be philosophically suspect. Yet the charge of indoctrination against Christian nurture is often made on the basis of this traditional modern concept of autonomy. If my critique of this liberal ideal is sound, it follows that in so far as the charge of indoctrination rests on this ideal, it too is philosophically suspect. We have here then a very important response to the frequent charge of religious indoctrination.

However, if we adopt instead the ideal of normal autonomy which I hope I have shown to be more philosophically defensible, then I believe Christian nurture is compatible with the goal of fostering autonomy. Normal autonomy, is, I believe, a Christian value.[11] From a historical perspective, we have already seen in chapter 1 that in the western world formal education was in the main initiated by the Christian church. One sees this also in the rise of universities in the Middle Ages, in Luther's appeal to the magistrates of Germany to ensure universal public education, and in the Puritan emphasis on establishing schools in England and the New World. Although the assumption was that these schools should promote biblical truth and values, the ideal of liberal education with its implicit ideal of autonomy was an equally obvious emphasis in all of these efforts to promote education (Ryken 1980; White 1986).

From a doctrinal perspective, we see the Christian Scriptures as supporting the key elements of normal autonomy. The individual person is given value, dignity, and worth (Genesis 1; Psalms 8, 139; Matthew 6:25-34; John 10). "And even the very hairs of your head are all numbered" (Matthew 10:30). Ultimately it is the individual who is called to respond to God and is whom God holds accountable (Ezekiel 3; Matthew 16:24-8), and the individual's right of refusal is respected (Luke 9:5, 55). This emphasis on the individual is of course balanced with an equal emphasis on our collective identity – the community and people of God as a community (Luke 10:25-37, Exodus 19:4-6; 1 Peter 2:9). But the emphasis on the individual still stands. There is also an emphasis on rationality, knowledge, and the development of the mind, as was argued in the previous chapter. In the next chapter I will also maintain that Christianity is compatible with the ideal of critical openness, an ideal that is closely related to the ideal of autonomy. John Hull comments on this aspect of autonomy after a review of New Testament Christianity, summing up his position thus: "The kind of critical openness which flows from Christian faith has many links with the secular educational ideal of autonomy, and yet ... it has distinctive flavour and colouring" (Hull 1984, 220, 190-5, ch. 18). Though Hull fails to make a clear distinction between the traditional secular/liberal ideal of autonomy and normal autonomy, I would suggest that it is the concept of normal autonomy which captures the distinctive flavour that he sees is the ideal of autonomy flowing from the Christian faith.

Here it might be objected that I am skirting an issue. At the heart of Christianity is a call to submit oneself to God and to his revealed Word, and it is precisely this call to submission that is often viewed as incompatible with the ideal of autonomy. It should be noted that the argument about the apparent incompatibility between submission to God and the ideal of autonomy too often rests on a caricature of what Christian obedience to God really means. We have seen that Peshkin, for example, describes Bethany Baptist Academy as aiming for "absolute acceptance" and "unquestioning obedience" to "absolute truth" (1986, 14, 55, 254, 258-9). Yes, orthodox Christianity does claim that God has revealed the truth and that this is in some way accepted as absolute, but nowhere does the Bible claim that human beings understand this truth perfectly. Instead we find in Paul's classic description of love a frank admission that we only "know in part," that we "see but a poor reflection" (1 Corinthians 13:9, 12). Yes, the Scriptures call for obedience to God's commands, but nowhere do they call for passive and unquestioning obedience. Instead there are frequent calls to test what God has said, to discern what his will really is (Isaiah 41:21, Romans 12:1-2; Philippians 1:9-11; 1 John 4:1). Surely it is entirely reasonable to obey a God who is thought to be good and wise and who ordered all Creation, and it is because of this that God's laws are found to be "fully trustworthy" by the Psalmist (Psalm 119). It should therefore come as no surprise that Peshkin is forced in places to acknowledge that thoughtful reflection and free response to God and his Word is encouraged and found at Bethany Baptist Academy (see examples in Peshkin 1986, 216, 220, 249-56, 253, 266, 297).

The argument concerning the incompatibility of submission to God and the ideal of autonomy further rests on a failure to make the distinction between substantive and procedural independence. Clearly Christianity advocates substantive dependence. But as long as people enter a relationship of commitment to God reflectively and from time to time reassess this commitment, they satisfy the requirements of procedural independence and hence must be described as autonomous.

To return to the central question of this chapter: Is Christian nurture indoctrinatory in the sense of failing to aim for autonomy? It all depends on what is meant by autonomy. Understood in its traditional strong and idealistic sense, then yes, Christian nurture is incompatible with the goal of fostering autonomy. But this traditional concept of autonomy is philosophically suspect. If we adopt instead the ideal of normal autonomy – which is philosophically defensible – then Christian nurture is compatible with the goal of fostering autonomy. Christian nurture aims for a free and independent response to the claims of the Christian gospel. It encourages authentic Christian commitment which is not steeped in mere traditionalism (see Mark 7:6-13). It promotes a spirit of constant evaluation and critical reflection so as to ensure that one's commitment remains authentic (James 1:22-5; 1 Corinthians 11:27-32).

Of course, Christian nurture also aims at conversion and edification in the Christian faith as was noted in the beginning of the chapter. And here seems to be the rub. Does not the specific intention that children are to grow up to become Christians rule out the possibility of promoting growth towards autonomy? Here again many opponents to Christian nurture commit the either-or fallacy. We are not necessarily stuck with a choice between *either* intending to convert a child *or* intending to foster autonomy. We can intend to do both. As McLaughlin points out, we can aim at "autonomy via faith" (1984, 79). But is this kind of intention coherent, it might be asked? It is, if the faith in question itself accepts autonomy as a value as has been argued is the case in the Christian faith. McLaughlin further defends the coherence of this two-pronged intention by distinguishing between the long-term and short-term aims of religious parents:

Their long-term, or ultimate, aim is to place their children in a position where they can autonomously choose to accept or reject their religious faith – or religious faith in general. Since, however, these parents have decided to approach the development of the child's autonomy in religion through exposing them to their own particular religious faith, their short-term aim is the development of faith; albeit a faith which is not closed off from future revision or rejection. So a coherent way of characterising the intention of the parents is that they are aiming at autonomy via faith. (McLaughlin 1984, 79)

McLaughlin's distinction between long-term and short-term aims is helpful in that it takes into account the fact that autonomy develops in stages. This "psychogenetic perspective" in the development of autonomy is missed in some accounts of autonomy, according to Haworth (1986, 19). I will have more to say on this shortly.

McLaughlin worries that religious parents "might not be committed to autonomy in a sufficiently strong sense to satisfy liberal demands" (1984, 79), and indeed one of his critics has argued that few religious parents would adopt his prescriptions for promoting autonomy (Gardner 1988, 98-9; cf. Callen 1985). The basic problem here is that both McLaughlin and his critics fail to distinguish between the traditional liberal ideal of autonomy and the ideal of normal autonomy. Christian parents will indeed not be committed to autonomy in a sufficiently strong sense to satisfy traditional liberal demands, but this ideal has been shown to be philosophically unsound. The ideal of normal autonomy is both defensible and consistent with Christian principles. Therefore it is coherent to say that Christian parents and teachers aim for "autonomy via faith."

Indeed, examination of the stated intentions of Christian parents and teachers reveals frequent references to the ideal of normal autonomy. For example, although Peshkin is very critical of Bethany Baptist Academy, he is forced to concede that students "can wonder why, seek explanations, raise questions on any topic, and, in the end, they can reserve judgment about what to accept as true" (1986, 59). Although Bible teacher Art Swanson honestly describes his goal as trying "to shape students' minds to one pattern," he also stresses that individuals "have the freedom to reject that system, to choose as they see fit" (260).

No doubt some critics, like Gardner, will remain unconvinced by the above, and their response to Christian parents and teachers claiming to aim for autonomy would be that they are being "hypocritical or disingenuous" (1988, 102). Unfortunately, this comes dangerously close to being an *ad hominem* argument which civilized people, especially philosophers, should never use. I would be so bold as to suggest that Christian parents and teachers (and religious parents and teachers generally) who frankly admit that they want their children to grow up to become Christians are perhaps more honest than most. After all, how would a liberal agnostic parent really feel if his or her child autonomously chose to become a committed Christian? And how about the atheistic parents who, in the interest of a liberal upbringing, faithfully take their children to Sunday school (but never enter a church door themselves) so that the children can choose for themselves? What message do the children really get? We all know that actions speak louder than words. What are the real intentions of these parents, particularly from a child's perspective? I would suggest that there is a certain "evangelistic" intent in all forms of upbringing and teaching. It is just that religious parents are a little more honest about their intentions.

NURTURING NORMAL AUTONOMY

A final question needs to be addressed with regard to the relation between Christian nurture and autonomy: How is autonomy best nurtured? My central concern here is to uncover some misguided notions about nurturing autonomy which underlie the charge of indoctrination.

Some, perhaps many, people assume that in order to foster autonomy in children we must place them in a free environment in which they can exercise their autonomy. This position is held, for example, by child-centred educationalists such as A.S. Neill and even more extremely by de-schoolers such as Ivan Illich (Dearden 1975, 11-12). Freedom is the fundamental principle governing Neill's famous school, Summerhill, and he went so far as to allow one student to absent himself from all lessons from the age of five to the age of seventeen, all in the name of freedom (Neill 1960, 29). Illich wants children to be free not only at school, but also to be free from school altogether, and again this is advocated in the interests of developing autonomy (1970).

One error made by these and other writers who stress freedom in education is that they assume that children are born autonomous. Children are assumed already to be discriminating and able to competently choose the kind of education they want (Dearden 1975, 13). However, most writers recognize the absurdity of this position. Children are not born autonomous, but need to be educated towards autonomy (Allen 1982, 199). They may display autonomy in a minimal sense, but certainly not at the level of normal autonomy expected of adults (Haworth 1986, 2, 55). This entails that children need to be treated as children and it is simply absurd to describe indoctrination as the violation of their autonomy (see ch. 4).

While children are not born autonomous, they certainly have the capacity and natural impulse to become so. But, as I noted, even here we must be careful not to move too quickly, because we are, as human beings, by nature also dependent on others. We want both to be loved, to belong, to be dependent on a group and to be autonomous, independent. It is this dual tendency within human nature that led me to make an important qualification to the ideal of normal autonomy earlier in this chapter. What needs to be underscored here is that, given these dual tendencies in human nature, there is a need to nurture development towards autonomy. Thalburg (1979) is therefore quite justified in suggesting that children need to be socialized towards autonomy. Doing nothing at all is not an option. We cannot help but influence children one way or another, and thus it is misguided both to label such socialization as indoctrination and to label as indoctrination socialization which tries to balance the ideals of autonomy and community, independence and dependence.

Another frequent error is the assumption that the conditions for the exercise of autonomy are the same as the conditions for the development of autonomy. Dearden (1972), among others, acknowledges that, while relevant freedoms are a necessary condition for the exercise of autonomy, such freedoms might not be necessary for its development. For at least some children, a strict upbringing with relatively little freedom might be most effective in developing autonomy (Dearden 1972, 61-2). Dearden considers the question of the best conditions for the development of autonomy to be largely an empirical one and he is cautious about expecting any general answers to this question. However, some generalizations can certainly be safely made.

First, it is important to note that this is not only an empirical question. There is a conceptual or logical point that needs to be made. It is logically impossible to nurture a child into critical reflection and openness alone. Criticism presupposes content to be criticized. It is only if a child has first been initiated into certain particular traditions that she or he can further develop toward autonomy in the sense of developing critical faculties. Liberal educators, especially those belonging to the current and widespread "critical thinking" movement, frequently seem to forget this point. Quite some time ago R.S. Peters warned against this error by giving a parody of Kant: "Content without criticism is blind, but criticism without content is empty" – indeed, I believe it is *absurd* (Peters 1965, 104).

Peters (1973b) also considers empirical argumentation when he draws on various findings in developmental psychology to show that a secure and non-permissive environment is essential to nurturing autonomy. Autonomous adults "seem to emerge from homes in which there is a warm attitude of acceptance towards children," an attitude which encourages trust in others and confidence in their own powers. Children also need a "firm and consistent insistence on rules of behaviour" and "a predictable social environment." This will encourage them to reflect on the consequences of their behaviour and to develop self-control, both of which are essential for autonomy (Peters 1973b, 130). Other writers have stressed the need for a stable and coherent primary culture in order for children to develop towards autonomy (Ackerman 1980, ch. 5; McLaughlin 1984). Exposing the young child to a variety of belief systems too soon will in fact prevent the development of abilities which are a key to later autonomy. Research in developmental psychology and psychiatry by individuals such as Michael Rutter and Urie Bronfenbrenner seem to confirm these conclusions.[12]

Peters also draws on the work of Piaget and Kohlberg and their theories of moral development which maintain that autonomy can only be achieved by children first passing through the earlier stages of moral development, what Peters calls the "good boy" and "authority-oriented" stages (1973b, 132). Such development is only possible in a non-permissive environment. This developmental approach to nurturing autonomy applies not only to the nurturing of moral autonomy but also to the nurturing of personal autonomy. What is important for our purposes is that development toward autonomy is best achieved if one begins with a relatively closed and non-permissive social, cultural, moral, and intellectual environment. There is therefore nothing inconsistent with raising children within a relatively closed Christian environment with the intent that eventually they will attain autonomy. In fact, nurture within such a stable and coherent primary culture, whether that be Christian, Buddhist or atheistic, is a prerequisite to normal development toward autonomy. It is thus a mistake to associate the provision of a relatively closed environment of Christian homes and primary schools with indoctrination. It is also a mistake to assume that parents who seek to provide a stable and coherent Christian primary culture for their children cannot at the same time intend that their children become autonomous.

Many questions remain about possible restrictions that might be placed on the notion of an acceptable primary culture as well as on the stages of development toward autonomy (see McLaughlin 1984, 78-9). Just how closed can and should primary cultures be? Are stability and coherence the only criteria for a primary culture? How long does the need for a stable and coherent primary culture last? How can and should children be gradually weaned from their primary culture?

Consideration of these questions appears in the final chapters. Here I am concerned to establish that there needs to be a nurturing toward autonomy, that such nurturing requires starting with the provision of a stable and coherent primary culture for the child, and that it is therefore folly automatically to associate such provision with indoctrination as so often occurs. We also need to be much more cautious in casting suspicions on the intentions of parents who are raising their children within a Christian environment and who hope that eventually their children will become Christians. It is possible to aim at autonomy via faith.

6 Consequences of Indoctrination and the Ideal of Critical Openness

I argued in the previous chapter that an analysis of "indoctrination" in terms of intention invariably seems to make reference also to the consequences criterion. Snook defines indoctrination as teaching with the intention that pupils believe something "regardless of the evidence" (1972b, 47).[1] McLaughlin follows J.P. White in describing indoctrination as intentional inculcation of unshakable beliefs (McLaughlin 1984, 77-8; White 1972a, 128). Although White and Snook object to the consequences criterion, what really carries the burden of their pejorative characterization of indoctrination is the way in which indoctrinated individuals hold their beliefs. Various other writers have suggested that consequences, frequently described as "a closed mind," are a key to defining indoctrination.[2] William Hare, for example, has written two books on the ideal of open-mindedness in liberal education (1979, 1985). Indoctrination, for Hare, "involves coming to hold beliefs in a closed-minded fashion" (1979, x, 8; 1985, 21; cf. Scruton, Ellis-Jones, et al. 1985, 25). Often the ideal of open-mindedness is associated with the ability to criticize one's beliefs, hence the frequent reference to "critical openness" (e.g., Halstead 1986, ch. 5; Hull 1984, ch. 18). Previous chapters have considered this emphasis on critical thought in relation to the ideals of rationality and autonomy. All these ideals are essential to what Kimball describes as the liberal-free ideal of liberal education which emerged during the Enlightenment (1986, ch. 5). Here we see how the various aspects of liberal education are so closely interrelated, and why it is difficult to treat each separately. It seems, however, that the ideal of critical thought is most closely re-lated to open-mindedness and hence I shall, in this chapter, focus on the combination, "critical openness." This would seem to cap-ture the heart of what is of concern to those who define indoctrina-tion in terms of consequences. Indoctrination involves the failure to produce minds that are open and critical. Indoctrinated persons are characterized as closed-minded and uncritical about their beliefs.

Concern about the consequences of indoctrination is often illus-trated by referring to religious instruction. Callan, for example, has argued that parents who rear their children within a particular reli-gion incur "a significant risk of indoctrinating them," because such an upbringing will have as its *effect* children who hold their beliefs "without due regard for relevant evidence and argument" (1985, 117, 115). Snook is even bolder when he concludes that indoctrina-tion is inevitable if religion is taught because parents or teachers ob-viously teach religious propositions with the intention that they be believed. Since the evidence for these propositions is inconclusive or even false, it is clear that parents or teachers want their children or pupils to believe these propositions "regardless of the evidence" (1972b, 75). A little later, Snook is more cautious, though still quite damning: "Many teachers of religion would think they had failed unless firm belief was the outcome. Such teaching clearly merits the title of indoctrination" (1972b, 81).

Here again it is necessary to keep in mind the distinction between two approaches to religious education to which I have repeatedly re-ferred. It is only the teaching *of* religion that is being condemned as indoctrinatory because it results in closed minds. By contrast, teach-ing *about* religion is often described as fostering critical openness and thus is a way to avoid religious indoctrination (see Hare 1979, 87-8; Hirst 1985, 14-15).

Sometimes the focus is on the closed atmosphere of a Christian school as a whole, as with Peshkin's description of Bethany Baptist Academy as a "total institution," an "organizational tyranny," a "closed universe" with a doctrinal foundation which "enslaves be-cause it constricts one's options" (1986, 261). Teachers at BBA are de-scribed as having rejected Jerome Bruner's ideal of schooling which favours "diversity and openness, not trying to shape minds to one pattern" (Peshkin 1986, 265-6). Hirst similarly describes church-re-lated schools as being "inconsistent with the principles that should govern an open, critical, rational and religiously pluralist society" (Hirst 1985, 15; cf. Callan 1985, 117-18).

"The most obvious hallmark of the indoctrinated person is that he has a particular viewpoint and he will not seriously open his mind to the possibility that that view-point might be mistaken. The indoctrinated man has a closed mind." (Barrow & Woods 1988, 73). It is in this same context that Barrow and Woods provide us with the paradigm case of indoctrination which we have been considering throughout – a Catholic school with Catholic teachers who "deliberately attempt to inculcate in their pupils an unshakable commitment to the truth of Catholicism and of the various claims or propositions associated with it" (70). Barrow and Woods conclude that it is "difficult to conceive of anyone seriously doubting that these teachers are indoctrinating" (70). Perhaps they are a little hasty with their conclusion! In beginning an examination of this aspect of the charge of indoctrination, we first need to look more closely at the meaning of "critical openness."

MEANING OF ''CRITICAL OPENNESS''

Despite the fact that much has been written about critical thinking and open-mindedness, there is confusion as to the precise meaning of these terms. It is generally assumed that there is a common meaning to such an expression as "believing regardless of the evidence," but as O'Leary has shown, there are at least four different ways to interpret this description of an indoctrinated state of mind (1979, 297). Such ambiguity is important to uncover, especially if the point is to subject the ideal of critical openness itself to scrutiny. In what follows, I would like to unpack some of the meanings associated with the ideal of critical openness as found in the literature on indoctrination. I will attempt to organize these meanings under broader headings for purposes of easier reference, though it should be remembered that classifications such as this are always somewhat arbitrary. Analyzing the strands of meaning in the ideal of critical openness will of course also unpack the meanings often associated with its opposite, uncritical closed-mindedness, which is associated with indoctrination.

Belief conditions

It might seem obvious that the indoctrinated or the closed-minded person must satisfy a belief condition – he or she believes a proposition or a set of propositions (O'Leary 1979, 295). There is some debate as to whether the open-minded person also can satisfy a belief condition. Hare, for example, argues that generally open-mindedness is ascribed to people who do have beliefs and even settled convictions (1979, ch. 2).

By contrast, open-mindedness is sometimes understood in terms of being neutral or uncommitted with regard to a certain position. The expression "to keep an open mind on the matter" seems to suggest that open-mindedness entails neutrality. Gardner associates being open-minded about alternatives with not thinking these alternatives to be true or false (1988, 92).

At times one even finds ignorance associated with open-mindedness. Whereas neutrality assumes some familiarity with the issue in question, ignorance does not and this is sometimes seen as better than a little learning which is a dangerous thing. Hare describes John Dewey as attempting to establish such a link between genuine ignorance and open-mindedness (Hare 1979, 41).

Epistemic conditions

Closed-mindedness is often described in terms of "believing regardless of the evidence." Green maintains that indoctrination will "produce persons who hold their beliefs non-evidentially" (1972, 35). By contrast, open-minded persons hold beliefs evidentially or on the basis of evidence. But these expressions can be interpreted in a variety of ways, as even Snook and Green recognize. (a) Snook suggests that indoctrinated persons with closed minds may believe what is true, but be unable to back up their belief (1973a, 56). (b) Open-minded persons take into account contrary evidence for beliefs held. Closed-minded persons on the other hand disregard contrary evidence (Snook 1973a, 56; Green 1972, 33). (c) Some philosophers are even more specific about the relationship between closed-mindedness and contrary evidence. They define closed-mindedness in terms of the failure to seek out contrary evidence. It was this readiness to *look for* weaknesses in his own position which the young Karl Popper detected in Einstein and which so impressed him, and which many would see as a sign of open-mindedness (see Hare 1979, 10). (d) Indoctrinated persons with closed minds are also sometimes described as simply completely uninterested in evidence for their beliefs (Snook 1973a, 56). The open-minded person, by contrast, forms or revises his beliefs in the light of evidence and argument.

Truth Conditions

One occasionally finds that open-mindedness is not only connected with having or being open to evidence for one's beliefs, but there is an even stronger implicit demand that these beliefs be true. Hare, for example, reminds us that people commonly say, "No open-minded person could believe that" (1979, 21). Snook gives, as one expression of the irrationality characteristic of the indoctrinated person with a closed mind, that he may believe what is false or doubtful (1973a, 56). What is being suggested here is that the possession of a certain belief is a sufficient condition for denying that the person is open-minded. By implication, the holding of the opposite belief is sufficient to call a person open-minded.

Snook's association of closed-mindedness with believing what is *doubtful* may also introduce another kind of restriction in terms of content. He may be suggesting that closed-mindedness involves making a commitment in areas of dispute, where evidence is ambiguous, or where issues are as yet not settled (cf. Hare 1979, 29).

Open-mindedness is sometimes associated with a denial of absolute truth. Peshkin, for example, finds the idea of absolute truth to be at the root of the closed atmosphere that characterizes Bethany Baptist Academy (1986, 258-61, 276). Even Hare on occasion seems to suggest that open-mindedness requires that one give up any claims to *exclusive* truth (1979, 89).

Methodological Conditions

It has already been suggested that open-mindedness is closely associated with critical thinking. For Hirst, liberal education stresses an open, rational, critical approach to all beliefs (1985). Open-mindedness means openness to critical reflection concerning one's own beliefs and those of others. The unexamined life is not worth living, according to Socrates, and this ideal of critically examining all that one believes is still very much present with us today.

Sometimes critical openness is associated with doubt. Hare (1979, 31) quotes Bertrand Russell: "When you come to a point of view, maintain it with doubt. This doubt is precious because it suggests an open mind."

At times open-mindedness is also associated with tolerance towards others and their beliefs (Rokeach 1960, 4-5).

Another methodological feature often associated with open-mindedness is that of objectivity and impartiality in assessing one's own beliefs or the beliefs of others (Hare 1985, 3).

Dispositional Conditions

More recently, various writers have expressed concerns about a preoccupation with the epistemic conditions of open-mindedness (O'Leary 1979; Hare 1979). They argue that we need to focus instead on attitudes or dispositions. (a) Hare therefore defines open-mindedness "in terms of a willingness to revise and reconsider one's views" (1979, x; cf. 129). (b) Hare then goes on to combine this dispositional condition with the epistemic conditions we have already considered. The open-minded person must be "disposed to form and revise his views in the light of evidence and argument" (Hare 1979, 9; 1985, 16). Siegel similarly describes the critical thinker as one who has "a well-developed disposition to engage in reason assessment." This is sometimes described as having a "critical spirit" (Siegel 1988, 39). (c) At times Hare adds another qualifier. Open-mindedness involves "a willingness to form and revise one's views as impartially and as objectively as possible in the light of available evidence and argument" (Hare 1985, 3).

What has been attempted above is to provide a fairly exhaustive list of features commonly associated with open-mindedness and its opposite. There will obviously be some features about which there is more agreement than others. However, all are being included for the sake of critical evaluation later. Before I engage in this task, however, I want to examine whether the attempt to establish a relation between indoctrination and consequences generally is successful.

INDOCTRINATION AND CONSEQUENCES

There seems to be an initial plausibility to including the consequences criterion in an analysis of "indoctrination." The word is surely a task-achievement term and thus it would seem that justice must somehow be done to the achievement aspect of indoctrination which would entail reference to consequences. It is further true that, if the outcome of teaching never resulted in closed minds, we should probably not worry about indoctrination (Snook 1972b, 38). We have also seen that Snook was forced to concede that the intent to indoctrinate is detected in consequences.

But here it is necessary to keep in mind what is involved in analyzing a concept such as "indoctrination." Philosophers are very careful to distinguish features contingently related to a concept from those which are necessarily related. Thus, while it might be "a psychological fact" that, if there were no people with closed minds, there would be no concept of indoctrination at all, this only establishes a *factual* relation between "indoctrination" and certain consequences, not the conceptual relationship philosophers are after in analyzing a concept (Snook 1972b, 38). And so I turn to a critical examination of the claim that the consequences criterion is essential to defining the concept of indoctrination.

Few if any philosophers think that "indoctrination" can be defined in terms of consequences alone, that the consequences criterion constitutes a sufficient condition of "indoctrination." Consequences alone cannot indoctrinate. They are rather the result of indoctrination. Reference has to be made to some other criterion such as methods or, as some would have it, intention. Even if we shift the focus to the notion of "an indoctrinated person," some reference still has to be made to the cause of this indoctrinated state of mind (Snook 1973a, 54). The consequences criterion cannot therefore be a sufficient condition of "indoctrination."

But there is a further problem here. It is difficult to establish a relationship between a closed mind and its cause. A closed mind can be caused by ways other than indoctrination. For one thing, such a state of mind may be due to nature – low intelligence, psychiatric disorder, diseases of the brain. Or a person may choose to behave or think irrationally, may choose to deceive her- or himself. In these cases, the irrational state of mind would be indistinguishable from the state of mind of an indoctrinated person. But if a person chooses to be irrational, that person would be blamed for irrationality. Nor is it possible to shift blame to someone else if an irrational state of mind is due to natural causes. Thus consequences alone are inadequate as a criterion of indoctrination.

Various writers have raised another decisive objection against the consequences criterion (Snook 1972b, 41; Wilson 1972b, 19). It is possible to attempt to indoctrinate and fail. Suppose a teacher is giving a biased presentation of a subject, suppressing contrary evidence, forbidding the reading of certain books, using threats, and so forth. But suppose, further, that despite this approach to teaching, students search out and read forbidden books on their own initiative, discuss topics on their own after class, and thus emerge with very open minds. In this case, might we not want to say that indoctrination has occurred even though the expected results are not forthcoming? We also allow for the possibility of freethinkers emerging from a system that would generally be deemed to be indoctrinatory: a Solzhenitsyn emerging from Russia, an atheist or agnostic emerging from a Catholic school, and perhaps even a Christian emerging from a strongly secular educational system. All these are examples about which we seem to be forced to say that it is possible for indoctrination to occur without the usually attendant consequences. This possibility arises because many other influences are at work which may counteract the indoctrinatory efforts of the teacher, such as the home environment, student peers, the student's own inquisitiveness and ability to question. People are seldom, if ever, in a position to *cause* someone to believe something, though at times the discussions of indoctrination seem to assume such a deterministic frame of reference. Summing up, indoctrination does not always result in closed and uncritical minds. It would seem to follow that the consequences criterion is also not a necessary condition of "indoctrination."

The final problem with defining "indoctrination" in terms of consequences concerns the notion of a closed uncritical mind itself. This will be dealt with in the next section. Regardless of whether or not it can be *precisely* defined in terms of consequences, it would seem that indoctrination must be related to consequences in some way. Further, quite apart from the problem of defining "indoctrination," it is important to deal with the concerns surrounding a closed, uncritical mind. The problem of the relation between Christian nurture and a closed uncritical mind also needs to be addressed. In the remainder of this chapter I therefore move to the more substantive questions concerning the consequences of indoctrination.

CRITIQUE OF THE ENLIGHTENMENT IDEAL OF CRITICAL OPENNESS

The examination earlier in this chapter of various features often associated with the ideal of critical openness should alert us to the fact that philosophers are not entirely clear about the meaning of critical openness. Harvey Siegel, in a recent book on critical thinking, concedes that despite widespread recent interest, there is no clear agreement concerning the meaning of this term (1988, 5). Hare too suggests that "open-mindedness" is a much misunderstood notion (1979, xi). Although Siegel and Hare go some way in overcoming the shortcomings in past treatments of the ideals of critical thinking and open-mindedness, there is still room for greater clarification. The basic thrust of this section is to show that the ideal of critical openness, as usually understood, is confused, ambiguous, and vague and needs to be seriously qualified in order to be philosophically defensible. Consequently appeal to it in making the charge of indoctrination against Christian nurture is to a large extent unwarranted. Once the ideal is clarified and properly qualified, it will be seen that Christian nurture can be quite compatible with critical openness.

Human Nature

I would like here to highlight a central criticism that will run through much of what is to follow. The vagueness inherent in the notion of critical openness lends itself to stretching the ideal to extremes which then becomes problematic. In other words, critical openness tends to be defined too idealistically. It fails to take into account the limitations of the human condition and the limitations inherent in the teaching situation. Joel Feinberg highlights this problem when he talks about "that corruption of the ideal of open-mindedness, where everything is always 'up for grabs,' and every conviction or allegiance is to be examined afresh each time it comes up, as if past confirmations counted for nothing" (1973, 166). This corruption is exposed in another way by G.K. Chesterton in his *Autobiography* in which he describes H.G. Wells as a man who "reacted too swiftly to everything," who was "a permanent reactionary," and who never seemed able to reach firm or settled conclusions of his own. Chesterton goes on: "I think he thought that the object of opening the mind is simply opening the mind. Whereas I am incurably convinced that the object of opening the mind, as of opening the mouth, is to shut it again on something solid" (Chesterton 1937, 223-4).

Critical thinking is similarly often viewed as an activity which is an end in itself, criticising infinitely, forever, or as Russell described the open mind, doubting infinitely, forever. But surely we can and should feel certain about some things. Surely we should respect authority to some extent. Surely criticism for the sake of criticism is pointless, unless it is put into the service of searching for something solid like truth. It simply is not possible or desirable to adopt "a policy of constant, sustained and intense critical onslaught" against one's beliefs (Hepburn 1987, 145). Instead, what is needed, according to Hepburn, is a golden mean "between on the one side such a relentless self-critical campaign, and on the other a complacent, or over-anxious, refusal ever to reappraise" (1987, 145). Critical openness needs to be defined as a realistic ideal, and only as such is it philosophically and practically defensible. As with the ideal of autonomy, I want to argue for a notion of "normal critical openness." The additional objections to the traditional ideal of critical openness that follow can also be seen as further clarifications of this revised notion of normal critical openness.

Another major problem with the ideal of critical openness as it is generally understood is that it fails to take human nature into account. This traditional ideal arose as a reaction to what is considered a basic weakness in human nature – the tendency to be dogmatic, closed, and trapped in tradition. Thus Hume, with various other philosophers, has described this basic tendency of the human mind to allow opinions to "take such deep root that 'tis impossible for us by all the powers of reason and experience, to eradicate them" ([1888]1965, Book I, Part 3, Section 9). Mill reminds us that "all rational creatures go out upon the sea of life with their minds made up" (quoted in Hare 1985, 2). And Socrates identified as a feature of the "young and tender" that "that is the time when they are easily moulded and when any impression we choose to make leaves a permanent mark" (Plato [1955]1974, 377b).

Several questions need to be addressed concerning this tendency: Is it good or bad? If bad, can it be eradicated? Should it be eradicated? It is significant that Hume, in exploring the deep-rooted habits of the mind and in adopting a program of systematic skepticism, nevertheless reminds us that it is important for us amidst all our skeptical philosophy to "be still a man" ([1748]1955, Section 1). And Mill, it should be noted, suggests that it is *rational* creatures who have their minds made up. Similarly Socrates, that master at dialectic and critical thought, nevertheless treats childhood beliefs with a certain tenderness and care – not until the age of thirty are children introduced to dialectic because it is harmful to introduce them to philosophy too soon (Plato [1955]1974, 539a/b). Modern educators have much to learn from these masters of philosophy and their insights into human nature.

The insights of these philosophers find abundant confirmation in the findings of the social sciences. Milton Rokeach (1960), in his classic study of the open and closed mind, concludes that all of us, including the liberal-minded, arrange the world of ideas, people, and authority along the lines of belief congruence. Rokeach also refers to the research of Leon Festinger and his theory of cognitive dissonance. "When dissonance is present, in addition to trying to reduce it, the person will actively avoid situations and information which would likely increase the dissonance" (Festinger 1957, 3, cf. 30). Writing shortly after Festinger, Peter Berger introduced his notion of "plausibility structures" to highlight the fact that all of us seek ways to reinforce the beliefs we hold (1969, 50). All these findings suggest that human beings of necessity have minds that are closed to some extent, and that we are less critically open than liberal educators often pretend.

Other dimensions of human nature point to the same conclusion. The limitations of human knowledge result in minds that are partially closed and uncritical. We are all ignorant about some things, and this demonstrates itself in closed minds, as defined in the beginning of this chapter. Further, our thinking necessarily starts with certain unquestioned assumptions which are for the time being at least closed to further scrutiny. Michael Polanyi has reminded us that all knowing has a tacit dimension to it, involving implicit knowledge which the subject is not aware of knowing and which is therefore not specifiable. One implication of this is that all knowing has an *acritical* aspect to it, and this would entail that a closed mind is unavoidable with regard to the beliefs which are tacitly held (see Allen 1978).

Another aspect of the limitations of the human mind comes to the fore when we consider the conclusions of our thought processes. People seldom, if ever, arrive at absolute certainty with regard to their beliefs. However, in order to live and make decisions in every-day life, we need to move beyond uncertainty – to make "leaps of faith" and come to some conclusions, however tentative. Our conclusions are and must be accepted as "functional absolutes" (Kaufman 1960, 86).

A final error underlying the ideal of critical openness which relates to human nature is that of individualism. The challenge to be critically open is typically made to individuals. It is individuals who are to criticize tradition and challenge authority. But who are these individuals? In fact they were once babies who were dependent on others, who were brought up within a particular way of life, who acquired a particular language, and who inherited particular values and beliefs. All of this left a "permanent mark" on these individuals, to quote Socrates once again (Plato [1955]1974, 377b). As these individuals grow up, they are to a large measure already defined by their historical and cultural context (Allen 1982, 206). To pretend that we can entirely escape this historical and cultural context, as is often presupposed by those who urge us to be critical and open, is to delude ourselves. We are by nature essentially finite, contingent, and situated, and our ability to be open and critical is therefore necessarily limited. This is not at all to adopt a deterministic or a Marxian view of human nature. Nor should it be thought that I am here advocating blind conformity to tradition. We can and should be open to evaluating critically the traditions we inherit, but such criticism must be carried out within the context of a "convictional community" (Halstead 1986, 50-1). I am arguing that our ability to be critically open is necessarily limited by virtue of who we are as human beings.

What is it possible to conclude from this review of various aspects of human nature, all of which suggest that a degree of uncritical closed-mindedness seems to be unavoidable? The central point I wish to make is that our ideal of critical openness needs to be appropriately qualified in order to take into account the above-mentioned aspects of human nature. Any ideal of critical openness that fails to take into account the psychological and sociological constraints on our attempts to be rational is simply unrealistic. Any ideal of critical openness that fails to take into account the human need for security or the need to come to some fairly definite conclusions ("functional absolutes") simply in order to live is being unrealistic. Critical openness taken to the extreme might be appropriate for the gods, but not for human beings. What is needed is a *new concept* of normal critical openness that is realistic, that recognises the limited degree to which human beings can and should be critical and have open minds.

So far I have been stressing those tendencies of human nature that suggest that the human mind is in part closed and uncritical. But I believe that human minds are by nature in part open and critical. Hare acknowledges this dimension of human nature when he points out that young children simply have not, as yet, come to be blindly committed to particular views (1985, 19). They are eager to learn and are constantly questioning. Hare seems to be suggesting that this tendency dies down as children grow older. But why? Might not this tendency continue? Rokeach, on the basis of his research, concludes that there are two opposing sets of functions to human belief systems.

On the one hand, they represent Everyman's theory for understanding the world he lives in. On the other hand, they represent Everyman's defense network through which information is filtered, in order to render harmless that which threatens the ego ... We do not agree with those who hold that people selectively distort their cognitive functions so that they will see, remember, and think only what they want to. Instead, we hold to the view that people will do so only to the extent that they have to, and no more. For we are all motivated by the desire, which is sometimes strong and sometimes weak, to see reality as it actually is, even if it hurts. (Rokeach 1960, 400-1)

Those who stress the need for critical thought often forget that the need might be less great than they think because there is a natural desire in human nature to know the truth. There are limits to the defence mechanisms at work with respect to our belief systems. All of us genuinely want to know the truth and are open to arguments and evidence which will bring us to the truth.

It also follows from this that people who want to condemn others as completely closed-minded are wrong. Christians, including

Christian teachers, are not the completely closed-minded bigots they are often made out to be. They, like everyone else, want to know the truth, and they want to help their students to see it. Closed- or open-mindedness is not an all-or-nothing affair (Hare 1979, 15, 17, 85; Rokeach 1960, 5). Yet discussions on this subject often paint such states of mind in these absolute terms. All of us are partly closed-minded and partly open-minded, partly critical and partly uncritical. The ideal of critical openness must acknowledge this very important truth.

Belief Conditions

Confusion about critical openness also arises about the belief conditions associated with this concept as described earlier in this chapter. I have noted that closed-mindedness is often associated with "unshakable commitment." While the emphasis is usually on the *unshakable* nature of the commitment, there are times where it would seem that commitment itself is viewed as a sign of closed-mindedness (see Siegel 1988, 50, 54). Critical openness is, as we have seen, also at times associated with neutrality or even ignorance, and here again concerns seem to centre on the fact of commitment to beliefs or to a belief system. With Hare (1979, ch. 2), I want to argue that the above associations are fundamentally mistaken. Critical openness is not only compatible with, but presupposes commitment.

"Open-mindedness is not empty-mindedness" Hare reminds us (1979, 53). Open-mindedness is both possible and necessary precisely because we ourselves or others are committed to certain beliefs which may not be correct. Similarly, critical thinking is only possible if there is first something to be critical about (Peters 1966, 53). Again it is because of a danger that the public traditions being passed on in education may be false or merely handed on as "inert ideas" that there is a need for critical assessment. In fact, we all have convictions, many of which we inherited from our culture, parents, and teachers, and it is especially with regard to these convictions that we should cultivate an attitude of openness and willingness to evaluate and criticize. Critical openness necessarily depends on our first having beliefs.

It is generally assumed that scientific inquiry is the paradigm of critical openness. (There has been some intense debate about the very possibility of critical openness in science, but this will not be my concern here as I will, for the time being, assume the traditional characterization of science as correct.[3]) While much is made of the tentativeness with which scientific hypotheses are held, it is frequently forgotten that commitment to hypotheses and theories plays an essential part in scientific inquiry. Tenacity of commitment is important for the growth of science. Various writers have pointed out that it is only if scientists vigorously defend their theories and try to protect them against objections for as long as possible that the full potential of such theories can be appreciated. Karl Popper, for example, while stressing that "science is essentially critical," qualifies this by giving approval to dogmatism in science: "But I have always stressed the need for some dogmatism: the dogmatic scientist has an important role to play. If we give in to criticism too easily, we shall never find out where the real power of our theories lies" (1970, 55; see also Hare 1979, 55-6). While Popper's use of the term "dogmatism" to describe the need for tenacious defence of scientific theories may be unfortunate, his point is well taken. Strongly held convictions and deep commitments to a theory are necessary in science, but this is in no way seen to be an endorsement of closed-mindedness in science. We see here that commitment, even strong commitment, is not only compatible with critical openness but also that the latter needs the former.

An interesting aspect of the notion of autonomy further substantiates the above point. Autonomy, as noted in the previous chapter, is often described as an educational ideal. It is a matter of degree and involves various dimensions of variability such as independent judgment and firmness in adhering to the judgments made (118-19). Yet autonomy also presupposes the ability to reflect critically on what one believes and does. Here again the compatibility of critical reflection and firm commitment is evident.

It follows that it is not necessary to be neutral (or ignorant) with regard to a certain position in order to be critically open. Neutrality is one way to be critically open, but it is not the only way (Hare 1979, 29-30, 40-1). We can also display critical openness in those areas where we have commitments, even strong commitments. Of course some people would argue that there are certain areas where the only appropriate stance is neutrality, for example in the area of religious beliefs where the evidence is ambiguous. But this is quite another issue, and will be dealt with a little later. What is important here is to realize that it is possible to be committed to religious beliefs and yet have an open and critical mind towards those beliefs. It is also important to note that it is not possible to be neutral with regard to everything. We need to be committed to all sorts of beliefs just to get on with ordinary living. And it is with regard to these commitments that we need also to cultivate the virtue of critical openness. Critical openness is not only compatible with commitment to certain beliefs, but ultimately it both depends on and is necessary to such commitment.

Epistemic Conditions

We turn next to problems that arise with regard to the epistemic conditions of critical openness described earlier. While the closed and uncritical mind is often described in terms of "believing regardless of the evidence," and this expression is open to a variety of interpretations, it should be noted that there is something very odd and unbelievable about the expression as a whole. Is it really possible to find anyone who believes regardless of the evidence? I have already pointed to the research of Rokeach (1960) which suggests that all of us are to some extent naturally concerned about arguments and evidence for our beliefs. Some writers have gone so far as to suggest that if a person can give no reasons for what he or she believes, it is difficult to know to what extent one can talk of beliefs at all (Snook 1972b, 39; Wilson 1972a, 102). In other words the very concept of believing necessarily entails some reasoning or evidence. Thus even the person with a closed mind will be able to reason or give some evidence in so far as he or she holds beliefs.

This is further substantiated in experience and ordinary language, since we find that so-called indoctrinated persons with closed minds do often thrive on arguments. Passmore (1967, 194) points out that drill in stock objections is often an important feature of the process of indoctrination, and research shows that people are more likely to discount future counter-arguments if they have been dealt with beforehand (Hare 1979, 77; Green 1982, 37-8). Thus again it seems necessary to admit that people with closed minds do reason and appeal to evidence.

Of course, it can be argued that the person with a closed mind only rationalizes and does not truly reason (Wilson 1972b, 19, 21). However, here we are back to the problem of evaluating reasons and evidence, and, as Smart points out, it is not so easy to distinguish between reasons and rationalizations (1973, 38). Green tries to overcome this problem by suggesting that the indoctrinated person with a closed mind "is betrayed in his *use* of reasons and evidence. He will use argument, criticism, evidence, and so forth, not as an instrument of inquiry, but as an instrument establishing what he already believes" (1972, 39). But the distinction between using reasons as an instrument of inquiry, as an instrument establishing what one already believes, or as a "weapon" of defence is just as problematic as the distinction between reasons and rationalizations. In fact, all rational people use arguments and reasons to establish what they already believe. Fundamental to the scientific method is the postulating of a preliminary hypothesis before one collects evidence. "As a matter of fact, it is strictly impossible to make any serious attempt to collect evidence unless one *has* theorized beforehand. As Charles Darwin, the great biologist and author of the modern theory of evolution, observed, ' ... all observation must be for or against some view, if it is to be of any service' " (quoted in Copi 1982, 477). There would therefore seem to be real difficulties distinguishing between indoctrinated persons with closed uncritical minds and rational persons with open and critical minds on the basis of believing or not believing "regardless of the evidence."

One final qualification should be noted with regard to the epistemic conditions of critical openness. It was noted earlier that closed-mindedness is sometimes defined in terms of the failure to seek out contrary evidence. But as Hare notes, to require that the open-minded person actually *look* for contrary evidence is surely to be too demanding in the ordinary case (1979, 10). All that we can require of open-minded persons is that they take objections to their position seriously when they are brought up. Of course there are additional problems with the notion of "paying serious attention to counter-objections," in that "serious" is a vague term. Callan, in a recent essay, joins Bertrand Russell in condemning Thomas Aquinas, that great medieval philosopher and defender of the Catholic faith, as closed-minded because he "clearly" displayed "a radical lack of seriousness" in assessing counter-evidence to his position, despite "an elaborate pretense of weighing pros and cons" (Callan 1985, 115). Russell, it might be remembered, labelled Aquinas an inferior philosopher because he did not, like Socrates, set out to follow wherever the argument would lead him. He always argued for a conclusion which he already knew in advance (Russell 1961, 453-4). One is tempted to ask whether Russell and Callan themselves are merely engaged in an elaborate pretense of weighing pros and cons as they try to establish the conclusion they have already chosen in advance, but it seems so unphilosophical even to ask such a question. However it is perhaps necessary in the face of such utter nonsense and obvious anti-religious prejudice. If ever there was a great thinker and philosopher, it surely was Thomas Aquinas, a point that is acknowledged by most rational philosophers today, including those who would disagree with Aquinas. To suggest that Aquinas was engaged in "an elaborate pretense of weighing pros and cons" is to commit an *ad-hominem* fallacy – a failure both in logic and morality. If ever there was a person who took arguments and counter-arguments seriously, it was Thomas Aquinas. In fact, he went well beyond the call of duty in displaying critical openness by constantly looking for counter-evidence to his convictions. For most ordinary mortals, it is sufficient to consider counter-evidence when it is brought to our attention. And, as even Callan admits in a less prejudiced moment, most of us are only able to examine our beliefs with "a rather frail and fitful seriousness" (Callan 1985, 115). But that is all that normal critical openness requires.

All this is not to rule out entirely the epistemic conditions normally associated with critical openness. I am simply suggesting that there is a need to recognize the limitations of rationality – the same limitations that were dealt with more generally in chapter 4. Clearly, critical openness does require assessment and revision of beliefs in the face of evidence. It is also important to connect these epistemic conditions to the dispositional conditions identified by Hare and Siegel. Thus for Hare, the open-minded person must "be disposed to form and revise his views in the light of evidence and argument" (1979, 9). And Siegel describes the critical thinker as one who has "a well-developed disposition to engage in reason assessment" (1988, 39). This emphasis on attitudes and dispositions is important because it helps to overcome the extremes in treatments of the epistemic conditions when taken by themselves.

Truth Conditions

I turn next to some truth conditions sometimes associated with critical openness. Hare notes that people commonly say such things as, "No open-minded person could believe that," suggesting thereby that believing certain content is sufficient to ascribe closed-mindedness to someone (1979, 21). Hare goes to some lengths to show that our use of the terms "open-minded" and "closed-minded" in ordinary language would suggest that these qualities are in no way restricted to certain content (1979, ch. 2). We do talk about critical openness in any area of belief. Critical openness, it would seem, does not have to do with *what* one believes, but rather with *how* one believes it. Rokeach similarly holds that even though most people cannot define precisely what is meant by a closed mind, it "can be observed in the 'practical' world of political and religious beliefs, and in the more academic world of scientific, philosophic, and humanistic thought" (Rokeach 1960, 5). Interestingly, even so-called "liberals" display closed minds at times, according to Rokeach (1960, 4, 121, 396).

Here it might be objected that I am being a little unfair to those who associate closed-mindedness with certain content. Surely the real point is that there is certain content about which the only proper response is to keep an open mind on the matter. For example, where expert opinion is divided, or where evidence is ambiguous, such as in the areas of religious or political beliefs, it is wrong to make a belief commitment (see p. 148). Instead, one should keep an open mind on such matters. The problem with such a restriction is that it rests on a prejudgment on the epistemological status of these beliefs, and this prejudgment is itself often in question. Dearden is forced to concede that the notion "controversial" is itself controversial (1988). In science, too, expert opinion is often divided on a matter or we find issues about which the evidence seems to be ambiguous – yet we do not necessarily call scientists who make a commitment on one side or the other of an issue closed-minded. In fact, it is most helpful in resolving such issues for scientists to make a commitment on one side or the other and then to defend it even against seemingly contrary evidence, as I have already noted. In all this, what we do still require is that these scientists keep an open mind on the matter, that they be willing to re-assess their belief in the light of further research. The need for critical openness is the same in science or religion, whether it be in areas where there are settled convictions or in areas where consensus has not yet been reached. Therefore any limitation of critical openness as applicable to a certain area of belief would seem to be arbitrary.

It is also a mistake to associate closed-mindedness with making absolute or exclusive claims to truth as does Peshkin in his critique of a Christian school (1986). Truth claims by their very nature are exclusive (or closed) in that they rule out the denials of these claims. But this has nothing to do with being closed-minded. If I believe that there is only one God, the Christian God, I am of course committed to believing that religions that deny this are false. But this does not make me closed-minded. I can be quite open to considering contrary evidence, despite my present commitment.

Nor should it be thought that religions which seem to avoid making exclusive claims are more open-minded than those which do. Hinduism, for example, is sometimes thought to be open-minded because it views various religions as simply being different revelations of the one divine reality, as different paths to reach the one Divine. But, as Harold Coward argues, to claim that all religions are simply different manifestations of the one Divine is still to make an exclusive claim (1985, 80). In fact, we cannot avoid making exclusive claims. This is the dilemma of relativism: to claim that all truths are relative is still to make one exclusive claim, namely, that all truths are relative (Kaufman 1960, ch. 1). Open-mindedness must not be confused with epistemological relativism, a theory which is itself problematic and which ultimately undercuts the need for critical openness (Hare 1979, 53). Making exclusive truth claims seems to be inescapable, and it is because we are fallible and may be in error about the claims we make that we need to be critical and open-minded about them.

Methodological Conditions

I come next to the methodological conditions often associated with critical openness. The primary focus here is on the "critical" aspect of critical openness. I have already touched on some aspects of critical thinking in my treatment of other dimensions of open-mindedness. For example, it has already been argued that we can only be critical if we have something to be critical about. Criticism depends on assertion, on humankind's having been initiated into the great traditions of thought that have usually characterized education (Passmore 1967, 200-1). As Wittgenstein said, "The child learns by believing the adult. Doubt comes *after* belief" ([1969]1972, para. 160).

It has also been argued that critical openness must not be confused with a persistent or open-ended questioning of all things in which everything is always "up for grabs" (Feinberg 1973, 166). Descartes's doubt is methodologically suspect. Surely past confirmations do count for something, and life is such that we need to come to settled convictions about many things.

But there are not only practical limitations to critical thinking and questioning. There are also some logical limitations. It is not logically possible to be critical about everything at one time.[4] There is always something that escapes one's present criticism. Certain axioms, definitions, and assumed truths are for the present immune to criticism (Hare 1985, 86). While we should encourage critical reflection concerning all our beliefs, the point in Neurath's metaphor of a ship being reconstructed while at sea is important (Haworth 1988, 4). A person's belief system, like a ship in mid-ocean, can be critically assessed and replaced part by part, but not all at once. This analogy further underscores the fact that criticism always takes place from within a certain tradition. I have already dealt with the tradition-bound nature of critical rationality in my treatment of normal autonomy and normal rationality where I noted Haworth's emphasis on "criticism internal to a tradition" (1986, 3-4). This means not that critical openness is entirely impossible but that normal critical openness is limited.[5] Critical openness is not so radical as is often assumed.

The above logical restriction on criticism simply makes the point that it is not possible to criticize everything at once. It is of course always possible to criticize presently unquestioned assumptions at some later time. Indeed, as Laura and Leahy have stressed, it is precisely these unquestioned assumptions or "epistemic primitives" that underlie any conceptual scheme that we need to become aware of so we can critically appraise them (1989, esp. 255-9, 263-4). It is here that the advocates of critical rationality often fail – they refuse to subject their own approach to critical evaluation. "The problem with critical doubt is that it is not doubtful enough. It does not subject itself to its own doubt" (Guinness 1976, 56; cf. Laura 1983, 54). Yet this doubt about critical rationality is needed because of the extremes to which this ideal is often taken. Hendrick Hart is surely justified in talking about the "impasse of rationality today ... its uncritical proclamation of the criticist framework, the critique of tradition and authority itself becomes an authoritative tradition" (1977, 4). In this section I have examined this tradition critically. It has been argued that the ideal of critical openness as it is usually understood is philosophically untenable and that it should be replaced by a more defensible ideal of normal critical openness.

My purpose above was not to analyze in detail the essential ingredients of this more defensible ideal of normal critical openness but to critique the traditional ideal of critical openness which is an essential element of the Enlightenment ideal of liberal education. I would suggest that much of the seeming force of the charge of indoctrination as it relates to this ideal and as it is applied to Christian nurture rests on what I have identified as untenable aspects of the ideal of critical openness. Before exploring this suggestion further, I want to examine briefly some questions relating to the justification of the ideal of critical openness.

JUSTIFICATION OF CRITICAL OPENNESS

How then should normal critical openness be described? To be a thinker who displays normal critical openness is to have a disposition to form and revise one's views in the light of evidence and argument. This is not incompatible with having convictions, even strong convictions, so long as there remains "the permanent possibility of reopening even settled issues" (Hare 1979, 30). Nor is this incompatible with having been brought up within a certain tradition, with having inherited certain beliefs and values – a condition which is in fact inescapable, given human nature. What is important is that there be an ongoing willingness to assess these traditions critically. Normal critical openness clearly involves a rejection of *blind* faith in tradition or authority, while at the same time remaining sensitive to the important function that tradition and authority play in each person's life. Critically open people are tolerant of others who hold viewpoints different from their own, listen to people who express differing viewpoints, and consider objections to their own viewpoints. At times they even look for such objections, though this characteristic is not essential for normal critical openness. Open-minded people display such intellectual virtues as honesty, humility, courage, impartiality, and objectivity. In short they are lovers of truth.

Brenda Watson, after a careful critique of "pseudo-openness" and extreme versions of critical-mindedness, suggests that we replace the term "critical openness" with "critical affirmation" (1987, chs. 4, 5). The word "affirmation" is warmer, according to Watson, and it does justice to the need to affirm one's past, one's own convictions, and one's desire to find insight. Critical affirmation still encourages "the rigorous use of critical faculties ... but not for the sake of destruction, as though skepticism were the be-all and end-all, but for the purpose of creating a larger grasp of understanding and commitment both for oneself and for others" (55). Watson's notion of critical affirmation captures the heart of what I have labelled normal critical openness. Omission of the word "openness" is unfortunate, though, and hence I prefer to retain the older terminology with the qualifier "normal" added to it. "Normal critical openness" affirms what is good in the traditional ideal and transforms what was indefensible.

Critical openness is generally held in high esteem, so much so that the question "Who could be against critical openness?" seems to be almost rhetorical (Hare 1979, 26). Yet some people reject this ideal, and I must therefore at least touch on the question of justification. Here I am only trying to justify *normal* critical openness. The traditional and extreme version of critical openness is, I believe, an arbitrary value, having come to us primarily through the Enlightenment and liberal revolts against tradition and the Church. Earlier sections of this chapter showed that the justification of this extreme version of critical openness would be indeed problematic. People who object to the value of critical openness are really only objecting to misconceptions of this ideal, a point that Hare stresses in his defence of open-mindedness (1979, 1985). But it is necessary to be careful not to think that we must therefore reject the ideal of critical openness in its entirety, an error at times made by those defending Christian nurture against charges of indoctrination. Critical openness when properly qualified is a legitimate educational ideal.

A complete justification of the ideal of normal critical openness is hardly possible here, nor is it necessary. It is not possible because such justification is a complex affair resting on an understanding of the nature of truth and what it means to be a human being or an educated person. Complete justification is also not necessary because I have already identified the basic presuppositions from which this study begins. I suggested in chapter 2 that I am generally sympathetic with such liberal ideals as autonomy and rationality, although these need to be qualified. Normal autonomy and rationality are at the heart of what it means to be human. Critical openness is intimately bound up with both these ideals, and thus can be justified by similar considerations.

Critical openness is essential because we are by nature fallible beings and therefore can never be absolutely certain that we have arrived at the truth. We are also by nature somewhat lazy intellectually and find it comfortable to be ruled by prejudice, authority, and prevailing traditions (Mitchell 1976, 101). All of this points to the need for openness and criticism. Here it would be good to reread John Stuart Mill's classic defence of freedom of thought and expression which is at the same time a defence of critical openness (*On Liberty*, [1859]1978). Of course the above characterizations of human nature are only part of the story. As I argued earlier, we are also by nature curious and open to the truth. But these qualities need to be encouraged in the light of the other tendencies of human nature described above.

Other justifications of the ideal of critical openness could be considered, but this must suffice.[6] More important here is whether the ideal of critical openness is compatible with the Christian faith. I wish to argue that it is not only compatible with but is in fact advocated by orthodox Christianity.

Closed-mindedness is repeatedly identified as a problem that needs to be overcome. The Old Testament prophets were constantly challenging established opinion, and in so doing were battling closed minds including attempts to silence the speaking of truth (see, for example, Isaiah 30:9-11; Jeremiah 25:4). This is described figuratively in terms of "eyes that will not see or ears that will not hear" (Isaiah 43:8; Jeremiah 5:21), and the hope is always expressed that someday "the eyes of the blind be opened and the ears of the deaf unstopped" (Isaiah 35:5). Jesus picks up these same prophetic themes and laments the closed-mindedness that comes from blind conformity to tradition (Matthew 13:14-5; Mark 7:1-13). Instead he taught that "the truth will set you free" (John 8:32). Paul similarly warns about the danger of suppressing the truth, about minds that have been blinded to the truth (Romans 1:18; 2 Corinthians 4:4). Open-mindedness is clearly a biblical ideal.

The Scriptures also include frequent exhortations to test and critically evaluate religious claims. Jesus tells us to be on the lookout for false prophets who will deceive many (Matthew 24:4-5, 10-11). John exhorts us to "test the spirits" (1 John 4:1). The author of Acts praises Paul's audience in Berea who, while they "received the message with great eagerness," nonetheless critically evaluated what was said, and "examined the Scriptures every day to see if what Paul said was true" (Acts 17:11). Even honest critical doubt is accepted as normal and is treated with respect in the Scriptures. Jesus does not condemn doubters like John the Baptist or "doubting Thomas" but provides them with the evidence that will overcome their doubts (Matthew 11:1-15; John 20:24-9; cf. Mark 9:14-27). We are even allowed to witness Jesus's own doubts, and it is for this reason that he is described as being able to sympathize with our own weaknesses (Matthew 26:36-46; 27:46; Hebrews 4:15).

John Hull, in a recent article entitled "Christian Nurture and Critical Openness," concludes: "Critical openness is a discipline which the Christian follows not in spite of his faith but because of it" (1984, 220; see also 190-5). Hull wrote his article in response to a recommendation in a British Council of Churches study of Christian nurture which recognizes that renewal in the church requires "a theology which sees critical openness as springing from Christian commitment" (1984, 145).

Some readers might feel that there is surely a fundamental incompatibility between genuine Christian commitment and the ideal of critical openness. Surely the notion of absolute Truth, which is at the heart of Christianity, and which Peshkin found to be foundational to Bethany Baptist Academy, is at odds with openness and critical thinking (Peshkin 1986, 55, 55, 259-60). Surely the authoritative nature of absolute Christian truth will of necessity discourage critical openness (59). Surely following Paul's example of taking "captive every thought to make it obedient to Christ" runs counter to the ideal I have been discussing (2 Corinthians 10:5; see also Peshkin 1986, 266). Surely there is no compromise possible between faith as "unshakable assent to dogma given by divine authority" and the rational-critical principle I have been dealing with (Callan 1988).

There are two fundamental problems with arguments such as the

above. They first rest on a distortion and often a caricature of orthodox Christianity. The Christian faith does not call for "unshakable"
assent. Doubt and uncertainty are a normal experience of all the he-
roes of faith, even of Jesus, the founder of the Christian faith, as has
already been pointed out. Fundamental to Christianity is a view of
human beings as finite, fallible creatures who, during their pilgrim-
age here on earth, can know the truth only in part (1 Corinthians
13:9, 12). Finality and completeness of truth must be understood es-
chatologically in orthodox Christianity (Hull 1984, 213-15). It is one
thing to claim that God has revealed the truth. It is quite another to
claim that one understands God's truth perfectly. Therefore, any
claims to know God's truth "unequivocally," "absolutely," or with
"no uncertainty" involve distortions of the Christian faith, a point
that Peshkin fails to acknowledge (1986, 259-60, 295). Some Christian traditions,[7] including some "fundamentalist" ones, may make
such claims. I would suggest that by doing so they are distorting orthodox Christian doctrine, and it is not at all my intent to defend
them.

Theology is not static: there is change and evolution in theology.
The Christian faith is constantly renewing itself, evaluating itself,
applying itself to new situations and contemporary problems. All
this requires openness and critical thinking (Hull 1984, 208). Furthermore, for many, including evangelical theologians, the Bible is a
book which demands historical, documentary, textual, and theological criticism (Hull 1984, 190).

Here it might be felt that I am still skirting the real issue. Surely
the very idea of a revelation from God as something given and therefore authoritative is somehow incompatible with true openness.
Surely the idea of revelation "enslaves because it constricts one's options" (Peshkin 1986, 261). Clearly, once a choice has been made to
accept God's revelation as authoritative, one has restricted one's options. But is this any different from a scientist who has opted for a
certain theory to explain some phenomena and who then commits
her- or himself to proving this theory for the remainder of her or his
life? The initial opting for a certain theory was of course not simply a
leap into the dark, but was made on the basis of a complex variety of
considerations, including "upbringing" and an open and critical
consideration of alternatives. Similarly, the Christian's initial acceptance of the authority of the Bible can be, and for many is, based on
rational grounds (Keller 1989). We must also always keep in mind
that commitment does not preclude critical openness, as I have already argued.

The second major error behind the claim that the Christian faith is incompatible with the ideal of critical openness is that it rests on a distorted view of the ideal of critical openness. I have already dealt with the basic misconceptions of the ideal in the previous section, so I need only show how these misconceptions lead to this error. One of the basic problems with the ideal of critical openness as it is usually understood is that it is viewed too idealistically. When this unrestricted notion of critical openness is then applied to Christian commitment, the two seem to be incompatible. But this unrealistic notion of critical openness is itself problematic, and once we realize the limitations inherent in our ability to be open and critical, the problems with Christian commitment disappear.

CHRISTIAN NURTURE AND NORMAL CRITICAL OPENNESS

To return to the central question of this chapter: Is Christian nurture necessarily indoctrinatory because it cannot satisfy the conditions inherent in the ideal of critical openness? It all depends on what is meant by the ideal of critical openness. Christianity and Christian nurture are clearly incompatible with the traditional liberal ideal of critical openness. But this traditional strong ideal of critical openness is itself philosophically problematic. Hence charges of indoctrination based on that ideal are unwarranted.

If instead we begin with the ideal of normal critical openness, then, as we found, Christianity is not only compatible with this ideal, but it is its advocate. It follows that Christian nurture can and should foster normal critical openness. Claims to the effect that indoctrination is inevitable in Christian nurture because such nurture fails to promote critical openness and results in unshakable beliefs are therefore unjustified (cf. Snook 1972b, 75). Even lesser claims of the high probability of indoctrination when engaging in Christian nurture are suspect in that they often rest on a problematic ideal of critical openness (Callan 1985, 117, 115). Contrary to Barrow and Woods (1988, 70), doubts can be raised as to whether Catholic schools with Catholic teachers who teach for commitment represent a paradigm of indoctrination. The argument of this chapter suggests that much more caution is in order when making the charge of indoctrination against Christian nurture.

Those who claim that Christian nurture is incompatible with fostering critical openness make another basic error: they assume that the conditions for the *exercise* of critical openness are the same as the conditions for the *development* of critical openness (the same error that occurs with regard to the ideal of autonomy which was considered in the previous chapter). This is no surprise, because critical openness is very intimately bound up with the ideal of autonomy. Just as with autonomy, it is necessary to entertain the possibility that critical openness might best be fostered in an environment that appears to be neither open nor critical. Dearden is cautious about expecting a definitive answer from empirical research on how best to foster autonomy (1972, 61-2). Hare similarly admits that the research findings on how to foster open-mindedness are often unclear and ambiguous because of the complexities of such empirical enquiries (Hare 1979, 103, 121). Based on evidence reviewed toward the end of the previous chapter, I believe the conclusions as to how best to nurture autonomy and critical openness are fairly certain. Here I only need briefly outline the relevant considerations and apply them specifically to the problem of nurturing critical openness.

I would like to repeat that the answer to the question of how to encourage development towards normal critical openness is in part conceptual. It is logically impossible to nurture critical openness alone. One can only be critically open about certain content that one has acquired in some way. The development of critical openness presupposes that children have first of all been initiated into certain traditions.

R.S. Peters draws on various findings in developmental psychology to show that a secure and non-permissive environment is essential to nurturing autonomy. Other writers stress the need for a stable and coherent "primary culture" in which children can develop toward autonomy (Ackerman 1980, ch. 2; cf. McLaughlin 1984).[8] Ackerman maintains that the need for cultural stability and coherence gradually declines as the child develops "dialogic competence" and the ability to face challenges to his or her primary culture without becoming disorientated. In fact, as children naturally develop the ability to question, parents have a responsibility to take this seriously and to provide them with "a liberal education – with cultural equipment that permits the child to criticise, as well as affirm, parental ideals" (Ackerman 1980, 117).

The above argument is even stronger than it might seem when we take into account the fact that all children do in fact grow up within a primary culture with at least some degree of stability and coherence. All children grow up in a particular environment, with some particular adults on whom they are completely dependant. Every child inherits a language and a host of attitudes, values, and beliefs. Rokeach talks of a constellation of "pre-ideological" primitive beliefs which all people acquire early in life, the validity of which they do not question and, in the ordinary course of events, are not prepared to question (1960, 40, 75). The development of critical openness must begin with this primary culture as a foundation. It cannot start from scratch.

The child will necessarily inherit a primary culture which entails a very specific orientation towards religion. Those parents who, under the guise of liberality, do not want to influence their children either way so that they will be able to make up their own minds later on, are really still relaying some very specific primitive beliefs about religion. Barrow is surely right in pointing to the curious phenomenon that it is always the religious parents or teachers who are placed in the dock about influencing towards belief. "There seems no good reason why those who advocate a non-religious environment should not equally be accused of cooking the books" (Barrow 1974, 57). The child is going to be influenced one way or the other, whether one likes it or not. Therefore this influence cannot in itself be deemed to be the deciding factor as to whether there will be development towards critical openness. It follows that Christian nurture in and of itself cannot be seen as hindering the development toward critical openness. Every child is nurtured into a primary culture of some sort, and such nurture is by its very nature uncritical and not open. Again it is important to remember that the closed and uncritical nature of such a primary culture is not a bad thing. It forms the necessary backdrop against which critical open-mindedness can and must grow.

Peter Gardner, in a recent article which highlights the apparent tension between a strong religious upbringing and the liberal ideal of autonomous reflection and assessment (i.e., critical openness), argues that a similar tension is not found in cases in which parents subject their children to an atheistic or agnostic upbringing. The reason is "that an atheistic or agnostic position is not, in our sense, as important as a religious one," the criterion of importance of beliefs being "their influence and pervasiveness." Important beliefs "tend to stick," and thus we find "that religious beliefs might prove more persistent than many other beliefs" (1988, 97).

There are a host of problems with this argument. For one, atheistic and agnostic positions are surely as important as religious ones – one only has to think of the implications of Marxist atheism. And, if Gardner wants to define the importance of beliefs as relative to the person who holds them, he needs to be reminded of the many crusading atheists and the many agnostic philosophers who use the classroom to persuade students of the evils of religious beliefs and the merits of agnosticism. The central problem with Gardner's position is that he fails to face up to the fact that *all* early beliefs tend to stick, and therefore the same supposed tension exists between the liberal ideal and atheistic and agnostic upbringing. In fact Gardner is forced to acknowledge this although he still wants to say that "stronger tensions are more likely to exist when the upbringing is of strong religious kind" (1988, 97). I would argue that the tensions are just as strong in a *strong* atheistic or agnostic upbringing (note Gardner's loaded term) as they are in a religious one.

Gardner also confesses at the end of his paper that there is a question that needs to be addressed: "If the psychology of belief is as we have described it, how attainable is the liberal goal?" (1988, 102). This is indeed a key question! And once this question is faced, the supposed tension between a religious upbringing (or an atheistic or agnostic upbringing) and the liberal ideal of autonomy and critical openness disappears. Every child is initiated into a very particular belief system which, given the psychology of belief, does persist and is to some extent "unshakable." This is simply inescapable given human nature. Therefore this in itself must not be seen to be in tension with the liberal ideal of critical openness. The problem is, what do we *do* with this belief system which every child inherits? The development of critical openness must begin with this heritage and arise out of it. It is unfair to single out religious nurture as being a problem when in fact this "problem" is shared by all, and when there really is no problem at all. To label religious parents "hypocritical or disingenuous" when they claim to be aiming for critical openness while at the same time giving their children a religious upbringing is not only to commit an *ad hominem* fallacy, but is to assume that there is a tension when in fact there is none (Gardner 1988, 102).

I have been focusing so far on the initial stages of Christian nurture. Perhaps we need to look at the final stages of Christian nurture to locate the real locus of the problem. Is there a tension inherent in the goals of Christian nurture? Christian parents and teachers obviously want their children or students to adhere to and grow in the Christian faith. Does this conflict with the aim of critical openness? These questions introduce considerations dealt with in the previous chapter, where I examined the problem of the intentions behind Christian nurture, particularly in relation to the ideal of autonomy (pp. 136-40). Since critical openness is an integral part of the ideal of autonomy, similar considerations apply to the questions raised here; therefore they will be dealt with only very briefly.

The basic problem is again one of assuming that there is a tension when in fact there isn't one. We have seen that commitment is compatible with critical openness. It follows that the goal of commitment to the Christian faith is compatible with the goal of critical openness.

Christian parents and teachers can hope that their children and students will both make a commitment or grow in their commitment to Christ and acquire a disposition to assess critically that commitment or be open to considering other alternatives. In fact, as has been argued, all commitment is to some degree critical and open, given the desire to know truth that seems to be inherent in human nature. It was further demonstrated that all teaching, whether in the home or in the school, is "evangelistic" in nature. Convictions about truth are by their very nature such that we want to persuade others of our convictions. To deny this is to be dishonest. But we can and should persuade others only in such a way that recognizes the need to be open and critical about these same convictions, because, after all, we only "see through a glass darkly," we only "know in part." Our concern for truth should therefore always combine teaching for commitment with teaching for critical openness.

Having examined both the starting point and the goal of Christian nurture, it is time to focus on the person who is teaching, whether that be a parent or a teacher in a school. It is sometimes maintained that Christian nurture is incompatible with the ideal of critical openness because of the convictions of the teacher. Barrow and Woods, for example, in their description of a paradigm case of indoctrination, call attention to the fact that all the teachers are committed Catholics (1988, 70). But as we have seen, committed Catholic teachers can still be open-minded and critical about their beliefs. Further, there is not even anything inconsistent about teachers' defending their convictions in the classroom in an open and critical manner (Hare 1979, 70, 88, 131). In fact modelling critical openness about the teachers' own convictions is probably a key to helping students acquire this intellectual virtue.

Hare is particularly concerned about the frequent association of neutrality with open-minded teaching, especially when dealing with controversial issues (1979, ch. 4). While neutrality might be appropriate in certain contexts, it is not a necessary condition for critical and open teaching: "The open-minded support of a particular view by the teacher is perfectly consistent with having the pupils treat all views according to consistent critical principles" (1979, 70). What is important here is that the teacher "among other things, entertains criticisms of his opinions which the students may have, looks at sources which conflict with the view he is defending, if there are any such, indicates where he thinks flaws may be found in his argument," though even here it is necessary not be too rigid in our requirements (Hare 1979, 76). All of this presupposes commitment on the part of the teacher, not an assumed neutrality.

There is of course the additional question as to whether neutrality is in fact possible in teaching. Much has been written about this, and it is neither possible nor necessary to get into this debate here (e.g., Hulmes 1979; Watson 1987, chs. 4 & 5). I believe that it is safe to say that it is difficult for a teacher to be entirely neutral in the classroom. This raises the question of whether it is not safer to admit frankly to one's convictions and then try to ensure that one demonstrates open-mindedness and critical thinking about these convictions. Commitment, as Edward Hulmes has argued, can be the teacher's "primary resource" (1979, 32). Be that as it may, I need here only maintain that critical openness in teaching does not require neutrality and that the commitment of the Christian parent or teacher is not necessarily incompatible with critical and open-minded teaching.

Hare goes on to stipulate a requirement of open-minded teaching in areas of controversy. In this case, "open-minded teaching demands that views which conflict with those of the teacher *not* be excluded." It is not enough for the teacher to have considered contrary views in an open-minded way. In the classroom he or she must, in addition to drawing students' attention to these contrary views, also *"explain* why he rejects them" (Hare 1979, 76). I have no problem with these requirements as long as it is acknowledged that this may not be possible with younger children and that there are some practical limits on how many contrary views are brought forward in the classroom. Here it should be noted that, while we cannot normally require open-minded people to actively go out and search for objections to their position, as was argued earlier, the requirements of open-mindedness in educational institutions may be somewhat more demanding (Hare 1985, 90). But here again it is important not to become unrealistic in the demands we make of educational institutions.

The concern of this chapter has been to defend Christian nurture against the charge that it involves indoctrination which results in uncritical closed-mindedness. The main thrust has been to show that this charge often rests on an unrealistic ideal of critical openness which is part of the Enlightenment concept of liberal education, and in so far as this is the case, the charge is unwarranted. What is needed is a more defensible ideal of normal critical openness. Christian nurture can of course still fail to measure up to this more realistic ideal, in which case we might want to make the charge of indoctrination. But I would suggest that the charge is not as strong as is generally assumed. Ursula King provides us with a fitting concluding statement for this chapter when she reminds us of the example of Ghandhi, "who spoke of opening the windows of his own house to the winds from the outside world without being swept off his feet. Every individual needs to be deeply rooted in his or her own tradition but also has to learn to grow upwards and outwards like the many branches of a large tree" (King 1985, 97).

7 Institutional Indoctrination and the Democratic Ideal of Liberal Institutions

So far I have examined four criteria often associated with indoctrination: content, methods, intention, and consequences. In the next chapter, I will come to a final assessment of these criteria as ways of defining "indoctrination." There is, however, another dimension of indoctrination which is by and large ignored in the literature. I want to suggest that, implicit in past treatments of indoctrination, there is really what might be considered a fifth criterion of "indoctrination" that deserves separate consideration.

I want to refer to this fifth criterion as the "institutional criterion." By labelling it the "institutional criterion," I call attention to the fact that the charge of indoctrination is most often made against institutions – what sociologists call social institutions: the family and educational, religious, and political institutions. Yet philosophers who attempt to define the concept of indoctrination have paid little attention to the typical institutional context of the charge of indoctrination, and this lopsided emphasis has, I believe, sidetracked attention from some issues that need to be addressed.

Analyses of "indoctrination" have been primarily concerned with a discussion of individuals shaping the beliefs of other individuals. This focus on the individual is of course to be expected given the Enlightenment ideal of liberal education from which concern about indoctrination arises. What is curious is that the institutional dimension of indoctrination comes to the fore more prominently when the charge of religious indoctrination is made. The institutions of the church and the home are seen as particularly vulnerable to the

charge of indoctrination. For example, in the paradigm case of indoctrination to which I have been referring throughout, Barrow and
Woods begin their description by highlighting two institutions:
"Imagine a Catholic *school* in which all the *teachers* are committed
Catholics and where all the children come from Catholic *homes* and
have *parents* who want them to be brought up as Catholics" (Barrow
& Woods 1988, 70; emphasis added). Barrow and Woods also make
reference to the use of *authority* by teachers as a way of reinforcing
the truth of the Catholic world view (70). Authority here obviously
has to do with the social structure of the school as an institution.

In fact it is in discussions of the notion of authority that the institutional dimension of indoctrination comes to the fore most clearly
in past treatments of the concept of indoctrination. For example, in
my discussion of the methods criterion, I noted that the misuse of
authority is frequently associated with indoctrination (p. 90). It was
the authoritarianism of political institutions, particularly as exemplified in the Nazi regime of Germany, that reinforced the pejorative
connotations that were increasingly being ascribed to the concept of
indoctrination (Gatchel 1972; Moore 1972). Davey (1972) and Benson
(1977) come closest to making the abuse of authority the fundamental characteristic of indoctrination, although Davey is more concerned about the detection of indoctrination than he is about defining the concept. Peters is similarly concerned about authoritarianism
in teaching and, interestingly, singles out Catholic educators as failing to condemn authoritarian methods of instruction (1973a, ch. 4;
1977, 48). Here again political and religious institutions are thought
to be most susceptible to abusing authority and hence to indoctrinating.

Another hint at institutional indoctrination is found in my analysis of the content criterion of "indoctrination." "No doctrines; no indoctrination," Flew announces, and thus "the outstanding paradigm case of indoctrination" involves the efforts of the Roman
Catholic Church to fix in the minds of their children, an unshakable
conviction in the truth of the churches' doctrines (1972b, 114; 1972a,
75-6). In chapter 3, I identified as one feature of "doctrines" that
they are beliefs backed by a group or an institution (p. 67). Thus Gregory and Woods make frequent reference to the Roman Catholic
Church and the Communist Party as the context out of which doctrines arise (1972, 166, 168, 187-8). It is because doctrines are backed
by the authority of an institution that they are susceptible to indoctrination.

As a final way to highlight the institutional dimension of the
charge of indoctrination when applied to Christian nurture, I refer to

Peshkin's recent careful sociological analysis and critique of Bethany Baptist Academy (BBA), as found in his book *God's Choice: The Total World of a Fundamentalist Christian School* (1986). Peshkin draws on the sociological concept of a "total institution" to highlight his basic criticisms of BBA. What worries him is the school's closed environment, its attempt to control all aspects of students' thought and behaviour, its rigid objectives, and its tight authority structure. In short, "BBA logically indoctrinates its students" because it is a total institution (Peshkin 1986, 284, ch. 10).

Peshkin's use of the notion of a total institution in order to make the charge of indoctrination against a Christian school provides a good basis for discussion of the institutional dimensions of indoctrination. Obviously there are differences between a "total institution" and an "institution," and I will have more to say about the relation between these two concepts later. However, I believe a careful review of the features which Peshkin finds objectionable in BBA as a total institution will help to isolate elements that belong to the institutional dimension of the charge of indoctrination generally.

PESHKIN, BETHANY BAPTIST ACADEMY, AND TOTAL INSTITUTIONS

The concept of total institutions is inseparably linked with Erving Goffman's study of asylums (1961). Goffman defines a total institution as a place "of residence and work where a large number of like-situated individuals, cut off from the wider society for an appreciable period of time, together lead an enclosed, formally administered round of life" (Peshkin 1986, 261). Goffman admits that all institutions have "encompassing tendencies," but some carry this to a considerable extent, erecting physical barriers to provide an effective "barrier to social intercourse with the outside" (Peshkin 1986, 275). He identifies five different groupings of such total institutions: homes for the blind, the aged, the orphaned; mental institutions; jails; convents and cloisters; and finally those established for the purpose of pursuing some task, such as army barracks, ships, and boarding schools (Peshkin 1986, 257). Peshkin includes Christian schools such as BBA in the latter category.

Total institutions are "anathema" to Peshkin (1986, 276). He quotes another writer to illustrate the use of the term as a pejorative: A total institution is "a symbolic presentation of organizational tyranny ... a closed universe symbolizing the thwarting of human possibilities" (1986, 261, 275).

What is it about total institutions that makes Peshkin colour them so negatively? Drawing on the work of McEwen (1980), he identifies six "dimensions of organizational variation" and he uses these to highlight his basic criticisms of BBA.

Shared Organizational Goals. A total institution is characterized by shared organizational goals exemplified in "the degree of staff coordination or consensus about work goals and practices" (Peshkin 1986, 261). Peshkin found BBA administration and teachers in remarkable accord with each other in "insuring the successful inculcation of their Truth," even to the point of sanctioning censorship (262). BBA's purposes are uniquely Christian, based on scriptural Truth (259, 78-80). Peshkin concludes that " 'work goals and practices' at BBA enjoy as much coordination and consensus as is humanly possible to achieve" (263).

Involuntariness. Total institutions are characterized by involuntary, if not coerced, participation, although there are differences in the degree of willingness to participate (Peshkin 1986, 264). At BBA, parents are not legally bound to enroll their children, "but they may feel theologically bound to do so" (264). Some of the students are coerced into attending. Closely related to the variable of voluntariness is the ability of an institution to select and expel its members (264). BBA clearly selects its students and reserves the right to expel students who do not comply with its objectives (264, 285).

Extent of totality. Under this category, Peshkin considers three closely related features that really deserve separate treatment. (a) Encompassing tendencies: Although all institutions are encompassing to some degree, total institutions are encompassing to a considerable extent (1986, 257). He describes BBA as establishing "the broadest possible control of its students. Indeed, the Christian school's hoped-for degree of totality surpasses that of all coercive total institutions ... Its aspiration to totality extends to most all behaviour and thought, everywhere, at all times, throughout the entire life of everyone affiliated in any capacity with their total institution. That, indeed, is totality!" (265). (b) Coercion: Total institutions not only achieve breadth of control but there is also an intensity to the control they exercise, even to the point of using coercive measures. BBA, like other Christian schools, has a "seemingly unlimited right to control students" (285). (c) Separation: In trying to achieve the broadest possible control over their participants, total institutions often erect physical barriers to preclude social intercourse with the outside world (257). Total institutions, it will be remembered, are places where a large number of like-situated individuals are cut off from the wider society for an appreciable period of time (26l). Although BBA is not a residential school and does not have physical barriers like walls to cut off its participants from contacts with the wider society, other kinds of barriers make it appropriate to classify it as a total institution. There are, for example, mental barriers which close students' minds to outside influences and alternative perspectives (266, 190). The principle of separation is fundamental to the theology that governs BBA. Students are, among other things, encouraged to attend Christian colleges when they graduate, not to have too close ties with non-Christians, not to date non-Christians, and of course never to marry non-Christians (270). "Indeed, one's capacity to exemplify total separation in one's personal life is a measure of personal and institutional success" (271).

Mortification practices. In order to achieve separation and control, total institutions attempt to reshape the inmates' sense of self, to break their spirit, by various mortification practices such as role-stripping, regimentation, and tyrannization of everyday life (Peshkin 1986, 271-2). Peshkin admits that Goffman's graphic description of these practices are too extreme to fit Christian schools, but there is a "counterpart" to them (271). BBA is "dedicated to the rebirth of its unredeemed youth," and the process of bringing about such a rebirth is surely one of reshaping the self and hence will involve the use of a kind of mortification (272). For children who come from Christian homes, the school's practices will not appear to be mortifying, but any outsiders, or any students who do not share BBA's values may indeed "feel humiliated by the academy's disrespect for their present religious status, by its rejection of their normal behaviour as 'worldly,' and by its demands that they change their appearance, their friends, their behaviour, and their response to authority" (272).

Subordinate-superordinate relationships. Another distinguishing feature of total institutions is the social distance between an organization's caretakers and those it cares for (Peshkin 1986, 272). Peshkin admits that BBA, like all schools, is characterized by a social distance between teachers and pupils by virtue of their age difference. However, a more profound subordinate-superordinate relationship exists at BBA involving the deference of all to the authority of Scripture; as long as the person in authority is not violating scriptural doctrine, the proper student response to authority at BBA is submission, "total and unqualified" (59).

Permeability to extra-organizational influences. Finally, total institutions are characterized by a certain degree of control by external forces that affect their operation (Peshkin 1986, 273). Prisons, for example, are creatures of the state; they use state funds and their workers are state employees. They are also subject to some extent to public opinion. Peshkin has some difficulty applying this feature to Christian schools because they are generally unresponsive to public opinion and struggle to stay free of governmental ties and regulations (274).

These are the basic characteristics of total institutions according to Peshkin, among others. These are the features that give total institutions their inherently "sinister" character (1986, 274). It is these features that lead Peshkin repeatedly to describe a Christian school such as BBA as an organizational tyranny, a closed universe, a rigid institution which enslaves and indoctrinates (32, 261, 275, 284). He concludes, "Benign though their total institution may be to Bethanyites, and awe-some their absolute Truth, total institutions and absolute Truth are nonetheless anathema to me" (276).

CRITIQUE OF PESHKIN'S ANALYSIS OF "TOTAL INSTITUTIONS"

It is to Peshkin's credit that he draws attention specifically to the institutional dimension of indoctrination. In evaluating his critique of BBA as a total institution, it is not my intent to come to a final conclusion as to whether or not indoctrination occurs at BBA. I want only to argue that the charge of institutional indoctrination is not so strong as Peshkin thinks it is. Nor do I want to suggest that the notion of a total institution is entirely inappropriate in helping us to understand the institutional dimension of indoctrination. I believe it is the key to capturing the meaning of institutional indoctrination, but, as will be argued later, much more work needs to be done in distinguishing between "normal institutions" and "total institutions" before we can make the charge of institutional indoctrination.

One weakness in Peshkin's analysis is that he tends to talk about total institutions as though they are all of one kind. McEwen, in his important review of two decades of research on total institutions, identifies this as perhaps the most important weakness of the total institution concept and the research connected with it (1980, 149). Although Peshkin does acknowledge, from time to time, that there are different kinds of total institutions, the overall thrust of his analysis is to generalize. He states that total institutions are anathema to him (Peshkin 1986, 276). In this he commits another frequent error in treatments of the concept of total institutions, that of trading on the pejorative overtones implicit in the very notion of a total institution (McEwen 1980, 147). I will have more to say about the pejorative meaning attached to this concept later.

For now it is important to note that, in order to use the notion of a total institution to critique BBA as severely as he does, Peshkin really has to say that all total institutions are bad. Given that he does sometimes qualify this claim, perhaps it is better to say that he is being selective in the kinds of total institutions he has in mind when he criticizes BBA. Clearly he is using the term as "an epithet, loosely employed to call attention to organizations that appear to isolate, degrade, and oppress their members" (McEwen 1980, 147). Clearly it is prisons, concentration camps, and army barracks that for Peshkin are the paradigms of total institutions (Peshkin 1986, 261, 257). Only these institutions include the strongly negative features that he finds so offensive. And he wants to prove that BBA can be properly classified as belonging to this particular kind of total institution so that it can be similarly condemned.

Another central problem of Peshkin's attempt to use the notion of a total institution to critique BBA comes to the fore in the number of qualifications that he himself makes. Here again he illustrates a general problem inherent in the previous studies of total institutions, the lack of precision in the concept itself (McEwen 1980, 145). Total institutions are characterized by involuntary, if not coerced participation. Peshkin, however, is forced to concede that only ten of the 114 students at BBA could be said to have been coerced to attend, and then it was not the state that made them attend (as is typical of many total institutions) but parents (1986, 264-5). BBA is really a voluntary institution, founded by private persons who decided to open a certain type of school (265). Nor does one of the central ideas behind the state's coercive total institutions – resocializing society's rejects – apply to BBA (265).

Another central feature of total institutions involves the physical separation of its participants from the rest of society. Peshkin concedes that BBA does not physically limit its participants' movements (1986, 265). It does not have a residence as do all other total institutions (261). Clearly there is an attempt to inculcate theological and moral separation at BBA, but that is very different from the separation typical of total institutions.

Peshkin is also forced to concede that Goffman's graphic description of the mortification practices typical of his paradigms of total institutions is "too extreme to fit Christian schools" (1986, 271). "I found little evidence to indicate that Bethany parents and students perceive their school's practices as mortifying" (271-2). Mouzelis identifies several other total institutions where alleged mortification practices do not have the sinister character which Peshkin ascribes to them (1971).

Total institutions, as we have seen, are also characterized by a sharply defined hierarchy. There is of course some social distance between students and teachers at BBA by virtue of differences in age, but this is typical of all schools (Peshkin 1986, 273). Indeed Peshkin is forced to admit that, because both "subordinate and superordinate alike, draw their prescriptions and proscriptions from the same ultimate authority," there is no "caste-like split" characterizing the student-teacher relationship, hence, again, BBA is very different from the typical total institution, where social distance and authoritarianism rule (273).

Peshkin identifies the final characteristic of total institutions as responsiveness to extra-organizational influences such as the state, which he admits is nearly completely inapplicable to BBA (1986, 274). This admission, along with his many other qualifications, raises the question of whether it is at all appropriate to classify BBA as a total institution. There would seem to be more differences than similarities, especially if we compare BBA with Peshkin's paradigms of total institutions – prisons, concentration camps, and army barracks. It is also important to keep in mind that the many qualifications Peshkin is forced to make weaken his critique. If BBA does not share many of the features of prisons, concentration camps, and army barracks, then he has no basis for criticizing the school as a total institution which indoctrinates.

Peshkin overlooks a further important disanalogy. The participants of total institutions typically are adults, whereas with BBA, and indeed with all public schools, we are dealing with children. Institutional participation of adults is usually expected to be voluntary. We expect only a minimal degree of control over adults, and are very careful not to cross the threshold of exerting too much authority over them.

But with children, these features become problematic. Children cannot choose to belong to the institution of the family. They are not given the opportunity to choose not to attend school. Except for a few radical educators such as A.S. Neill (1960), it is generally assumed that adults can and should exert authority over children. There is of course some debate about these differences in the way we treat children and adults, especially in the literature concerning children's rights (see, for example, Wringe 1981; O'Neill & Ruddick 1979), but even the most liberal defenders of such rights should concede that children can and must be treated somewhat differently from adults. This idea was covered in the discussion of autonomy in a previous chapter. Haworth, for example, argues that, because children possess an underdeveloped capacity for living autonomously, they are necessarily subject to a degree of coercion for their own good (1986, 127; cf. White 1973, 22). These differences between children and adults are critical when total institutions are being discussed. What Peshkin finds offensive concerning adults may not at all be offensive when applied to children. Lack of choice, as well as control, and even coercion, as Haworth argues, are necessary and quite acceptable with children. Therefore it is really inappropriate to impose the notion of a total institution, which normally applies to adults, onto children.

This inappropriateness of applying the total institution concept to children can be illustrated in one other way. I have noted in earlier chapters that children need a stable and coherent primary culture in order to develop into mature autonomous individuals. But a home with a stable and coherent primary culture is by its very nature all-encompassing, separate, and controlled. A normal good home is surely a paradigm of a total atmosphere for an infant. Does Peshkin really want to criticize the home as a total institution? To be consistent he should, and yet most people, including the most liberal minded, would have difficulty in attributing to a good home all the negative characteristics Peshkin gives to total institutions.

In fact, even when applied to adults, there is some question as to whether the features Peshkin finds so offensive about total institutions are really always offensive. There is, first of all, the problem of the unique status of the adult participants at some of the total institutions he deals with. For example, people in jails and prisons are denied various rights because of some crimes they have allegedly committed. Thus it can be argued that the lack of voluntariness and the unusual level of control found in these institutions is not necessarily bad. Of course this is a debatable point, but it is raised to show that Peshkin's ascription of pejorative features to total institutions is less obvious than he thinks it is.

Then there are the other kinds of total institutions. Homes for the blind and the aged, for example, are also characterized by a high degree of control over their participants. But again, such control, when responsibly exercised, is surely necessary and good, given the special needs of the participants. Thus there is a problem with understanding the concept of total institutions as necessarily pejorative, as has also been argued by Mouzelis (1971). In fact it would seem that scholars are increasingly viewing traditional total institutions in a more positive light (McEwen 1980, 167). Peshkin's critique of BBA rests on the pejorative overtones he builds into the concept. But if the pejorative conceptualization of total institutions is itself problematic, then his criticisms of BBA as an organizational tyranny, as a school which thwarts human possibilities, is indeed "debatable" – as he himself admits on one occasion (1986, 261).

Further problems with Peshkin's analysis of BBA as a total institution emerge as we examine more closely the specific characteristics he finds so objectionable in total institutions. McEwen, in his review of the study of total institutions over a period of two decades, suggests that there is a tendency to overstate the effects of total institutions and that this "derives in part from the exaggerated portrayal of totalitarian control implied somewhat ambiguously by the concept itself" (1980, 149). Peshkin falls prey to such exaggeration when he talks about the "seemingly unlimited right to control students" in Christian schools (1986, 285). Surely no Christian school can be described in this way either in theory or in practice, and Peshkin himself is forced to concede that BBA "neither desires nor has automatons for students" (220, cf. 297). In fact he includes a section describing the "intellectual independence of students" (249-50; cf. 216, 253).

Peshkin also describes the level of shared organizational goals in extreme terms. BBA, he says, enjoys "as much coordination and consensus as is humanly possible to achieve" (1986, 263). This is nonsense! There are many examples of greater degrees of coordination and consensus in institutions, such as factories, political parties, unions, and sometimes even colleges run by dictatorial college administrators.

Peshkin goes to great lengths to describe the primary goal of BBA in terms of "schooling for spirituality" (ch. 6). Quoting several writers, he argues that the purposes that shape Christian schools such as BBA have to do with spirituality, *not* with "the development of informed thinking citizens, concern for a pluralistic society, or learning-how-to-learn" (259). But this is again an absurd over-statement. Surely BBA can promote spirituality in addition to the other common purposes of public schools as indeed Peshkin concedes elsewhere in the book.

Peshkin is particularly hard on BBA's commitment to separation and in this context expresses "distress at the impact of their arrogance on them, on me, on all of us" (1986, 287; cf. 270-1). But is separation necessarily a bad thing? Some total institutions such as homes for the blind, the aged, and the mentally handicapped exist as separate institutions so they can better meet the needs of their participants. Here separation is surely a good thing. Might the separation of BBA not similarly be good?

One important dimension of BBA's separation is moral in nature.

"Be ye separate, saith the Lord," is a biblical principle which Peshkin correctly identifies as central to the operation of BBA (1986, 270). He also admits that the students at BBA "get the moral education that many American parents say they want for their children. BBA parents can revel in a school that is explicitly, exultantly moral" (281). What is wrong with this kind of separation? Is it wrong for parents to want to separate their children from those whom they perceive as corrupting them? Is it wrong for parents to ask their teen-agers to stay away from peers whose lives are pre-occupied with drugs, alcohol, sex, vandalism, and whose attitudes are shot through with dishonesty, laziness, hatred, and disrespect for all authority? Surely any morally sensitive parents with sincere concerns about the moral development of their children want to separate them from such corrupting influences. Surely the most liberal educator recognizes the concerns of these parents as legitimate. Unfortunately our public schools, in the opinion of many, are failing in the area of moral education. Peshkin himself admits that our public schools might want to emulate BBA's programs in order to promote improved student moral standards and behaviour (279). Further, given the open door policy of public schools, all types of children, including many with very distorted values and behaviour, attend. Thus parents with a concern for a proper moral education for their children, both by way of teaching and in terms of positive moral influences, see the need to send their children to *separate* institutions where these objectives can be met. Surely there is nothing wrong with such institutional separateness.

Another kind of separateness about BBA worries Peshkin – doctrinal separateness. But even here, is there anything inherently wrong with separate institutions being formed to promote their views of truth? Liberals seem to have no problems with various other institutions established for this very purpose – political institutions with very distinctive views about political truth: economic institutions, think tanks committed to a very narrow view of economic truth, and so forth. To call these institutions "arrogant" seems terribly unfair because any group committed to a certain view of truth thinks it is right. This belongs to the very nature of making truth claims. To maintain that such institutional separateness promotes divisiveness and intolerance, as Peshkin maintains (1986, 286-99), begs for evidence, and further rests on a false notion of intolerance, as I have argued elsewhere (Thiessen 1985c, 1987a). Indeed we can and must distinguish between judging a belief as unacceptable and condemning the holder of that belief as unacceptable, as Peshkin notes at one point (1986, 289). But what is more to the point, such institutional separateness should not automatically be associated with institutional indoctrination. In fact Peshkin's own liberal starting point forces him, in the final pages, to admit that institutional pluralism is a sign of ideological health (296-9). In other words, we need to protect separate institutions in order to satisfy liberal ideals. I will say more on this in the final chapter.

Closely related to doctrinal separateness is the all-encompassing nature of BBA's view of absolute truth. The school is clearly committed to shaping students' minds to one pattern of truth, and thus seems to be opposed to diversity and openness which characterize non-total institutions (Peshkin 1986, 266). But Peshkin fails to do justice to the fact that all of us view truth as absolute and monolithic in some sense, although he does hint at this at one point (260). All of us make truth claims and are thereby committed to eliminating the pluralism of other truth claims. The task of scientific research, for example, can be interpreted as trying to achieve consensus with regard to the truth. Science does not want a "multitude of competing doctrines to thrive" because its truth too is singular (293).

Peshkin would like to see students presented with alternative perspectives in order to avoid the totality of absolute truth (1986, 266). But here again we are in danger of under-estimating the extent to which all teachers in all schools aim to help students arrive at truth in the singular. Yes, various perspectives should be presented, and more of this could have been done at BBA, though some of this was indeed found (156), and I suggest more of this would have been found if students had been questioned specifically on this point. But even when a teacher presents a variety of perspectives in a public school, the aim of considering all these perspectives is to shape students' minds so they will arrive at truth, unless of course the teacher is a relativist. Although Peshkin wants to avoid relativism (260), it would seem that, in his opposition to BBA's concept of absolute truth, he is in constant danger of flirting with relativism – a "Jeffersonian marketplace of contending ideas," a democratic determination of truth (190, cf. 59). But truth is ultimately one, and absolute, and total! To affirm this is in no way to deny the need for open-mindedness, as was argued in the previous chapter. Here again Peshkin fails to see that commitment to absolute truth is quite compatible with open-mindedness and critical thinking.

In summing up, despite its weaknesses, Peshkin's analysis of total institutions makes a significant contribution to the discussion of indoctrination. Not only has he called attention to the institutional dimension of indoctrination, but he has also identified some of the key aspects of institutions that might cause concern. The overall thrust of my criticisms so far is to show that what Peshkin has failed to do is to define precisely at what point each of the six aspects of an institution is to be considered extreme enough to become a defining characteristic of a total institution in the pejorative sense. When does the co-ordination and consensus of work goals and practices of an institution become extreme? How much voluntariness is required in order to escape the charge of being a total institution? Can separation be carried to the extreme? When does control within an institution become too much? When does the exercise of authority become authoritarianism? That this is a problem in Peshkin's analysis is not surprising. "Lack of precision and of consistency in identifying their essential characteristics have plagued the study of total institutions," writes McEwen in his excellent review of research on total institutions (1980, 145).

Peshkin recognizes that there is a danger in calling an institution a "total institution," because totality is very much a matter of degree (1986, 265). He also admits that BBA's total institution is "imperfectly total" (297). Without a clear definition of the degree of totality which makes an institution total, Peshkin's critique of BBA fails. The need for a clear definition of "totality" is accentuated by the fact that all institutions have "encompassing tendencies," as Peshkin recognizes (257). Furthermore, the variables that can be applied to total institutions are also applicable to non-total institutions (McEwen, 1980). All institutions by their very nature are "total" institutions to some degree. Or it might be better to say that all institutions have some degree of power or control over individuals. We therefore need to define clearly the distinction between a *normal* degree of "totality" (or power or control) and an extreme degree of totality. This task has been completed neither by Peshkin nor by sociologists in general (McEwen 1980, 152). And until such time as it is completed, we should be much more cautious in making the charge of institutional indoctrination against schools like BBA.

In his concluding chapter, Peshkin does a final cost benefit analysis of Christian schools, contrasting them with the public schools of North America, which for him are obviously non-total institutions. In this context he teases the reader with an interesting suggestion that merits further attention: he concedes that indoctrination "is not uncommon in public schools" (1986, 284). Unfortunately, Peshkin confuses matters here by relying on the traditional definition of indoctrination I considered in the earlier chapters, and in so doing, detracts from his central and more insightful focus on institutional indoctrination. Be that as it may, his suggestion that public schools may indoctrinate needs to be explored further. In the next section I want to examine more closely the public school as a paradigm of a liberal (non-total) institution.

"LIBERAL INSTITUTIONS" AND STATE PUBLIC SCHOOLS

Peshkin is certainly not alone in viewing the state-run public school as the exemplar of a liberal institution (cf. Ackerman 1980; Gutmann 1987). In showing how public schools differ from total institutions such as BBA, Peshkin highlights the following dimensions:

Most public schools have built-in diversity in the heterogeneity of their students and teachers, as well as the relatively unrestrained access to libraries and the media which they offer. Moreover, they do not make a conscious, planned, determined effort to control the employees hired, the students admitted and retained, the instructional and library materials available, and the operating rules and regulations according to the dictates of one, uncontested, overarching belief system. (Peshkin 1986, 284-5)

In this description of public schools, Peshkin is obviously trying to show that they do not share those features which make BBA a total institution. They do not have the same extent of shared organizational goals. There is a greater degree of voluntariness at public schools. There is also a greater degree of plurality of students, teachers, beliefs taught, library materials, and so on. Nor do public schools have the tight authority structure that evolves from the acceptance of one, uncontested, overarching belief system, as exists at BBA (cf. Peshkin 1986, 273). Clearly, according to Peshkin, the public school is a non-total or liberal institution; it is therefore not generally guilty of institutional indoctrination.

But is this a fair generalization? Have Peshkin and those who concur with him overlooked some dimensions of public education? Should Peshkin be encouraged to do a follow-up study on a public school, following the same format, and using the same paradigm of a total institution as he did with BBA? But perhaps he is not the right person to do this study, since he is well aware of the problems of objectivity involved (1986, ch. 1). What is needed is a researcher whose "world" is as far from the public school as Peshkin's is from the Christian school (ix). My purpose in this section is not to do such a study, but rather to outline some considerations that might suggest that the public school can be characterized in ways that Peshkin ascribes to a total institution. In so doing, I further want to call into question Peshkin's pejorative description of BBA as a total institution.

Many writers, from a wide variety of backgrounds, describe the public school in ways very similar to the way in which Peshkin describes BBA. Rothbard notes, "It is remarkable that the old libertarian right and the New Left, from very different perspectives and using very different rhetoric, came to a similar perception of the despotic nature of mass schooling" (1973, 134). Rothbard, writing from a libertarian perspective, refers to Paul Goodman and other New Left critics of education, who "have trenchantly exposed the nation's public schools – and to a lesser extent their private appendages – as a vast prison system of the nation's youth, dragooning countless millions of unwilling and unadaptable children in the schooling structure" (Rothbard 1973, 132). Here is a comparison of public schools to one type of total institution – prisons. Everett Reimer and Ivan Illich of deschooling fame draw a similar comparison when they object to public schools taking on the multiple functions of custodial care, social role selection, indoctrination, and education which puts them "well on the way to joining armies, prisons and insane asylums as one of society's total institutions" (Reimer [1971]1972, 16).

Some people will want to dismiss the above comparisons as rhetorical over-generalizations and exaggerations made by the radical left or right (see Barrow 1978). But we must not be too hasty. Instead, it is necessary to examine carefully those features of public schools which lead these writers and others of less radical bent to make such comparisons. In what ways are public schools like total institutions?

One often-highlighted feature is that public schools are subject to state control and state laws. Some writers have expressed alarm about the increasing centralization and control of education by the state in Great Britain and elsewhere (Hartnett & Naish 1986; West 1970). Others have pointed to the inherent tensions that exist between such state control and liberal democratic principles, some frankly admitting that such control leans toward totalitarianism and bears suspicious resemblance to the education of a communist state (Dewart 1965).

State control of education exists because the state has very definite objectives in mind. Various writers, especially of Marxist and neo-Marxist persuasion, have pointed to the dominance of economic objectives in state education, one going so far as to talk of the death of democracy in education in the face of "the rise of the tyranny of manpower needs defined by a centrist bureaucracy" (Hartnett & Naish 1986, ix). Oakeshott expresses alarm about the way in which the state has corrupted education, replacing it with "a systematic apprenticeship to domestic, industrial and commercial life in a 'modern' State" (1972, 37). West similarly talks about "the present feverish emphasis on the idea of education for economic growth," along with other commonly made reasons for state involvement in education such as social cohesion, reduction in crime, promotion of equality of opportunity, and the fostering of common values (1970, 111, chs. 3-6). The point of all this is to show that public education too is governed by "shared organizational goals," a feature that Peshkin ascribes to total institutions (1986, 261). And the state goals for education affect every dimension of the educational enterprise, including the determination of the criteria used in the selection of employees, the control of the curriculum, the supervision of classroom performance, the testing of educational outcomes, and the careful monitoring of any alternative schools and systems of education. Indeed, it would seem that, in terms of "work goals and practices," the public school system of education "enjoys as much coordination and consensus as is humanly possible to achieve," to use a phrase of Peshkin's (263). Given the amount of state control in education, it would not seem to be inappropriate to talk about the public system of education as an "organizational tyranny," another phrase Peshkin and others have used to describe total institutions (261).

If we apply the criterion of voluntariness, public schools again can be characterized as total institutions, since attendance is compulsory in most western countries. Thus it is ironic when Peshkin praises the public schools for not making a determined effort to control the students as do schools such as BBA, because in fact there is control — total control – in public schools. All children must attend schools for some twelve or thirteen years of their lives. Hence the sarcastic title of Goodman's critique of public education, *Compulsory Miseducation* (1971). And from a very different perspective and background, Rothbard generalizes: "Indeed, if we look into the history of the drive for public schooling and compulsory attendance in this and other countries, we find at the root not so much misguided altruism as a conscious scheme to coerce the mass of the population into a mould desired by the Establishment" (Rothbard 1973, 135). Of course liberals have tried to justify the compulsoriness of education in terms of the future benefit of the child, and such arguments no doubt have a good deal of validity (Peters 1977, 80-1; J.P. White 1973, 22; Haworth 1986, ch. 7). But the fact remains that there is a significant degree of lack of voluntariness in public education, and if this is a criterion of a total institution, then consistency demands that public schools must be classified as total institutions.

Another aspect of liberal educational institutions lauded by Peshkin is the "built in diversity in the heterogeneity of their students and teachers" (1986, 284-5). While there would seem to be more diversity in public schools than in Christian schools such as BBA, there is much more uniformity (totality) in our public schools than is most often acknowledged. The teachers have all been educated in accordance with state-maintained standards at institutions supported and "controlled" by the state. The student population of public schools is less heterogeneous than most people would like to admit, as schools reflect the generally homogeneous population of the neighbourhood. The diversity argument also completely overlooks the fact that "one of the major motivations of the legion of mid-nineteenth century American 'educational reformers' who established the modern public school system was precisely to use it to cripple the cultural and linguistic life of the waves of immigrants into America, and to mould them, as educational reformer Samuel Lewis stated, into 'one people' " (Rothbard 1973, 138-9). Although some lip-service is paid to enhancing multi-culturalism in our schools, the "social cohesion" argument is still one of the dominant justifications for public education today (West 1970, xxxix, ch. 4). As evidence for this, one has only to think of the frequency with which the social cohesion argument is used against independent/private schools (see Thiessen 1987a). What is also most frequently ignored is the extent to which the social cohesion argument violates the principle of "freedom of association" which is so fundamental to a liberal and democratic society. Surely the freedom to associate implies the freedom to dissociate (West 1970, xxxix). Social cohesion via government decree seems again to make the public school system of education resemble a total institution.

Similar concerns arise when one considers the supposed diversity of beliefs allowed and taught in our public schools. Here again is a lack of voluntariness in that many aspects of the curriculum are compulsory. Further, there are limitations in terms of the number of viewpoints that can be taught in the classroom, especially with young children. Similar limitations apply to library holdings. There *is* censorship in our public schools, in that decisions are being made with regard to library holdings, course design, and textbook selection, all of which entail that some ideas and books are excluded from the curriculum and the library. There would seem to be a real discrepancy between what librarians say in public about intellectual freedom or censorship and how they go about making decisions in private in their libraries (Manley 1986). "Librarianship is censorship," argues Swan in an article by this title (1979). These and other writers realistically acknowledge the validity of Sue Jansen's thesis that "censorship is an enduring feature of all human communities" and that it is "the knot that binds power and knowledge" (1988, 4).

Jansen also argues at length that the Enlightenment did not abolish censorship, but "merely transferred the office of Censor from a civic to a private trust" (1988, 4). It merely replaced church censorship with market censorship. This would seem to be confirmed in another study by Fitzgerald, who has documented how the history textbooks of America have changed over the twentieth century, so much so that students of one decade grow up with "a completely different version of American history" from students of another decade (1979, 59). This occurs because a host of very non-academic factors are at work in determining the content and choice of text-books used in public schools – factors which make "textbook publishers see themselves as beleaguered, even persecuted people" (42). Fitzgerald's analysis of these factors would again confirm that censorship is very much alive in our public schools.

Of course liberal educators want to deny that this is censorship, but as Stephen Arons has pointed out in his book aptly titled *Compelling Belief: The Culture of American Schooling* ([1983]1986), this does not appear to be censorship only because it is done within the framework of established orthodoxy. Arons maintains that "the health of American public education depends almost entirely on the existence of a rough consensus of values among families on a local basis" (16). When this consensus seems to be weakening, a battle for the control of socialization in the schools ensues. In that battle, minority attempts to gain control appear to be what is traditionally considered censorship. But surely these censors "do nothing fundamentally different from what is done by the 'selectors' of books or designers of curriculum" (27). What we have is a battle over the control of orthodoxy in our schools; and this battle really began with the entrenchment of universal compulsory schooling, according to Arons (17-8). "Once the audience became virtually captive and the control became majoritarian, it was necessary for a variety of social groups to contest with each other over whose values and world view" would be adopted by the local public school (xi). The battles exist because curriculum is determined by the "tyranny of the majority" (Mill [1859]1978, 4). Arons reminds us that J.S. Mill warned us over a century ago that schools controlled by the state are a "despotism over the mind," an attempt to mould future beliefs and culture to serve political majorities or public officials (Arons [1983]1986, 195). How paradoxical it is, Arons remarks, that the institution widely acclaimed to be the bulwark of a liberal democracy in America is used to stifle dissent and to repress intellectual freedom (vii). And again, how like a total institution!

Contrary to Peshkin, it can be argued further that the public school espouses a world-view which is masked by the alleged doctrine of neutrality, and which Christian and other religious adherents often identify as a secular/humanist world view (see Peshkin 1986, 29, 292, 294; Reese 1985, 178-9). This is a topic in its own right and I will here provide only an outline of some considerations that would lend support to this position.

In chapter 2, I distinguished between secularization and secularism. Secularization is "the process through which, starting from the center and moving outward, successive sectors of society and culture have been freed from the decisive influence of religious ideas and institutions" (Guinness 1983, 51). Secularism is a philosophy, a world view, which accepts and advocates the principles underlying the process of secularization.

There is little, if any, quarrel about the secularization of western societies – indeed of all modern societies (see Berger 1969; Martin 1978). Today we live in what R.J. Neuhaus has picturesquely described as "The Naked Public Square" (1984), a society that has excluded religion and religiously grounded values from the conduct of public business and hence is naked and secular. Even liberal educators admit as much. It is less readily acknowledged that this process of secularization is intimately related with secularism as a philosophy or world-view. Historically, however, it is obvious that the secularism of the Enlightenment was an important contributor to the modern process of secularization. Secularism is also the end product of this process of secularization. The secularization of society and culture leads, eventually, to the secularization of consciousness, and as the latter matures, it becomes expressed as a philosophy, a world-view (Berger 1969, 107-8). Hence the prevalence of the philosophy of secular humanism.

The process of secularization has also affected our schools and our view of education, as was noted in chapter 1. The sciences, morality, art, and social and political thought are now seen as autonomous – as functioning in their own right – independent of any religious considerations (Hirst 1974b, ch. 1). Liberal educators like Paul Hirst have no quarrel with this; however, what they fail to appreciate is the extent to which this process of secularization has transformed the structure as well as the hidden and the overt curricula of public education. When the process of secularization is accepted as a given, when it is explicitly adopted as a norm in education, then surely it follows both that education is controlled by the philosophy of secularism and that children in secularized schools are being taught that philosophy. In other words, our public schools are dominated by "the dictates of one, uncontested, overarching belief system," to use a description Peshkin applies to Christian schools (1986, 285).

Of course, this is disputed by secular educationists like Peshkin and Hirst who like to highlight the pluralism inherent in our public schools. I have already argued that less diversity is allowed in our public schools than is often assumed. More significant, however, is the fact that the adoption of a pluralistic approach to values and basic beliefs itself rests on an ideological base. Hirst is very frank in identifying some of the assumptions underlying a secular pluralistic society and educational system (1974b, ch. 1). Religious beliefs and values are relegated to the private personal domain. Personal religious beliefs and values are "never allowed to determine public issues" (3). Pluralism of values and religious beliefs is accepted and viewed as good. There is a tendency to think of all beliefs in this area as equally justifiable, as simply being matters of personal choice and decision. Religious beliefs and values are also not accepted as a proper basis for scientific, moral, aesthetic, or other beliefs. It is important here to note that these claims are by no means self-evident. They belong to a very particular ideological outlook – an outlook that many intelligent people question. The pluralism advocated by secularists is therefore deceptive. Underlying the principle of pluralism is a unified and complex world-view, the philosophy of secularism.

Some people conclude on the basis of careful historical analysis that our public schools are dominated by the philosophy of secularism or secular humanism (e.g., Dawson 1961; McGarry 1980). Others support this claim by an examination of textbooks used in public schools (e.g., Vitz 1986; Roques 1989).[1] Other writers have attempted to establish this conclusion by comparing the history, philosophy, curriculum, and practices of the public schools with the credal formulation of secular humanism as found in the *Humanist Manifestos I and II* (Kurtz [1933] [1973]1976; see McCarthy et al. 1981; Oppewal 1981).[2] McCarthy et al. (1981), Oppewal (1981), and others have further argued that secular humanism is itself a religion.[3] Even if one rejects the claim that secular humanism is a religion, the basic thrust of the last few paragraphs remains: children are being initiated into one world view in our public schools – a secular world view, or a secular "Cosmology and Way," as Allen prefers to call it (1976).[4]

Our public schools are not neutral, as is so often claimed, because the very omission of religion from the curriculum and structure of the school reinforces the outlook children already absorb by living in a secular society. The introduction of "religious studies" courses in our public schools does not overcome the problem because this approach is basically secular and pluralistic in outlook, and it is only as such that it is acceptable to liberal educationalists like Paul Hirst (1974a, 173-89). This is not to say that Hirst is not justified in addressing the problem of what it means to provide a "moral education in a secular society" (1974b). However, he fails to be sufficiently aware that this kind of moral education is also implicitly and explicitly conveying a secular world view. The supposed ideological neutrality of liberals and liberal institutions is "a gigantic piece of bad faith" (Corbett 1965, 152). There would seem to be an increasing recognition that "liberal neutrality" is not quite as neutral is has often been assumed. Gutmann sums it up this way: "All sophisticated liberals recognize the practical limitation of neutrality as an educational ideal: it is, in its fullest form, unrealizable" (Gutmann 1987, 35; cf. Crittenden 1988, 125).

If, as I have attempted to show, the philosophy and the curriculum of public schools are dominated by secular humanism, it follows that public schools are also captive to a closed system of belief – the philosophy and/or religion of secular humanism. It further follows that public schools are not liberal but total institutions, given Peshkin's description of total institutions as captive to a particular philosophical/religious outlook. Indeed, if I may be granted the liberty to distort a sentence of Peshkin's, which he uses when discussing the totality of BBA's Truth, "To those outside their fold, the secular/humanist's all-embracing doctrine enslaves, because it constricts one's options; to those inside, freedom lies in Truth's domain" (1986, 261).

I turn now to some additional specific factors that would further support the conclusion that public schools are total institutions. Total institutions, as I have noted, are institutions in which a large number of individuals are cut off from the wider society for an appreciable period of time (Peshkin 1986, 261). This surely applies to public schools just as much as it applies to Christian schools, for as Oakeshott has noted, an essential characteristic of all schools is that of "detachment from the immediate, local world of the learner" (1972, 24).

Peshkin, drawing on Goffman, also calls attention to the mortification practices of total institutions: attempts at reshaping the self, breaking the spirit, humiliating the inmates (Peshkin 1986, 271-2). Though Goffman's graphic description of this process is perhaps too extreme to fit public schools, a concession which Peshkin also makes with regard to Christian schools, something very much akin to mortification goes on in our public schools, especially for those children who do not belong to the school's prevailing culture. Children who have been brought up in a Christian home may, in a first grade singing period in a public school, suggest that the class sing some songs they have learned in Sunday school or in church. Even if the teacher ever so gently tells these children that this is not appropriate in this secular setting, they will feel humiliated, and their self is being reshaped. Think of the frequent experience of the seventeen- or eighteen-year-old Christian student taking a first course in philosophy at college or university, in which long held and cherished religious convictions are systematically undermined, even ridiculed, all under the guise of teaching critical reflection in a neutral manner. Again, is this not mortification? Is this person's self not being reshaped?

Further general considerations could be used to show that public schools are not really so liberal as is generally assumed. Much more could be said, for example, about the hidden curriculum, about which so much has been written since the late 1960s. While the adjective "hidden" is perhaps unfortunate, conjuring up ideas of some sort of a conspiracy, and while philosophers have quibbled much about the exact meaning of a "hidden curriculum," the term is useful in calling attention to the fact that schools by virtue of their being institutions with a physical, social, and symbolic environment teach an implicit, latent, tacit, and unstudied curriculum (Gordon 1982; Cornbleth 1984). The hidden curriculum functions as a very effective form of socialization and social control, affecting behaviour, thinking, and values (Vallance 1974). Now that most people have acknowledged that there is a hidden curriculum, we begin to see how pervasive the influence of a public school can be and how much like a total institution it is. To refer again to Peshkin, the public school, just like a Christian school, "establishes the broadest possible control of its students ... Its aspiration to totality extends to most all behaviour and thought, everywhere, at all times, throughout the entire life of everyone affiliated in any capacity with their total institution. That, indeed, is totality!" (Peshkin 1986, 265).[5]

Space does not permit a consideration of a whole range of additional closely inter-related arguments which can be seen as extensions of the hidden curriculum argument and could be used to provide additional support for the conclusion that public schools are total institutions. One such argument involves research on classroom communication patterns which leads one writer to conclude "that the dominant pattern of classroom communication is indoctrinational" (Young 1984, 236). Other arguments include the Marxist and neo-Marxist critiques of education (e.g., Harris 1979), the contributions of sociologists of knowledge such as Berger and Luckmann ([1966]1967), the "new" sociology of education (e.g., Young 1971), and the more recent school of "radical" or "critical" pedagogy which draws extensively from the Marxist tradition as well as from recent continental European philosophy (e.g., Aronowitz & Giroux 1985; Freire 1973; Giroux 1985). There is not space here to deal with the problems inherent in these schools of thought, their tendencies towards economic and psychological determinism, relativism, and association with conspiracy theories. But despite these problems, which I believe can be overcome, these theories share a central theme that cannot be dismissed: that what counts as "real knowledge" in our schools is in part determined by society, social institutions, and the power structures of a society. Society and social institutions do structure individual consciousness. Public schools do function as agencies of social, economic, and cultural reproduction and are subject to the imperatives of the dominant social order. This would suggest that our public schools are less liberal than is often assumed and that they share many of the features often associated with total institutions. Public schools are in part subject to outside forces and dominant ideologies which serve to create a "total atmosphere" from which students cannot entirely escape.

In this section I have attempted to show that liberal rhetoric surrounding the public school is quite misleading. My central thrust is captured well in the title of Stephen Arons' *Compelling Belief: The Culture of American Schooling* ([1983]1986). North American schools, indeed schools anywhere, constitute, to a much greater degree than is commonly realized, a total culture which compels children to believe certain things. The "marketplace of ideas" that is supposed to exist in our public schools ignores the reality of schooling as a socializing institution (Arons 55-6). The marketplace model "becomes a robe of secular sanctity under which school officials can hide (57). It creates the illusion that schooling can be value neutral and it obscures the fact that children are subject to "institutionalized indoctrination" (58).

People who have faith in our public schools as liberal institutions will want to reject this conclusion as too extreme, will maintain that it is fundamentally wrong-headed to describe public schools as total institutions in the pejorative sense. It might surprise some readers that I have a good deal of sympathy with such a position. The central thrust of this section is not to join the many who enjoy public-school bashing. Rather, I have tried to argue that *if* total institutions are described in the way in which Peshkin describes them in his critique of Christian schools, then public schools must also be characterized as total institutions. Public schools share many of the features of Christian schools, though in different ways. By the same token, if, with Peshkin, we do not want to label public schools total institutions, understood pejoratively (despite the fact that they seem to resemble such institutions in many ways), then consistency demands that we also refrain from labelling Christian schools as total institutions guilty of institutional indoctrination. This would suggest that the distinction between total institutions and liberal institutions is less sharp than Peshkin assumes, and that much more work needs to be done to clarify this distinction. Until such time as this work has been completed, we should be much more cautious in charging Christian schools with institutional indoctrination.

NORMAL LIBERAL INSTITUTIONS

Some readers will feel uncomfortable with the conclusions of the previous section. Is it not possible, and preferable, to talk about the ideal of liberal education apart from institutions? Has Peshkin misled us by focusing on the institutional dimension of Christian schools? Is there something wrong with the very notion of "institutional indoctrination"? Should this chapter have even been written?

As an introductory response to these questions, let me refer to *Pravda: A Fleet Street Comedy* (Brenton & Hare 1985). In this delightful play, a satire on journalism, a young idealistic editor, Andrew, has the misfortune of having his newspaper shut down because of some quarrels about wanting to report the "truth" ("Pravda" means "truth"). After nearly giving up on journalism altogether, Andrew contemplates an opportunity to get back at the man who fired him by joining a group which is thinking of purchasing the now defunct newspaper. His wife protests, even though she also hates the man who fired Andrew. "But the way to fight him is with ideas," she says. Andrew responds: "How can you say that? You need institutions. How else can you make ideas real? We must have the means and the courage to buy the means. And that's what we're doing" (Brenton & Hare 1985, 108).

Ideas need institutions; ideas are inevitably transmitted *via* institutions; human beings need institutions; human beings are necessarily shaped by institutions; any attempt to ignore the institutional context of liberal education is foolish; we do need to talk about institutional indoctrination. These are the claims I want to try to establish in the concluding section of this chapter. Here it might be well to repeat that I am using the term "institution" to refer to what sociologists call a social institution – "an interrelated system of social roles and norms organized about the satisfaction of an important social need or function" (Theodorson 1969, 206-7). Commonly defined institutions include the family institution, the economic institution, the educational institution, the political institution, and the religious institution.

In order to explore the problem of institutions, it will be helpful to return to Haworth's discussion of autonomy (see chapter 5). Haworth (1986) is one of few scholars writing from a liberal perspective who squarely faces the problem of institutions. He reminds us that autonomous decision-making always occurs within the context of a "task environment" which has an institutional structure (107). Haworth objects to the naïve frontier conception of the task environment often met in philosophical and economic literature, in which the environment is represented as formless. "In this view the individual conceives of purposes and goals he *brings to* the world of action. There he encounters resources necessary or useful for realizing his purposes and obstacles that impede him" (108).

Haworth considers this view naïve for two reasons. First, it fails to grasp the fact that there are institutional structures behind all the resources and obstacles an agent confronts – institutional structures which gain a momentum of their own. The idea of an uninstitutionalized frontier is largely mythical, according to Haworth (1986, 111). It is also important to realize that there are two faces to these institutional structures: the face of constraint and the face of opportunity. A library, for example, despite the fact that it is governed by all kinds of constraining regulations, nevertheless opens up endless opportunities for self-education. The fact that institutions do provide opportunities, that they actually "institute" the possibility of doing things that could not otherwise be done, is frequently forgotten (112). Therefore the common assumption that institutions limit personal autonomy more or less by definition is false according to Haworth (113). I agree with Haworth that institutions, properly understood, must be seen as also opening up opportunities, as enhancing personal autonomy.

The frontier view of the task environment is also naïve because it fails to see the agent as integrally related to the world (Haworth 1986, 108). The individual does not conceive of purposes and goals quite apart from the institutions of which he or she is a part. The task environment itself shapes an individual's goals to some extent. It gives purpose. There are both contraint and opportunity in this dialectic between the individual and the task environment.

Haworth's account of institutions is really a restatement of a very old theory of human nature. It was Aristotle who said that man is by nature a social or political animal. We are by nature institutional animals. We are born into a family. This is the first institution a child encounters or belongs to, and it represents both constraint and opportunity. This might seem like begging the question. Surely the institution of the family is an antiquated notion that is, in any case, dying.[6] But we must not be too hasty. Suppose we eliminate the family. Does that in any way de-institutionalize the child? Obviously not. If not the traditional family, some other institution will nurture the child. Children simply cannot exist on their own. Social institutions are inescapable.

Looking beyond the infant within the institution of the family to the problem of educating a child after infancy again brings up concern about the institutional context of education. While some writers advocate the deschooling of society, it is not always clear whether they are arguing for a deschooled society or a de-institutionalized society. Illich (1970), for example, makes repeated references to institutions, often with pejorative qualifiers attached. Here an interesting problem arises when considering Illich's alternative to schools – a system of learning webs. Has Illich really de-institutionalized society, or has he merely replaced one type of educational institution – the school – with another type of educational institution – a system of learning webs? This raises an even more basic question as to whether education can be thought of apart from institutions.

One of the basic problems surrounding discussions of liberal education is that such discussions all too often deal only with the abstract ideal. There is nothing wrong with considering an ideal in the abstract, as long as one remembers that it is an abstraction. But the ideal of liberal education is not concrete, it is an abstraction, and when discussing liberal education, it is necessary to address some very practical questions: Where does liberal education occur? How do we provide a liberal education? And, in answering these questions, we will necessarily have to talk about institutions. Even the self-educated person cannot acquire a liberal education apart from institutions, libraries, for example.

It is to R.S. Peters's credit that he recognizes the inevitability of the institutional context of liberal education. Peters is very much aware of the status of the child. In chapter 2 I noted that Peters stresses that the development of the mind only occurs as the child is initiated into "public traditions enshrined in the language, concepts, beliefs and rules of a society" (1966, 49). "All education," Peters writes, "can be regarded as a form of 'socialization,' " in so far as it involves initiation into such public traditions (1965, 89). In other words, all education, including liberal education, involves initiating individuals into the institution of society as a whole, it involves getting the "barbarian outside the gates ... inside the citadel of civilization" (Peters 1965, 107). This initiation is of course mediated through various institutions of society such as the family and the schools. It is for this reason that Peters keeps talking about schooling and education in the same breath. Though there are dangers in this (Harris 1977), there is something healthy about interchanging schooling and education. It recognizes the necessary institutional context of a liberal education.

Oakeshott (1972), to whom Peters is much indebted, is even more explicit. Education, he maintains, including liberal education, properly speaking only begins when, after the casual encounters with learning, "there supervenes the deliberate initiation of a newcomer into a human inheritance of sentiments, beliefs, imaginings, understandings and activities. It begins when the transaction becomes 'schooling' and when learning becomes learning by study, and not by chance, in conditions of direction and restraint. It begins with the appearance of a teacher with something to impart which is *not* immediately connected with the current wants or 'interests' of the learner" (Oakeshott 1972, 23). Oakeshott may be going too far when he states that liberal education begins only in schools. Surely the institution of the family is a significant factor in initiating the child into the human inheritance of beliefs and values, and as such, the family is also the bearer of liberal education. But in either case, education occurs within an institutional context.

There are many other illustrations of the inevitability of institutions. The institutional dimensions of science – often viewed as the paradigm of free and open inquiry and thus seen as essentially linked to a liberal education[7] – provide an interesting example. More generally, Mary Douglas, in her controversial book, *How Institutions Think* (1986), attempts to clarify how all thinking is dependent on institutions.[8] The institutional dimension of shaping beliefs indeed seems to be inescapable.

Christian homes or Christian schools are frequently accused of being guilty of indoctrination, and I began this chapter by examining how the charge of indoctrination often focuses on the institutional dimension of Christian nurture. The paradigm of indoctrination I have been referring to throughout this book involves a Christian school in which Christian teachers teach church doctrines to students from Christian homes. The problem with most contemporary philosophical discussions of indoctrination, based as they are on the Enlightenment ideal of liberal education, is that they fail to focus specifically on this institutional context of indoctrination. As we have seen, typical analyses of "indoctrination" are more concerned with the teaching of individual beliefs to individual students by individual teachers via specific non-rational methods.

Even Peshkin flirts with this kind of a narrow approach to defining "indoctrination" when he specifically introduces the term (1986, 284). However, as a sociologist, Peshkin is mainly concerned with describing Bethany Baptist Academy as an institution, and he uses the notion of a total institution to highlight what he finds objectionable about this fundamentalist Christian school. I therefore used Peshkin's own criteria of a total institution to characterize "institutional indoctrination," when this term is understood in its pejorative sense. An attempt was then made to defend BBA against the charge of institutional indoctrination.

The problems uncovered in Peshkin's attempt to level this charge against BBA might suggest that there may be some problems with the criteria used to make the charge of institutional indoctrination. This was substantiated when I applied these same criteria to what Peshkin, along with many other liberals, considers to be a liberal institution – the public school. I argued that, under Peshkin's criteria, the public school looks indeed like a total institution and that therefore the public school is also guilty of institutional indoctrination. Since most liberals would want to deny this rather damning conclusion, there must be a problem with the definition of institutional indoctrination itself.

I finally argued that it is not possible to get around this problem by simply ignoring or denying that there is an institutional component to education wherever it occurs. While careful to avoid determinism, we need to acknowledge that cognition is, to a large extent, socially conditioned. Knowledge is similarly defined by institutions to a large extent, as various writers have argued. What is needed, therefore, is a new theory of institutions, a new epistemology, and a new theory of liberal education which amends the current unsociological view of human cognition (See Douglas 1986, ix; Halstead 1979, 73-5).

All this further entails that the distinction between total institutions and liberal institutions also needs to be redefined. What is needed especially is a recognition that institutional "totality" (power or control) is inescapable and very much a matter of degree, and that there is therefore a need to define the level of "totality" that is acceptable for a *normal* liberal institution. Unfortunately, although the tasks of defining the central features of a normal liberal institution and distinguishing it from a total institution are important ones, they are beyond the scope of this book. I can at most point sociologists and philosophers of education in the right direction. Once these tasks are completed, we will be in a position to define more precisely what is meant by "institutional indoctrination" understood in its pejorative sense. Until these tasks are completed, we should be much more cautious in charging Christian homes or Christian schools with institutional indoctrination.

8 Religious Indoctrination vs. Liberal Education: Some Conclusions

We have seen that concern about indoctrination grows out of the Enlightenment ideal of liberal education. Indoctrination is generally understood to be the very antithesis of liberal education. As such, indoctrination is considered to be immoral. My primary concern has been to examine the charge of indoctrination applied to Christian nurture as it occurs in Christian homes and schools. Christian nurture is also sometimes identified as a confessional approach to Christian religious education. While my arguments could for the most part also be applied to Hindu nurture or to a confessional approach to religious education that would be used in a Buddhist home, I have limited myself to Christian nurture since that is the kind of religious education with which I am most familiar. What is of concern to those who make the charge of religious indoctrination is that a child is being nurtured into a particular religion, whatever that religion may be.

Chapter 1 examined the charge of religious indoctrination as it occurs in the context of analytic philosophers attempting to clarify the meaning of the concept of indoctrination. Such conceptual analysis is very much concerned with analyzing the meaning of words as they occur in ordinary language, and thus it can be safely assumed that philosophical concerns about religious indoctrination reflect the concerns of the non-philosopher as well. Whenever the charge of religious indoctrination is made, concerns about the non-scientific status of religious beliefs, non-evidential teaching, the failure to aim for autonomy in students, and the production of closed minds are the focus. These concerns are reflected in each of the four criteria normally associated with indoctrination, which have been dealt with in the previous chapters. I have, in addition, considered a possible fifth criterion – an institutional criterion – which philosophers have tended to neglect. The primary thrust of this book is to answer the charge of religious indoctrination based on concerns such as are expressed in these five criteria of indoctrination. It is now time to draw some conclusions about how to reply to the charge of indoctrination as it is specifically applied to Christian nurture.

REPLIES TO THE CHARGE OF RELIGIOUS INDOCTRINATION

The basic conclusion I have been arguing for throughout is that the charge of religious indoctrination is less strong than generally assumed, and that this charge should be made with much caution. It is now time for more specific responses to this charge as made against Christian nurture. Some writers maintain that there is a necessary relation between Christian nurture and indoctrination. Others are more cautious and argue only for a contingent relation, for example, that indoctrination is more probable in the religious domain. I shall first examine the stronger claim of a necessary relation, which will be broken down into two different claims.

Many philosophers claim that indoctrination is necessarily limited to the teaching of doctrines such as occur in religion or politics. "No doctrines, no indoctrination," Flew states (1972b, 114). This connection was dealt with extensively in chapter 3 and therefore I need only summarize the conclusions of my treatment of the content criterion of indoctrination. I argued that there is no logical connection between "indoctrination" and doctrines. Affirmations of a connection were found to rest on etymological considerations; however, these cannot be used to establish conceptual links in contemporary usage. We do talk of indoctrination in non-doctrinal areas, and even Flew is forced to concede such a secondary usage of the concept of indoctrination (1972a, 87). I further argued that, even if we do limit it to doctrines, indoctrination is still not limited to the teaching of religious or political beliefs. A careful examination of the criteria associated with "doctrines" led to the conclusion that science or history also contains doctrines, however these be defined. It was finally argued that it is strategically safer not to build any content restriction into the concept of indoctrination. Only in this way will we avoid both the danger of biases in our accusations against others, and the danger of a false sense of security about our own teaching in areas we think are immune to indoctrination. Indoctrination is therefore not necessarily limited to areas of religious or political beliefs which are commonly thought to be the only ones containing doctrines or ideologies.

The second kind of logically necessary connection between Christian nurture and indoctrination reverses the order of the first. It is here maintained that Christian nurture necessarily, in some logical sense, involves indoctrination. This would seem to be the way in which the charge of religious indoctrination is expressed at times, though it is not always clearly stated. Snook, for example, argues that, because the evidence for *all* religious propositions is inconclusive, and because a religious parent or teacher teaches these inconclusive propositions with the intention that they be believed, "indoctrination is inevitable if religion is taught," and therefore the teaching *of* religion (i.e., Christian nurture) is an immoral activity (1972b, 75-6; cf. White 1972a, 129). What seems to be at issue here is the nature of religion itself. It is because religious doctrines are, in Flew's words, "either false or at least not known to be true," that any attempt to implant firm convictions in the truth of such doctrines *must* be indoctrination (1972a, 86, cf. 75; 1972b, 113).

In reply, it needs to be pointed out, first of all, that to state that there is a logically necessary relation between Christian nurture and indoctrination is to make a very strong claim which is, for that very reason, vulnerable to attack. In order to establish such a strong claim, it would be necessary to show the self-contradiction in claiming that there is such a thing as Christian nurture but that it does not involve indoctrination in the pejorative sense. It will not do merely to find some people who think that this is contradictory. It must be demonstrated that Christian nurture really is logically incompatible with true education, that all rational people would find it to be so.[1] Unfortunately for those who make this claim, many rational people, even philosophers, do not find Christian nurture to be necessarily indoctrinatory in the logical sense of necessary. Of course, critics will maintain that these so-called rational thinkers are not really rational. But who has the final verdict? Who is to say that maybe the critics themselves are not entirely rational when they make such an extreme claim?

Interestingly, the critics sometimes seem to be suggesting that Christian nurture may not always involve indoctrination in the pejorative sense. For example, Snook does at times allow for the possibility of non-indoctrinatory Christian nurture – with the very young child, for example (1972b, 95-6). Here Snook is contradicting his earlier position and we are not sure which pole of the contradiction he would have us accept. The arguments of the previous chapters point to further contradictions on the part of those who maintain that Christian nurture necessarily entails indoctrination. If these same critics are forced to allow for non-rational teaching in other areas, if they concede that children are not autonomous and that we are right to restrict their freedom now so as to provide as much autonomy as possible later on, if they have to admit that conviction is compatible with critical openness in areas like science, then surely we must allow for these possibilities in the area of Christian nurture as well. Hence Christian nurture does not necessarily entail indoctrination in the pejorative sense.

The fundamental issue has to do with the status of religious beliefs themselves. In order to show that Christian nurture necessarily involves indoctrination, critics would have to *prove* that *all* Christian beliefs are somehow suspect. I believe enough has been said in the previous chapters to cast doubt on this extreme position. This is not the place to enter into a detailed refutation of such a position, though it should be pointed out that many reputed scholars claim that there is good evidence for Christian beliefs, and that these beliefs are true and known to be true. Throughout I have compared science and religion, showing either that in many ways science is as irrational as religion or that religion is as rational as science. If the irrational features of science do not make us conclude that indoctrination is necessary in science, neither should they make us draw this conclusion in the area of religion. And if religion is in many ways as rational as science, then again indoctrination should not be considered inevitable in the area of religion.

The primary thrust of the previous chapters has been to show that it is logically possible for Christian nurture to satisfy the ideals of a defensible form of liberal education. In chapter 3 I argued that Christian nurture can satisfy the concerns of verification that are so fundamental to the scientific ideal. I then argued that Christian nurture can be rational (chapter 4) and that it is possible for Christian parents and teachers to aim for both autonomy and Christian commitment (chapter 5). In chapter 6 I tried to show that Christian conviction is compatible with critical openness. In chapter 7 I argued that the institutional dimension of Christian nurture can be liberal. I conclude that Christian nurture does not necessarily involve indoctrination. Christian nurture and liberal education are not necessarily incompatible.

I turn next to a less extreme position which is perhaps the more common expression of the charge of religious indoctrination. This argument maintains that, instead of a necessary relation, there is a strong contingent relation between Christian nurture and indoctrination. Again there are two variations of this claim. Some people, while denying that indoctrination is necessarily restricted to doctrines, would nevertheless concede that indoctrination is much more likely to occur in doctrinal areas such as religion. Others maintain that, when a Christian parent or teacher is nurturing a child in the Christian faith, there is a high probability that they are indoctrinating. Paul Hirst, for example, associates Christian nurture with his traditionalist concept of education, which is concerned with the transmission of a body of specific concepts, beliefs, and values within a particular tradition and which in its methods "is likely to favour the procedures of exposition, instruction, catechesis and indoctrination" (1985, 7). Similarly Snook, who at times makes the stronger claim of a necessary connection, at other times only argues that "indoctrination is most likely to occur in the areas of morals, religion and politics, for these are matters upon which informed people differ" (1972b, 68).

I will deal with both the above claims at the same time, since they are closely related in that both involve a *probable* connection between Christian nurture and indoctrination, and since similar considerations are involved in establishing or refuting each claim. The arguments of the third chapter, dealing with the content criterion of indoctrination, also serve to weaken the claims of probable connections between Christian nurture and indoctrination. The basic approach of chapter 3 involved consideration of similarities between scientific and religious beliefs using various criteria generally associated with doctrines and hence with indoctrination. In effect, the argument showed that scientific beliefs are just as "irrational" as religious beliefs, or, that scientific believing is just as "irrational" as religious believing. A study of the history of science shows that false beliefs, or beliefs based on insufficient evidence or even on no evidence at all occur in science just as they do in religion. Both areas contain beliefs for which the evidence is ambiguous. I argued at length that there are "non-verifiable" first-order principles in science just as in religion. In both areas, people hold on to beliefs despite the existence of seemingly contrary evidence. The history of science is also replete with examples of beliefs about which there are varying levels of public disagreement. In both areas we find examples of dogmatism, closed minds, evangelistic zeal, and lack of objectivity.

If, therefore, indoctrination is associated with any or all the above features, it should be concluded that indoctrination is also likely in the domain of science. However, the critics of Christian nurture generally assume that the teaching of science is immune to indoctrination, or at least that it is highly unlikely that indoctrination occurs in science (see Barrow & Woods 1988, 76; Kazepides 1987, 229). But if we want to say that indoctrination does not occur, or that it is very unlikely in science (despite its irrational features), then we should not make the charge of indoctrination about Christian nurture on the basis of these same irrational features which have been shown to be common to both science and religion. It follows that those making the charge of indoctrination with regard to Christian nurture will be forced to admit, if they want to be consistent, that there is less indoctrination accompanying Christian nurture than they generally assume.

This argument can be recast by focusing on the positive features shared by science and religion. I argued in chapter 3, by doing justice to the complexities of scientific verification, it will be found that religious claims also satisfy the demands of this more sophisticated notion of verification. Similarly, a more sophisticated notion of rationality reveals that religion is also rational, like science (see chapter 4). Also, religious claims can be, and often are, held in such a way as to satisfy the demands of critical openness – qualities often associated with science (chapter 6). If, therefore, religion shares with science, many of these positive features which are thought to make indoctrination highly unlikely in the teaching of science, consistency demands that we then concede that indoctrination is also unlikely in the teaching of religion. Again the supposed probability of indoctrination in Christian nurture has been lessened.

Let us now proceed to another kind of argument which emerges from my treatment of the methods criterion of indoctrination in chapter 4. After a careful analysis of various teaching methods commonly identified as "non-rational" – and hence indoctrinatory – I argued at length that these non-rational teaching methods are inevitable, particularly when teaching young children. The use of non-rational teaching methods is not unique to religious or Christian nurture; it applies equally well to the teaching of science, history, and mathematics. If therefore we do not want to label as indoctrination (pejorative sense) the use of non-rational teaching methods when initiating children into the scientific or historical traditions, then we should not, if we are consistent, accuse Christians of indoctrination when they use these same non-rational teaching methods which, in fact, are unavoidable. Thus much of the charge of indoctrination (understood in the pejorative sense and as applied to

Christian nurture) simply dissipates when we acknowledge that it is based on a non-rational component of teaching which in fact is inescapable and hence cannot be seen as immoral.

The arguments of chapters 5, 6, and 7 similarly have shown that the probability of indoctrination in Christian nurture is lower than is often assumed. I argued in chapter 5 that the charge of indoctrination, when focusing on the failure of Christian parents and teachers to promote autonomy, is based on a problematic definition of autonomy. With proper qualifications, it can be shown that Christian parents and teachers can and do intend that their children and students mature towards autonomy, and hence more caution was urged in making the charge of indoctrination against Christian nurture. A central argument of chapter 6 was to show the compatibility of Christian commitment with critical openness. Generalizations about the high probability of indoctrination in Christian teaching are often based on a notion of critical openness that is philosophically suspect. Fewer charges would result with the more defensible notion of normal critical openness. In chapter 7 I argued that charges of indoctrination based on the fact that Christian nurture takes place in the context of institutions are often unwarranted because they rest on an unnecessary identification of Christian institutions with total institutions. All education has an institutional component to it, and until we can clearly distinguish between total institutions and liberal institutions, we should be more cautious in making the charge. All these arguments serve to show that the probability of indoctrination in Christian nurture is lower than is often assumed.

The above conclusion is obviously not very precise. To what extent has it been demonstrated that indoctrination is less probable in Christian nurture than is often assumed? Greater precision is simply not possible in the kind of argument being used here. I would further point out that charges concerning the probability of indoctrination are themselves very imprecise. What is meant when Hirst claims that Christian nurture is "likely" to favour procedures of indoctrination, or when Snook maintains that indoctrination is "most likely" to occur in areas such as religion? How likely is indoctrination? And where is the empirical evidence, given that probability claims generally require such documentation? The difficulty of answering questions such as these is, no doubt, behind the frequent tendency to slip from probability claims about indoctrination to claims suggesting that indoctrination is inevitable or necessary when engaging in Christian nurture. But charges made in these stronger terms have already been shown to be unwarranted.

Finally, the charge of indoctrination against Christian nurture is

often expressed by appealing to paradigms. I have refered throughout to a description in Barrow and Woods of a Catholic school with
Catholic teachers instructing students from Catholic parents, who,
with the teachers, are determined to bring up these children as devout Catholics with an unshakable commitment to the truth of Catholicism. Barrow and Woods suggest that it "is difficult to conceive
of anyone seriously doubting that these teachers are indoctrinating"
(1988, 70). This is meant to be "an uncontentious example" – a paradigm case – of indoctrination. Similarly, Nielsen has cited much of
what occurs on Christian television stations in the United States and
on Iran Television as "paradigmatic" or "unequivocal" instances of
religious indoctrination (1984, 70). It should be clear that I do not see
these supposed paradigms as clear, uncontentious, unequivocal instances of religious indoctrination. And this is not due to a peculiar
bias on my part. I have argued that the very ingredients that lead
these writers to identify the above examples as paradigms of indoctrination are found in other contexts (e.g., public schools, secular
television in the United States), contexts which these writers probably would not identify as indoctrinatory. If they therefore wish to be
consistent, they should not treat Catholic schools or Christian television as obvious paradigms of indoctrination.

It is also curious that these writers themselves disagree on their
paradigms. Nielsen, for example, argues that his paradigms stand in
"firm contrast to the teaching of Karl Barth or Cardinal Newman
where we have teachings which should not be described as indoctrination. And indeed some of the characteristic practices, though by
no means all, of the mainline Protestant Churches and of the Catholic Church should also not be described as indoctrination" (Nielsen
1984, 70). Yet for Antony Flew, "the outstanding paradigm case of
indoctrination" is the effort by a traditional Christian church to teach
children the truth of its specific distinctive doctrines (Flew 1972b,
114). While Nielsen maintains that the teaching of Cardinal Newman should *not* be described as indoctrination, Barrow and Woods
give as their paradigm case of indoctrination the behaviour of a
Catholic school which probably subscribes to the model of liberal education espoused by Cardinal Newman. Thus we see significant disagreement concerning paradigm cases of religious indoctrination.
While Nielsen's target is Moslem and Christian fundamentalists,
Flew, Barrow, and Woods single out the Catholic Church. Even
Christian fundamentalists have their own unique targets which they
like to cite as paradigms of indoctrination – humanists like Nielsen
and Flew, for example, and the extremist cults (see Enroth 1977).
The vicious circle of charges and counter-charges goes on and on. It

all seems quite subjective, dependent on the peculiar biases of the person making the charge. Caution is therefore again in order when identifying paradigm cases of indoctrination.

Careful examination of the way in which charges of indoctrination tend to be made suggests that they are indeed sometimes based on prejudices. Broad generalizations, rhetoric, and ad hominem arguments are all too common in discussions of indoctrination. To describe religion as "superstition," religious education in the home as "primitive" or "sub-human," and Christian parents as "hypocritical or disingenuous" or "misguided," as has been done in some philosophical writings on indoctrination, would seem to be accounted for only in terms of disrespect and prejudice (Gardner 1988, 102; Hirst 1981, 86; 1985, 10; Kazepides 1983, 264). The strong anti-religious sentiment that keeps surfacing in discussions of indoctrination does cause one to ask: Might it be that those who are so strongly opposed to Christian nurture have themselves been indoctrinated? Are we dealing here with what Peter Berger calls "the unexamined prejudice" of most moderns and liberals, namely the evolutionary assumption that the search for identity and meaning in one's ethnic, cultural, and religious heritage is part of our primal, primitive, prerational past out of which we are evolving (1974, 199)? Of course these must remain questions, because in order to answer them I might find myself engaging in the very kind of rhetoric to which I have been objecting.

There is another way in which my arguments can be used to answer the charge of indoctrination as applied to Christian nurture. Before one attempts to answer a charge, it is important to understand clearly what the charge is. Here, we need to ask what is meant by "indoctrination." That there are real difficulties in clarifying the meaning of the term creates a fundamental problem. Although, as noted in chapter 1, my approach has not been to focus on the definition of the concept of indoctrination, I have used the criteria generally associated with "indoctrination" to get at the substantive questions that need to be addressed in assessing whether Christian nurture is incompatible with liberal education and immoral. However, it should be clear from my treatment of the issues surrounding each of the four criteria traditionally associated with indoctrination as applied to Christian nurture that there are some very real problems with the concept of indoctrination itself. I have uncovered a host of inconsistencies in the way in which the notion of indoctrination is understood and applied. Moreover, since the concept of indoctrination is itself vague, ambiguous, and confused, the charge of religious indoctrination really suffers from the same problems.[2] Thus the question arises: Is there really a coherent charge to answer?

Dunlop sums up the problem this way:

Although indoctrination has perhaps attracted more attention from contemporary analytic philosophers of education than (almost) any other reasonably self-contained and isolated topic, there is still far from being general agreement about it. Method, content, states of mind, with or without teacher's intention – various combinations of these standard ingredients still emerge from philosophers' kitchens with astonishing regularity, but nobody has yet apparently managed to digest anyone else's concoction. (1976, 39)

I believe that this continuing philosophical disagreement surrounding the correct analysis of the concept of indoctrination is significant and cannot simply be dismissed as a misguided search for an elusive essential meaning, as Nielsen has claimed (1984).[3] The concept of indoctrination is riddled with problems regardless of how the task of conceptual analysis is defined. It will not do to try to overcome these problems by suggesting that we know the meaning of indoctrination because we can point to paradigm cases (Nielsen 1984), for, as has already been argued, the paradigm cases of indoctrination themselves are contentious. Philosophers have no clear and coherent notion of indoctrination when they make the charge against Christian nurture.

Charges of religious indoctrination outside the philosophical literature (examined in chapter 1) are generally based on the same ingredients, assumptions, and ideals as occur in philosophers' attempts to analyze the concept of indoctrination. Hence, whether made by the philosopher or by someone else, the charge of religious indoctrination itself is confused.

This then leads to another kind of reply to the charge of religious indoctrination: If the concept of indoctrination is unclear, then the charge of religious indoctrination is unclear. Until a more adequate concept of indoctrination is forthcoming, there is a problem in understanding the charge, and there is therefore no clear charge to answer. Of course, a word whose cognitive meaning is confusing can still have emotive meaning. Charges of religious indoctrination all too frequently express the critics' feelings of disapproval. Rational defence against such expressions of emotion is not only futile but unnecessary.

This is not to suggest that the Christian should totally ignore the charge of indoctrination. I believe that there are certain unacceptable forms of religious instruction which merit the label "indoctrination," and, in what follows, I will attempt to reconstruct the notion of indoctrination so as to overcome the problems of the past. But until there is a more adequate and coherent concept of indoctrination, we should be cautious in charging anyone with indoctrination. Surely it is not too much to expect the critics to be a little less vehement in their attacks against Christian nurture if they, or anyone for that matter, are unclear as to precisely what it is they are objecting to.

The final reply to the charge of indoctrination will emerge as I attempt this reconstruction of the concept of indoctrination. With the reconstructed notion, many typical objections to Christian nurture will no longer apply. Thus again the charge will be found to be weaker than is generally assumed. Before I begin, I will reconstruct the ideal of liberal education which is the context out of which the charge of indoctrination in its pejorative sense emerges (see chapter 2).

TOWARD A RECONSTRUCTION OF THE IDEAL OF LIBERAL EDUCATION

In the previous chapters, I have criticized various aspects of what I have labelled the Enlightenment ideal of liberal education. In each case, I argued that it was these problematic aspects of the ideal of liberal education which lay behind the largely unjustified charge of indoctrination against Christian nurture. In most cases an attempt was made to move beyond criticism to a reconstruction of those aspects of the ideal of liberal education under consideration so as to overcome the problems uncovered. It is now time to pull all this together with a view to working toward a reconstructed ideal of liberal education which is more philosophically defensible than past accounts of this ideal. I want first to examine some of the key assumptions underlying the ideal of liberal education. I will then be in a position to consider a reconstruction of the ideal itself. It needs to be stressed that I can at most provide a bare outline of such a reconstruction here. In effect I am providing some suggestions for the directions future discussion concerning liberal education and indoctrination should take.

I have been assuming throughout that a neutral, value-free, or non-ideological analysis of liberal education is impossible.[4] Peters, in his later writings, urges philosophers to move on to a more constructive, integrative approach to thinking about education. This would be more in line with a classical approach such as Plato's, whose educational theory is "exemplary in structure because he had a worked-out theory of knowledge, an ethical theory and a theory of human nature. No educational theory can be viable without these three major components" (Peters 1977, 120). Similarly, John White has pointed to the need for a supporting web of metaphysical beliefs for the ideal of liberal education, without which the ideal seems to be without foundation (1982, ch. 2). "Man is a metaphysical animal," Allen reminds us, and it is important that the study of education investigate the metaphysical dimensions that are an inescapable part of human education (1989, 168).

Peters and White have thus identified some of the fundamental questions that need to be answered in order to provide a reconstruction of the assumptions underlying the ideal of liberal education. Which metaphysics, which theory of human nature, which theory of knowledge, and which ethical theory do we accept as providing an adequate foundation for liberal education? I want to argue that there are some basic flaws in the way in which these questions have been answered in the past.

It is most important to note that a reconstruction is precisely that – a reconstruction – and not a complete destruction or rejection of the ideas and values underlying liberal education. My approach is very similar to that found in *Elements of a Post-Liberal Theory of Education* (Bowers 1987). Bowers very deliberately uses the word "post-liberal" to show that his theory has some connection with the past (vii). One could of course invent a new word for a new theory, as the scientists often do, but that would seem to be inappropriate here. With Bowers, I too am questioning many of the assumptions that are at the root of the Enlightenment ideal of liberal education. But I am not prepared to reject these assumptions entirely. Rather, I want to revise them.

I have argued that many of the ideas and values underlying liberal education have their roots in liberalism (chapter 2). Although, as should be evident from my own critique of liberal ideas and values, I agree with much of the communitarian critics of liberalism such as MacIntyre ([1981]1984), Sandel (1982), and Hauerwas (1983), I also agree with Amy Gutmann's major objection to these communitarian critics, when she maintains that they fall prey to "the tyranny of dualisms" (1985, 316-18). One does not have to choose between adopting *either* liberal *or* communitarian values because liberal values can be reconstructed so as to accommodate the important insights of the communitarian critics. Along with Gutmann, my objective is not to *replace* liberal ideas and values but to *improve* them (1985, 322). Given my approach, I am assuming, of course, some compatibility between liberal ideas and values and those of orthodox Christianity. I have in fact been arguing for such compatibility and will not say more here.[5]

Metaphysics

The contemporary ideal of liberal education first needs a new metaphysics or theory of reality. At the turn of the century there was no problem of justifying the possession or pursuit of knowledge for its own sake – a key element of the ideal of liberal education – because the dominant philosophy in Britain during this time was a version of Hegelian idealism (White 1982, 11-12). Men like T.H. Green and F. H. Bradley, who had a lasting influence on the shaping of the British national education system, based their ideas on a wider metaphysics. They believed in God, and their philosophy of education was rooted in a religious philosophy.

Similar considerations apply to another aspect of liberal education, namely the ideal of all-round development. R.S. Peters relates his analysis of the concept of education (i.e., the concept of liberal education) to the nineteenth-century notion of "educated," "as characterizing the all-round development of a person morally, intellectually, and spiritually" (Peters 1972, 9). Here again is the assumption that there is a spiritual dimension to human nature and to reality as a whole. Liberal education at various times in history allowed for a transcendent reality. In fact the ideal of liberal education was at times based on the premise that God exists.

However, as noted in chapter 2, western society has undergone a process of secularization which involves a gradual erosion of the influence of religious ideas and institutions on all aspects of society, culture, and thought. This process was related to the growth of science and the acceptance of the scientific ideal as the norm for all areas of thought, and it has influenced the ideal of liberal education. Hence the increasing reluctance to acknowledge that initiation into a particular religion might be an essential element of a liberal education. We see this, for example, in Peters's and Hirst's questioning whether religion is really a form of knowledge, and hence an acceptable part of the curriculum (Peters 1966, 155; Hirst 1974a, 180-8). We see this also in Peters's strange neglect of the spiritual dimension of liberal education even though this was included in his original description of liberal education as all-round development (see B.A. Cooper 1973).

If it is generally felt that God does not exist, then any aspect of education that might relate to God would obviously be viewed with suspicion. I suggest that much of the suspicion that surrounds Christian nurture is grounded in a naturalistic metaphysics. Charges of indoctrination against Christian nurture beg some important questions. Does God exist? Or, might he exist? It should therefore not surprise us that discussions of indoctrination are invariably coloured by strong anti-religious sentiments.

As I have argued, however, there are problems with the dogmatic empiricism that often underlies the scientific ideal and the secularist frame of mind. What I am proposing in my reconstruction of the ideal of liberal education is that we do not beg any metaphysical questions and that we therefore allow for the possibility of a broader metaphysics which acknowledges a transcendent reality. This is not at all to suggest that liberal education *must* include initiation into a particular religion. Secularists should certainly be free to fill the ideal of liberal education with secular content. I am only insisting that religious people be allowed similar privileges. I am therefore calling on liberals to be true to their liberalism and to avoid making dogmatic assumptions in defining the metaphysics underlying the ideal of a liberal education.

Human Nature

A revision of metaphysical assumptions will necessitate some revisions in the assumptions we make about human nature, the second dimension of educational theory that I have suggested needs some reconstruction. We have seen that Peters describes the nineteenth-century ideal of liberal education in terms of "the all-round development of a person morally, intellectually and spiritually" (1972, 9). Unfortunately, most analytic philosophers of education, including Peters and Hirst, have focused primarily on the intellectual dimension of education. Concerns about indoctrination too are expressed primarily in terms of a concern for human rationality (Snook 1972b, 108). It would therefore seem that these writers still hold to the Greek notion of reason as defining the essence of human nature. B.A. Cooper, for one, calls for a return to a fuller notion of human nature when he criticizes Peters who "seems to be so concerned with the intellectual dimension of education that he virtually ignores those other physical, emotional, and spiritual activities which together make up a comprehensive definition of man" (B.A. Cooper 1973, 61, cf. 71-2). Christian educators join Cooper in calling for a return to a broader conception of human nature which will also allow for the possibility of spiritual development as an essential component of liberal education (see also Plunkett 1990; Thiessen, 1991b).

Our conception of human nature not only needs to be fuller or broader but also more holistic. It is a grave error to think that we can abstract reason from the other components that make up human nature, as is done in most discussions of liberal education and indoctrination. Our rational nature is intimately bound up with the emotional, physical, moral, and spiritual aspects of who we are. And all these dimensions of our nature are in turn influenced by our history, both individual and social.

Related to this is the need to recognize human existence as "necessarily situated in a contingent historical, cultural and social context" (Allen 1982, 205). Communitarian critics of liberalism are particularly concerned to stress this point. Instead of autonomous individuals, atomistic selves, dislocated strangers, they prefer to see humans as defined in part by others, as attached to others, as essentially social beings (Sandel 1982). Education must therefore also be seen as essentially social in nature as Langford (1985) stresses. We are born into a particular home, a particular culture, a particular nation, and these define in part our loves, interests, and beliefs. And all of this particularity must be accepted as good, not necessarily something we need to be liberated from. In chapter 5, I dealt at length with a critique of the liberal ideal of autonomy and argued instead for an ideal of normal autonomy which does justice to the finiteness, contingency, and dependency of human nature. Here again it is necessary to be careful to avoid extremes. We need to find a balance between individualism and community, between independence and dependence.

Epistemology

The above redefinition of human nature will also have significant implications for one's epistemology. Beliefs and moral principles must not be seen as "chosen by lonely, autonomous agents in an emotionally empty state of rational reflection," but by those "who have some feeling of what it is to be a person among other persons" (O'Hear 1982, 127-8; cf. Code 1987, 8). Langford correctly makes the following observation: "What sets man above the rest of sensible beings, then, is not simply that he thinks, but that he thinks in accordance with a way of thinking which is both the product of and shared with many others" (Langford 1985, 168; cf. Code 1987, ch. 7). The contingency and dependency of human existence will also entail that we need to do justice to the human need for security in tradition and authority (Allen 1987). Of course there are dangers here, and therefore there is a need to emphasize some of the ingredients typically associated with liberal education, such as independent critical reflection. But this emphasis needs to be balanced by a proper regard for the limitations inherent in human nature.

As I noted in chapter 4, accounts of liberal education have generally been based on a foundationalist approach to epistemology, an approach which is increasingly being questioned by philosophers. This calls for a new definition of knowledge which in turn will have significant implications for our understanding of liberal education. Various writers have bemoaned the fact that these new developments in epistemology are not being reflected in the analysis of key educational concepts by philosophers of education (Page 1980, 37; Young 1984, 221; Laura and Leahy 1989, 255). Some early exceptions to this were the works by Soltis (1979) and Pring (1976). More recently there is the work of Young (1988), Laura and Leahy (1989), Cooling (1992), and Bowers (1987). Stephen Toulmin's *Cosmopolis*, [Cooling 1992] although not focusing specifically on education, points in the right direction by calling for a reconciliation between the epistemologies of modernism and post-modernism (1990, ch. 5). This is essentially the thrust also of Kimball's historical analysis of the idea of liberal education and his call for a restoring of the balance between the oratorical and liberal-free concepts of liberal education (1986, 240).

What is needed is an epistemology that recognizes that all observation is theory laden, and that theorizing is an incredibly complex process involving the justification of whole belief systems, rather than individual claims. Theorizing also depends on a host of ingredients such as concepts, observations, presuppositions, past theorizing, and present public agreement. Epistemology must also be seen as in part related to certain personal, social, historical, and material factors (Page 1980, 37, 141). We need an epistemology that stresses human fallibility and yet does not give up the notion of absolute truth as an ideal, as a regulative principle. Laura describes this as an epistemology of "fallibilistic realism" (1983, 46). We need an epistemology that acknowledges the creative tension that must exist between tradition and renewal, between authority and autonomy, between individual thought and community affirmation, between conviction and critical openness.

Values

I turn finally to the question of the values that underlie any theory of education, including my reconstruction of the ideal of liberal education. I have from the beginning stated that I am roughly in agree-

ment with the liberal values inherent in the ideal of liberal education, though some need to be qualified in important respects. I have
no quarrel with R.S. Peters's description of the normative aspect of
"education" (i.e., "liberal education") as implying "that something
worth while is being or has been intentionally transmitted in a morally acceptable manner" (1966, 25). I agree that knowledge and understanding are worthwhile, though one must be careful not to assume that knowledge and understanding in themselves will lead to
moral virtue and the salvation of society, as seems to be implied by
some advocates of liberal education. I wholeheartedly agree with the
intellectual virtues often associated with liberal education such as
truth-telling, courage in defending the truth, consistency, impartiality, tolerance, clarity, respect for evidence, respect for persons as
possible sources of points of view that may be right, and humility in
acknowledging that one may be in error. (see Crittenden 1972, 141;
Peters 1977, 131).

I agree with Peters that not only the content but also the manner
of education must be in accordance with the moral principles of liberty and respect for persons. Hence such processes as conditioning,
brainwashing, and indoctrination are ruled out as immoral (Peters
1966, 35-43). Obviously I differ as to what should count as indoctrination, but I agree that indoctrination, properly defined, is immoral.
I have also noted that we need a more sophisticated notion of the
principles of liberty and respect for persons. For example, it has
been argued that the ideal of autonomy, as usually understood by
the liberal, is indefensible, and hence must be revised as per my notion of "normal autonomy." We must also be careful not to put too
much value on autonomy, recognizing that there are other equally
important values such as dependence, love, goodwill, benevolence,
and harmony. But I do accept normal autonomy as one ideal among
others, and as a moral principle that needs to govern education.

I have from time to time also dealt with the difficult question of
the justification of these values. While I agree with some aspects of
the liberal justification of values, I feel that there needs to be a broadening of approach so as to include the possibility of utilitarian and
religious justifications. While I agree that these liberal values (properly qualified) must be viewed as absolute and universal in some
sense, I try to be careful to avoid the arrogance of treating one's own
interpretation of these values as the only correct one. There is a
sense in which values are in part historically conditioned, a point the
communitarian critics of liberalism stress. Much more would need to
be said to show how one can acknowledge this point without falling

into a vicious kind of relativism, but that is beyond the scope of this book (see Kaufman 1960).

One way to summarize the needed reconstruction of the assumptions underlying the ideal of liberal education is to refer again to the paradigm of the "normal." I have argued that the ideal of autonomy, one of the central values underlying the ideal of liberal education, needs to be qualified to that of normal autonomy so as to become philosophically defensible. I also argued for normal science, normal rationality, and normal critical openness, all of which have to do with a revision of the epistemological and normative assumptions underlying liberal education. Thus what is needed in this reconstruction is a normal epistemology which is especially sensitive to the limitations inherent in the human quest for knowledge. Some of the arguments for "normal science" also have metaphysical implications, and so it is possible also to talk of a need for normal metaphysics. This is appropriate in that a reference to the transcendent would indeed seem to be part of the normal outlook of human beings throughout the world (cf. Hudson 1973, 195). All these qualifications relate of course to human nature, and thus it would be appropriate also to say that liberal education needs to be based on a normal view of what it means to be a human being.

TWO CONCEPTS OR PHASES OF LIBERAL EDUCATION

The previous section looked at a reconstruction of the assumptions underlying the Enlightenment ideal of liberal education. We are now in a position to look at the ideal itself and to examine ways in which this ideal needs to be reconstructed. In the previous chapters, I have been uncovering various specific problems with the Enlightenment ideal of liberal education as expressed in making the charge of indoctrination. We now need to look more generally at the problems in the ideal of liberal education itself. Why the need for a reconstruction of this ideal? What is essentially wrong with the way in which educators, philosophers, and the informed public look at liberal education?

I suggest that the fundamental problem with present conceptions of liberal education is the failure to see that it is an abstraction. Again we have here the fallacy of mistaking the abstract for the concrete. Of course we cannot think without abstractions. But serious error will result from forgetting that we are dealing with an abstraction, and that is what has happened in our thinking about liberal education. Liberal education, as currently understood, is necessarily part of a much broader process; it is necessarily dependant on other occurrences. It is part of a larger whole, and we are fundamentally mistaken to pretend that liberal education is in itself the whole, that it can stand on its own. In other words, it is a mistake to treat a mere abstraction – liberal education – as though it were a concrete whole.

This can be illustrated by a description of liberal education which captures the essence of the way in which this ideal is currently understood. Charles Bailey describes liberal education as an education which liberalizes a person and moves him or her "beyond the present and the particular," a phrase that is used as the title of his book (1984). But Bailey does not address the question of how children get into the present and the particular in the first place. It is rather obvious that children must be initiated into a particular home, a particular language, a particular culture, a particular set of beliefs before they can begin to expand their horizons beyond the present and the particular. Liberal education is therefore necessarily parasitic on something else. It is not concrete and self-contained. It is an abstraction from a larger whole, and to forget this leads to endless confusions such as noted in the previous chapters.

R.S. Peters writes of a suggestion made by Oxford philosopher, Richard Hare, "that many of the dark places in ethics might be illuminated if philosophers would address themselves to considering the question 'How should I bring up my children?' " (Peters 1973a, 38). This advice is equally applicable to the area of education. Many of the confusions with regard to liberal education would be overcome if philosophers would seriously address the question: How should I educate my two-year-old child at home? It is only if we honestly face the question of educating young children that we will begin to see the whole picture. It is only if we acknowledge that a child's education begins on day one, and that initiation into the language, beliefs, and values of a culture is an essential part of education, that we will begin to see that liberal education is an abstraction from a larger whole.

It is revealing to see how philosophers and educationists tend to look at the early education of the child. One tendency is to introduce a host of different words to describe the early years of a child's "education": "socialization" or even "cognitive socialization," "enculturization," "transmission," "initiation," providing a child with the "preconditions of education," etc. (Kazepides 1982, 157, 160, 161). Any word is used except the word "education." It is further generally thought that what goes on in socialization or enculturization is very different from education. It is therefore felt that we must keep the concept of education sharply distinguished from these other concepts. For example, Kazepides warns against the strategem of the advocates of religious indoctrination who "relax the criteria of education so as to render it indistinguishable from that hazy, all-embracing and confusing term 'socialisation' " (1982, 156).

Other writers do use the word "education" in relation to a child's early years of learning, but they then contrast this type of education with another kind of education, that is, true liberal education. This contrast has been made repeatedly and perhaps most forcefully by the eminent British philosopher of education, Paul H. Hirst (1974b, 1981, 1985). Hirst refers to the "primitive or traditionalist concept of education" which is merely concerned with "the transmission of a body of specific concepts, beliefs, values, skills and so on within a particular tradition" (1985, 6-7, 16). The second, "much more sophisticated view of education," according to Hirst, is by contrast "concerned with passing on beliefs and practices according to their objective status and with their appropriate justification. It is dominated by a concern for knowledge, for truth, for reason, distinguishing these clearly from belief, conjecture, and subjective preference" (1981, 86). This second concept of education clearly refers to the ideal of liberal education whose central aim is the development of rational autonomy and critical openness. Hirst stresses that these two concepts of education are "quite different," operating on "different principles," each resting on "a distinctive view of the foundation of knowledge and belief," and thus they should be kept separate and distinct (1974b, 79, 89; 1985, 6). There is also a strong evaluative component in this contrast between the "primitive concept" and the "much more sophisticated view of education." The first concept is associated with indoctrination and a ghetto mentality; it is opposed to rationality and autonomy, and hence must be viewed as "inadequate," "anti-educational," committed to goals that can only be described as "improper, even sub-human" (Hirst 1981, 87, 92; 1985, 7, 10, 15).[6]

There are a host of problems with this contrast between these two concepts of education, or with the contrast between socialization and education. I can only highlight a few of them.[7] The first has to do with the strongly pejorative overtones ascribed to the traditionalist concept of education or to the socialization of the young. Hirst's traditionalist concept of education clearly applies to the home because it is here that we have a paradigm case of transmitting beliefs and values from a particular tradition. In fact Hirst says as much (1974b, 90). But we need to pay careful heed to precisely what is being said here. What Hirst is really saying is that the process of a one-year-old child's absorbing or being taught the language, values, beliefs of her or his parents is "primitive," "improper, even subhuman." He is saying that, because the child is being brought up in a particular home, with particular beliefs and particular values, what goes on in the home is "ghetto-istic" and "anti-educational." This frankly is extreme, if not absurd. Far from being sub-human, education in the home is the process by which a child becomes fully human. This was the great insight of Emile Durkheim who saw that, in an important sense, education *must* be socialization. All education is centrally concerned with developing children's minds and this development is largely a social matter (P.A. White 1972, 113). It is a matter, as Oakeshott has said, of helping children to take possession of their human inheritance – an inheritance of feelings, thoughts, beliefs, values, languages, works of art, books, and so forth, in short, what Dilthey called "a geistige Welt" (Oakeshott 1967, 158). To enter this inheritance "is the only way of becoming human, and to inhabit it is to be a human being" (Oakeshott 1967, 158). So, far from being "sub-human," education in the home is essential to becoming human. Far from being "anti-educational," the initial process of socialization captures the essence of education. Far from being "ghetto-istic," it is essential for a child to acquire a particular language, a particular culture, and a particular outlook. Far from being "primitive," the child's initial education involves a sophistication bordering on the miraculous, as anyone reflecting on the complexity of learning a language will acknowledge.

Another problem with attempts to drive a sharp wedge between socialization and liberal education or between a traditionalist and a sophisticated concept of liberal education is that the distinctions invariably become blurred. Education in the home is never quite so irrational as liberal educators describe it. As any parent knows, the young child is curious, constantly asking questions and demanding reasons. And liberal education is never quite so rational and open as liberal educators tend to describe it. Tradition and authority play an important part in scientific education, which is often seen as the paradigm of a liberal education. Hirst's sharp distinction between knowledge, truth, and reason, on the one hand, and belief, conjecture, and subjective preference, on the other, is philosophically suspect and simply not so neat and tidy as he would have us believe (1981, 86). Moreover, this distinction's being at the heart of Hirst's contrast between his two concepts of education calls the contrast into question. Much of the argumentation of the previous chapters serves to further blur the distinctions that are so dear to liberal educators.

The fundamental problem with the distinction between socialization and liberal education is that liberal education necessarily depends on this very socialization or the traditionalist kind of education. Children can learn to be critical only if they have first been given something to be critical about. Liberal education, as typically understood, can only become a reality if children have already acquired a language, together with the host of concepts, values, and feelings that are necessarily part of learning a language. The development of the mind is very much a social event, or, as Oakeshott puts it, a "transaction between the generations" – a transaction "in which newcomers are initiated into an inheritance of human achievements of understanding and belief" (1972, 22). Page draws on this point and applies it to the ideal of autonomy: "To socialize a person is therefore a necessary part of helping that person to think at all, much less to 'think for himself.' Autonomy requires socialization" (Page 1980, 149). Liberal education is therefore dependent on socialization (the transmission of beliefs and values), and those who try to drive a wedge between these two notions are invariably forced to admit the relation (see Hirst 1974b, 83; Kazepides 1982, 160; P.A. White 1972, 113-4).

How then do we reconstruct the ideal of liberal education? The central requirement is to develop a more holistic understanding of liberal education which addresses the question of how children are first educated, and which includes this dimension of education as an essential component of liberal education. We need to look at the primitive traditionalist approach to education and contemporary notions of liberal education, not as two radically different concepts of education, but rather as two equally important and necessary phases of a broader and more inclusive concept of liberal education. It is necessary to recognize that socialization is an essential component of liberal education. Nurture must be acknowledged as the cradle of liberal education (Watson 1987, 9).

I suggest that thinking in terms of two phases instead of two concepts of education involves a significant shift in understanding. To speak of two concepts of education suggests separateness, differences, whereas to speak of two phases suggests continuity. This reconstruction will also force us to look at the development of critical rational thought not as completely different from the transmission of values and beliefs in childhood but as building onto such transmission. The two-phase approach will also make us evaluate the early transmissionist component of education very differently – not as primitive, inadequate, improper, sub-human, but as healthy and a positive necessary dimension of becoming human. Education in the home will now be looked at not as something the child needs to be liberated from, but as something we need to build on as the child matures. University professors will now be seen not as practising "a kind of intellectual colonialism as they set about their task of rescuing the natives from their ignorance and savagery" but as building on the student's past learning, of stretching the student's horizons, "without at the same time destroying the student's roots or his sense of self" (Silberman 1970, 394).

It is curious that the philosophical writings I have been considering contain hints of this new way of understanding liberal education. Hirst, for example, admits that "education must start within some system of beliefs" (1985, 13). He also suggests that the two concepts of education can be seen as complementing each other, though this clearly contradicts his overall description of them as radically different and opposed (1974b, 89-90).

R.S. Peters comes even closer to my reconceptualization of liberal education when he suggests that education needs to be described in terms of initiation (1965, 102-110; 1966, ch. 2). However, there seems to be a definite break in his treatment of the three criteria of education, which parallel the more typical understanding of liberal education, and his treatment of education as initiation, even though the latter follows immediately after the former. He simply does not provide us with an account of how these two rather different descriptions of liberal education can be combined into a coherent whole. Peters also, unfortunately, tends to forget his description of education as initiation, relying almost entirely on his other more standard description of liberal education which, he later confesses, leads to various ambiguities and dilemmas he cannot resolve (1977, 84-5, 66-7).

Peters follows Oakeshott in describing education as initiation. He maintains that education involves the development of the mind, and such development is "the product of the *initiation* of an individual into public traditions enshrined in the language, concepts, beliefs and rules of a society" (1966, 49; emphasis mine). The child must be initiated into "a public inheritance" so as to get the barbarian outside the gate inside "the citadel of civilization" (Peters 1965, 107). He even criticizes those who see education as more concerned with critical thinking than with the transmission of a body of knowledge. Critical thought without content is vacuous, Peters argues, and besides, it is absurd to think that critical procedures can be handed on without content (1966, 53-4).

We see here that education (i.e., liberal education), for Peters, necessarily includes a transmissionist component. Rationality and critical thinking can only be developed *after* initiation into certain content. And he is quite clear that such initiation depends on learning by example, and involves mechanisms of imitation and identification (1977, 83; cf. 1966, 60). In other words, there are non-rational elements in the process of initiation. Various other writers have had to concede that there is a non-rational transmissionist, instructional, informational component to liberal education (Passmore 1967; Oakeshott 1967).

Ackerman (1980), clearly writing from a liberal perspective, is perhaps even clearer in facing the problem of the unique status of children in his treatment of liberal education. Ackerman argues that children need a stable and coherent "primary culture" and that this is a precondition of their subsequent development into autonomous liberal citizens. In Chapter 5 I reviewed the findings in developmental psychology which provide abundant support for this claim.[8] This need for a stable and coherent primary culture suggests that children must be exposed neither to too many ideas nor to too much uncertainty too soon.

While an infant may learn English or Urdu or both, there are limits to the cultural diversity he can confront without losing a sense of the meanings that the noises and motions might ultimately signify. Exposing the child to an endless and changing Babel of talk and behaviour will only prevent the development of the abilities he requires if he is ever to take his place among the citizenry. (Ackerman 1980, 141)

Ackerman further points out that this need for a stable and coherent primary culture gradually loses force as the child develops "dialogic competence" and the ability to face challenges to the primary culture without becoming disoriented. Indeed, Ackerman maintains that parents have a responsibility not only to take the natural questioning on the part of child seriously but also to provide the child with "a liberal education – with cultural equipment that permits the child to criticise, as well as affirm, parental ideals" (117). This is clear affirmation of the need for a developmental understanding of liberal education. Ackerman sees that the transition from the initiation phase to the critical reflective phase of liberal education is a gradual one. He does not provide a definite answer as to how much cultural coherence and stability is needed at the various stages of a child's development, but he assumes that all would agree that *some* is needed. There further seems to be evidence suggesting that the need for some coherence and stability continues even into adulthood.[9]

I am here only providing a sketch of a reformulation of the ideal of liberal education. Sketches by their very nature require oversimplifications and generalizations. For example, in arguing for a stable and coherent primary culture for a child, I have been assuming the typical child. Clearly there are exceptional children for whom this requirement might not be so stringent. In general, though, children do require a degree of stability and coherence. I have also been talking primarily about two phases of liberal education. Again this is an oversimplication. Clearly, these two phases need to be broken down into several more phases, taking into account the work of Jean Piaget and other developmental theorists (see Crittenden 1988, 89-92). For my purposes here, however, I can simplify and speak broadly of only two phases of liberal education – initiation and liberation. I will provide a little more detail on stages of development in the next section.

One objection to this reconstruction of the concept of liberal education must be considered. Kazepides (1982, 1983, 1989) has been most insistent in objecting to both the association of education with socialization and the use of the initiation metaphor. He accuses people who try to make such associations of having a "programmatic intent," of "seeking to alter the meaning of 'education' for some hidden purposes," and of being "politically motivated" (Kazepides 1982, 156, 160, 161; 1989). What, according to Kazepides, are the supposed nefarious intentions underlying attempts to associate education with socialization or initiation? The intentions belong to people "who blindly or wickedly support ignominious social orders, institutions or policies" (1982, 159). They belong to people who are trying to defend programs of religious and political indoctrination. According to Kazepides, there seems to be "no limit to the arbitrary, absurd and dangerous suggestions" that people make when governed by such hidden agendas (1982, 164).

I have deliberately quoted Kazepides at some length in order to give the reader a feeling for the kind of language that colours his argument. It is evident that we have here an unfortunate example of an *ad hominem* argument. It is never, never appropriate, in doing philosophy, to speculate about the intentions or the motivations that lie behind an argument. Obviously anyone, including Kazepides, has certain motivations for providing an argument, but these are entirely irrelevant to the evaluation of the argument itself. The inflammatory language and the vehemence with which Kazepides states his opposition to religious nurture is not only "faintly ridiculous" as Hudson notes, but a tragic betrayal of the standards of good philosophical argument as well as a failure to live up to the liberal and Christian ideal of tolerance (Hudson 1982, 172).

Much of Kazepides's argument rests on an examination of the way in which words such as "education," "socialization," and "initiation" function but, as is typical of so many analytical philosophers, he assumes that language is more precise than it is. Various counter-examples to Kazepides's specific linguistic arguments have been provided elsewhere and will not be reviewed here (Hudson 1982, 168-9; Thiessen, 1985b, 231-3). However, it should be noted that, at times, it almost seems that his argument rests on the false assumption that, because "education," "socialization," and "initiation" are different words, they must have three different meanings. But different words can surely be used to describe the same phenomenon.

The fundamental problem with Kazepides's argument is that, while he wants to object to any attempts to associate the concept of education with the concepts of socialization or initiation, he is forced to concede that there must be some sort of connection: "One cannot be overimpressed by the extent to which particular societies and social groups determine the way the young come to think, feel, relate to people, evaluate things and express themselves" (1982, 157). He even allows for "cognitive socialization" (163). Moreover, he admits that some aspects of the process of socialization do have educational significance, for example, learning to speak, which should be described as providing the "preconditions of education" (160). "Like any other high-level intellectual engagement, education has its prerequisite foundation; and the acquisition of this foundation is the result of primary socialization – not the result of education" (1989, 389). In these statements, Kazepides is clearly acknowledging that education (liberal education) requires initiation or socialization as its foundation. He wants to say that this is not part of education, but this exclusion is surely arbitrary. Providing children with "the riverbed of our thought," that is, the logical and methodological prerequisites for rational thinking, surely should be seen as a necessary and hence an essential part of education (1989, 394-5). It is true that the acquiring of this foundational equipment is best described in terms of an "apprenticeship model" in which one learns by imitation, but this in itself is no reason to divorce such apprenticeship from true education (1989, 389-90). Instead, apprenticeship into the language and the modes of thought and action of the older generation is foundational to, and hence an essential part of, education. One can arbitrarily define education so as to exclude socialization and initiation, but this is to create an abstraction from a larger whole. Unfortunately, Kazepides forgets that socialization and initiation are abstractions.

The arbitrariness and inconsistency of Kazepides's argument can be illustrated in another way. In a description of his concept of education, he makes the following claim:

To be educated is *not merely* to have acquired certain skills, habits, beliefs, attitudes and values that are deemed desirable or useful by the particular social group to which a person belongs or by the larger society; *it is rather* to have one's mind and character disciplined by the logic and the standards of excellence immanent in the various disciplines of thought and actions as we know them today. (Kazepides 1982, 156; emphasis mine)

I have highlighted the words "not merely" and "it is rather" to emphasize a basic logical error made by Kazepides (see Hudson 1982, 168). To say that education is *not merely* initiation or socialization suggests that it is *more than* just initiation or socialization. But Kazepides's additional requirement for education – having one's mind and character shaped by the logic and standards of excellence immanent in various disciplines of thought – is not given as *an addition to*, but rather as an *alternative to*, these requirements of socialization and initiation. To be educated, according to Kazepides, *is rather* to have one's mind and character shaped by the logic and standards of excellence immanent in various disciplines of thought. But there is no need to provide an alternative definition of education because Kazepides's two concepts of education are much better seen as two phases of the ideal of liberal education, as he himself acknowledges again and again.

I contend that to say that education is "not merely" socialization is to suggest that socialization is at least one part of education. Kazepides quotes a similar statement from R.S. Peters as support for his own position. "I am constantly irritated," says Peters, "by having my view of education represented [baldly] as just involving 'initiation' into worthwhile activities" (Kazepides 1982, 162).[10] But Peters includes initiation as a necessary condition of education. He is objecting only to any misrepresentations of his writings which would make initiation alone a sufficient condition of education. This captures the heart of my own reconstruction of the ideal of liberal education, and this is also what Kazepides is saying in the first statement quoted above.

In fact, when Kazepides refers to the logic and standards of excellence immanent in the various disciplines of thought and action *as we know them today*, he is inadvertently suggesting that his "pure" ideal of education is, in effect, relative to today's standards. This sounds suspiciously like the social science definition of education which he is so vigorously opposing (see Hudson 1982, 171). Any conception of liberal education will necessarily have to make reference to what is generally accepted in a society. Even our notion of rationality cannot, as noted in previous chapters, avoid reference to what is generally accepted in a society. Of course, we must include objective truth as an ideal, a heuristic principle, but we must never be so vain as to assume that our present understanding of truth has the status of objective truth. This is the error of people like Kazepides who assume that their own understanding of the standards of excellence immanent in the various disciplines of thought and action is the only possible and correct one.

In fact, as Hudson notes, Kazepides's own understanding of these standards is rooted in a very specific world-view: the doctrinal outlook of scientific humanism.

[Kazepides] has persuasively redefined 'education' (or 'educated') so that it excludes everything he is going on to deride as 'socialisation' and includes only such ways of thought and evaluation as are comprehended within the scientific humanism of which he approves. The object of the exercise is to convince us that this is what 'education' really means as contrasted with indoctrination. But it is, of course, a patent, if unwitting, attempt at indoctrination itself. (Hudson 1982, 168)

I have argued in this section that the concept of liberal education, as typically understood in educational writings, is in need of a major overhaul. To describe the unifying idea behind various conceptions of liberal education as "that of the unimpeded and unconstrained development of the mind," as does Peters, at times, is unrealistic because it assumes absolute freedom (Peters 1977, 46, 48). The development of the mind always occurs within the context of a particular tradition and culture. To think of liberal education in terms of an education which liberalizes is incomplete. Liberalize from what? To characterize the essence of liberal education in terms of helping a person to move "beyond the present and the particular," as does Bailey in the title of his book, raises the question of how we get into the present and the particular in the first place (Bailey 1984). To characterize the present and the particular as "limitations" from which we need to be liberated begs some important questions. Why should the present and the particular be viewed in such a pejorative light? What is needed is a reconstruction of the prevailing Enlightenment ideal of liberal education, a reconstruction which recognizes the initiation into the present and the particular as healthy, as a necessary preliminary to the broadening of one's horizons. Drawing on the notion of "normality" used throughout, I feel that what is needed is a normal holistic ideal of liberal education which incorporates both the unavoidable initiation phases and the "liberating" phases of education. The early stages of a child's education are never completely superseded; "rather they are, ideally speaking, caught up in and transformed by the next stage" (Peters 1973b, 136). What is needed is a developmental understanding of liberal education. In short, what is needed is the recognition that teaching for commitment is a foundational phase of liberal education.

Another dimension of the needed reconstruction of the ideal of liberal education concerns its inevitable institutional context which was dealt with in chapter 7. To think of liberal education apart from institutions is again an abstraction. What is required is a consideration of the nature of liberal education as it occurs in institutions such as the family, schools, and universities. I suggested in chapter 7 that a monolithic state system of education can hardly be described as very liberal. Since I will argue in the next chapter that a pluralistic school system is a fundamental requirement of a liberal system of education. I will not pursue it any further here.

TOWARD A RECONSTRUCTION OF A THEORY OF INDOCTRINATION

Given the above proposal for a reconstruction of the ideal of liberal education, it is now possible to look at a reconstruction of the notion of indoctrination. The charge of indoctrination, as we have seen, grows out of the Enlightenment ideal of liberal education. The latter provides the context for the former. Indoctrination is commonly understood as a violation of the criteria of liberal education. We should therefore expect that a reconstruction of the foundational ideal of liberal education will necessitate a reconstruction of the notion of indoctrination.

Before beginning this task, I wish to mention some limitations to my attempt to reconstruct the theory of indoctrination, as well as the parameters within which this discussion will take place. My aim is not to present a careful analysis of the concept of indoctrination in terms of logically necessary and sufficient conditions. There would seem to be a growing recognition that language simply is not precise enough to enable philosophers to fit analysis into a "logically tight straitjacket" (see chapter 1). Given the theory-ladenness of language, it would seem more appropriate to aim for a "theory of indoctrination," rather than an analysis of the concept of indoctrination. Hence the modest title of Ralph Page's dissertation, "Some Requirements for a Theory of Indoctrination" (1980). Hence also the modesty of my attempt merely to make some suggestions about how indoctrination might best be understood.

I reiterate that I am attempting a reconstruction of our understanding of indoctrination. It might well be that past philosophical analyses of "indoctrination" reflect the way in which this word is used in ordinary language. But ordinary language "should never be treated as a repository of unquestionable wisdom," as even Peters and Hirst recognize (1970, 8). And, as J.L. Austin has observed, the ordinary language which helps us to understand one another may also be "infected with jargon of extinct theories" (1964, 47). I have attempted to show that our present understanding of indoctrination is indeed infected with the jargon of a liberal theory of education that needs to be at least revised. Further, while I have identified some aspects of the theory of liberal education that need revision, I have by no means completed this task. Hence again the incompleteness of the present task. Given the pervasiveness of the present understanding of "indoctrination," it would be unwise to propose too radical a reconstruction of the concept or theory of indoctrination. I will therefore make my suggestions relate as closely as possible to past analyses of the concept of indoctrination – analyses which have attempted to capture the meaning of this word as used in ordinary language.

While there is a danger in beginning the reconstruction of the theory of indoctrination with an attempt to provide a short description or "definition" of indoctrination, it will nonetheless help to provide a focus for the remaining discussion which attempts to sketch a theory of indoctrination. I would suggest that the core idea of indoctrination be thought of as *the curtailment of a person's growth towards normal rational autonomy.*[11]

Several things should immediately be noted about my short description of indoctrination lest it be misinterpreted. No reference is made here to a teacher because I believe indoctrination can occur in a host of ways, some of which do not involve teachers or a classroom context. It is furthermore most important to note the qualifier "normal" before "rational autonomy." This is intended to draw attention to all the qualifications I have made to the Enlightenment ideal of rational autonomy in order to overcome the problems I found with this ideal. It should also be noted that I am not making reference to "normal science" and "normal critical openness," dealt with in chapters 3 and 6 respectively, as these ideals are really implicit in the notion of rational autonomy. There is, in any case, considerable overlap in these notions, and making reference simply to normal rational autonomy helps to simplify the treatment. My short description of indoctrination also makes reference to *growth* toward normal rational autonomy, such reference being made to highlight the importance of the development of the mind. I will therefore argue for a developmental view of indoctrination. I now want to consider some aspects of this revised notion of indoctrination in more detail.

My proposal to think of indoctrination as the curtailment of the growth of a person towards normal rational autonomy focuses on people rather propositions. Page has highlighted the remarkable agreement of analytic philosophers that indoctrination involves the "shaping of beliefs," and that beliefs should be construed in terms of propositions (1979, 77; 1980, 28-41).

By emphasizing the shaping of belief, and construing belief in strictly propositional ways, these philosophers tend to view indoctrination as essentially an *epistemological* issue where epistemology is conceived as essentially distinct from psychological or sociological conditions under which beliefs develop. The disagreements about the proper analysis of the concept of indoctrination become essentially disagreements about the proper justification of propositions. (Page 1980, 35)

Page, along with several other writers, suggests that the problems in past discussions of indoctrination will only be solved if we give up this epistemological focus (Young 1988). The suggestion here is that, when we talk about indoctrination, we change our focus from the shaping of belief to the shaping of the believer. Instead of arguing about the proper way to justify propositions in abstraction from persons, we need to focus on whole persons, whose believing and whose approach to justifying beliefs is intimately bound up with their history, the sociological context in which they live, their psychological make up, and so forth.

In changing our focus in this way, it is important to note further that indoctrination does not involve only a manipulation of a person's mind or reason (which tends to be the emphasis of past analyses) but rather a manipulation of the *whole* person. Our minds and the ways in which we reason are intimately related to our whole being – our past, our social connections, our feelings, our physical well-being. This would suggest that the usual distinction between indoctrination, conditioning, brainwashing, and physical coercion is less sharp than has generally been assumed.[12]

Despite the interrelationships of these concepts, and despite the need to consider the whole person, I believe it is appropriate to link the term "indoctrination" centrally with the mind – as long as it is remembered that this is an abstraction, and as long as it is remembered that the mind is affected by the other dimensions of human make-up. Once this is acknowledged, it needs to be underscored that my reconstructed theory of indoctrination links the notion of indoctrination centrally to the hampering of the *development* of the mind. As well, it is important to contrast this with past treatments of indoctrination in which there is a tendency to think of the mind as a static entity, or when development is acknowledged, to judge whether "a person's development has been oppressively controlled by 'fixed' epistemological standards" (Page 1980, 154).

Several aspects of this developmental understanding need to be briefly underscored. The development of the mind, at its early stages, requires socialization, initiation, or the acquiring of a primary culture, as was discussed in the previous section. It is therefore a fundamental error to associate these early stages of the development of the child with indoctrination (understood pejoratively), on the grounds that such initiation is non-rational and that there is a lack of critical openness. It is precisely here that past treatments of indoctrination have foundered. It is fundamentally wrongheaded to associate the initiation or socialization phase of the development of a child's mind with indoctrination, because a child requires a stable and coherent primary culture as a foundation for further development. The development of a child's mind necessarily begins within the context of a particularity, and it is simply mistaken to associate the particularity of such an upbringing with indoctrination as Callan (1985), among others, has recently done.

A developmental approach to our understanding of indoctrination will further entail that the meaning of the term will change as a child matures. A full theory of indoctrination would therefore require a detailed theory of cognitive development, a task which is clearly beyond the scope of my objectives here. Roughly, I would suggest the following as an outline of a developmental view of indoctrination: we begin with an initiation phase which is necessarily narrow, non-rational and "coercive" in the sense that children simply cannot decide which particular culture, language, and so on they will be initiated into. The all-important process of acquiring a language, together with the host of beliefs and values implicit in a language, is essentially a non-rational process. As children mature, they begin to ask questions, and these need to be encouraged and taken seriously. But what children want are answers, not doubts, and it is as absurd as it is cruel to treat children at this stage with a heavy dose of "critical thinking." Two-year-olds are simply not graduate students in philosophy! It is this initiation phase which provides the necessary foundation for further development. Or, to use another image, nurture is the "cradle" of education (Watson 1987, 9).

After the initiation or nurture phase of children's development, there should be a gradual opening-up phase where they are exposed to other influences, other beliefs, though still from the vantage point of the tradition into which they were first initiated. To fail to encourage this opening-up phase should be labelled indoctrination. Still later, perhaps at adolescence, young people should be encouraged to begin to reflect critically on the traditions into which they were first initiated. Maturing individuals should also be taught to reflect critically on the alternative traditions, past and present. At a final stage, vigorous critically reflective skills are developed, though, even here, the extreme of "critical skepticism," which even Hirst recognizes as a danger, should be avoided (Hirst 1985, 13). The notion of indoctrination will therefore change from one stage to another.

These stages should not be viewed as absolute or as precisely defined. Obviously, there is overlap and gradual transition from one phase to the next. It is important to note that, throughout these stages, there will always be some degree of nurture or a traditionalist approach to learning and education, as we can never dispense entirely with the need for some security, the acceptance of socially constructed knowledge, and an appeal to authority. Here again the paradigms of normal rationality and normal autonomy come into play in order to make us realistic in our expectations of how much growth is possible. It would seem, though, that growth toward reflective and independent thinking should be ideally accompanied by a lessening dependence on the traditionalist approach to learning and education. Any attempt to increase rather than lessen dependence on the traditionalist approach to learning and education should be called indoctrination.

It should further be remembered that cognitive development will vary from person to person. Hence, what is an indoctrinative practice for one child might not be for another. The suggestion of a developmental understanding of indoctrination introduces a variety of empirical considerations about what will best foster growth toward reflective and independent thought, and thus no philosophical argument alone can determine what is or is not indoctrination at the various stages of development.

So far, I have focused on growth and development in my reconstruction of the theory of indoctrination. What goal, what end result, does indoctrination frustrate? Indoctrination hinders growth towards normal rationality. Clearly normal rationality incorporates some elements of the traditional liberal ideal of rationality such as an understanding of the various forms of knowledge, a concern for evidence for beliefs held, and the acquiring of intellectual virtues like critical openness. However, the qualifier "normal" is added to show that the conception of rationality has been modified so as to overcome some of the problems of the traditional conception of rationality as discussed in earlier chapters. Normal rationality acknowledges the focus on persons rather than propositions as discussed in the previous section of this chapter. It also recognizes the limitations inherent in our attempts to achieve objective rationality. It acknowledges that the human pursuit of knowledge, based largely on the five senses, might not exhaust all there is to know. There might be more to reality than empirical reality. Normal rationality recognizes that justification of beliefs, while important, is intimately linked with the psychological and sociological conditions under which beliefs develop. In addition it is sensitive to the need for human beings to have convictions, while at the same time recognizing the need for some degree of critical openness about these convictions. Normal rationality acknowledges that growth towards reflective, critical, and independent thought necessarily takes place within the context of "a convictional community" (Halstead 1986, 50-1). Indoctrination therefore involves the hampering of growth toward this ideal of normal rationality.

Indoctrination, in my reconstructed model, also involves the failure to encourage growth toward normal autonomy. The necessary limitations in my ideal of autonomy must be kept in mind if we want an ideal that is philosophically defensible. We are not aiming for absolute autonomy which is an empty ideal. Normal autonomy recognizes the importance of a certain level of dependence on others in normal human relationships. It acknowledges that growth toward autonomy necessarily begins within a contingent historical context. Normal autonomy also allows for the possibility that one may choose to submit to another person, even to God. What is important is that there be a degree of procedural independence in making this decision of substantive dependence. Indoctrination stops growth toward such procedural independence and limited autonomy.

I earlier examined some psychological factors that need to be taken into account in my reconstruction of the notion of indoctrination. It is also necessary to take into account some sociological factors. Indoctrination cannot simply be conceived in terms of the frustration of the development of normal rational autonomy within the individual psyche, because such development is very much a social process. We must therefore look at the sociological and institutional context within which individual development takes place – a theme which was explored in chapter 7. It has been argued that knowledge is in part socially constructed. All human beings, including the liberal minded, need "plausibility structures" in order to maintain some level of credibility for the beliefs they accept as true (Berger & Luckmann [1966]1967, 154-63). Thus it is fundamentally mistaken to associate the existence of institutions *per se* with indoctrination. We need to examine, instead, the character of these institutions. Is there growth of reflective thought within the institution as such? Is there a certain *degree* of freedom within the institution (realizing that complete freedom is impossible)? Is there a creative tension between the necessary constraints of the institution as a whole and the adult individual within that institution? Is there freedom for creative thinkers, innovators, and leaders? Here the institution of science is, I believe justifiably, often lauded as being exemplary in terms of encouraging independent thinking. What is forgotten is that powerful constraints are imposed on individual thinking and research even within the scientific community, and it is simply mistaken to associate these constraints automatically with indoctrination (see p. 82).

I suggested in chapter 7 that past treatments of indoctrination have been particularly weak in recognizing the sociological and institutional dimensions of definitions of knowledge and education. Much more work needs to be done in this area, and my treatment of this aspect of a reconstructed theory of indoctrination is at best very sketchy. It should be stressed, though, that indoctrination must not be thought of as occurring only within educational institutions. We also need to look at the influences of society as a whole on the development of the mind of its children. We need to look at the powerful influences of television and the other media in shaping our thinking. We need to look at advertizing and the kind of narrow world-view this imposes on its often unwary subjects. We need to look at propaganda, especially if Ellul is correct in arguing that propaganda is inevitable and even necessary for modern democratic society (1969). It is in fact the possibility of providing a broader and more complete illumination of a variety of contemporary issues such as these which, according to Page, suggests some advantages of this reconstructed theory of indoctrination over past work on this concept (1980, 164-73).

The psychological and sociological aspects of the reconstruction of the theory of indoctrination also have implications for a reconstruction of the epistemology of indoctrination. I have already dealt with the problem of conceiving of indoctrination primarily in epistemological terms, as has been the case in analytical treatments of this concept heretofore. Indoctrination is not primarily concerned with beliefs, but with believers as persons. While it is important for persons to hold beliefs with proper regard for their justification, such justification must be understood as being intimately linked with the psychological and sociological conditions under which beliefs develop. This, of course, adds to the complexity of the notion of indoctrination, but one of the basic problems of past analyses of "indoctrination" is that they rested on a simplistic and what is increasingly recognized as an antiquated epistemology.

It should finally be noted that indoctrination is very much a matter of degree. Charges of indoctrination are far too often made as though indoctrination were an all-or-nothing affair. Persons, institutions, and practices are simply condemned in a wholesale fashion. But surely there are degrees of indoctrination, especially given a developmental approach to understanding this concept. All charges of indoctrination should therefore be coupled with some indication of the severity of indoctrination.

I conclude this section by reviewing the relationship of my reconstruction of the theory of indoctrination to the four criteria traditionally associated with "indoctrination." It needs to be stressed that the alignment of a *theory* of indoctrination with past analyses of a *concept* of indoctrination will at best be very loose since the approaches are very different.

It is interesting to note that some of the key ideas in my proposed theory of indoctrination are already present in a paper written by R.M. Hare in 1964, a paper which was one of the first to spark the interest of ordinary language philosophers in the concept of indoctrination. Hare maintains that "indoctrination only begins when we are trying to stop the growth in our children of the capacity to think for themselves" (1964, 52). This emphasis on growth is captured again when Hare goes on to say that "the educator is trying to turn children into adults; the indoctrinator is trying to make them into perpetual children" (69). Hare himself rejected the possibility of defining indoctrination in terms of method or content and suggested shifting the focus to purpose or aim (50). My proposed theory of indoctrination can therefore be seen to include elements of concern that have been raised by those writers who have wanted to define indoctrination in terms of intentions. Clearly we can and should be concerned about the intentions of any teachers (advertisers, politicians), and if we find no evidence of their aiming toward some growth in reflective and independent thinking on the part of their students, then we might be justified to charge them with a degree of indoctrination.

My proposed theory of indoctrination, along with Hare's original proposal, includes implicit reference to consequences. The result of indoctrination is to stop growth towards normal rational autonomy. We do not want students (consumers, voters) to end up with closed minds, though this can really only be assessed in the light of people's intellectual capacities, previous and ongoing development, and the environment in which they live. Closed minds must also not be identified with having convictions, even strong convictions, as I argued in chapter 6. Only if individuals fail to exercise *normal* rational autonomy can we begin to suspect that they might have been subjected to a degree of indoctrination.

Does indoctrination involve the use of certain methods of teaching or influencing people? Yes, teaching methods which stop growth towards normal rational autonomy should be labelled indoctrinatory. But what teaching methods do this? As I argued in chapter 4, we cannot simply identify the use of non-rational teaching methods as indoctrinatory. Drill, rote memory, and learning from authority all have a legitimate and necessary role in education, especially at the initiation phase, as long as these are part of an over-all process of development toward normal rational autonomy. But obviously, if a teacher of a class of fifteen-year-old students cultivates excessive reliance on his or her authority, if this teacher teaches only by drill and rote memory and fails to allow students to question what is being taught, then this teacher will be stopping growth toward normal rational autonomy, and hence should be charged with a degree of indoctrination. Although it is beyond the scope of this work to spell out inappropriate teaching methods, I will make a few more suggestions in the final chapter. What should be noted here is that such identification is made more complex because of the developmental nature of my theory of indoctrination.

In chapter 3, I rejected the content criterion as a defining feature of indoctrination. My theory of indoctrination focuses on persons rather than beliefs. We cannot simply label certain content as suspect, as in itself hindering growth towards normal rational autonomy. What is needed instead is to ask whether there is a dynamic process of inquiry going on in the area in question, and to realize that this is possible in all areas of inquiry, even in religion. If by "doctrines" we mean presuppositions, first-order principles, epistemic primitives, or world-views, then I would agree that we need to be especially careful about the way in which we teach these doctrines. We need to ensure that our students are given the tools to become critically aware of the fundamental assumptions underlying a belief system or a form of knowledge. Failure to do so is to indoctrinate (cf. Laura 1983; Leahy 1990). But all belief systems, all forms of knowledge contain doctrines as defined above, and hence indoctrination is possible in all areas. Given that scientific rationalism is the establishment position in education today, I would suggest that we should be particularly concerned about failing to cultivate critical awareness of the presuppositions underlying scientific rationalism, thereby failing to foster growth toward normal rational autonomy, that is, indoctrinating (see p. 75).

My expression of caution about establishment positions touches on the final criterion of indoctrination considered in chapter 7: institutional indoctrination. Growth toward normal rational autonomy never occurs in isolation. Individuals always grow within an institutional context. It is therefore most important to ensure that this institutional context of learning is itself dynamic, open, and growing.

CONCLUSION

This completes my tentative sketch of a reconstructed theory of indoctrination. Some, perhaps many, readers will be dissatisfied with this proposal. There is little here of the pretended precision of past conceptual analysis. There are no clear-cut criteria by which one can decisively label this to be liberal education, and that to be indoctrination. Instead, I have argued for the need for a complete *theory* of indoctrination. It was not my intent to provide such a complete theory, but only to suggest a tentative outline of some ingredients of a reconstructed theory of indoctrination. My critique of past work on the concept of indoctrination is, I believe, sufficient to show that we need to strike out in new directions. But the working out of a complete theory of liberal education and indoctrination will be left to others with a greater bent and ability to construct theories. Or perhaps we need to look again at some of the educational theories of the past (such as Dewey's) as Ralph Page (1980) has suggested.

This chapter began by looking at various possible responses to the charge of religious indoctrination. Based on my critique of past analyses of the concept of indoctrination, I concluded that the charge of indoctrination against Christian nurture was not nearly so strong as is often assumed by liberal educators and others. Having completed an outline of a reconstruction of the theory of indoctrination, it should be evident that another kind of response is now possible to the frequent charge of religious indoctrination. If by indoctrination we mean the curtailment of a person's growth toward normal rational autonomy, it should be obvious that this is possible to avoid also in Christian nurture. Christian nurture therefore does not necessarily entail indoctrination. I further believe that indoctrination is less prevalent than is often assumed, though this is an empirical generalization which is difficult to substantiate. However, the above outline of a reconstructed and, I hope, more adequate theory of indoctrination does have the effect of undermining many of the "fixed" platforms from which charges of indoctrination were made. The charge is therefore weaker than is often assumed.

This is not to suggest that indoctrination never occurs in Christian nurture. In the final chapter I want to examine some current practices in Christian homes and schools which should be charged with a degree of indoctrination. The ability to distinguish between educative Christian nurture and that which is indoctrinative will in fact provide further grounds for recommending my outline of a reconstructed theory of liberal education and indoctrination. This should also help to assuage the fears of those who feel that my analysis is too indeterminate. I hope to show that even my brief outline of a theory of indoctrination and my abbreviated description of the nature of indoctrination provides us with a sharp enough instrument to distinguish cases of indoctrination from cases of true religious education.

9 Some Practical Suggestions

"Ideas have consequences." This ancient and profound truth, captured in the title R.M. Weaver ([1948]1971) gave his oft-reprinted book, also serves as a fitting introduction to this final chapter. Philosophers need to be reminded that ideas really *do* have consequences when they remain in their proverbial ivory towers absorbed in abstract and theoretical arguments, without ever demonstrating the important differences their ideas make in the ordinary lives of people. The purpose of this chapter is to show the concrete implications of the often abstract arguments of the previous chapters concerning our understanding of liberal education and indoctrination.

Not only do ideas have consequences, but ideas can be tested by their consequences. I have demonstrated that past conceptions of liberal education and indoctrination are inadequate, and this has led to proposals for the reconstruction of these two concepts. The central objective of this chapter is to show how my reconstruction of the notions of liberal education and indoctrination works itself out in practice, especially with regard to Christian nurture. Indoctrination, it will be recalled, was defined in the previous chapter as "the curtailment of a person's growth towards normal rational autonomy." I will argue that this reconstruction of the notion of indoctrination is indeed better able to identify indoctrinative practices in Christian nurture than was possible with past analyses of the concept.

In chapter 8 I noted that Kazepides, for one, tends to be very critical of "programmatic definitions" in education, though, he does admit that our ordinary understanding of concepts may be defective and hence may need to be "supplemented and improved upon and superseded" (1989, 388). Kazepides goes on to suggest that a key to evaluating a proposed reconstruction of a concept is to work out the application of the reconstructed term and to show the advantages and disadvantages of such a reconstruction. I intend to do this.

Because much more needs to be done by way of working out a full theory of liberal education and indoctrination, I can at most outline some of the practical implications and advantages of the reconstruction. It is not possible here to respond to all the vast literature on the theory and practice of religious education which, unfortunately, is largely ignored by philosophers writing on liberal education and indoctrination. Nor is it possible here to develop a complete theory of Christian religious education.[1] Instead, I will suggest some implications that specifically grow out of my critique of past analyses of "indoctrination" and my outline of a reconstruction of this concept. I will begin by identifying some practical principles that should govern the initiation phase of Christian nurture.

THE INITIATION/SOCIALIZATION PHASE/ COMPONENT OF CHRISTIAN NURTURE

1 Christian parents should boldly initiate their children into the Christian faith.
Here it needs to be stressed that I am talking about the initiation phase of liberal education with a particular focus on what roughly takes place in the education of a child from birth to the age of five or six. I am further assuming that parents have the fundamental right and responsibility to determine the nature of the primary culture into which their children are initiated.[2] The previous chapter argued that liberal education necessarily begins with an initiation or socialization phase which involves young children acquiring a specific language, customs, beliefs, and values from their immediate primary society. This process is essentially non-rational, depending on imitation and on the mechanism of identification (Peters 1966, 60). A child growing up in a Christian home will therefore unavoidably be initiated and socialized into the language, beliefs, practices, and values of the Christian religion.

The principle that I put forward is that such initiation should be done *boldly*. Why? Because Christian parents are often made to feel guilty about doing so by liberal educators and educationalists. Callan, for example, maintains that "parents who rear their children within a particular religion incur a significant risk of indoctrinating them" (1985, 117). Charges such as these, I would suggest, have led many religious parents to be very hesitant to bring up their children within a particular religious tradition. It is this fear of indoctrination that leads some religious parents to take an approach to child rearing in which they go to great lengths trying to avoid the imposition of their religion on their children. This fear of indoctrination makes some parents so concerned about ensuring that their children will move beyond the present and the particular that they hesitate to provide a solid mooring in the present and the particular from which their children can then expand their horizons.

More specifically, Christian parents are so intent on ensuring that their children are brought up within a liberal environment that they fail to provide them with a Christian environment in which they can be nurtured in the Christian faith. Christian schools are so intent on ensuring that their students get a liberal religious education that they fail to give them a Christian religious education. I want to suggest that Christians have in fact sold their Christian birthright for a mess of "liberal" pottage.[3]

I would further suggest that the fear and the guilt imposed on Christian parents by those of a "liberal" mind is by and large unjustified. It is based on the Enlightenment ideal of liberal education and on a traditional notion of "indoctrination" which I have shown to be incoherent and indefensible. Initiation and socialization are inescapable. Indeed they are essential to children's well-being, to their becoming fully human. Thus one finds again and again that liberal educationalists are forced to concede that indoctrination of some sort seems to be unavoidable, as was argued at length in chapter 4. But what is often forgotten in making this concession is that the meaning of "indoctrination" has changed. If initiation and socialization are unavoidable and essential to a child's well-being, then "indoctrination" applied to these same processes can no longer have a pejorative meaning. We are in fact using the word in two quite different ways. Liberals like Callan are trading on the pejorative meaning to make Christian parents feel guilty about a process which is healthy and good. Christian parents have nothing to worry about because every child is necessarily initiated and socialized into a particular religious (or irreligious) tradition.

Here an important question arises. Can the charge of indoctrination, understood pejoratively, be applied at all to the initiation/socialization phase of liberal education? Callan attempts to do so by distinguishing between "being brought up within a particular belief system," which he deems to be indoctrination, and "being brought up in a family where one is merely exposed to the fact that one's parents adhere to certain beliefs" (1985, 111). The problem with this distinction is that it is vacuous for a two-year-old child. An infant is not only exposed to the beliefs and values of the parents but it inherits them, absorbs them completely. Callan simply refuses to face up to what is really involved in an infant's acquiring a language together with the beliefs, values, and even prejudices built into a language. Callan also tends to talk about older children, or about children in a school context, thus skirting the problem of the inevitability of "total" socialization into a particular way of life for an infant. Infants are not merely "spectators" (McLaughlin 1985, 122), as Callan has to assume, they are necessarily totally immersed in their parents' life, language, and culture, as McLaughlin points out (1985, 122).

Gardner (1988) suggests another way to maintain the distinction between indoctrination and non-indoctrination at the initiation stage by contrasting parents who expose their preschool children to only one religious tradition with those who expose their children to several or to none at all. Gardner argues that parents who are committed to the liberal ideal of autonomy and "who do not want to be responsible for predetermining their children's subsequent religious stances would seem best advised to avoid subjecting their children to an upbringing which inculcates a particular set of religious beliefs" (1988, 96).[4] One problem with this, as Barrow has noted, is that it is difficult to see "why those who advocate a non-religious environment should not equally be accused of cooking the books" (1974, 57). In fact Gardner admits as much (1988, 94).

The more basic problem with Gardner's position is that he fails to see that it is simply not possible to raise children without a particular set of religious or irreligious beliefs. Even the parents who give their children an agnostic upbringing, which Gardner seems to favour (1988, 94, 105), or who try to expose their children to a variety of religious beliefs at an early age nonetheless predispose them to a particular position with regard to religion – that all religions are equally valid, or that they are unimportant, or that there is no rational way to assess religions. Gardner, in fact, raises a possible fatal objection to his position when he asks whether the psychology of belief (i.e., the fact that early beliefs tend to persist) is such that the liberal ideal is unattainable (102). Indeed, that is the key problem! Philosophers need to face up to the fact that children will, by and large, continue to remain in the traditions in which they have been brought up. To label that phenomenon "indoctrination" makes indoctrination inescapable, even for the most liberal parent.

McLaughlin further points out that Callan's (or Gardner's) attempt to define a liberal non-indoctrinatory kind of upbringing fails to take into account the need for a stable and coherent primary culture for a young child, a need which can only be adequately provided within the context of a home which achieves an "organic unity" in which all share a common world-view, common loyalties, and commitments (1985, 122-3). From this it would seem to follow that a so-called "liberal" upbringing is in fact inadequate – if not immoral – in that it fails to meet the basic needs of children.

I would therefore suggest that the concept of indoctrination understood in its pejorative sense simply cannot be applied to very young children. One can obviously condemn certain types of treatment of young children from a moral point of view. For example, it is wrong to beat children if they ask too many questions, or if they use the wrong word to identify a certain object. It is also wrong to expose children "to an endless and changing Babel of talk and behaviour" (Ackerman 1980, 141). But I'm not at all sure we would want to label these as instances of indoctrination: they are simply immoral ways to bring up children.

Considerations such as these lead McCloskey, in his analysis of liberalism, to question "whether a meaningful distinction can be drawn here between education and indoctrination in respect of the child of 12 or less, and in such a way that the liberal can opt for education alone" (1974, 27). I believe that the concept of indoctrination can be applied before the age of twelve, but I agree with McCloskey that the concept is inapplicable to the training or education of very young children.

Therefore, parents should have the courage to be bold in the initiation/socialization of their children. They should not hide from the awesome responsibility of passing on a particular inheritance of ideas and values which will to a large extent shape their children's outlook for the rest of their lives. It will not do to try to escape this responsibility by trying to be more liberal than it is possible to be with infants. Parents necessarily choose the primary culture for their children. This of course means that they should choose wisely, but what they cannot do is escape this choice. Nor should they let others determine what is or is not an acceptable primary culture for their children. Here liberals are inconsistent. On the one hand, they admit as a foundational principle of their liberal democratic theory that "there are no moral experts on the good life for individuals," but then promptly forget about "this agnosticism about the good life" when they make pronouncements about the unacceptability of providing children with a religious upbringing (see White 1983, 10-11, 87, 146-7). Consistency demands that we allow parents to determine the kind of upbringing they give to their children without creating shackles of fear of indoctrination. Consistency demands that we acknowledge that Christian parents of necessity initiate their children into the Christian faith. Therefore the advice: initiate boldly, without fear or hesitation.

2 Christian nurture (recognizing the developmental nature of religious understanding, and while acknowledging that religious instruction should be adjusted to the stage of a child's cognitive development) sees initiation into the language, concepts, and stories of the Christian faith as contributing to a child's religious development. Christian nurture will therefore again boldly initiate a child into the language, concepts and stories of the Christian faith.

This second principle really is a corollary of the first, but it is being singled out for separate treatment as a response to a prevalent error in contemporary thinking about religious education which grows out of the extensive research in the psychology of religion. Greer, in two important articles reviewing "Fifty Years of the Psychology of Religion in Religious Education" (1984a; 1984b), highlights the many empirical studies which, influenced by the work of Piaget, have shown that children pass through various stages in their religious thinking. Ronald Goldman's influential *Religious Thinking from Childhood to Adolescence* (1964) was one of the first of these studies, and subsequent research has generally confirmed his overall conclusions. Goldman identified three basic stages in children's cognitive religious development: an intuitive stage, ending at about seven to eight years; a concrete operational stage, ending at about thirteen or fourteen years; and a formal or abstract operational stage.

This research would seem to have some important implications for religious education and is summarized by Greer as follows:

The Piagetian-type research made it clear that religious educators needed to examine concepts involved in understanding material chosen for any given age group and to consider if pupils were capable of the level of thinking necessary for religious insight. If, as Goldman claimed: 'the truths to be gleaned from most biblical stories are generally abstract, are of a propositional nature and are dependent upon the capacity to see analogies from one situation to another and to understand the metaphors in which religious narratives abound' then 'the recommendation may have to be faced that very little biblical material is suitable before Secondary schooling.' (Greer 1984a, 96)

Goldman and others are correct in concluding from this Piagetian-type research that religious educators need to adjust their teaching to a child's level of mental development. This principle was already affirmed by Socrates in the fifth century B.C. and reaffirmed again by the nineteenth-century educator Friedrich Froebel who said that "the child has the right to be at each stage what that stage requires" (Greer 1984a, 94-5).

But there is a fundamental error in the conclusions Goldman and many others have drawn from this kind of research. It is sheer nonsense to claim that a child should not be exposed to biblical material before secondary schooling. Children love stories and are perfectly capable of understanding biblical stories *as stories*. Much of the early education of a child, a large part of which is the acquiring of a language, involves the reading and telling of stories. Children cannot catch all the nuances of metaphors and analogies in such stories, but they still appreciate stories as stories. And we do not stop reading or telling these stories because the children do not completely understand the metaphors and analogies in them. Biblical stories too can be "grasped validly and creatively at a concrete level" as various writers have pointed out, and thus it is foolish to abandon the use of the Bible in religious education (Greer 1984a, 97). Even abstract concepts can be translated into terms which communicate with the thought patterns of the child, as the work of Jerome Bruner shows (see Cooling 1987, 154).[5]

It should further be noted that there is considerable controversy concerning the assumptions underlying this Piagetian-inspired approach to religious development and religious education (see Greer 1984a). Peters challenges one such assumption – its treatment of mental structure as being innate or simply the product of maturation. "What is lacking," says Peters, "is the notion that such a structure develops out of and is a response to public traditions enshrined in language" (1966, 51). In other words, the development of the mind is fundamentally a "product of initiation into public traditions enshrined in a public language" (49). Therefore, if we want children to grow and to be able to think in the area of religion, we need first to initiate them into the language and the concepts not of abstract, but of concrete religion. Christian parents therefore need to tell their children the stories that are part of the Christian tradition. Children need to be initiated boldly into the linguistic religious inheritance parents are inviting them to share. This admonition to initiate boldly is again necessary because lurking in the background of Piagetian-inspired recommendations regarding religious education is the implicit charge of indoctrination. To initiate a child into the language and the stories of a particular religion is not to indoctrinate, but to provide him or her with the necessary tools for further growth and development in the area of religion.

3 Christian nurture should occur within the context of a faith-supporting community and faith-supporting institutions, one of which is the Christian school.

This principle rests on the fact that the development of the mind never occurs in isolation. This is most clearly seen at the initial stages of a child's mental development, but what is frequently forgotten, especially by advocates of the Enlightenment ideal of liberal education, is that the need for a social context for mental development persists throughout a person's lifetime. Without a social world, the individual will not only "begin to lose his moral bearings, with disastrous psychological consequences, but he will become uncertain about his cognitive bearings as well. The world begins to shake in the very instant that its sustaining conversation begins to falter" (Berger 1969, 22). All of us, including the liberal minded, need "plausibility structures" in order to maintain sanity, according to Berger. The provision of Christian plausibility structures should not therefore in itself be associated with indoctrination in the pejorative sense.

Various writers have stressed the role of the community in Christian learning and growth. John H. Westerhoff III is one of the most influential exponents of the faith community approach to Christian education today.[6] "Westerhoff is a radical critic of methods of Christian education based on conventional education theory and practice, which he refers to as the 'schooling-instructional paradigm', preferring what he calls a 'community of faith-enculturation paradigm', or more briefly, 'catechesis' " (Heywood 1988, 65). He prefers the language of socialization in which the learner is perceived as "a communal being whose identity and growth can only be understood in terms of life in a community that shares a common memory, vision, authority, rituals and family-like life together" (Westerhoff 1983, 50).

Westerhoff is certainly justified in countering the individualism that underlies much of the schooling-instructional paradigm, which is prevalent in discussions about liberal education. He also clearly does justice to the initiation/socialization component of Christian education – indeed of all education. I have noted that the hidden curriculum plays an important part in education, and Westerhoff's emphasis on the importance of the total life of the Christian community for Christian education really builds on this notion of the hidden curriculum.

One problem with Westerhoff's approach is that he goes too far in rejecting the schooling-instructional paradigm. Surely schools play an important part in enculturation in faith.[7] Why does a society have schools? Obviously, schools have to do with education. But what kind of education? Within a liberal democracy schools are, or at least should be, concerned with liberal education. But, as I argued in the previous chapter, initiation/socialization is a significant component of liberal education. Schools, therefore, are thought to be necessary to continue the process of initiation/socialization begun by the parents. Oakeshott, for example, describes schooling as "the deliberate initiation of the newcomer into a human inheritance of sentiments, beliefs, imaginings, understandings and activities" (1972, 23). Schools involve serious study and orderly initiation within a context of detachment from the immediate local world of the learner and under conditions of direction and restraint imposed by teachers. The idea of "school" "is that of an historic community of teachers and learners, neither large nor small, with traditions of its own, evoking loyalties, pieties and affections, devoted to initiating successive generations of newcomers to the human scene into the grandeurs and servitudes of being human" (Oakeshott 1972, 26).

It is interesting to note that in this same article Oakeshott identifies the substitution of "socialization" for education as one corruption of the educative role of schools (1972, 33-47). But here he gives a very special meaning to the term. The socialization which he sees as frustrating the educational engagement of the school is the reduction of teaching and learning to serving an extrinsic end, namely, "a systematic apprenticeship to domestic, industrial and commercial life in a 'modern' State" (37). Oakeshott is not at all rejecting the initiation/socialization that is necessarily a component of education and the development of the mind as the newcomer is helped to share the human inheritance of sentiments, beliefs, imaginings, understandings, and activities. Nor is he ruling out conceiving of education and schooling as the initiation of children into a Christian inheritance. In fact, he specifically points out that, when rulers of modern European states (beginning in the late seventeenth century) imposed confessional qualifications upon both teachers and learners in schools and universities, "they did not otherwise seriously modify the educational engagement" of these institutions (35). Oakeshott would therefore seem to sympathize with the idea that schools are needed to initiate/socialize newcomers *systematically* into a Christian inheritance, though he is of course also concerned about further growth toward rationality and autonomy, about which I will say more later.

Christian parents who have initiated their children into a Christian inheritance of sentiments, beliefs, imaginings, understandings, and activities will and should want this process to continue in a systematic and orderly way in a Christian school. In the brief review of the history of education in chapter 1, I pointed out that there had been a time when it could be assumed that all schools in countries like Canada, the United States, and the United Kingdom would be initiating/socializing children into a broadly conceived Christian inheritance. This was accepted because it was generally assumed that there was a kind of Christian consensus in society at large. However, with the growing pluralism and secularization of western societies, the assumption of a Christian consensus is increasingly being called into question, and the common schools of these societies have had to adapt to the new reality around them by becoming increasingly secular and pluralistic. It is no doubt awareness of this shift in the nature of socialization in our public schools that is leading more and more Christian parents to withdraw their children from these schools and to send them to Christian schools where they will be initiated/socialized into the Christian tradition.

My point in reviewing some of the developments in schools in western societies is to show that there is nothing unusual in the desire of Christian parents who want to send their children to Christian schools. Such a desire is quite in keeping with the ideal of liberal education because the initiation into the human inheritance of beliefs and practices begun in the home needs the support of schools where such initiation is continued in a more systematic way. Obviously, schools should do more than *merely* continue the initiation/socialization begun in the home, but that is another question about which more will be said later. Here I want to underscore the fact that systematic initiation/socialization in schools is necessary and good. If one's conception of the human inheritance into which children should be initiated includes Christian sentiments, beliefs, imaginings, understandings, and activities, then we need schools which systematically initiate children into this Christian inheritance, *though this is by no means an exhaustive description of what these schools are about*.

Many liberal educators would no doubt argue that there is no need for Christian schools because Christian parents have already had the opportunity to initiate their children into Christian beliefs and values, and that surely such initiation in the home should be adequate. They would argue further that by the time a child reaches school age the emphasis should be on growth, exposure to other traditions, liberation, and so on. In reply, it needs to be pointed out that there is a curious inconsistency on the part of these "secular" liberal educators who argue in this way. On the one hand, they acknowledge the need for schools in which there is a deliberate, systematic, and serious *initiation* of the newcomer into the human in-heritance of sentiments, beliefs, imaginings, understandings, and activities; on the other hand, they fail to acknowledge a similar need for deliberate, systematic, and serious initiation into one's religious inheritance. If schools are needed to continue the process of initia-tion into the human inheritance begun in the home, surely they are also needed to continue the process of initiation into a Christian in-heritance, which for Christian parents is an important part of the hu-man inheritance they are inviting their children to share.

4 Christian nurture necessarily includes an initiation/socialization compo-nent at all stages of a Christian's development, though in lessening degrees as a Christian matures. The Christian parent and teacher, as well as the Christian church and school, will therefore boldly and openly initiate and socialize into the Christian tradition.

The first practical principle of Christian nurture dealt only with the initial phase of a child's education, the initiation/socialization phase. We now move beyond this initial phase to affirm that *some degree* of initiation/socialization continues throughout a person's lifetime. Throughout the previous chapters I have called attention to research in psychology, sociology, and anthropology, all of which bear on our understanding of knowledge and education and have contrib-uted significantly to our reconstruction of the theory of liberal edu-cation. Peter Berger, for example, has been particularly forceful in reminding us that a person's own identity and that of the world around him or her are very much dependent on a person's being in conversation with others. Hence the title of his important work, co-authored with T. Luckmann, *The Social Construction of Reality* ([1966]1967). Berger goes on to maintain that this implies "that so-cialization can never be completed, that it must be an ongoing pro-cess throughout the lifetime of the individual" (1969, 16).

Many words have been used to describe this ongoing component of a person's education: initiation, socialization, formation, encultur-ation, transmission, instruction, catechesis, an informational com-ponent to education, etc. Obviously there is another component of liberal education – the development of rationality and critical open-ness – about which I will say more later, but we must not let this detract from the importance and the inevitability of initiation/socialization. Of course, it is possible to distinguish conceptually be-tween these two components, but we must not forget that these are abstractions, and that in real life they are always found side by side.

Within the Christian community, therefore, there will be continu-ing efforts boldly and openly to initiate members into the language, culture, and values of the Christian faith. Christian nurture will continue to include the transmission of information as an essential component of education, and it will be very open about the fact that it begins from a commitment to Christian truth and seeks to nurture such commitment in others. This initiation/socialization component of Christian nurture will continue throughout a Christian's life, although it will give way more and more to the other components of a liberal education as a person matures. I will have more to say about the balance between initiation/socialization and "liberalization" in a later section.

I have treated the above four principles of Christian nurture, all concerned with initiation/socialization, first and separately in order to highlight one central point. Initiation/socialization in and of itself should not be looked upon in a negative light. It is a fundamental error to treat the initiation/socialization phase or component of Christian nurture as indoctrination (understood pejoratively). If all education necessarily includes an initiation/socialization component, and if this is essential for normal and healthy cognitive development, then it is an error to think of this component as in itself "primitive," or "sub-human," or "ghetto-istic," as Hirst has done (1981, 86; 1985, 7, 10). There is nothing wrong per se with initiating a child into a *particular* religion – a false assumption that is all too frequently made by liberal educators. Nor is it wrong to teach for Christian commitment. Christian schools are not necessarily "total institutions" which indoctrinate, because there is co-operation between them and the home and church (Peshkin 1986). All human beings need plausibility structures in order to avoid a "crisis of credibility" which ensues when we are exposed to an endless and changing Babel of talk and behaviour or when we are exposed to people and beliefs that threaten our subjective world.

The charge of indoctrination cannot be made simply because an initiation/socialization component is present in Christian nurture. For children brought up in Christian homes and schools, initiation and socialization into Christian beliefs, values, and practices is a necessary foundation of a liberal education. Of course, if some Christian teacher or school conceives of education *only* in terms of initiation/socialization, and if *only* those methods appropriate to initiation/socialization are used when dealing with students at a later stage of cognitive development, then and only then should we say that indoctrination is occurring. As long as the initiation/socialization component is combined with other components of liberal education such as growth toward normal autonomy and rationality, about which I will say more later, we cannot make the charge of indoctrination.

Most Christians will no doubt find the above set of implications of my reconstructed notions of liberal education and indoctrination quite palatable, while many advocates of the traditional ideal of liberal education will no doubt have some serious concerns about what I have said. I turn now to a second set of practical implications which I suspect will cause a reversal of reactions on the part of some Christians and some liberal educators. These varied reactions are, I believe, significant in that they point to the radical nature of my reconstruction of the ideal of liberal education. This second set of implications concerns that phase or component of liberal education traditionally associated with "liberation" and growth toward rational autonomy. In my reconstruction of the ideal of liberal education, of course, both phases are seen as essential to nurturing growth toward normal rational autonomy.

CHRISTIAN NURTURE IN RELATION TO RATIONALITY AND AUTONOMY

5 *The goal of Christian parents and teachers for Christian nurture should be both Christian commitment and normal autonomy. (This dual goal includes the hope that children or students will eventually make an "independent" choice for or against Christian commitment.)*

The previous section dealt only with principles arising from the initiation/socialization phase or component of liberal education as applied to Christian nurture. I noted that the initial stages of children's education can only be described in terms of initiation/socialization and suggested that it is impossible to distinguish between indoctrinative and non-indoctrinative ways to initiate or socialize very young children. However, if the focus changes from the process of initiation/socialization to the intention of the parents/teachers involved in this process, there might still be a way of making the charge of indoctrination.

I believe that it is possible to talk about an indoctrinative intent, though it is necessary to remember that intentions alone cannot indoctrinate (see chapter 5). I am assuming that one goal of Christian parents will be that their children will eventually commit themselves to the Christian faith. But this goal is in itself not sufficient to satisfy the requirements of our reconstructed ideal of liberal education. Christian parents should also have as a central goal that their children grow toward normal autonomy (cf. McLaughlin 1984, 75, 79). Christian parents will therefore aim for both autonomy and Christian commitment on the part of their children. That such a dual intention is possible was defended in chapter 5, so there is no need to establish the coherence of this notion here.

I need to stress once again that I am here talking about *normal autonomy*, as defined in chapter 5. Absolute autonomy or completely independent choice is impossible. Freedom always occurs within a certain context. Choice is always made by persons with a history. It is for this reason that the term "independent" appears in quotation marks in my statement above of this principle. The goal of Christian parents and teachers, as indeed of all parents and teachers, should be that their children and students will grow toward normal autonomy, that they will eventually make relatively independent choices, that they will achieve as much independence as is humanly possible. Christian parents and teachers have the additional goal that their children or students will eventually also make a Christian commitment.

Unfortunately, such dual intentions are not always present. I suggest that Christian parents who do not have as a goal that their children will grow toward normal rational autonomy, and/or that their children will at some point make their own "independent" decision for or against Christian commitment, can legitimately be charged with having indoctrinative intent. Of course, Christian parents "may well hope that their child's eventual autonomy will be exercised in favour of faith; but ... this must remain a hope rather than a requirement" (McLaughlin 1984, 79). Christian parents therefore need to entertain seriously the possibility that their children will reject the Christian heritage into which they have been initiated. The parents will of course be saddened by this, but respect for the individuality and freedom of their children will entail respect for this negative decision.

Indeed, examination of the stated intentions of Christian parents, teachers, and clergy, reveals frequent references to the ideal of normal autonomy as one of their goals. For example, Lewis B. Smedes, professor of theology and ethics at Fuller Theological Seminary, in *Caring and Commitment*, devotes a chapter to the subject of commitment of parents to children (1988, ch. 9). While acknowledging that the commitments of parents put them in control, Smedes goes on to highlight the principle that "parents are committed to their children's freedom from their commitment" (Smedes 1988, 95). Father Henri J.M. Nouwen writes in a similar vein from a Catholic perspective: "The difficult task of parenthood is to help children grow to the freedom that permits them to stand on their own feet, physically, mentally and spiritually and to allow them to move away in their own direction" (1975, 83).

Although Peshkin is very critical of Bethany Baptist Academy and describes it as a total institution which indoctrinates, there is a very clear affirmation of the dual goal under consideration in a statement of one of the BBA teachers. Although Bible teacher Art Swanson honestly describes his goal as trying "to shape students' mind to one pattern," he also stresses that individuals "have the freedom to reject that system, to choose as they see fit ... If they don't accept what I teach, I feel they're making a mistake. But they have that freedom and I would defend their freedom to make that choice. I think God does, too" (Peshkin 1986, 266). These statements surely satisfy the requirement of having a dual goal of commitment and autonomy.

Peshkin is, however, quite justified in expressing concern about a seeming preoccupation with "spiritual" goals as found in a statement of the American Association of Christian Schools (1986, 259, cf. ch. 5). Some of the teachers' own accounts of their aims in the classroom seem to be rather one-sided, with little acknowledgment of the goal to promote growth toward normal autonomy and rationality (80). Concern about indoctrinatory intent would therefore seem to be justified, if indeed Peshkin has given an accurate and complete account of the goals involved in each of the above cases. Unfortunately, he tends to treat spiritual goals and educational goals as mutually exclusive. He states, for example, that it is these spiritual purposes that shape Christian schools, "not the development of informed thinking citizens" (259). But this is patently false, and commits the fallacy of either-or. Surely BBA and its teachers can and do aim for both "spirituality" and growth towards rationality and autonomy, as indeed Peshkin is forced to concede on a number of occasions (9, 79, 156, 266). In so far as both goals are present, the charge of indoctrinatory intent should not be made.

6 *Christian parents and teachers should actively promote both Christian commitment and growth toward normal autonomy. Although their children and students are brought up within a context of Christian commitment, they will be taught and nurtured toward an eventual "independent" choice for or against Christian commitment.*
This principle moves beyond intentions (which are often rather difficult to uncover in any case) to a consideration of the way in which Christian parents and teachers actively engage in Christian nurture. I am assuming that they will be actively seeking to promote Christian commitment. They will be initiating and socializing the child

into the beliefs and practices of the Christian faith. As the children mature, there will be formal instruction concerning Christian beliefs, obviously with the intent that this will further encourage Christian commitment. Christian parents and teachers cannot be faulted for this, as has already been argued in the first section of this chapter. However, what I am now demanding is that they must also be actively promoting growth toward normal autonomy. Children need to be nurtured toward autonomy (see pp. 140-3, 223-9). McLaughlin has suggested that little philosophical or empirical research has been done to show what parents must actually *do* to ensure growth in autonomy and rationality while at the same time providing the necessary security of a stable and coherent primary culture (1984, 80). Here again we see the failure of philosophers to address the question of what is involved in educating the small child.

What is the relationship between teaching for commitment and teaching for autonomy during the initial initiation phase of liberal education? In a recent article, Callan expresses a common view. He maintains that parents who want to promote growth toward rational autonomy in a child in such complex and important areas as religion and politics should "discourage her from making any firm commitments until she is capable of doing so in an informed and mature manner" (1985, 111). One fundamental problem with this approach to child rearing is that it fails to satisfy children's need for the security that is found in commitment to the primary culture within which they are raised. Further, children are by nature committed to this same culture. It is therefore a fundamental mistake to pretend that one can encourage children to leave open decisions and commitments on such questions. Instead, as McLaughlin has argued, "The child should be encouraged to make – or is brought up to have – an initial commitment" (120). It is, however, of utmost importance that children should further be repeatedly reminded that there will come a time when they will need to make an adult decision about this early "immature" commitment.[8]

In normal adolescence children go through "a period of differentiation from the main 'life guidance' agencies of their earlier years – parents, church, and school" (Rossiter 1982, 34). During this time Christian parents and teachers need to be especially sensitive to their children's growing independence and need to achieve personal identity and autonomy. It is during this time that Christian parents and teachers should respect the freedom of their children to refuse to participate in the religious practices that were part of their Christian upbringing (McLaughlin 1984, 81). Only if Christian parents and teachers gradually and sensitively move toward freeing their children and students to affirm or deny the Christian heritage within which they were nurtured can those parents and teachers be said to be encouraging growth toward normal rational autonomy, thus avoiding indoctrination.

It should be evident that I am not disagreeing entirely with Callan. A child's commitment should be treated quite differently from an adult's. Callan simply fails to acknowledge the possibility of a child-like commitment. However, he is right in insisting that "firm," or perhaps better, "full," commitments should postponed until children mature (1985, 111). Laura and Leahy have spelled out another implication of this principle. After reminding us that a child's capacity for acceptance or rejection of a religious faith grows as the child matures, they maintain that genuine commitment supposes a considerable degree of maturity. "The early Christian church implicitly acknowledged this fact in its practice of initiating only adults to membership of the community. The continuing practice of infant baptism in most Christian churches is at odds, in our view, with the belief that the capacity for commitment is dependent upon maturity of the kind acknowledged in the early church" (1989, 259). I would concur that while infant baptism does not preclude the possibility of subsequent "*critical* initiation" (259), the persistence of the practice of infant baptism (or its evangelical variety of child dedication) can certainly discourage parents and educators from seeing the need for children to critically reflect on and reaffirm or reject the faith into which they were initiated. This danger of indoctrination can be eliminated by postponing institutional expressions of religious commitment such as baptism until adulthood.

It should finally be noted that, from an orthodox Christian perspective, Christian commitment or conversion cannot itself be nurtured, as Westerhoff reminds us (see Heywood 1988, 67). Parents, teachers, and the Christian community can at most seek to nurture an individual toward commitment, to invite an individual to consider Christian commitment. But the process by which the individual internalises or "owns" the faith is not one that can be controlled or planned for in the educational framework. It is finally the individual who must choose to be "open to the mystery of the transcendent" (Heywood 1988, 67).

7 *Christian parents and teachers should actively promote cognitive growth with respect to the Christian faith. This is seen as an essential part of growing toward normal rationality.*
This principle is included because of the tendency of many advocates of liberal education to assume that growth toward rational au-

tonomy will be growth away from Christian commitment. Growth toward rational autonomy is frequently defined only in terms of independent questioning or critical thinking about the primary culture into which one has been nurtured. While this is certainly part of what growth toward rational autonomy means (I will say more about this later), it is only one aspect of such growth. Growth toward normal rational autonomy also includes growth in understanding one's Christian faith, in the ability to use Christian concepts, and in the ability to think from a Christian perspective.

When Christian parents and teachers do not encourage and facilitate growth beyond a child-like understanding of the Christian faith, they can and should be charged with indoctrination. Hudson cites the following example: "It was said of Lord Shaftesbury that his nurse impressed her own religious beliefs on him so firmly that he never changed them and at the age of eighty he believed exactly what he had believed at the age of eight" (1973, 191). While it is true that Lord Shaftesbury firmly retained the Christian faith within which he was first nurtured, this is surely a gross caricature of a man who provided strong and intelligent leadership in the fight against the evils of industrial capitalism and who clearly saw this fight as growing out of his Christian convictions (Lovelace 1985, 55-6). This caricature further rests on the assumption that commitment is incompatible with openness and growth – an assumption I criticized in chapter 6. However, some examples could no doubt be provided in which Christians at the age of eighty believe nearly exactly what they had believed at the age of eight. When this is a result of a certain approach to Christian nurture, such nurture should be condemned as involving a degree of indoctrination.

Sören Kierkegaard, great nineteenth-century Christian philosopher and frequent critic of the Christian church of his day, described another example of the failure to promote cognitive growth. "There are many people who reach their conclusions about life like school boys: They cheat their master by copying the answers out of a book without having worked the sum out for themselves" (Bretall 1946, 19). Far too much Christian nurture closely resembles this kind of cheating – the copying of answers out of a book, the passing on of information which students are required to regurgitate, the giving of pat answers to pat questions. This too deserves to be condemned as indoctrination.

Although Ninian Smart is speaking about religious education within a pluralistic context, much of what he says can also be applied to Christian nurture. Religious education, Smart says, "must transcend the informative" (1968, 105). He further points out that too much religious education takes the form of authoritative teaching *that*. Just as in other areas of study, religious education should also involve teaching *how* to think and reason within the religious form of knowledge (Smart 1968, 95; for verification of Smart's concerns see Kerry 1982). Yet the aim of all liberal education is to foster growth toward higher cognitive skills. Teaching in all areas should not only be concerned with the acquisition of facts, but should also facilitate the ability to collect, organize, and evaluate data, to construct hypotheses, to draw conclusions, and so on. This also applies to Christian nurture. Students must move to levels of analysis, synthesis, and evaluation with regard to their Christian beliefs. Without the facilitation of such growth, Christian nurture is reduced to indoctrination.

One of the first signs of natural growth toward rational autonomy is the endless questioning for which toddlers are famous. At first this questioning is very elementary, and the child will simply accept the answers that are given. This is the stage where the initiation/socialization component of liberal education is still dominant. But we see here the beginnings of growth, and it is important that "parents should encourage the child to ask questions and be willing to respond to the questioning honestly and in a way which respects the child's developing cognitive and emotional maturity" (McLaughlin 1984, 81).[9]

This is only one way in which parents can nurture growth towards rationality and autonomy. Parents also need to encourage independent thinking, criticism, and openness to new ideas. In the following sections, I will further explore ways in which this can and should be done. Here I want to stress only the general point that Christian parents and teachers have a responsibility to nurture actively the growth toward normal rationality with regard to the Christian belief system itself.

If this component of growth toward normal rational autonomy is missing in Christian nurture, one can legitimately make the charge of indoctrination. A further example of where this charge might be appropriate occurs in Rose's study of two evangelical schools in upstate New York (1988). I want to suggest that one of these schools indoctrinates, while the other exemplifies all that is best in the ideal of liberal education.

Covenant School, an independent charismatic school, "stresses the acquisition of analytical skills, flexibility, self-direction, and the persuasive use of language. Group work, discussions that explore a spectrum of values and beliefs, and various strategies for formulating and resolving problems characterize school life" (98). "The Covenant educators are ... process oriented, wanting their students to explore ideas and express their creativity" (164). By contrast, educators at Lakehaven Academy, a fundamentalist Baptist school which uses the Accelerated Christian Education (A.C.E.) curriculum, are "task and content oriented, wanting their children to know specific pieces of information. This is manifested in the emphasis on recitation rather than interpretation and in the objective testing (multiple choice, true-false, fill-in-the-blank) that characterizes A.C.E. materials" (164). "The curriculum allows little room for individuals to raise questions or to explore answers to the questions asked" (139; cf. 128, 179). Various other studies have verified this assessment of the A.C.E. approach to education (Alberta Education 1985; Fleming & Hunt 1987; Van Brummelen 1989, 10-16). Given the orientation to information recall, the discouragement of discussion and questioning, one can only conclude that schools such as Lakehaven Academy are weak in fostering growth toward rational autonomy and hence should be charged with a degree of indoctrination. By contrast, Covenant School, though committed to Christian nurture, clearly fulfills the requirements of liberal education.

8 Christian nurture should seek a balance between the cognitive and affective/dispositional dimensions of religious development.
In my reconstruction of the ideal of liberal education, I stressed that we need a more holistic view of human nature which will then entail a more holistic view of education. Past treatments of liberal education and indoctrination have been justifiably criticized for being too preoccupied with the intellect. However, care should be taken to avoid the opposite extreme of disregarding it. Rationality still has an important part to play in my reconstructed ideal of liberal education. I have defined "indoctrination" as a failure to promote growth toward normal *rational* autonomy. While an essential part of this ideal of *normal* rational autonomy is a recognition of the limits of rationality and the need to keep a balance between rationality and the other dimensions of human nature, growth in rationality is still important. Christian parents must therefore also "ensure that the affective, emotional and dispositional aspects of their child's religious development takes place in appropriate relationship with the cognitive aspect of that development, so that irrational, compulsive or neurotic forms of religious behaviour or response are guarded against" (McLaughlin 1984, 81).

An emphasis on the cognitive component of religious development is necessary in light of the anti-intellectual forces often found within the Christian church. Richard Hofstadter, in his classic study,

Anti-intellectualism in American Life (1963), devotes three chapters to documenting these anti-intellectual forces in early American Protestantism, particularly as found in evangelical revivalism. Though his analysis suffers from too narrow a definition of "anti-intellectualism," and though he himself is forced to make a number of qualifications, Hofstadter's overall thesis is secure.[10] There was, and still is, an unfortunate tendency on the part of many Christians to discredit learning, to oppose theological education for ministers, to look upon piety and intellect as being in open enmity, to rely on emotions in evangelism, and to fail to see growth toward rational autonomy as an essential component in religious development.[11] Such tendencies within the Christian church clearly invite the charge of indoctrination.

However, religious development, as indeed all human development, cannot be defined only in cognitive terms. Humans are more than rational animals. Indeed, according to Poewe and Hexham (1986, ch. 7), it is precisely modern western society's preoccupation with the rational and the scientific, and the accompanying disregard for the emotional dimension of human experience, that is leading to the proliferation of new cults, new religions, astrology, prophecy, futuristic speculation, the occult, charismatic religion, and a general rise in superstition, even and perhaps especially among the educated. What is needed in Christian nurture is a balance between reason and emotion, theology and devotion, the cognitive and the affective dimensions of the Christian faith (Groome 1980, 74-5; Hudson 1973, 182, 192).

9 Christian nurture should attempt to foster both growth in a rational grounding of Christian convictions and honest and serious grappling with doubt, questions, and objections to Christian convictions.
As has already been mentioned, there is a danger, when thinking about growth toward rational autonomy in relation to Christian nurture, to think of such growth only in negative terms, as necessarily involving the questioning of Christian convictions or the raising of objections to such convictions. This is too narrow and too negative a view of growth toward normal rational autonomy. Growth must also be seen in terms of a possible strengthening of people's Christian convictions. Christian nurture seeks to increase understanding of Christian beliefs and concepts. It seeks to enhance the ability to use Christian concepts and to reason within the context of Christian presuppositions. A major aim of Christian nurture is to enable individuals to be able rationally to justify their own Christian convictions. Such an aim is not only narrowly based on a theological ratio-

nale or on the desire to protect one's faith, it is rooted in the very nature of a liberal education. There must be growth toward normal rational autonomy, and such growth must be conceived also in terms of strengthening a person's understanding of and commitment to the Christian faith.

Indoctrination can occur when Christian parents or teachers fail to promote growth toward normal rational autonomy either in the sense of increasing children's understanding of and ability to justify their Christian convictions or in the sense of allowing for independent questioning, doubts, and the raising of objections to the Christian belief system. From an educational point of view, such questioning, doubts, and a consideration of objections must be seen as having positive value in terms of fostering growth towards normal rational autonomy.

Unfortunately, Christians all too often look upon doubt, questioning, and the raising of objections in exclusively negative terms. Children and students are often told that they must repress their questioning and that doubting is sinful. This kind of teaching about doubt, questioning, and the raising of objections hinders growth toward normal rational autonomy and therefore lends itself to "indoctrination."

Other Christians, however, do foster growth toward normal rational autonomy by encouraging honest questioning and doubting. For example, the philosophical statement in the faculty handbook of the evangelical Ontario Bible College includes this sentence: "Believing that 'all truth is God's truth,' we hold that honest inquiry and Christian faith commitment are fully compatible and therefore support the development and exercise of critical thinking" (1989, II-8). This philosophy is presumably put into practice at this college.

Similarly, from quite another Christian perspective, Thomas Groome, in his widely acclaimed *Christian Religious Education* (1980), advocates a "shared praxis approach" to religious education which includes a healthy emphasis on critical reflection and consciousness (122-7, 185-8, 237). However, very much in keeping with my description of *normal* critical openness, Groome stresses that such criticism must not be understood in the narrowly negative sense, but in a dialectical sense in which criticism is balanced with affirmation, confrontation with consolation (217).

Os Guinness, in his classic treatment of doubt from a Christian perspective (*In Two Minds*, 1976), attempts to develop a positive and constructive approach to doubt by reminding us that it is not a uniquely Christian problem, but a human one (39). Bertrand Russell agrees: "All our knowledge of truths is infected with *some* degree of doubt and a theory which ignored this fact would be plainly wrong" ([1912]1959, 135). Doubt arises because we only "know in part," and hence it is wrong to associate doubt with sin (1 Corinthians 13:12). Not only is doubt natural, it is healthy. "Doubt acts as a sparring partner both to truth and error. It keeps faith trim and helps to shed the paunchiness of false ideas ... To a healthy faith doubt is a healthy challenge," says Guinness (1976, 48-9). It leads to growth toward normal rationality and autonomy.

We must be careful, however, to distinguish this natural doubt from the methodological doubt often advocated by philosophers and educationalists (see Guinness 1976, ch. 4). Methodological doubt follows Descartes in attempting to arrive at truth by systematically doubting everything. This kind of doubt is problematic, as was argued in chapter 6. It fails to realize that all thinking, including doubting, necessarily takes place within a context in which certain beliefs remain unquestioned. It fails to satisfy the requirements of normal rational autonomy which I have defended throughout this work.

My opposition to methodological doubt should not be taken, however, as a rejection of raising objections to Christianity as part of Christian nurture – these are appropriate and necessary in fostering growth toward rational autonomy, as long as there is awareness of the constraints I have argued for in my defence of the ideal of *normal* rational autonomy. Callan, although he often strongly opposes religious upbringing, is justified in demanding the following, as one way to lessen the risk of indoctrination in denominational schools: "The very formidable arguments which some western philosophers have developed against theism might be presented in all their disturbing force as soon as students reached a stage where these arguments were comprehensible, and it might be stressed that the arguments should be accepted if they were found to be cogent" (1985, 117-18). We see here a recognition of the need to adjust teaching approaches to a child's development: counter-arguments should only be raised when students have reached a stage where counter-arguments are comprehensible. Callan is quite correct in demanding that students be encouraged to accept these counter-arguments if they are found to be cogent. This surely is necessary both for teaching with integrity and for teaching that respects children's eventual achievement of normal rational autonomy. All adults need to be encouraged to go where the wind of the argument carries them, to paraphrase Socrates.

One might be a little concerned, however, that the emphasis in Callan's requirement that these objections should be presented in "all their disturbing force" fails to satisfy children's need for a stable and coherent primary culture (1985, 117-18). Counter-arguments will disturb, and they should disturb, but the aim is never to disturb for the sake of disturbing. Teachers should always take into account children's psychological need for some *degree* of security and stability. The raising of such counter-objections within the context of a Christian school does, I believe, provide this kind of security. This would no doubt worry Callan in that it would fail to satisfy his requirement that alternative beliefs and objections be given "serious attention" (1985, 115, 118). There are, however, some problems with this requirement of Callan's which I have already dealt with in chapter 6.

The need for security and stability lessens, of course, as the child matures, though it never entirely disappears, as has already been argued. Hence, if we shift our focus to post-secondary Christian education, Callan's requirement that alternative beliefs and objections be given more serious attention is justified to a greater degree. Unfortunately, Christian parents sometimes criticize Christian colleges for allowing too much by way of honest grappling with doubts, questions, and objections to the Christian faith. Such criticism stems from an inadequate understanding of the nature of liberal education. It further is in conflict with biblical principles which stress the need for growth toward normal rational autonomy. Christian colleges need strenuously to resist the "hot-house" mentality which, when carried to an extreme, justly deserves to be labelled indoctrinatory.

10 *Christian nurture, in addition to the ongoing nurture of the child within the Christian tradition, must also open a child's horizons to alternate religious/philosophical belief systems in ways appropriate to the level of development of the child.*
This principle is closely related to the previous one in that questioning, doubt, and a consideration of objections to one's beliefs often arise in the context of being exposed to other belief systems. Thus these two emphases are often combined in the ideal of critical openness, which focuses on the need for a gradual opening up of a child's horizons. There is a need to expand the child's horizons "beyond the present and the particular" as Bailey has highlighted in his description of liberal education (1984).

Children should be made aware in the home, McLaughlin argues, of the fact that religious beliefs alternative to those held by the family do exist, and that there is much disagreement in this area (1984,

81; 1985, 120). Other writers have suggested that the foundations for critical openness are best laid in the play world of young children, "by providing for actual and imaginative participation in the life of different communities of faith" (Schools Council Project 1971, 25-6). As children mature, there is a need for serious study of other religions or religious experience in general, often described as a phenomenological approach to religious education. Although the last two suggestions are generally made within the context of the common school (or the state-supported public school in North America), they can be applied equally well to Christian schools.

I am suggesting here that Christian nurture that does not include this gradual opening up of children's awareness and understanding of other religious/philosophical traditions fails in a significant way to foster growth toward normal rational autonomy. Such nurture can and should be charged with a degree of indoctrination.

Obviously, the above suggestions for fostering critical openness, when applied to a Christian context, will differ from the phenomenological approach to religious education typically found in common schools. In Christian schools, teaching for openness occurs at the same time that children are nurtured within the Christian tradition. Some liberal educators will no doubt worry that this combination undermines the integrity of the opening up process (see Callan 1985, 117; Gardner 1988, 91-4), but this worry is rooted in an unrealistic ideal of critical openness. Given a realistic ideal of *normal* critical openness, there is nothing incoherent in being committed and open at the same time, nor in combining teaching for commitment with teaching for openness. In fact, in my reconstruction of the ideal of liberal education I argue that this is the only way in which education can proceed. Education beyond the present and the particular necessarily builds on the present and the particular.

11 *Christian schools should offer a broad curriculum, initiating students into all the traditional forms of knowledge, thus satisfying the breadth requirement of liberal education. However, each of these forms of knowledge can and should be interpreted as a revelation of God's truth.*
This principle is really an extension of the previous one. Not only should children from Christian homes and students in Christian schools be made aware of and come to understand other religious traditions, they also need to be initiated into all the traditional forms of knowledge. Christian education is, or at least should be, fully in agreement with the breadth requirement of liberal education as advocated by Peters and Hirst and as discussed in chapter 2. However,

since initiation into all there is to know is impossible, since there are limits to the breadth that any school education can achieve, students should be initiated into the *traditional* forms of knowledge.

One writer, attempting to show that the Puritans of the sixteenth and seventeenth centuries advocated general education, goes on to lament the narrowness of some Christian education today (Ryken 1980, 29). As an example, he cites a graduate of a prestigious Bible college who maintained that he had never heard of John Milton. Ryken further suggests that there are Christian schools in which reading in English courses consists solely of missionary biographies (29). Hofstadter provides other examples of narrowness in educational ideals among evangelicals. Charles Finney, the outstanding Presbyterian revivalist of the nineteenth-century United States, had this to say about literature: "I cannot believe that a person who has ever known the love of God can relish a secular novel" (Hofstadter 1963, 94). Dwight L. Moody shared similar sentiments, denigrating all education that did not serve the purpose of religion. "I have one rule about books. I do not read any book, unless it will help me to understand *the* book" (108). When such attitudes determine the policies of Christian schools, they can and should be condemned as indoctrinatory.

One caution, however, is in order. One must be careful not to define the forms of knowledge in such a way as to preclude their being interpreted from a Christian point of view. Contrary to Hirst, the forms of knowledge are not autonomous (which he equates with being secular) (1974a, 84; 1974b, 77; 1981, 87). Treating them as secular is, in fact, a kind of interpretation, and one that goes contrary to a Christian interpretation. Interpretation of the forms of knowledge from a certain world-view or *Weltanschauung* is inescapable. Hirst prefers a secular interpretation, Christians prefer a Christian interpretation. For the Christian, all truth is God's truth, or as Comenius stated 300 years ago, "All truth is one – and leads to God" (Schools Council Project 1971, 56). Hirst is quite justified in suggesting that the Roman Catholic doctrine of Natural Law allows for the possibility of discovering truth apart from revelation, but he fails to realise that such truth will still be interpreted from a Christian perspective by the Christian (1981, 88-9).[12] Christian scholars join their secular counter-parts in the search for truth, but for Christians, any discovery of truth will point to God as the source of that truth.

McLaughlin, in a recent defence of the "breadth and diversity of curriculum" principle for religious schools, seems to agree with my formulation of the above principle, but then is led into an error. He states that "whilst the general curriculum of the religious school might have a particular flavour or series of emphases, it must not be domesticated to religious ends" (McLaughlin 1987, 77). What McLaughlin fails to realize is that every part of the curriculum will serve a religious end within a Christian school, because the orthodox Christian sees all truth as leading to God. Perhaps McLaughlin's worry is that the study of the forms of knowledge in a Christian school should not continually be used for evangelistic purposes. While I sympathetize with McLaughlin's concern about the presence of overt evangelistic emphases in the study of all subjects in a Christian school, there is a sense in which all study is "evangelistic" for the Christian. If all knowledge is rooted in God, then the exploration and teaching of knowledge in any area will point to God, and hence will be implicitly evangelistic. Much more needs to be done by way of an examination of the conditions, situations, and methods for inviting or commending faith, as Rossiter notes (1982, 34), but it is surely obvious that constant explicit appeals for commitment when teaching history, science, or arithmetic are inappropriate. But it *is* appropriate for a Christian teacher to suggest that mathematical truth is ultimately dependent on God.

12 Christian nurture should seek to maintain an appropriate balance between the individual's psychological need for stability and coherence and the educational requirement of growth toward normal rational autonomy.
I have maintained that all children need a stable and coherent primary culture, and that this is in fact a necessary foundation for growth toward rational autonomy. This need for some degree of stability and coherence persists to some extent throughout a person's lifetime, as Berger, among others has argued (1969, 16). As a person matures, the need for stability and coherence lessens, though it never totally disappears.

This need for stability and coherence is in tension with the educational requirement of growth toward rational autonomy. Such growth involves movement beyond the safety and security of a primary culture. It involves risk, independent thinking, stretching of the mind, openness to new ideas, and openness to criticizing old ideas. It is therefore important to establish an appropriate balance between these two sets of demands (McLaughlin 1987, 73). I believe contemporary discussions of liberal education tend to skew the balance by not paying sufficient attention to the psychological need for stability and coherence. I will therefore say more about this violation of the balance principle.

Growth must take place within a context of respect for traditions and authority. It is wrong to foster growth at a rate which leads to children's becoming disoriented. Too much emphasis on critical thinking can also create this kind of disorientation. These practical principles really grow out of my reconstructed ideal of *normal* rational autonomy, where I attempted to outline the parameters of a realistic ideal of rational autonomy. They are well illustrated by means of a botanical analogy which Peshkin found used by the teachers at Bethany Baptist Academy:

Students are like young plants. If they are pre-maturely exposed to the natural elements of wind and rain and sun, they may perish. Better to bring them along slowly, in a carefully controlled environment, so they become strong enough to withstand the impact of the world's uncontrolled environment. (Peshkin 1986, 85)

This principle of the need for an appropriate balance between the need for stability and coherence and the educational requirement for growth towards normal rational autonomy leads to another argument in support of Christian schools for children from Christian homes. Children first entering school have a great need for stability and coherence. Too radical a break with the past or with the inheritance children receive from their parents invites disastrous psychological consequences. Certainly there needs to be growth toward independence and critical reflection about the primary culture children have inherited, but I would suggest that such growth is best fostered within a context of basic continuity with the religious/ philosophical tradition into which they have first been initiated. Much more needs to be done by way of empirical support to justify how much continuity is required, and for how long.[13] But I believe it can be safely concluded that children from Christian homes should be sent to Christian schools, especially at the primary level where the need for stability and coherence is particularly acute.

McLaughlin further worries whether the common school (or the state-supported public school in North America) can adequately satisfy the needs for stability and coherence for children (1987, 75). He expresses his worry in a series of rhetorical questions:

Might not self-identity, self-esteem, psychic and emotional unity, moral development, critical capacity, emotional security and so on be threatened by too high a level of 'openness' (in its various aspects) in the common school; by a 'Babel of values' at the school level? Is it not arguably the case that the greater degree of interim coherent stability in the religious school might not better facilitate the development of the autonomy of its pupils? Might it not have other advantages, too, for example, in counterbalancing for pupils prevailing and dominant conceptions and prejudices in society? (McLaughlin 1987, 75)

The truth of McLaughlin's last question is frequently forgotten by critics of Christian schools. There is indeed a desperate need to provide a counter-balance to the dominant consumer-oriented values of our society, values which are all too often simply reinforced in our public schools.[14]

However, there is a also a danger of placing too much emphasis on the need for the security of a stable and coherent primary culture. The above defence of Christian schools can all too easily be corrupted by a protectionist kind of rationale that fails to give equal emphasis to the need for growth toward rational autonomy. Unfortunately, this kind of rationale is at least implicit in the earlier quote describing the botanical analogy used by the teachers of Bethany Baptist Academy. Peshkin, in this same context, points out that these teachers "without exception" agree that the academy shelters its students. They also justify the academy in terms of providing a "hothouse" for Christian students (1986, 85). Where then is the emphasis on growth toward rational autonomy? Christian schools must not only protect or provide security. There is also a need to disturb, to open up students to the outside elements of "wind and rain and sun," to expose them to the "world's uncontrolled environment" if growth is to be nurtured. Without this, the balance described in the above-mentioned principle is not met, and such a school can indeed be criticized for indoctrinating to some degree.

The principle of balance between the need for stability and coherence and the educational requirement of growth toward normal rational autonomy also has some implications for "secular" higher education. As has already been pointed out, even adults need some degree of stability and coherence in their belief systems. I suggest that there is something wrong with the all too common experience of colleges and university students who are forced to endure a systematic undermining of everything they believe by professors who take upon themselves the task of liberating these students from their supposedly narrow upbringings. Of course, this is all done in the name of teaching critical thinking or by an appeal to Descartes's celebrated method of doubt. But it is forgotten that not only is Descartes's method of doubt philosophically suspect, but such an approach violates the principle of balance. My reconstructed ideal of liberal education further implies that it is fundamentally mistaken to think of students' upbringing as something from which they must necessarily be liberated. Instead, it must be used as a foundation for further growth toward normal rational autonomy.

13 *Christian nurture should seek to maintain a balance between formation and reformation, or between initiation and critical/creative thinking, in terms both of individuals who are being nurtured and of the Christian tradition within which they are being nurtured.*

I have emphasized throughout that Christian parents and teachers need make no excuses for initiating their children and students into the Christian faith. "Faith-formation" is part of what Christian nurture is all about (see Warren 1987). "Initiation," "faith-formation," "transmission of the Christian faith" all have a rather conservative ring to them. But liberal education, even secular liberal education, is in part necessarily conservative, a point about which not all liberal educationalists are sufficiently aware.[15] Certain traditions are necessarily transmitted to the next generation. Liberal education does involve initiation and socialization.

However, it is of utmost importance to realize that liberal education also includes the possibility of reformation of the traditions being transmitted. Students must be encouraged to reflect critically on these traditions. Teachers and students alike must acknowledge the possibility of creative renewal of these traditions. Institutions which foster certain traditions must themselves be subject to criticism and open to renewal. Without these additional dimensions, dangerous stagnation sets in, both in the traditions themselves and in the individuals who are a part of these traditions. If initiation/conservation is not balanced with critical renewal, there is a danger of indoctrination.

This also applies to the overall Christian tradition and to the various particular traditions that comprise that tradition. Education within each tradition must maintain a balance between faithfulness to and a critical/creative reformation of that tradition. The tradition itself and the entire community which supports this tradition must reflect this balance, a point stressed by Westerhoff (see Heywood 1988, 68).

Groome similarly maintains that in the task of Christian religious education there is a need to "call in question and counteract much of the socialization that is already taking place" (1980, 122). He gives three reasons for making such "critical consciousness" essential to religious education: "In brief, it is necessary for the transformation of society, for the reformation of the Church, and for the maturation in faith of individual Christians" (122). Groome concludes with a warning that has been made repeatedly in this book: "For Christian becoming it is not a question of either socialization *or* education. We need a socialization process *and* a critical education in the midst of it" (127).

TOWARD EDUCATIONAL PLURALISM

The primary purpose of this chapter is to explore some of the practical implications for Christian nurture that grow out of my critique of past conceptions of liberal education and indoctrination as well as my reconstruction of these concepts. Clearly, the arguments of the preceding chapters also have implications for state-maintained schools and public education generally. In fact, I have from time to time already hinted at those implications. I do not intend to explore these and other implications in detail, since that would take us beyond the central focus of this book. However, I do want to touch on one implication for public education that does, I believe, grow out of the preceding discussion.

I suggest that much of what has been said in the previous chapters points to a greater degree of educational pluralism as philosophically more defensible than our present state-maintained system of education in Canada, the United States, and other parts of the world. It seems to me that this system is to a large extent inspired by the traditional ideal of liberal education criticized in the preceding chapters.[16] Public education today is very much governed by principles that are in keeping with the Enlightenment liberal ideals of science, rationality, autonomy, and critical openness. However, I have argued that each of these liberal ideals must be seriously qualified in order to be philosophically defensible. Hence there is also a need to reassess the system of state-maintained education that we, in most of the western world, have come to take for granted.

One of the fundamental conclusions of this book is that it is a mistake to view liberal education primarily in terms of liberation. Liberal education is not simply concerned with liberating children from the present and the particular. Instead, our understanding of liberal education needs to be reshaped so that nurturing children into a present and a particular will be seen as an essential and foundational component of liberal education. Obviously, there are many conceptions of the present and the particular. Given that schools are essential to providing liberal education, it would seem to follow that we need a plurality of schools, each beginning with its own conception of the present and the particular, but each also committed to fostering growth toward normal rationality and autonomy.

Some of the principles enunciated earlier in this chapter also point in this direction. It has been argued that Christian nurture needs to occur within the context of a faith-supporting community and institutions. The same applies to Hindu nurture, Jewish nurture, Marxist nurture, and even secular nurture. Without plausibility structures, people's sense of identity is bound to crumble. Schools play an important role in providing plausibility structures for children as well as for adults. Of course, schools do more than this if they are, as they should be, committed to liberal education. But, as we have seen, initiation/socialization is one important aspect of liberal education and hence an important ingredient of schooling committed to liberal education. We therefore need a variety of schools reflecting different belief traditions, schools which will not only provide the plausibility structures necessary for the mental and psychological health of their students, but which will also stretch their students, broadening their horizons and enabling them to think critically and openly about the traditions into which they have been nurtured.

I also argued, earlier in this chapter, that it is important to maintain an appropriate balance between the individual's psychological need for stability and coherence and the educational requirement of growth towards rational autonomy. I raised serious questions as to whether the state-maintained common/public school can adequately satisfy the need for stability and coherence for young children. Might it not be that the anomie and rootlessness so pervasive in our societies is in part related to our liberating children too soon from the present and the particular in which they are raised? Are they exposed too soon to a "Babel of values" in our public schools? It has been suggested that a greater degree of interim coherence and stability will better facilitate growth towards normal rational autonomy, but this is again only possible if it occurs in the context of a plurality of schools reflecting the plurality of traditions in our society.

In chapter 7 I argued that our public schools are less liberal than is often assumed and that they share many of the features often associated with "total institutions." But we must not think that it is possible to escape this problem by eliminating institutions. Ideas need institutions. Institutions are inescapable. What we must ensure is that the institutional context for ideas is liberal. I would suggest that a key requirement for such a liberal institutional context is that it be pluralistic. The best guarantee against institutional indoctrination is that there be a plurality of institutions. This also applies to education. A liberal institutional context for education entails educational pluralism. I would also suggest that a fundamental characteristic of a truly liberal society is that it allows for and supports a variety of educational institutions, each committed to teaching for commitment, while at the same time being committed to fostering growth toward normal rational autonomy.

Other considerations need to be taken into account in order to come to a final conclusion concerning the desirability of educational pluralism.[17] There is, for example, the question of religious freedom for both the believer and the non-believer. There is a need to balance the rights of parents with the rights of the state in education. Economic considerations would need to be taken into account. Then there are also problems in defining the relation between church and state or between society and the individual. Space does not allow consideration of these additional factors; therefore, I am only tentatively suggesting educational pluralism as an implication of the arguments of the previous chapters.,

This educational pluralism could be achieved in a number of ways. It might be conceivable to arrange for a variety of schools within a city or school district, each with its own distinctive approach and curriculum, but all operating under the umbrella of the state-maintained system of education. Or we might want to dispense entirely with the notion of a state-supported and controlled system of education and provide for a more comprehensive pluralism that encompasses both the content and structure of education. These suggestions are in no way a complete departure from the wisdom of the past, for they are one with a long line of advocates, perhaps none more distinguished than John Stuart Mill:

All that has been said of the importance of individuality of character, and diversity of opinion and mode of conduct, involve, as of the same unspeakable importance, diversity of education. A general state education is a mere contrivance for moulding people to be exactly like one another: and as the mould in which it casts them is that which pleases the predominant power in the government, whether this be a monarch, a priesthood, an aristocracy, or the majority of the existing generation: in proportion as it is efficient and successful, it establishes a despotism over the mind, leading by natural tendency to one over the body. An education established and controlled by the State should only exist, if it exist at all, as one among many competing experiments, carried on for the purpose of example and stimulus, to keep the others up to a certain standard of excellence. (Mill [1859]1978, 104-5)

While I believe that Mill goes too far in stressing individuality, much in this statement relates to various concerns of this section. Possibly the real question we need to face is whether we are willing to examine critically our present system of education and consider alternatives, or whether the present monolithic system of state-maintained education is a sacred cow.[18]

CONCLUSION

Many people will no doubt object to my tentative suggestion by raising the familiar objection that such a system of educational pluralism will only breed fanaticism and intolerance. Indeed, some readers will consider my defence of Christian schools throughout this work deficient because it fails to take into account the dangers of such schools serving as breeding grounds for fanaticism and intolerance. But such fears are based on a failure to distinguish between commitment and fanaticism or intolerance.[19] The latter are perversions of healthy commitment, as has been so ably argued by Jay Newman (1982; 1986; see also Thiessen 1987a). It is true that teaching for commitment can foster these perversions, but it need not. And we must not let the fear of such perversions make us miss out on the benefits of healthy commitment. Love has its perversions too, but we do not let this stop us from praising the virtues of love.

And what are the benefits of healthy commitment? For the individual, healthy commitment is "a *sine qua non* of happiness, self-realization and peace of mind," according to Newman (1986, 9). Healthy commitments are also the key to the promotion of civilization. "A civilized society," writes Newman, "is dominated by people who have a healthy and socially constructive commitment to some reasonably plausible and morally efficacious world view. A society in which such people gradually lose influence drifts towards a condition of barbarity" (1986, 9). Indeed, as is being increasingly argued by both serious social critics and casual observers of the contemporary scene, we are facing a "crisis of commitment" in our own society (Newman 1986, 9).[20]

If we want to avoid this crisis of commitment, or if we want to stop the drift toward barbarity, we need schools that openly teach for healthy commitment. There is clearly a risk involved, but we must not let the risk rob us of that which is good and necessary for a civilized society. Allan Bloom, in his widely reviewed and popular book, *The Closing of the American Mind*, which he describes as "a meditation on the state of our souls," also talks of crises: "an intellectual crisis," "the crisis of liberal education," and "the crisis of our civilization" (1987, 346). At bottom, Bloom is describing a crisis of commitment. One reviewer says this about Bloom's book: "Its enormous and surprising popularity suggests that there is a deeper longing for lost ideals among Americans – and Canadians too, I suspect – than we in the academy are comfortable acknowledging" (Downey 1988, 16). Downey urges us "to listen for the ground bass in [Bloom's] requiem. That ground bass is an insistent reminder of what we all know but, in our reflex wish to obviate criticism, we deny or ignore: that there is too much joyless, convictionless teaching and learning in our universities" (1988, 16).[21]

Not only in our universities but in all our schools, and in our homes too, we need to restore the dignity of teaching for commitment. Healthy commitment should be the goal of all education. True, all our beliefs and even our knowledge claims are tainted with a degree of uncertainty. We are, after all, fallible human beings. But despite our fallibility, despite the deep-rooted uncertainty that colours even our most unequivocal claims, we need to dare to believe. We also need to dare to teach for commitment.[22]

"Hell is a forever without commitment" (Smedes 1988, 153). What is so desperately needed in our day is the restoration of a defensible ideal of liberal education which will allow parents and teachers once again to teach for commitment and which will spare our children and students the hell of non-commitment.

Notes

1 Ieuan Lloyd (1981, 253) cites another fascinating example of the charge
of indoctrination being made within the context of state-maintained
education in Greece where education is still closely linked to one
religion. Over a decade ago, A.C. Kazepides published an article
in the journal of the Secondary Education Teachers' Confederation
of Greece entitled "The Ideological Confusion and the Indoctrination
of the Young in Greek Education." "The response to the article was
hostile as evidenced by the 2,500 telegrams sent to the Government
protesting over the publication of the article. Some of the passages of
the article were regarded as vulgar and insulting and as 'undermining
the Greek-Christian foundations of Greek education.' The public prose-
cutor agreed with the public response and a trial is to be held in Athens later this year. The prosecution witnesses are six Greek Orthodox
theologians who claim that the distinction between education and
indoctrination cannot be made in the case of Greece, because the doctrines of the Greek Orthodox Church, unlike other religions, are the
correct ones" (Lloyd 1981, 253). It should be noted that Kazepides
won his case and has subsequently achieved considerable notoriety
in Greece.

2 There are other more recent developments in religious education, but
since they all still include a significant focus on a study of other religions, justified on educational rather than theological grounds, they

can be subsumed under the general rubric of a non-confessional approach to religious education (see Hammond, Hay, et al., 1990; Cooling 1992, chs. 1-4).

3 As further evidence of Hull's tendency to colour Christian nurture negatively, consider the following: At one point he links religious nurturers with evangelists and indoctrinators (1984, 184). Christian nurture is described as occupying "a middle ground" between education (a term of approbation) and indoctrination (a pejorative term) (39). The traditional approach to religious education as nurture is described as "evangelistic in general intention and doctrinaire in tone" (65). Religious nurture is grouped together with evangelism and indoctrination as a "convergent" teaching process where there is a convergence of personal commitment on the part of the teacher with his lesson content and his teaching aims (176-7). Education, by contrast, is characterized by divergence, which "is itself a value, or a bundle of values," and which therefore possesses several marks of "superiority" over convergence (181-2). Nurture is again and again contrasted with religious education where the latter is understood in the sense of an open, critical study of world religions, which for Hull is the only acceptable approach to religious education in state maintained schools.

Paul Hirst, a prominent British philosopher of education, is also an advocate of the new directions in religious education. He repeatedly tries to draw a sharp distinction between a traditionalist concept of education which is concerned with the transmission of a body of specific concepts, beliefs, and values within a particular tradition, and a liberal concept of education which is critical and rational. The former tends to be linked with catechesis, the latter entails that religious education should involve an open, critical, and rational study of religion(s) (Hirst 1974b, 1981, 1985). Hirst defends the latter approach to religious education as essential to education within state-maintained schools, but he clearly rejects the traditionalist approach to religious education as indoctrinatory (see also note 9 below and Snook 1972b, 81, 86, 88).

4 Roger Marples (1978), for example, has argued that the teaching-about-religion approach, in order to be successful, must get pupils to acquire a kind of "religious understanding," which entails some sort of commitment to religion generally. All this leads Marples to conclude that the new approach to religious education is sufficiently like indoctrination that it should not be part of a program of education. Eric Johns (1981) has similarly expressed concern about a "pan-religious confessionalism" that pervades the phenomenological approach to religious education.

5 Susan Rose (1988) reviews some of the statistics concerning Christian day schools in the United States. Various estimates would suggest that

such schools have been established at the rate of two per day since 1960. According to one writer, there has been approximately a 630 percent increase in Christian school enrolments since 1965. Estimates further suggest that there are between fifteen and eighteen thousand Christian schools, with a student population of approximately one million (Rose 1988, 34-9; cf. Carper 1984; Reese 1985).

6 The report in Great Britain is commonly referred to as the Swann Report (1985). The Canadian report, commissioned by the government of Alberta, was submitted by the Committee of Tolerance and Understanding (1984). I have responded to the charge made in both these reports – that independent religious schools foster intolerance – in Thiessen (1987a).

7 T.H. McLaughlin (1984) reviews this challenge and provides an interesting defence of the rights of Christian parents to nurture their children in the Christian faith.

8 I have attempted to refute Hirst and to defend the possibility of a distinctively Christian curriculum in Thiessen (1985a).

9 Hirst is in fact not entirely consistent on this point. He clearly objects to Christian nurture in schools, frequently condemning it as indoctrination. For example, church-related schools, according to Hirst, "offer an indefensible form of religious education" and "are not even in principle committed to the demands of open, critical, rational education" (1985, 15). In other words, such schools indoctrinate, Hirst claims, because they are committed to a "primitive" or "traditionalist" concept of education, or because they are committed to Christian catechesis, where "the aim is from the stance of faith, the development of faith" (1981, 86, 89, 91; 1985, 6-7). At times, however, Hirst seems to want to allow for the possibility of rational and open Christian nurture in the home and in Christian schools (1985, 13-14). The basic problem with this is that by Hirst's own criteria there cannot be such a thing as rational and open Christian nurture. The central feature of nurture is that it is committed both in terms of its starting point and in terms of its aims, and it is precisely this element of commitment that Hirst finds so objectionable. Hirst is further dubious that religion is a rational form of knowledge (1974a, ch. 12). Thus there is an inherent contradiction in the very idea of rational Christian nurture, for Hirst, and it is therefore difficult to see how he can look upon Christian nurture in the home and the church in a favourable light even though they belong to a supposedly "private" domain.

Similar ambiguity occurs in the Swann Report. While allowing for a confessional approach within the Christian community, features clearly belonging to the confessional approach are condemned as indoctrination. For example, it is argued that "under no circumstances does edu-

cation become simply a process of indoctrinating a child into one particular way of thinking as the only 'right and proper' view, since in
so doing, his or her capacity to make reasoned and rational judgments may, in effect, again be undermined" (Swann 1985, 14-15). Further, the confessionalist approach to religious education is described as
in keeping with assimilationist tradition which is condemned in the
report, "since it regards the faiths of ethnic minority groups as inferior
to Christianity and seeks therefore, in a 'missionary' spirit, to replace
these faiths with a commitment to the 'superior' Christian religion"
(474).

10 For a review of this phenomenon, see Enroth (1977).

11 In an essay reviewing anti-intellectualism within the Mennonite
church, the charge of indoctrination is made on a number of occasions
(Wiebe 1980). Wiebe calls for reform of Mennonite institutions from
"indoctrination centres" to true education centres (152).

12 John Dewey maintained that "philosophy is the theory of education ...
education is the laboratory in which philosophic distinctions become
concrete and are tested" ([1916]1966, 332, 329).

13 See, for example, Callan (1985), Gardner (1988), Kazepides (1987),
Laura and Leahy (1989), Marthaler (1987), McLaughlin (1985), Neiman
(1989), Scruton, Ellis-Jones, et al. (1985), Spiecker (1987), and Young
(1988).

CHAPTER TWO

1 I concur with Neiman who has recently suggested that the only way
"we can escape the sterility characteristic of the present impasse over
indoctrination" is to undertake a contextualist approach which recognizes "that all inquiry is shaped at least to some extent, by historical
and social realities ... Meaning is not there to be found; it is created in
social situations (Nieman 1989, 53, 54).

2 There would seem to be a resurgence of the older oratorical ideal of
liberal education in the current crusade for a new classicism (see, for
example, Bloom 1987; Hirsch 1988).

3 Paul Hirst, a close associate of R.S. Peters, has written extensively on
these forms of knowledge (Hirst 1974a).

4 In essence, the transcendental justification for liberal education maintains that the basic elements of liberal education such as rationality,
critical thinking, and the pursuit of truth are inescapable. In questioning them one is necessarily presupposing them. To ask for a justification of liberal education is already to be committed to rationality and
the pursuit of truth (Hirst 1974a, 41-2; Peters 1966, 164).

CHAPTER THREE

1 For example, Snook (1972b, 37; 1972c, 152), Flew (1972a, 70-1, 81-2, 85-6), and Green (1972, 37-8), all tend to use "doctrine" and "ideology" interchangeably. Siegel, after reviewing the "semantic disarray" surrounding the term "ideology," proposes the following as capturing the central meaning of the term: "a general framework that shapes individual consciousness, guides and legitimates belief and action, and renders experience meaningful" (1988, 64). This would also capture the essential meaning of "world-view" though some writers stress that world-views are pretheoretical in nature (Walsh & Middleton 1984; Holmes 1983, 31). While sympathetic with this position, I would argue that pretheoretical world-views are always finally given theoretical expression, and thus I believe we need to focus on doctrines or ideologies, which I see as the theoretical expression of world-views.

  Since it is generally assumed that there is an etymological connection between "indoctrination" and "doctrines," I will interpret the content criterion in terms of a limitation to doctrinal beliefs, rather than to ideologies. This restriction should not affect the soundness of my critical evaluation of the content criterion, since, as will be shown later in my analysis of the meaning of "doctrine," there is clearly some overlap in the meaning of the two terms. Further, my arguments can easily be extended to include the notion of ideology but such extrapolation will not be undertaken in this chapter.

2 Flew, in an essay, "The Jensen Uproar," describes the reaction of the scientific community to Arthur Jensen's studies on IQ, and his suggestion "that genetic factors are strongly implicated in the average Negro-White intelligence difference … The original publication occasioned an enormous coast-to-coast brouhaha of protest and denunciation; including tyre-slashing, slogan-painting, telephoned abuse and threats, and strident demands to 'Fire' or even to 'Kill Jensen' " (1973, 63).

3 J.S. Mill, in commenting on the disagreement over first principles in morality, points out that "similar discordance exist[s] respecting the first principles of all the sciences, not excepting that which is deemed most certain of them – mathematics" ([1861]1957, ch. 1).

4 It should also be noted that this description of doctrines might be suggested by a certain view of religious language arising out of the positivist challenge. Instead of focusing on the cognitive aspect of religious belief, meaning is here located in the believer's response. However, this view of religious language is by no means accepted by all philosophers and theologians, and it would surely be inadvisable to base a

definition of "doctrines" in a certain view of religious language which is itself a point of debate.

5 Some versions of the design argument for the existence of God, for example, suggest that the only adequate explanation as to why the universe is intelligibile to the human mind is the postulate of God as the source of such intelligibilty. Alvin Plantinga has argued that belief in God should be viewed as a basic belief which is foundational to a rational noetic, or cognitive, structure. He further reminds us that Augustine argued that reason is ultimately reliable just because God has created us and is not a deceiver (Plantinga 1979).

6 *Webster's Third New International Dictionary* (1976) hints at this limitation of "doctrine" when it defines "indoctrinate" as "to give instruction esp. in fundamentals or rudiments." Snook also argues that "the basic assumptions and postulates of an empirical science qualify as doctrines" (1972b, 35).

7 In *Theism in an Age of Science* (1988), Phillip Wiebe also attempts to show that Judaeo-Christian theism can be construed as a theory which posits a god as a theoretical entity in order to account for various inter-subjectively observable events.

8 Whitehead, for example, argued that "the faith in the possibility of science ... is an unconscious derivative from medieval theology" ([1925]1967, 13). The idea of "the detailed providence of a rational personal God was one of the factors by which the trust in the order of nature had been generated" (61).

9 See, for example, Colwell (1979), Heimbeck (1969), and McKinnon (1970).

CHAPTER FOUR

1 Snook (1972b), for example, attempts to analyze indoctrination in terms of the intention criterion alone, but a careful analysis of his intention criterion will reveal that it includes reference to teaching methods. In a later essay, Snook admits that reference to the teacher's activity may be all that is necessary in explaining an indoctrinated state of mind (1973a, 57, 59).

2 White (1973, 35, 104) attempts to answer possible objections by distinguishing between compulsion and coercion but this surely flies in the face of common usage.

3 Schwartz (1979), in dealing with the problem of children not being able to choose, objects to the Kantian ideal, implicit in the writings of John Rawls and Jean Piaget, that we must be radically free from all social influences. Schwartz uses arguments in Aristotle's writings showing that children only become rational if they have first been *influenced* in

this direction by way of adult choice and example. Initially, however, they do not choose to be rational.

4 Brent (1978) has argued that the forms of knowledge can be justified transcendentally as some kind of a priori structure of the mind itself, and that we are therefore justified in imposing these public traditions on the child. Brent's defence, however, is problematic in that he appeals to "the Chomskyan notion of certain semantic structures that are presupposed by any human language," a notion which "is almost universally rejected by his followers." See a critical review of Brent's work by Hendley (1980).

5 In an excellent review of Kuhn's thought, Fennell and Liverette (1979) examine Kuhn's argument that "normal science" operates within a set of presuppositions and techniques which are seldom if ever critically examined. This also carries over into the teaching of science. Allen (1978) reviews Polanyi's argument that there is a tacit dimension to knowing which, according to Polanyi, entails that all knowing and teaching has an acritical foundation.

6 Peters himself argues that it is "absurd to foster an abstract skill called *critical thinking* without handing on anything to be critical about" (1966, 53-4). Elsewhere he writes, "Logically speaking, too, criticism must take certain presuppositions for granted. Not everything can be questioned at once" (1977, 64). Peters, however, fails to see that these comments entail that indoctrination is unavoidable on his own criteria.

7 Pring (1976, ch. 4) reviews these "new directions" in the sociology of education.

8 Gadamer (1975) provides another illustration of the inevitability of non-rational, indoctrinative teaching methods in his discussion of prejudice. He maintains that the historicity of our existence entails not only that prejudices are unavoidable, but that they belong to the very possiblity of understanding, and hence the Enlightenment ideal of objective knowledge is an illusion.

9 For excellent discussion on the validity of Reichenbach's distinction, see Siegel (1979), Halstead (1979), and Page (1979).

10 Mavrodes (1970) argues for this same conclusion by way of analyzing the concept of knowledge. The concept of knowledge is both objective and subjective, according to Mavrodes. It is objective in that "N knows p" logically entails "p is true." The latter claim is objective in that it does not entail any statement about the psychological state of any person or group. The concept of knowledge is also subjective in that "N knows p" logically entails "N believes that p." The latter claim is subjective in that it refers to a certain type of psychological state. Knowledge is therefore a mixed concept and hence is person-relative and person-variable, according to Mavrodes. Much of the

confusion engendered in epistemological discussions today arises from the failure to recognize the mixed character of crucial epistemological concepts such as the concept of knowledge, according to Mavrodes.

More recently, Lorraine Code (1987) has raised similar concerns. "Epistemologists," Code complains, "in their analysis of the meaning and justification of knowledge claims, rarely ask, 'But whose claims? When? And in what circumstances?' " (ix). Code develops an alternate way to approach epistemological questions by focusing on cognitive activity and process rather than products or end-states of cognition (8). She is also very concerned about the individualism of most contemporary epistemology, and offers instead a "socialized" approach to epistemology because humans are "cognitively interdependent" (115, 167). Hence her chapter, "Epistemic Community" (ch. 7).

11 A regulative or heuristic principle serves as an ideal model towards which we strive. Habermas himself is forced to treat his ideal speech situation as a heuristic principle in the face of the objection that his theory is too utopian (1979).

12 For other comments on the need to develop an epistemology that does justice both to its normative and historical/situational character, see Code (1987, ch. 6) and Stout (1981, ch. 8).

13 Susan Haack (1990), building on the work of Quine, seeks a compromise between foundationalist and coherentist epistemologies. She classifies her attempt as a reformist naturalistic epistemology and coins the awkward term "foundherentism" to label her theory. My notion of normal rationality would be built on an epistemology somewhat akin to Haack's foundherentism.

14 Unfortunately, Hofstadter's definition of "anti-intellectualism" is too narrow in that it rests on a purist and idealistic notion of rationality which I have been criticising. He also fails to acknowledge that many evangelicals were not opposed to learning *per se*, but to "humanistic" learning which begins with presuppositions which are counter to Christian presuppositions. Hofstadter is also forced to acknowledge that there were evangelicals, like John Wesley, who were well educated, well read, and who defended the importance of the intellect and education for the church (see Hofstadter 1963, 72, 80, 95-6, 101). He also admits that the revivalists and Methodist circuit preachers at that time were attempting to bring the gospel to the poor, the uneducated, and often the uncivilized, and thus they had to adapt themselves to their audience to some extent in order to be able to communicate, thereby appearing to be anti-intellectual (75, 79-80, 97).

CHAPTER FIVE

1 Snook (1972b, 1972c), for example, who has paid considerable attention to the concept of indoctrination, defines it in terms of intention alone. According to Snook (1972b, 41), one of the first writers to stress the intentions criterion of indoctrination was William Heard Kilpatrick, a disciple of John Dewey and one of the leading Progressivists in the United States during the first half of this century. Among analytic writers in addition to Snook, R.M. Hare (1964) and J.P White (1972a, 1972b) argue that intention is a fundamental ingredient in a proper analysis of "indoctrination." More recently, McLaughlin (1984), following White, defines indoctrination as the intentional inculcation of unshakable beliefs.

2 Callan, in responding to McLaughlin, objects to defining indoctrination in terms of intentions. However, he agrees with McLaughlin in emphasizing the importance of autonomy. "Indoctrination curtails personal autonomy and thereby infringes upon the right to self-determination or at least devalues that right for the individual" (Callan 1985, 116).

3 Hirst is not entirely consistent in making this contrast. At times he seems to suggest that there can be a rational form of Christian nurture which is not indoctrinatory (Hirst 1981, 92; 1985, 13-14). The problem with this concession, however, is that on Hirst's own criteria, there cannot be such a thing as rational Christian nurture. In a later essay, he bluntly states that religious schools "are not even in principle committed to the demands of open, critical, rational education" (Hirst 1985, 15). This is entirely in keeping with Hirst's overall thrust, which associates the intentions of Christian nurture with indoctrination.

4 For a careful treatment of the problems involved in defining indoctrination in terms of intentions, see D.E. Cooper (1973).

5 R.S. Peters (1977, 83) gives another example of unintentional indoctrination relating to the authority teachers naturally hold by virtue of their position: "Even those who regard their role as authorities as merely a transitional device for helping their pupils to learn, may have, quite unintentionally, a profound influence on them which fixates them with a set of beliefs. Their intention may be to initiate others into a form of thought in such a way that they may become critical and learn to think for themselves. But they may find, even after many years, that their pupils are still inordinately influenced by their views on particular issues."

6 This point is also made by Feinberg (1973, 166) and Allen (1982, 200). Allen cites Paul Hirst as an example of someone demanding too much

by way of autonomy – who admits that many people are not capable of autonomous judgments, yet does not amend his ideal in the light of this (Allen 1982, 206, 207; Hirst 1974b, 60, 98). Callan, in *Autonomy and Schooling* (1988), attempts to free the concept of autonomy from some perfectionistic elements often associated with it, such as the propensity to engage in endless criticism and rational justification. But Callan doesn't go far enough with his realism and he fails to draw on recent work in epistemology calling for what I have termed normal rationality. Callan also fails to achieve realism in balancing autonomy with interdependence and community.

7 Haworth argues that a community just by virtue of being a community has no value whatsoever because it may be a band of Nazis with a shared purpose to annihilate Jews (1986, 207). By the same token, an autonomous person just by virtue of being autonomous has no value whatsoever because he or she may be a Nazi determined to annihilate Jews. Moral requirements obviously need to be added to the values of both community and autonomy, a point that is most often forgotten by those advocating the ideal of autonomy.

8 See also White (1973, 82), who, in reviewing Dearden's attempts at justifying the value of autonomy, concludes that acceptance of this ideal would seem to be a "subjective matter," a matter of "individual preference." Halstead (1986, 34, 37-42) also points to the arbitrariness of valuing autonomy in his excellent review and critique of five arguments for strong autonomy.

9 Unfortunately, Haworth does not limit himself to justifying normal autonomy, but proceeds to justify the value of autonomy as an ideal condition, that is, the traditional liberal ideal of autonomy (1986, ch. 12). He argues that "the reasons we have for valuing normal autonomy in ourselves and others are equally reasons for valuing autonomy as an ideal condition" (195). But this is surely false. It may be natural to grow toward normal autonomy, but not beyond it. Haworth here undermines the important contribution to the discussion of autonomy he has made with his concept of normal autonomy.

10 Wood (1980), in an essay reviewing the research literature on cognitive development, identifies three images of the child: the child as actor in the world; the child as essentially and primarily a social being; and the child as observer. The first and third images focus on the child's desire for autonomy and individuality. The second image focuses on the child's dependency and need for community. There is truth in all three images.

11 Halstead (1986, ch. 4) argues in a similar way for the compatibility of his weak form of autonomy with Islamic principles.

12 Michael Rutter, Professor of Child Psychiatry at the Institute of Psychi-

atry, University of London, provides an overview of the research literature on "maternal deprivation" since the classic work of John Bowlby (1951). In his study for the World Health Organization, Bowlby's claim that "mother love in infancy and childhood is as important for mental health as are vitamins and proteins for physical health," was first greeted with a storm of controversary (Rutter 1972, 13, 123). Some of Bowlby's earlier claims have been modified, but the basic claim – that lack, loss, or distortion of child care has very important negative effects on psychlogical and cognitive development – has received substantial support in subsequent research according to Rutter (1972, ch. 6). Children need a stable, enduring, and loving relationship with a few care-givers (Rutter 1972, 28). They also need rich, distinctive, and meaningful conversational interchange with adults. Linguistic chaos creates problems for normal child development (86-92). Although there is controversy in the field of child development, as is documented in an important anthology reviewing the research literature in developmental psychiatry (Rutter 1980), the basic claim that a child needs a stable and coherent primary culture for development towards eventual autonomy seems to be generally accepted by researchers.

This conclusion is also confirmed by the work of Urie Bronfenbrenner, Professor of Human Development and Family Studies and of Psychology at Cornell University (1979, 1980). For a more detailed description of the work of Bronfenbrenner, among others, see chapter 8, notes 8 and 9.

CHAPTER SIX

1 In a later essay, Snook asks us to shift our focus from indoctrination to the indoctrinated person or the indoctrinated society, and here again, what is highlighted is the non-rational way in which beliefs are held (1973a; cf. O'Leary 1979). The irrationality characteristic of indoctrinated persons can take many forms: they may believe what is false or doubtful, they may believe what is true but be unable to back up their belief, or they may disregard contrary evidence or simply be uninterested in evidence (Snook 1973a, 56).
2 Gardner, for example, has recently suggested "that indoctrination involves the production of a certain effect" (1988, 94). The effect Gardner has in mind is the reluctance to change one's position in the face of arguments and reasons (cf. Beehler 1985; Callan 1985, 115; Watson 1987, 12).
3 The debate concerning the possibility of open-mindedness in scientific inquiry centres particularly on the work of Thomas Kuhn ([1962]1970).

See also Lakatos and Musgrave (1970). For an effective defence of the possiblility of critical openness in science in relation to education see Hare (1985, ch. 7) and Siegel (1988, ch. 6).

4 Wittgenstein makes the point in this way: "If you tried to doubt everything you would not get as far as doubting anything. The game of doubting itself presupposes certainty" ([1969]1972, para. 115).

5 Hare recognizes the problem of the tradition-bound nature of our thinking and treats it as an objection to the logical possibility of critical openness (1979, ch. 3). He tries to get around the problem by suggesting that there can still be some openness within a tradition (1979, 49, 53). But surely the real problem has to do with the possibility of moving beyond the tradition to which we are presently bound. Fortunately, Hare does address the real problem in his treatment of scientific paradigms, in which he recognizes that it is always possible at some *later time* to be open and critical about what was assumed earlier (see note 3 above).

6 For example, Siegel considers a pragmatic justification of critical openness – it is useful as a defence against unscrupulous advertisers, idealogues, and other potential manipulators of opinion (1988, 51). Siegel himself is more interested in a philosophical justification which sees critical openness as an expression of the autonomy and dignity of the person (1988, ch. 3). Some philosophers have justified the ideal of critical openness with a kind of transcendental argument – to question critical openness is in fact to presuppose it. Critical openness seems somehow to be inescapable (Hare 1979, 17-18). Closely related is Hare's claim that "for anyone with a concern for truth, anxious to arrive at true, reasonable, or morally sound conclusions, there must be a presumption in favour of open-mindedness (1985, 4, 87; 1979, 60).

7 Spiecker cites an example of a Dutch cardinal who is strongly opposed to criticism in the church. "Some with all their criticism think that in the church something like 'loyal opposition' is possible. Now if bishops did behave in an obscene way – I do not know any one who does – yes, then opposition certainly is necessary, but opposition against the doctrines of the church and her sexual morality, that are supposed to be backward, that is inadmissible, that is not loyal, because it goes against the authentic Christian doctrine" (1987, 263). Not only is this claim false – some bishops do behave in obscene ways – but we have here a clear case of stifling critical openness, a case of attempted indoctrination.

8 This appears to be confirmed by the research of Rokeach who found some correlation between closed-mindedness and childhood anxiety, insecurity, and feelings of inadequacy (1960, chs. 4, 19).

CHAPTER SEVEN

1 As might be expected, some of these studies suffer from rhetoric and unsupported exaggeration; however, some are supported by extensive and systematic research. One such study, funded by the National Institute of Education (u.s.), concludes that public school textbooks commonly exclude the history, heritage, beliefs, and values of millions of Americans who are committed to the Judeo-Christian religion (Vitz 1986). Further, religious persons, beliefs, and values are often portrayed in a negative light. While rejecting any suggestion of a conscious conspiracy, Vitz does maintain that it is a very widespread secular and liberal mindset that is responsible for the anti-religious bias in textbooks (1986, 1).

2 These studies conclude that several "doctrines" of the *Humanist Manifestos* (Kurtz [1933][1973]1976) were found in a sampling of government funded and approved textbooks in each of four subject areas – biology, history, social studies, and civics – as well as in the stated objectives or editorial comment of the companion teachers' guides (McCarthy et al. 1981; Oppewal 1981).

3 I have argued this point elsewhere by examining the definition of "religion" and looking at the evolution of legal definitions of religion (see Thiessen 1982b; see also Oppewal, 1981; "Towards a Constitutional Definition of Religion," 1978). Interestingly, Ivan Illich has pointed out that "the school is becoming the established church of secular times" (Arons, [1983]1986, 49). And John Dewey, among others, agrees that secular humanism should be viewed as a religion (Dewey 1934; Kurtz [1933, 1973]1976).

4 R.S. Peters also illustrates my argument that all education involves teaching a cosmology and a way, and that, for him as a liberal philosopher of education, this is a secular cosmology and way. According to Peters, "Our basic predicament in life is to learn to live with its ultimate pointlessness. We are monotonously reminded that education must be for life, so obviously the most important dimension of education is that in which we learn to come to terms with the pointlessness of life" (1973c, 1). This is certainly quite different from a Christian cosmology and way which affirms the ultimate meaningfulness of life.

5 It should be noted that those attempting to show that public schools inculcate secular humanism need to pay more attention to the hidden curriculum. It is because much of the anti-religious influence is latent or implicit that it is difficult to substantiate such claims. Interestingly, some of the empirical work being done to prove that an unwritten curriculum does affect people's thinking has focused on the concept of

psychological "modernity," a concept related to secularization and its variant – secularism. Dreeben (1976) reviews some studies that have shown that, even though most, if not all, schools do not explicitly design the curriculum to increase the level of psychological modernity, formal schooling emerges as the single most powerful influence towards psychological modernity (116).

6 Indeed much educational philosophy follows the assumptions of modernism, which views the family and the values closely tied to the family – ethnicity, culture, and religion – as part of the primal, primitive, pre-rational past out of which humans are evolving (Berger 1974, 199; Greeley 1974, 14). R.S. Peters, for example, in tracing the consequences of "social progress" on the family, is led to entertain the disintegration of the family as a "logical alternative" (1973a, ch. 3). After all, we are only bound to the family "by irrational bonds of love and loyalty" (36). But Peters recognizes that if we are unable to rehabilitate the traditional family structure, it will have to be replaced by another institution, because children (and adults) cannot exist without institutions. Thus Peters sees the state as taking on many of the functions traditionally associated with the family.

7 Michael Polanyi ([1946]1964) has done much to show the institutional aspects of the scientific enterprise. See also Feyerabend, 1975. For some comments on this see my discussion of science in chapter 3.

8 See also chapter 4 where I argued that epistemology is in some way related to the psychological, sociological, and historical dimensions of the knower, in which case it again could be argued that epistemology is in some way related to institutions.

CHAPTER EIGHT

1 I am drawing on a distinction made by Mavrodes between a logical contradiction and an epistemic dilemma (1970, ch. 4). It is not enough for the critic of Christian nurture to show that it and true education are *believed* to be contradictory. It must be shown that they really are logically contradictory. An epistemic dilemma has a subjective component to it, whereas the notion of a logical contradiction is a purely objective notion.

2 I made a claim in earlier writings to the effect that the concept of indoctrination is meaningless (Thiessen 1980; 1984a). Nielsen (1984) is surely correct in pointing out that a concept cannot be declared meaningless just because philosophers are unable to provide a clear analysis of it. We need to distinguish between a concept's being confused, and its being meaningless.

3 See my response to Nielsen (Thiessen 1984b; see also Thiessen 1984a).

4 This is of course a debatable point, but I believe it is now generally recognized that analysis is value laden. Snook, for example, after suggesting that all analyses of concepts are biased in that "they presuppose and carry with them an ideological component, a social theory and (perhaps) a metaphysic," concludes, "There is no neutral analysis of a concept in a normative domain." He adds, "My heart is no longer in this approach to philosophy" (personal correspondence, 9 April 1979). More recently, and in response to Neiman's plea for a new contextualist approach to discussing the problem of indoctrination (1989), Snook claims that the context-free approach to doing philosophy of education "ceased some ten years ago" (Snook 1989, 62).

5 See, for example, my reference to G.K. Chesterton, on p. 55. It should be noted that my observations about liberalism could equally well be applied to the broader context of the contemporary ideal of liberal education – modernism. Here also my objective is not to replace modernism with radical post-modernism. Rather, with Toulmin, I want to seek reconciliation between modernist and post-modernist ideas. In exploring the antecedents of the modern age, Toulmin remarks, "We are not compelled to *choose between* 16th-century humanism and 17th-century exact science: rather, we need to hang on to the positive achievements of them both" (1990, 180).

6 This contrast is also implicit in Peters's distinction between the older undifferentiated concept of education and the more recent, more specific concept of education in which education is seen as leading up to the emergence of a liberally educated person (see chapter 2).

7 See Thiessen (1987b) for a more detailed critique of Hirst's contrast between the primitive and sophisticated concepts of education.

8 Urie Bronfenbrenner, Professor of Human Development and Family Studies and of Psychology at Cornell University, in a review of the research conducted over the past half a century regarding the environmental conditions necessary for the emotional development of human beings from early childhood, concludes that a fundamental requirement of such healthy development is a secure and stable home, which is supported in its activities (and world-view) by other adults in the child's environment (1979, 1980). Sociologist Peter Berger similarly warns against the danger of anomie and homelessness which result from modern man's failure to take into account the need for a primary culture and to provide for institutions which satisfy this need (1977, 1974). See also the work of Michael Rutter, Professor of Child Psychiatry at the Institute of Psychiatry, University of London (1972, 1980). For some comments on his work, see chapter 5, note 12.

9 Bronfenbrenner, in his review of the research regarding the child's need for a stable and secure home environment, raises the question of

the age of the child who has such a need. His reply: "The matter is debatable, but I would suggest anyone under the age of, say, 89" (1980, 1). Bronfenbrenner argues that this need is simply part of the human condition, because we are by nature social animals. Karl-Ernst Nipkow, a leading German expert in religious education, draws on research from various quarters in order to argue that not only the small child but also the older child "needs the basic experience of living in a reliable, safe and unambiguous world which is not permanently questioned," and it is within this secure nurturing context that a liberalizing and opening up process can best occur (Nipkow 1985, 31-5). Berger also argues that the need for security, which a primary culture provides, continues well beyond childhood (1974, 1977). Watson acknowledges this point in her plea for a more positive approach to critical thinking. She argues that for adults as well as children there is a need for *self-assurance* as a basis for further intellectual development (1987, 58). Hence, also her more positive concept – "critical affirmation" (54-61).

10 It should be noted that Kazepides misquotes Peters when he omits the word "baldly" which again underscores Peters's main concern: liberal education cannot be defined *only* in terms of initiation, but initiation is certainly an essential part of liberal education (Kazepides 1982, 162; Peters 1973d, 144).

11 This reconstructed definition of indoctrination comes fairly close to the suggestion of Ralph Page, who in turn suggests that we look to John Dewey as providing the needed correctives to past ordinary language analyses of "indoctrination" (Page 1979; 1980; 1985). More recently, Watson has described indoctrination as nurture which is conducted without due regard and sensitivity to the awakening maturity of the child (1987, 13). Interestingly, some of the key ideas in my proposed definition of indoctrination are already present in a paper written by R.M. Hare in 1964. I will say more on this later in the text. Similarly, Kleinig, in an article reviewing past work on the concepts of education and indoctrination, sums up by describing various kinds and methods of teaching as "educative and acceptable insofar as they are directed towards the development of rational autonomy." Indoctrination, by contrast, "constitutes a chronic frustration of this ideal" (Kleinig 1973, 31). Other examples could be provided to show that implicit and, at times, explicit references are made in past analyses of "indoctrination" to the concerns that I am suggesting lie at the core of my reconstruction of the theory of indoctrination. Unfortunately, past work on the concept of indoctrination was based on an indefensible ideal of liberal education, thereby introducing a host of problems which I have reviewed in previous chapters.

12 John Wilson, for example, makes these distinctions in a crisp statement: "Roughly, if I illegitimately (whatever this may mean) persuade
a child to think that God will punish him for masturbating, this is indoctrination; if I give him a feeling of fear and repulsion about it, this
is conditioning; if I tie his hands behind his back, this is force" (1972a,
101; 1972b, 17). But surely the first example involves appeal to fear and
even a kind of coercion. Wilson himself is unable to maintain these
sharp distinctions when he talks about indoctrination in terms of a person holding "psychological" power over another, and when he admits
that "there are all sorts of ways in which we can compulsively direct
another person's thinking," and when he states: "The model cases of
indoctrination are obvious: brainwashing people to believe in Communism, teaching Christianity by the threat of torture or damnation, forcing people by early training to accept social roles as in Huxley's *Brave
New World*" (Wilson 1972b, 18; 1972a, 103; 1964, 26). These difficulties
come up again and again and they are based on an inadequate conception of human nature. Green, for example, acknowledges that making
a sharp distinction between conditioning and indoctrination may not
always be possible. He further introduces psychological dimensions in
his analysis of "indoctrination" when he stresses that it has less to do
with *what* we believe and more to do with *how* we believe, and even
that there may be a "psychological or spatial order" to a belief system
(Green 1972). Snook, in commenting on the conditioning-indoctrina-
tion distinction, writes that perhaps "the distinction cannot be entirely
sustained" (1970, 85).

Given a holistic view of human nature, a theory of indoctrination
should at the same time consider a whole cluster of related concepts
such as conditioning, brainwashing, propaganda – concepts which are
in fact often interchanged in the literature. For examples where the
terms "indoctrination," "brainwashing," "conditioning," and "propaganda," are interchanged, see Ellul (1969), White (1972b, 194), and
Green (1972, 27).

CHAPTER NINE

1 Thomas Groome's widely acclaimed *Christian Religious Education* (1980)
picks up on several themes that I outline in my reconstruction of the
theory of liberal education. Groome's "shared praxis" approach to religious education stresses the importance of relating to the the past, the
present and the future. He also takes a developmental approach to religious education, stressing the importance of growing toward a mature Christian faith which is able to critically reflect on one's own and
other's religious experiences. See also two recent anthologies, one ed-

ited by Leslie J. Francis and Adrian Thatcher, *Christian Perspectives for Education: A Reader in the Theology of Education* (1990) and the other edited by Jeff Astley and David Day, *The Contours of Christian Education* (1992).

2 Debate concerning parental rights with regard to a child's education most often centres on the right to determine a child's later education, and I agree that this is indeed a complex problem. However, with regard to the early initiation phase of a child's education, the problem is surely a good deal simpler, and a combination of a biological argument and the argument regarding a child's need for a stable and coherent primary culture is sufficient to establish this parental right (see McLaughlin 1984; Crittenden 1988).

3 I am here drawing on the biblical metaphor of Esau selling his birth-right to Jacob for a mess of pottage (Genesis 25:29-34). As one example of hesitation about the religious orientation of Christian schools, I would refer the reader to a recent report of the Catholic Committee in the Province of Quebec (1989). The Committee reports that many of the people surveyed admitted "that they hesitate to say they are Catholic or to qualify their school as Catholic ... it does not seem realistic to believe that a Catholic public school today should attempt to educate students in Christianity" (Catholic Committee 1989, 26, 20; cf. 13, 23, 25, 27). At times the reports of the British Council of Churches seem to go out of their way to identify with secular approaches to religious education while seeming to apologize for the apparent "rather parochial, rather narrow" appearance of Christian nurture. The question is asked as to whether Christian nurture may even appear to be a process of indoctrination, and every effort is made to distance the religious instruction of ecumenical churches from sectarian patterns of instruction (British Council of Churches 1984, 46). See also the example of John Hull, chapter 1, note 3, and an example from within a Canadian Mennonite Christian community, chapter 1, note 11.

4 The results of such an upbringing were vividly illustrated for me in a conversation with a young business woman occupying a seat beside me on a plane bound for Boston. After I had mentioned my interest in religious education, she informed me that her parents had been upset about the division between Protestants and Roman Catholics and had decided not to expose their children to religion at all. She confessed that as a result she knew nothing about religion. She wouldn't even know where to begin in order to get information about religion. She further admitted to feeling short-changed by the kind of upbringing she had received. The question that secularists like Gardner have to face with regard to situations like this is: does such an upbringing allow for growth toward rational autonomy in the area of religion?

5 For a corrective to Goldman's negative application of Piagetian-type research to religious education, see Groome (1980, Part V).

6 See Westerhoff (1976, 1983). For an excellent review article on Westerhoff, see Heywood (1988). Groome (1980, ch. 6) reviews various other writers who, like Westerhoff, take a socialization approach to religious education.

7 Westerhoff is thinking primarily in terms of the dominance of the schooling paradigm in church education, e.g. Sunday School programs. Thus Rossiter considers it unfortunate that Westerhoff's faith-enculturation approach has been applied so widely and uncritically to Catholic schools (1982, 28).

8 I am well aware that my treatment of mature and immature commitment suffers from oversimplification. A fully developed theory of religious education would need a much more sophisticated treatment of faith development such as has been worked out by James Fowler. See an excellent review of Fowler in Groome (1980, ch. 4).

9 McLaughlin further reminds us of the work of writers such as G.B. Matthews (1980), who describes the philosophical significance of the questioning of young children. Matthews argues that it is important for parents to encourage this embryonic philosophizing which is a key to fostering growth toward independent intellectual enquiry. Groome similarly stresses the need for an ever-deepening and expanding capacity for critical reflection in religious education (1980, 237).

10 For further comments on Hofstadter's analysis of anti-intellectualism in evangelicalism, see chapter 4, note 14.

11 Rose, in her study of two evangelical schools, uncovered a pervasive anti-intellectualism at Lakehaven Academy (1988, 107).

12 See Thiessen (1985a) for a detailed refutation of Hirst's argument concerning the autonomy of the forms of knowledge.

13 For a review of some empirical studies on the need for a stable and coherent primary culture, see "Nurturing Autonomy," chapter 5, note 12, and chapter 8, notes 8 and 9.

14 Unfortunately, Christian schools all too often seem to simply mirror the consumer-oriented values of our society. In her critique of evangelical schooling in America, Rose points out that although the many new Christian schools are often "constructed as fortresses to protect children from unhealthy 'worldly' influences, their unintended effect on future education may be far different ... The product could be far more 'secular' than any educational system ever imagined by the founders of the 'sacred' schools" (1988, 218). Groome also warns about the danger of Christian religious education being used as a source of legitimation for sinful social arrangments rather than being a liberating/redemptive/critiquing force (1980, 123). See also Warren on the need to

counter the influence of "the marketeers and panderers to consumer lust" (1987, 522-3).

15 Penny Enslin (1985), for example, claims Peters and Hirst should not be called liberal philosophers of education because of their emphasis on initiation.

16 For an analysis of some other roots of the state-maintained system of universal, compulsory education see McCarthy, Oppewal, et al. (1981) and Russell (1976).

17 McCarthy, Oppewal, et al. (1981), in their defense of educational pluralism from a Christian perspective, provide a fine treatment of various considerations that need to be taken into account in defending such pluralism. In chapter 1 they also draw on the social/political analysis of Berger and Neuhaus (1977) and their notion of "mediating structures" as a way of defending educational pluralism. Coons and Sugarman (1978) have treated the economic aspects of educational pluralism. Crittenden (1988) deals with the issue of parental rights.

18 Rose, in reviewing the historical developments leading to the proliferation of Christian schools in America, says this about the public schools in the mid-nineteenth century: "The public school, an important socializing institution, became the substitute for the American national church" (1988, 29). Richard Russell quotes American sociologist Peter Berger: "A good case could be made for seeing in the public school the principal agency in our society representing our politically established cultural religion in almost pure form ... If one is to look for a catechism that states these religious suppositions of the public school John Dewey's *A Common Faith* will probably be the best choice" (1976, 116).

19 It is interesting to note that the identification of commitment with intolerance can be traced back to the emergence of the Enlightenment ideal of liberal education. Kimball (1986, 121) identifies tolerance as an essential component of the liberal-free concept of liberal education, based on the assumption that "certainty is the mother of intolerance ... Appearing at the turn of the eighteenth century, this was 'a new virtue,' for the notion of tolerance had previously implied weakness or cowardice, that is, lack of commitment to one's professed beliefs. The new virtue thus depended centrally on the epistemology of skepticism, as Locke demonstrated forcefully about religion" (Kimball 1986, 121).

20 See also the study of Robert Bellah and his associates on the loss of commitment in American life, *Habits of the Heart: Individualism and Commitment in American Life* (1985).

21 Bloom, along with Hirsch (1988) and other advocates of the current crusade for a new classicism, assumes that liberal education needs a revival of the study of the classics of western civilization. This smacks of cultural imperialism given the pluralistic nature of modern societies,

and these writers have been rightly criticized for assuming that we can return to the glorious past and again teach for commitment to a specific world view in our state common schools and universities. This is also the error of Bowers's attempt to develop a post-liberal theory of education which attempts to correct the excesses of liberalism by introducing some conservative themes (1987). What all these writers fail to do is carry their argument to its logical conclusion – a return to teaching for commitment within a pluralistic society requires a pluralistic educational system.

22 All our beliefs and knowledge rest upon acritical convictions and commitments as has been argued by Michael Polanyi, among others. It was Polanyi's great aim "to restore to us once more the power for the deliberate holding of unproven beliefs" so that "we may firmly believe what we might conceivably doubt, and may hold to be true what might conceivably be false" (1958, 268, 312). Allen suggests this thrust of Polanyi's work can be summed up in terms of the injunction *credere aude* – "dare to believe." He continues, "Ours should be the extension of this to *docere aude* – 'dare to teach,' and the restoration of the ability to teach beliefs which we cannot prove and which we know might conceivably be false. Belief, faith, commitment – these are inevitable while life lasts, and neutrality is a fraud and delusion" (Allen 1976, 14).

Bibliography

Abington v. Schempp, 374 U.S. 203 (1963).

Abraham, William J. 1985. *An Introduction to the Philosophy of Education.* Engelwood Cliffs, NJ: Prentice-Hall.

Ackerman, Bruce. 1980. *Social Justice in the Liberal State.* New Haven: Yale University Press.

Alberta Education. 1985. *An Audit of Selected Private School Programs.* Edmonton: Alberta Education.

Allen, R.T. 1976. "Neutral Against Faith." *Spectrum* 9(1):12-14.

– 1978. "The Philosophy of Michael Polanyi and Its Significance for Education." *Journal of Philosophy of Education* 12:167-77.

– 1982. "Rational Autonomy: The Destruction of Freedom." *Journal of Philosophy of Education* 16(2):199-207.

– 1987. " 'Because I Say So!' Some Limitations upon the Rationalization of Authority." *Journal of Philosophy of Education* 21(1):15-24.

– 1989. "Metaphysics in Education." *Journal of Philosophy of Education* 23(2):159-69.

Archambault, R.D., ed. 1965. *Philosophical Analysis and Education.* London: Routledge & Kegan Paul.

Aronowitz, Stanley, and Henry Giroux. 1985. *Education Under Siege: The Conservative, Liberal and Radical Debates over Schooling.* South Hadley, MA: Bergin and Garvey.

Arons, Stephens. [1983]1986. *Compelling Belief: The Culture of American Schooling.* Amherst: University of Massachusetts Press.

Astley, Jeff, and David Day, eds. 1992. *The Contours of Christian Education.* Great Wakering, Essex: McCrimmons.

Astley, Jeff, and David Day. 1992. "The Contours of Christian Education."
In *The Contours of Christian Education*, ed. Jeff Astley and David Day, 13-25.
Great Wakering, Essex: McCrimmons.

Austin, J.L. 1964. "A Plea for Excuses." In *Ordinary Language*, ed. V.C.
Chappell, 41-63. Englewood Cliffs, NJ: Prentice-Hall.

Bailey, C. 1984. *Beyond the Present and the Particular: A Theory of Liberal Education*. London: Routledge & Kegan Paul.

Barbour, Ian. 1971. *Issues in Science and Religion*. New York: Harper & Row.

Barrow, Robin. 1974. "Religion in the Schools." *Educational Philosophy and Theory* 6:49-57.

– 1978. *Radical Education: A Critique of Free Schooling and Deschooling*. London:
Martin Robertson.

– and Ronald Woods 1988. *An Introduction to Philosophy of Education*. 3rd. ed.
London and New York: Routledge.

Baynes, K, J. Bohman, and T. McCarthy, eds. 1987. *After Philosophy: End or Transformation?* Cambridge, MA and London: MIT Press.

Beehler, R. 1985. "The Schools and Indoctrination." *Journal of Philosophy of Education* 19(2):261-72.

Bellah, Robert, Richard Madsen, William M. Sullivan, Ann Swidler, and
Steven Tipton 1985. *Habits of the Heart: Individualism and Commitment in American Life*. Berkeley: University of California Press.

Benson, T.L. 1977. "The Forms of Indoctrinatory Method." *Philosophy of Education 1977: Proceedings of the Thirty-Third Annual Meeting of the Philosophy of Education Society*. Worcester, MA: Philosophy of Education Society, 333-43.

Berger, Peter L. 1969. *The Sacred Canopy: Elements of a Sociological Theory of Religion*. Garden City, NJ: Anchor.

– 1974. *Pyramids of Sacrifice: Political Ethics and Social Change*. New York: Penguin.

– 1977. *Facing up to Modernity: Excursions in Society, Politics & Religion*. New
York: Penguin.

– and T. Luckmann [1966]1967. *The Social Construction of Reality: A Treatise on the Sociology of Knowledge*. New York: Doubleday.

– and Richard J. Neuhaus 1987. *To Empower People: The Role of Mediating Structures in Public Policy*. Washington, DC: American Enterprise Institute.

Blair, A.G. 1986. *The Policy and Practice of Religious Education in Publically-Funded [sic] Elementary and Secondary Schools in Canada and Elsewhere: A Search of the Literature*. Toronto: Queens Printer for Ontario.

Bloom, Allan. 1987. *The Closing of the American Mind*. New York: Simon and Schuster.

Bowers, C.A. 1987. *Elements of a Post-Liberal Theory of Education*. New York
and London: Teachers College Press.

Bowlby, John 1951. *Maternal Care and Mental Health*. Geneva: World Health Organization.

Brent, A. 1978. *Philosophical Foundations for the Curriculum*. London: George Allen and Unwin.

Brenton, Howard, and David Hare. 1985. *Pravda: A Fleet Street Comedy*. London and New York: Methuen.

Bretall, Robert. 1946. *A Kierkegaard Anthology*. New York: Modern Library.

British Council of Churches Consultative Group in Ministry among Children. 1984. *The Child in the Church: Reports of the Working Parties on the Child in the Church and Understanding Christian Nurture*. n.p. British Council of Churches.

Bronfenbrenner, Urie. 1979. *The Ecology of Human Development: Experiments by Nature and Design*, Cambridge, MA: Harvard University Press.

– 1980. "On Making Human Beings Human." *Character: A Periodical about the Public and Private Policies Shaping American Youth* 2(2):1-7.

Brown, S.C., ed. 1975. *Philosophers Discuss Education*. London: Macmillan.

Brunner, Emil. 1939. *Man in Revolt: A Christian Anthropology*. Translated by Olive Wyon. Cambridge: Lutterworth.

Buechner, Frederick. 1982. *The Sacred Journey*. San Francisco: Harper & Row.

Callan, Eamonn. 1985. "McLaughlin on Parental Rights." *Journal of Philosophy of Education* 19(1):111-18.

– 1988. *Autonomy and Schooling*. Kingston and Montreal: McGill-Queen's University Press.

Carper, James C. 1984. "The Christian Day School." In *Religious Schooling in America*, ed. J.C. Carper and T.C. Hunt, 110-29. Birmingham, AL: Religious Education Press.

– and Thomas C. Hunt, eds. 1984. *Religious Schooling in America*. Birmingham, AL: Religious Education Press.

Catholic Committee. 1989. *The Catholic School: Challenge of its Educational Project*. Government of Quebec: Ministry of Education.

Chesterton, G.K. 1937. *Autobiography*. London: Hutchinson.

Clark, Kelly James. 1990. *Return to Reason* Grands Rapids, MI: William B. Eerdmans.

Clouser, Roy A. 1991. *The Myth of Religious Neutrality: An Essay on the Hidden Role of Religious Belief in Theories*. Notre Dame, IL: University of Notre Dame Press.

Code, Lorraine. 1987. *Epistemic Responsibility*. Hanover and London: University Press of New England.

Colwell, Gary G. 1979. "Biblical Theism and the Question of Factual Significance." Ph.D. diss., Department of Philosophy, University of Waterloo.

Committee on Tolerance and Understanding. 1984. *Final Report of the Com-*

mittee on Tolerance and Understanding. Edmonton: Department of Education, Government of Alberta.

Cooling, Trevor. 1992. "The Epistemological Foundations of Contemporary Religious Education: A Study with Special Reference to the Evangelical Christian Tradition." Ph.D. diss., Department of Religious Education, University of Birmingham.

– and Margaret Cooling. 1987. "Christian Doctrine in Religious Education." *British Journal of Religious Education* 9(3):152-9.

Coons, John E., and Stephen D. Sugarman. 1978. *Education By Choice: The Case for Family Schooling.* Berkeley: University of California Press.

Cooper, B.A. 1973. "Peters' Concept of Education." *Educational Philosophy and Theory* 5:59-76.

Cooper, David E. 1973. "Intentions and Indoctrination." *Educational Philosophy and Theory* 5(1):43-55.

Copi, Irving M. 1982. *Introduction to Logic.* 6th ed. New York: Macmillan.

Copley, Terence. 1990. "Teacher or Preacher: Tutor or Neuter." *Resource* 12(2):6-8.

Corbett, J.P. 1965. "Teaching Philosophy Now." In *Philosophical Analysis and Education,* ed. R.D. Archambault, 141-56. London: Routledge & Kegan Paul.

Cornbleth, Catherine. 1984. "Beyond Hidden Curriculum?" *Journal of Curriculum Studies* 16(1):29-36.

Corporation of the Canadian Civil Liberties Association et al. v. Ontario (Ministry of Education) and the Board of Education of Elgin County, 37 A.O.C. 71; O.R. (2d) 341 Ontario Court of Appeal (1990).

Coward, Harold. 1985. *Pluralism: Challenge to World Religions.* Mary Knoll, NY: Orbis Books.

Crittenden, B. S. 1972. "Indoctrination as Mis-education," In *Concepts of Indoctrination,* ed. I.A. Snook, 131-51. London: Routledge & Kegan Paul.

– 1988. *Parents, the State and the Right to Educate.* Carlton, Australia: Melbourne University Press.

Dale, A.S. 1982. *The Outline of Sanity: A Life of G.K. Chesterton.* Grand Rapids, MI: Eerdmans.

Davey, A.G. 1972. "Education or Indoctrination?" *Journal of Moral Education* 2(1):5-15.

Dawson, Christopher. 1961. *The Crisis of Western Education.* New York: Sheed & Ward.

D'Cruz, J.V., and P.J. Sheehan, eds. 1973. *Concepts in Education: Philosophical Studies.* Melbourne: A Mercy Teacher's College Twentieth Century Publisher.

Dearden, D.F. 1972. "Autonomy and Education." In *Education and the Development of Reason,* ed. R.F. Dearden, P.H. Hirst, and R.S. Peters, 448-65. London: Routledge & Kegan Paul.

– 1975. "Autonomy as an Educational Ideal." In *Philosophers Discuss Education*, ed. S.C. Brown, 3-18. London: Macmillan.

– 1988. "Controversial Issues and the Curriculum." In *Philosophy of Education: Introductory Readings*, ed. William Hare and John P. Portelli, 167-75. Calgary: Detselig Enterprises.

Dearden, R.F., P.H. Hirst, and R.S. Peters, eds. 1972. *Education and the Development of Reason*, London: Routledge & Kegan Paul.

Dewart, Leslie 1965. "Education and Political Values: The Dilemmas of Liberal Democracy." In *The Prospect of Change: Proposals for Canada's Future*, ed. Abraham Rotstein, 286-307. Toronto: McGraw-Hill.

Dewey, John. [1916]1966. *Democracy and Education.* New York: The Free Press.

– 1934. *A Common Faith.* New Haven, CT: Yale University Press.

Diamond, M.L. 1975. "The Challenge of Contemporary Empiricism." In *The Logic of God: Theology and Verification*, ed. M.L. Diamond and T.V. Litzenberg, 1-54. Indianapolis: Bobbs-Merill.

Diamond, M.L., and T.V. Litzenberg, eds. 1975. *The Logic of God: Theology and Verification.* Indianapolis: Bobbs-Merill.

Douglas, Mary. 1986. *How Institutions Think.* Syracuse, NY: Syracuse University Press.

Downey, James. 1988. Review of *The Closing of the American Mind. University Affairs* 29(2):15-16.

Doyle, J.F., ed. 1973. *Educational Judgments: Papers in the Philosophy of Education.* London: Routledge & Kegan Paul.

Dreeben, Robert. 1976. "The Unwritten Curriculum and Its Relation to Values." *Curriculum Studies* 8(2):111-24.

D'Souza, Dinesh. 1991. *Illiberal Education: The Politics of Race and Sex on Campus.* New York: Free Press.

Dunlop, Francis. 1976. "Indoctrination as Morally Undesirable Teaching." *Education For Teaching* 100:39-42.

Eddington, Sir Arthur. [1939]1958. *The Philosophy of Physical Science.* Ann Arbor: University of Michigan Press.

Ellul, Jacques 1969. *Propaganda: The Formation of Men's Attitudes.* trans. Konrad Kellen and Jean Lerner. New York: Knopf.

Enroth, R. 1977. *Youth, Brainwashing and the Extremist Cults.* Grand Rapids, MI: Zondervan.

Enslin, P. 1984. "The Liberal Point of View." *Educational Philosophy and Theory* 16(2):1-9.

– 1985. "Are Hirst and Peters Liberal Philosophers of Education?" *Journal of Philosophy of Education* 19(2):211-22.

Feinberg, Joel. 1973. "The Idea of a Free Man." In *Educational Judgments: Papers in the Philosophy of Education*, ed. J.F. Doyle, 143-69. London: Routledge & Kegan Paul.

Felderhof, M.C., ed. 1985. *Religious Education in a Pluralistic Society*. London: Hodder & Stoughton.

Fennell, Jon, and Rudy Liverette 1979. "Kuhn, Education and the Grounds of Rationality." *Educational Theory* 29(2):117-27.

Fernhout, Harry. 1979. "Education versus Indoctrination: Religious Education in Ontario's Public Schools." In *Education and the Public Purpose*, T. Malcolm and H. Fernhout, 19-35. Toronto: Curriculum Development Centre.

Festinger, Leon. 1957. *A Theory of Cognitive Dissonance*. Evanston, IL: Row, Peterson.

Feyerabend, Paul. 1975. *Against Method: Outline of an Anarchistic Theory of Knowledge*. London: Verso Edition/NLB.

– 1988. "How to Defend Society Against Science." In *Introductory Readings in the Philosophy of Science*, ed. E.D. Klemke, R. Hollinger, et al., 34-44. Buffalo, NY: Prometheus Books.

Fitzgerald, Francis. 1979. *America Revised: History Schoolbooks in the Twentieth Century*. Boston and Toronto: Little, Brown.

Fleming, D.B., and J.C. Hunt 1987. "The World as Seen by Students in Accelerated Christian Education Schools." *Phi Delta Kappan* 68(7):518-23.

Flew, Antony. 1972a. "Indoctrination and Doctrines." In *Concepts of Indoctrination*, ed. I.A. Snook, 67-92. London: Routledge & Kegan Paul.

– 1972b. "Indoctrination and Religion." In *Concepts of Indoctrination*, ed. I.A. Snook, 106-16. London: Routledge & Kegan Paul.

– 1973. "The Jensen Uproar." *Philosophy* 48:63-9.

Francis, Leslie, and Adrian Thatcher eds. 1990. *Christian Perspectives for Education: A Reader in the Theology of Education*. Leominster, Herfordshire: Fowler Wright Books.

Freire, Paulo. 1973. *Education for Critical Consciousness*. New York: Seabury.

Gadamer, Hans-George. 1975. *Truth and Method*. New York: Seabury.

Gardner, Peter. 1988. "Religious Upbringing and the Liberal Ideal of Religious Autonomy." *Journal of Philosophy of Education* 22(1):89-105.

– 1991. "Personal Autonomy and Religious Upbringing: The Problem." *Journal of Philosophy of Education*. 25(1):69-81.

Gatchel, R.H. 1972. "The Evolution of the Concept." In *Concepts of Indoctrination*, ed. I.A. Snook, 9-16. London: Routledge & Kegan Paul.

Giroux, Henry. 1985. *Ideology, Culture and the Process of Schooling*. Philadelphia: Temple University Press.

Goffman, Erving. 1961. *Asylums: Essays on the Social Situation of Mental Patients and Other Inmates*. Garden City, NJ: Anchor.

Goldman, R. 1964. *Religious Thinking from Childhood to Adolescence*. London: Routledge & Kegan Paul.

Gooch, P.W. 1987. *Partial Knowledge: Philosophical Studies in Paul*. Notre Dame, IL: University of Notre Dame Press.

Goodman, Paul. 1971. *Compulsory Miseducation*. Harmondsworth, Middlesex: Penguin.

Gordon, David. 1981. "The Immorality of the Hidden Curriculum." *Journal of Moral Education* 10(1):3-8.

– 1982. "The Concept of the Hidden Curriculum." *Journal of Philosophy of Education* 16(2):187-98.

Gourlay, David. 1990. "Quebec." In *Catholic School Systems Across Canada*, ed. Carl J. Matthews, 21-6. Willowdale, Ont: Canadian Catholic School Trustees Association.

Greeley, A. M. 1974. *Ethnicity in the United States: A Preliminary Reconnaissance*. New York: Wiley.

Green, T.F. 1972. "Indoctrination and Beliefs." In *Concepts of Indoctrination*, ed. I.A. Snook, 25-46. London: Routledge & Kegan Paul.

Greer, J.E. 1984a/b. "Fifty Years of the Psychology of Religion in Religious Education." Part 1, 2. *British Journal of Religious Education* 6(2):93-8; 7(1):23-8.

Gregory, I.M.M., and R.G. Woods 1972. "Indoctrination: Inculcating Doctrines." In *Concepts of Indoctrination*, ed. I.A. Snook, 162-89. London: Routledge & Kegan Paul.

Groome, Thomas H. 1980. *Christian Religious Education*. San Francisco: Harper & Row.

Guinness, O. 1976. *In Two Minds: The Dilemma of Doubt and How to Resolve It*. Downers Grove, IL: InterVarsity Press.

– 1983. *The Gravedigger File: Papers on the Subversion of the Modern Church*. Downers Grove, IL: InterVarsity Press.

Guthrie, Stewart. 1980. "A Cognitive Theory of Religion." *Current Anthropology* 2(2):181-203.

Gutmann, Amy. 1985. "Communitarian Critics of Liberalism." *Philosophy and Public Affairs* 14(3):308-22.

– 1987. *Democratic Education*. Princeton: Princeton University Press.

Haack, Susan. 1990. "Rebuilding the Ship While Sailing on the Water." In *Perspectives on Quine*, ed. R.B. Barrett and R.F. Gibson, 111-270. Cambridge, MA: Blackwell, 111-27.

Habermas, Jurgen. 1979. *Communication and the Evolution of Society*. Boston, MA: Beacon.

Halstead, J.M. 1986. *The Case for Muslim Voluntary-Aided Schools: Some Philosophical Reflections*. Cambridge: The Islamic Academy.

Halstead, Robert 1979. "The Relevance of Psychology to Educational Epistemology." In *Philosophy of Education: 1979: Proceedings of the Thirty-Fifth Annual Meeting of the Philosophy of Education Society*, ed. Jerrold R. Coombs, 65-76. Normal, IL: Philosophy of Education Society.

Hammond, J., D. Hay, J. Moxon, B. Netto, K. Raban, G Straugheir, and C. Williams. 1990. *New Methods in RE Teaching*. Harlow: Oliver and Boyd.

Hare, R.M. 1964. "Adolescents into Adults." In *Aims in Education: The Philosophic Approach*, ed. T.H.B. Hollins, 47-70. Manchester: Manchester University Press.

Hare, William. 1979. *Open-Mindedness and Education*. Kingston and Montreal: McGill-Queen's University Press.

– 1985. *In Defense of Open-Mindedness*. Kingston and Montreal: McGill-Queen's University Press.

– and John P. Portelli, eds. 1988. *Philosophy of Education: Introductory Readings*. Calgary: Detselig.

Harris, Kevin. 1977. "Peters on Schooling." *Educational Philosophy and Theory* 9(1):33-48.

– 1979. *Education and Knowledge*. London: Routledge & Kegan Paul.

Hart, Hendrick. 1977. "The Impasse of Rationality Today: A Précis." Toronto: Institute for Christian Studies.

– , Johan van der Hoeven, and Nicholas Wolterstorff, eds. 1983. *Rationality in the Calvinian Tradition*. London, MD: University Press of America.

Hartnett, Anthony, and Michael Naish, eds. 1986. *Education and Society Today: Contemporary Analysis in Education Series*. Lewes, East Sussex: Falmer.

Hauerwas, S. 1983. *The Peaceable Kingdom: A Primer in Christian Ethics*. Notre Dame, IL: University of Notre Dame Press.

Haworth, Lawrence. 1986. *Autonomy: An Essay in Philosophical Psychology and Ethics*. New Haven and London: Yale University Press.

Haydon, Graham. 1983. "Autonomy as an Aim of Education and the Autonomy of Teachers." *Journal of Philosophy of Education* 17(2):219-28.

Heimbeck, Raeburne S. 1969. *Theology and Meaning: A Critique of Metatheological Skepticism*. Stanford: Stanford University Press.

Hendley, B. 1980. "Knowledge and the Curriculum." *The Review of Education* 6(1):35-41.

Hepburn, Ronald. 1987. "Attitudes to Evidence and Argument in the Field of Religion." In *Philosophers in Education*, ed. Roger Straughan and John Wilson, 127-46. Basingstoke: Macmillan.

Her Majesty's Government. 1988. "Education Reform Act." London: Her Majesty's Stationery Office.

Heywood, David. 1988. "Christian Education as Enculturation: The Life of the Community and its Place in Christian Education in the work of John H. Westerhoff III." *British Journal of Religious Education* 10(2):65-71.

Hick, John. 1966. *Faith and Knowledge*. 2nd ed. Ithaca: Cornell University Press.

Hirsch, E.D. 1988. *Cultural Literacy: What Every American Needs to Know*. New York: Vintage.

Hirst, Paul H. 1972. "Christian Education: A Contradiction in Terms." *Learning for Living* 11(4):6-10.

– 1974a. *Knowledge and the Curriculum: A Collection of Philosophical Papers.* London: Routledge & Kegan Paul.

– 1974b. *Moral Education in a Secular Society.* London: Hodder & Stoughton.

– 1981. "Education, Catechesis and the Church School." *British Journal of Religious Education* 3(3):85-93.

– 1985. "Education and Diversity of Belief." In *Religious Education in a Pluralistic Society,* ed. M.C. Felderhof, 5-17. London: Hodder & Stoughton.

– and R.S. Peters 1970. *The Logic of Education.* London: Routledge & Kegan Paul.

Hofstadter, Richard. 1963. *Anti-intellectualism in American Life.* New York: Knopf.

Holley, Raymond. 1978. *Religious Education and Religious Understanding: An Introduction to the Philosophy of Religious Education.* London: Routledge & Kegan Paul.

Hollins, T.H.B., ed. 1964. *Aims in Education: The Philosophic Approach.* Manchester: University Press.

Holmes, Arthur F. 1983. *Contours of a World View.* Grand Rapids, MI: Eerdmans.

Holmes, Mark. 1985. "The Funding of Private Schools in Ontario: Philosophy, Values and Implications for Funding." In *The Report of the Commission of Private Schools in Ontario,* B.J. Shapiro, 109-52. Toronto: Department of Education, Government of Ontario.

Hudson, W.D. 1973. "Is Religious Education Possible?" In *New Essays in the Philosophy of Education,* ed. G. Langford and D.J. O'Connor, 167-96. London: Routledge & Kegan Paul.

– 1982. "Educating, Socialising and Indoctrination: A Reply to Tasos Kazepides." *Journal of Philosophy of Education* 16(2):167-72.

Hull, John, ed. 1982. *New Directions in Religious Education.* Lewes, Sussex: Falmer.

– 1984. *Studies in Religion and Education.* London: Falmer.

– 1987. "Religious Education and Modernity." *British Journal of Religious Education* 9(3):117-23.

– 1989. "School Worship and the 1988 Education Reform Act." *British Journal of Religious Education* 11(3):119-25.

Hulmes, Edward. 1979. *Commitment and Neutrality in Religious Education.* London: Geoffrey Chapman.

Hume, David. [1748]1955. *An Inquiry Concerning Human Understanding.* ed. C. W. Hendel. Indianapolis: Bobbs-Merrill.

– [1888]1965. *A Treatise of Human Nature.* ed. L. A. Selby-Bigge. Oxford: Clarendon.

Illich, Ivan. 1970. *Deschooling Society.* New York: Harper & Row.

James, William. 1902. *The Varieties of Religious Experience: A Study in Human Nature*. New York: Modern Library.

– [1948]1968. *Essays in Pragmatism*. New York: Hafner.

Jansen, Sue Curry. 1988. *Censorship: The Knot That Binds Power and Knowledge*. New York: Oxford University Press.

Johns, Eric. 1981. "The Unacceptable Aim of Religious Education." *British Journal of Religious Education* 4:28-30.

Kaufman, G.D. 1960. *Relativism, Knowledge and Faith*. Chicago: University of Chicago Press.

Kazepides, Tasos. 1973. "The Grammar of Indoctrination." In *Philosophy of Education 1973: Proceedings of the Twenty-Ninth Annual Meeting of the Philosophy of Education Society*, ed. B. Crittenden, 273-83. Edwardsville, IL: Studies in Philosophy and Education.

– 1982. "Educating, Socialising and Indoctrinating." *Journal of Philosophy of Education* 16(2):155-66.

– 1983. "Is Religious Education Possible? A Rejoinder to W. D. Hudson." *Journal of Philosophy of Education* 17(2):259-65.

– 1987. "Indoctrination, Doctrines and the Foundations of Rationality." In *Philosophy of Education 1987: Proceedings of the Forty Third Annual Meeting of the Philosophy of Education Society*, ed. Barbara Arnstine and Donald Arnstine, 229-49. Normal, IL: Philosophy of Education Society.

– 1989. "Programmatic Definitions in Education: The Case of Indoctrination." *Canadian Journal of Education* 14(3):387-96.

Keller, James A. 1989. "Accepting the Authority of the Bible: Is it Rationally Justified?" *Faith and Philosophy* 6(4):378-97.

Kerry, Trevor. 1982. "The Demands Made by RE on Pupils' Thinking." In *New Directions in Religious Education*, ed. John Hull, 161-70. Lewes, Sussex: Falmer.

Kierkegaard, S. [1936]1967. *Philosophical Fragments*. trans. David F. Swenson. Princeton: Princeton University Press.

Kimball, Bruce A. 1986. *Orators and Philosophers: A History of the Idea of Liberal Education*. New York: Teachers College Press.

King, Ursula. 1985. "A Response to Howard W. Marratt." In *Religious Education in a Pluralistic Society*, ed. M.C. Felderhof, 92-100. London: Hodder & Stoughton.

Kleinig, John. 1973. "Educating and Indoctrinating." In *Concepts of Education: Philosophical Studies*, ed. J.V. D'Cruz and P.J. Sheehan, 23-31. Melbourne: A Mercy Teacher's College Twentieth Century Publisher.

Kuhn, Thomas. [1962]1970. *The Structure of Scientific Revolutions*. Chicago: University of Chicago Press.

– 1977. *The Essential Tension*. Chicago: University of Chicago Press.

Kurtz, Paul, ed. [1933][1973]1976. *Humanist Manifestos I and II*. Buffalo, NY: Prometheus Books.

Lakatos, I., and Alan Musgrove, eds. 1970. *Criticism and the Growth of Knowledge*. Cambridge, MA: Cambridge University Press.

Landesman, C., ed. 1970. *The Foundations of Knowledge*. Englewood Cliffs, NJ: Prentice-Hall.

Langford, Glen. 1985. *Education, Persons and Society: A Philosophical Inquiry*. London: Macmillan.

– and D.J. O'Connor, eds. 1973. *New Essays in the Philosophy of Education*. London: Routledge & Kegan Paul.

Laura, R.S. 1978. "Philosophical Foundations of Religious Education." *Educational Theory* 28(4):310-17.

– 1981. "Philosophical Foundations of Science Education." *Educational Philosophy and Theory* 13(1):1-13.

– 1983. "To Educate or to Indoctrinate: That is still the Question." *Educational Philosophy and Theory* 15(1):43-55.

– and Michael Leahy 1989. "Religious Upbringing and Rational Autonomy." *Journal of Philosophy of Education* 23(2):253-65.

Leahy, Michael. 1990. "Indoctrination, Evangelization, Catechesis and Religious Education." *British Journal of Religious Education* 12(3):137-44.

Lloyd, Ieuan. 1981. "Teaching Religious Understanding." *Religious Studies* 17:253-9.

Lovelace, Richard F. 1985. *Renewal as a Way of Life*. Downers Grove, IL: InterVarsity Press.

McCarthy, Rockne, Donald Oppewal, Walfred Peterson, and Gordon Spykman. 1981. *Society, State and Schools: A Case for Structural and Confessional Pluralism*. Grand Rapids, MI: Eerdmans.

McCloskey, H.J. 1974. "Liberalism." *Philosophy: The Journal of the Royal Institute of Philosophy* 49(187):13-32.

McEwen, C.A. 1980. "Continuities in the Study of Total and Non-total Institutions." *Annual Review of Sociology* 6:143-85.

McGarry, D.D. 1980. "Secularism in American Public Education and the Unconstitutionally of its Exclusive Government Support." St Louis, MO: Educational Freedom Foundation.

MacIntyre, A. [1981]1984. *After Virtue: A Study in Moral Theory*. Notre Dame, IN: University of Notre Dame Press.

– 1988. *Whose Justice? Which Rationality?* Notre Dame, IN: University of Notre Dame Press.

MacKinnon, Alistair. 1970. *Falsification and Belief*. Reseda, CA: Ridgeview Publishers.

McLaughlin, T.H. 1984. "Parental Rights and the Religious Upbringing of Children." *Journal of Philosophy of Education* 18(1):75-83.

– 1985. "Religion, Upbringing and Liberal Values: A rejoinder to Eamonn Callan." *Journal of Philosophy of Education* 19(1):119-26.

– 1987. " 'Education for All' and Religious Schools." In *Education for a Plu-*

ralistic Society: Philosophical Perspectives on the Swann Report, ed. G. Haydon, 67-98. Bedford Way Paper no. 30. London: University of London Institute of Education.

Manley, Will. 1986. "Facing the Public." *Wilson Library Bulletin* 60(5):41.

Marples, Roger. 1978. "Is Religious Education Possible?" *Journal of Philosophy of Education* 12:81-91.

Marthaler, B. 1987. "Dilemma for Religious Educators: Indoctrination or Indifference." *Religious Education.* 82(4):555-68.

Martin, David. 1978. *A General Theory of Secularization.* Oxford: Blackwell.

Matthews, G.B. 1980. *Philosophy and the Young Child.* Cambridge, MA: Harvard University Press.

Matthews, M. 1980. *The Marxist Theory of Schooling.* London: Routledge & Kegan Paul.

Mavrodes, G.I. 1970. *Belief in God: A Study in the Epistemology of Religion.* New York: Random House.

Mill, J.S. [1859]1978. *On Liberty.* Indianapolis: Hackett.

– [1861]1957. *Utilitarianism.* Indianapolis: Bobbs-Merrill.

Miller, J.F. 1975. "Science and Religion: Their Logical Similarity." In *The Logic of God: Theology and Verification*, ed. M.L. Diamond and T.V. Litzenburg, 351-80. Indianapolis: Bobbs-Merrill.

Mitchell, Basil. 1973. *The Justification of Religious Belief.* New York: Seabury.

– 1976. "Reason and Commitment in the Academic Vocation." *Oxford Review of Education* 2(2):101-9.

Moore, Willis. 1972. "Indoctrination and Democratic Method." In *Concepts of Indoctrination*, ed. I.A. Snook, 93-100. London: Routledge & Kegan Paul.

Morgan, K. 1974. "Socialization, Social Models and the Open Education Movement: Some Philosophical Considerations." In *The Philosophy of Open Education*, ed. D. Nyberg, 110-39. London: Routledge & Kegan Paul.

Mouzelis, N.P. 1971. "Critical Note on Total Institutions." *Sociology* 5:113-120.

Muggeridge, Malcolm. 1975. *Jesus: The Man Who Lives.* London: Fontana/Collins.

Neill, A.S. 1960. *Summerhill: A Radical Approach to Child Rearing.* New York: Hart.

Neiman, Alven M. 1989. "Indoctrination: A Contextualist Approach." *Educational Philosophy and Theory* 21(1):53-61.

Neuhaus, Richard John. 1984. *The Naked Public Square: Religion and Democracy in America.* Grand Rapids, MI: Eerdmans.

New International Version of the Holy Bible. 1978. Grand Rapids, MI: Zondervan Bible Publishers.

Newman, Jay. 1982. *Foundations of Religious Tolerance.* Toronto: University of Toronto Press.

– 1986. *Fanatics & Hypocrites.* Buffalo, NY: Prometheus Books.

Nichols, Kevin. 1992. "The Logical Geography of Catechesis." In *The Con-*

tours of Christian Education, ed. Jeff Astley and David Day, 54-65. Great Wakering, Essex: McCrimmons.

Nielsen, Kai. 1984. "On Not Being at Sea About Indoctrination." *Interchange* 15(4):68-73.

Nipkow, Karl-Ernst. 1985. "Can Theology have an Educational Role?" In *Religious Education in a Pluralistic Society*, ed. M.C. Felderhof, 23-38. London: Hodder & Stoughton.

Nouwen, Henri J.M. 1975. *Reaching Out: The Three Movements of the Spiritual Life*. New York: Doubleday.

Nyberg, D., ed. 1974. *The Philosophy of Open Education*. London: Routledge & Kegan Paul.

Oakeshott, Michael. 1962. *Rationalism in Politics and other Essays*. London: Methuen.

– 1967. "Learning and Teaching." In *The Concept of Education*, ed. R.S. Peters, 156-76. London: Routledge & Kegan Paul.

– 1972. "Education: The Engagement and its Frustration." *Education and the Development of Reason*, ed. R.F. Dearden, P.H. Hirst, and R.S. Peters, 19-49. London: Routledge & Kegan Paul.

O'Hear, A. 1982. *Education, Society and Human Nature: An Introduction to the Philosophy of Education*. London: Routledge & Kegan Paul.

O'Leary, P.T. 1979. "The Indoctrinated State of Mind." *Philosophy of Education 1979: Proceedings of the Thirty-Fifth Annual Meeting of the Philosophy of Education Society*, ed. Jerrold R. Coombs, 295-303. Normal, IL: Philosophy of Education Society.

O'Neill, Onora, and William Ruddick, eds. 1977. *Having Children: Philosophical and Legal Reflections on Parenthood*. New York: Oxford University Press.

Ontario Bible College. 1989. *Ontario Bible College Faculty Handbook*. Toronto: Ontario Bible College.

Oppewal, Donald. 1981. "Humanism as the Religion of Public Education: Textbook Evidence." *Christian Legal Society Quarterly* 7(9):31-3.

Page, Ralph C. 1979. "Epistemology, Pyschology, and Two Views of Indoctrination." In *Philosophy of Education: 1979: Proceedings of the Thirty-Fifth Annual Meeting of the Philosophy of Education Society*, ed. Jerrold R. Coombs, 77-86. Normal, IL: Philosophy of Education Society.

– 1980. "Some Requirements for a Theory of Indoctrination." Ph.D. diss., Graduate College, University of Illinois at Urban-Champaign.

– 1985. "Towards Some Serious Entertaining." In *Philosophy of Education 1985: Proceedings of the Forty-First Annual Meeting of the Philosophy of Education Society*, ed. D. Nyberg, 107-10. Normal, IL: Philosophy of Education Society.

Passmore, John. 1967. "On Teaching to Be Critical." In *The Concept of Education*, ed. R.S. Peters, 192-211. London: Routledge & Kegan Paul.

Peshkin, Alan. 1986. *God's Choice: The Total World of a Fundamentalist Christian School*. Chicago and London: The University of Chicago Press.

Peters, R.S. 1965. "Education as Initiation." In *Philosophical Analysis and Education*, ed. R.D. Archambault, 87-111. London: Routledge & Kegan Paul.

– 1966. *Ethics and Education*. London: George Allen and Unwin.

– , ed. 1967a. *The Concept of Education*. London: Routledge & Kegan Paul.

– 1967b. "What is an Educational Process?" In *The Concept of Education*, ed. R.S. Peters, 1-23. London: Routledge & Kegan Paul.

– 1972. "Education and the Educated Man." In *Education the Development of Reason*, ed. R.F. Dearden, P.H. Hirst, and R.S. Peters, 3-18. London: Routledge & Kegan Paul.

– 1973a. *Authority, Responsibility and Education*. 3rd ed. London: Allen and Unwin.

– 1973b. "Freedom and the Development of the Free Man." In *Educational Judgments: Papers in the Philosophy of Education*, ed. J.F. Doyle, 119-42. London: Routledge Kegan & Paul.

– 1973c. "Farewell to Aims?" *London Educational Review* 2(3):1-4.

– 1973d. "Values in Education." In *New Essays in the Philosophy of Education*, ed. Glenn Langford and D.J. O'Connor, 135-46. London and Boston: Routledge & Kegan Paul.

– 1977. *Education and the Education of Teachers*. London: Routledge & Kegan Paul.

Phillips, D.C. 1975. "The Anatomy of Autonomy." *Educational Philosophy and Theory* 7(2):1-12.

Plantinga, Alvin. 1979. "Is Belief in God Rational?" In *Rationality and Religious Belief*, ed. C.F. Delany, 7-27. Notre Dame, IN: University of Notre Dame Press.

Plato. [1955]1974. *The Republic of Plato*. 2nd. ed. trans. Desmond Lee. Harmondsworth, Middlesex: Penguin.

Plunkett, Dudley. 1990. *Secular and Spiritual Values: Grounds for Hope in Education*. London & New York: Routledge.

Poewe, K., and I. Hexham. 1986. *Understanding Cults and New Religions*. Grand Rapids, MI: Eerdmans.

Polanyi, Michael. [1946]1964. *Science Faith and Society*. Chicago and London: University of Chicago Press.

– 1958. *Personal Knowledge*. London: Routledge.

Popper, Karl. 1970. "Normal Science and its Dangers." In *Criticism and the Growth of Knowledge*, ed. I. Lakatos and A. Musgrove, 51-8. Cambridge, MA: Cambridge University Press.

Prado, Carlos G. 1980. *Illusions of Faith: a Critique of Non-Credal Religion*. Dubuque, IA and Toronto: Kendal Hunt.

Pring, Richard. 1976. *Knowledge and Schooling*. London: Open Books.

Quine, W.V. [1953]1961. *From a Logical Point of View*. 2nd ed. Cambridge, MA: Harvard University Press.

– 1970. "The Basis of Conceptual Schemes." In *The Foundations of Knowledge*, ed. C. Landesman, 160-72. Engelwood Cliffs, NJ: Prentice-Hall.

– and J.S. Ullian 1978. *Web of Belief*. 2nd ed. New York: Random House.

Ratzsch, Del. 1986. *Philosophy of Science: The Natural Sciences in Christian Perspective*. Downers Grove, IL: InterVarsity Press.

Raywid, Mary Anne. 1980. "The Discovery and Rejection of Indoctrination." *Educational Theory* 30(1):1-10.

Rich, John Martin, and Joseph L. DeVitis. 1985. *Theories of Moral Development*. Springfield, IL: Charles C. Thomas.

Reese, William J. 1985. "Soldiers for Christ in the Army of God: The Christian School Movement in America." *Educational Theory* 35(2):175-94.

Reichenbach, Hans, 1938. *Experience and Prediction*. Chicago: University of Chicago Press.

Reimer, Everett. [1971]1972. *School Is Dead*. Garden City, NJ: Anchor.

Rokeach, Milton. 1960. *The Open and Closed Mind: Investigation into the Nature of Belief Systems and Personality Systems*. New York: Basic.

Roques, Mark. 1989. *Curriculum Unmasked: Towards a Christian Understanding of Education*. Eastbourne, East Sussex: Monarch.

Rose, Susan D. 1988. *Keeping Them out of the Hands of Satan: Evangelical Schooling in America*. New York and London: Routledge.

Rossiter, G.M. 1982. "The Need for a 'Creative Divorce' between Catechesis and Religious Education in Catholic Schools." *Religious Education* 77(1):21-40.

Rothbard, Murray N. 1973. *For a New Liberty*. New York: Macmillan.

Russell, Bertrand. [1912]1959. *Problems of Philosophy*. New York: Oxford University Press.

– 1961. *History of Western Philosophy*. London: George Allen & Unwin.

Russell, Richard. 1976. *Reason and Commitment in Education*. Masters thesis. Department of Education, University of Bristol.

Rutter, Michael. 1972. *Maternal Deprivation Reassessed*. Harmondsworth, Middlesex: Penguin.

– , ed. 1980. *Developmental Psychiatry*. Washington, DC: American Psychiatric Press.

Ryken, Leland. 1980. "Puritan Piety and the Liberated Mind." *Christianity Today* 24(19):26-9.

Sandel, M. 1982. *Liberalism and the Limits of Justice*. New York: Cambridge University Press.

Schools Council Project on Religious Education. 1971. *Religious Education in Secondary Schools: Schools Council Working Paper 36*. London: Evans/Methuen Educational.

Schwartz, A. 1979. "Aristotle on Education and Choice." *Educational Theory* 29(2):97-107.

Scruton, R., A. Ellis-Jones, and D. O'Keeffe. 1985. *Education and Indoctrina-*

tion: An Attempt at Definition and a Review of Social and Political Implications. Harrow, Middlesex: Education Research Centre.

Shapiro, Bernard J. 1985. *The Report of the Commissioner on Private Schools in Ontario.* Toronto: Department of Education, Government of Ontario.

Shils, Edward. 1981. *Tradition.* Chicago: University of Chicago Press.

Siegel, Harvey. 1979. "Can Psychology Be Relevant to Epistemology?" In *Philosophy of Education: 1979: Proceedings of the Thirty-Fifth Annual Meeting of the Philosophy of Education Society,* ed. Jerrold R. Coombs, 55-64. Normal, IL: Philosophy of Education Society.

– 1988. *Educating Reason: Rationality, Critical Thinking and Education.* New York and London: Routledge.

Silberman, Charles E. 1970. *Crisis in the Classroom: The Remaking of American Education.* New York: Random House.

Slee, Nicola. 1989. "Conflict and Reconciliation between Competing Models of Religious Education: Some Reflections on the British Scene." *British Journal of Religious Education* 11(3):126-35.

Smart, Ninian. 1968. *Secular Education and the Logic of Religion.* London: Faber & Faber.

Smart, Patricia. 1973. "The Concept of Indoctrination." In *New Essays in the Philosophy of Education,* ed. Glenn Langford and D.J. O'Conner, 33-46. London: Routledge & Kegan Paul.

Smedes, Lewis B. 1988. *Caring and Commitment: Learning to Live the Love We Promise.* San Francisco: Harper & Row.

Smith, J.W.D. 1975. *Religion and Secular Education.* Edinburgh: The Saint Andrew Press.

Snook, I.A. 1970. "The Concept of Indoctrination." *Studies in Philosophy and Education* 7:65-162.

– , ed. 1972a. *Concepts of Indoctrination: Philosophical Essays.* London: Routledge & Kegan Paul.

– 1972b. *Indoctrination and Education.* London: Routledge & Kegan Paul.

– 1972c. "Indoctrination and Moral Responsibility." In *Concepts of Indoctrination,* ed. I.A. Snook, 152-61. London: Routledge & Kegan Paul.

– 1973a. "Indoctrination and the Indoctrinated Society." *Studies in Philosophy and Education* 8(1):52-61.

– 1973b. "Teaching Pupils to Think." *Studies in Philosophy and Education* 8(2):146-61.

– 1989. "Contexts and Essences: Indoctrination Revisited." *Educational Philosophy and Theory* 21(1):62-5.

Soltis, Jonas F. 1979. *Education and the Concept of Knowledge.* New York: Teachers College, Columbia University.

Spiecker, Ben. 1987. "Indoctrination, Intellectual Virtues and Rational Emotions." *Journal of Philosophy of Education* 21(2):261-6.

Stott, John R.W. 1972. *Your Mind Matters: The Place of the Mind in the Christian Life*. Downers Grove, IL: InterVarsity Press.

Stout, Jeffrey. 1981. *The Flight from Authority: Religion, Morality and the Quest for Autonomy*. Notre Dame, IL: University of Notre Dame Press.

Straughan, Roger, and John Wilson, eds. 1987. *Philosophers in Education*. Basingstoke: Macmillan.

Swan, John C. 1979. "Librarianship Is Censorship." *Library Journal* 104(17):2040-3.

Swann, Lord. 1985. *Education for All: The Report of the Committee of Inquiry into the Education of Children from Ethnic Minority Groups*. London: Her Majesty's Stationery Office.

Taylor, Philip. 1986. "General Editor's Preface." In *Education and Society Today: Contemporary Analysis in Education Series*, ed. Anthony Hartnett and Michael Naish, xi. Lewes: Falmer.

Thalburg, Irving. 1979. "Socialization and Autonomous Behaviour." *Tulane Studies in Philosophy* 28:21-37.

Theodorson, George, and Achilles G. Theodorson. 1969. *Modern Dictionary of Sociology*. New York: Thomas Y. Crowell.

Thiessen, E.J. 1980. "Indoctrination, Education and Religion: A Philosophical Analysis." Ph.D. diss., Department of Philosophy, University of Waterloo.

– 1982a. "Indoctrination and Doctrines." *Journal of Philosophy of Education* 16(1):3-17.

– 1982b. "Religious Freedom and Educational Pluralism." In *Family Choice in Schooling: Issues and Dilemmas*, ed. M.E. Manley-Casimir, 57-69. Lexington, MA: Lexington Books.

– 1984a. "Indoctrination and Religious Education." *Interchange* 15(3):27-43.

– 1984b. "Paradigms of Religious Indoctrination: A Response to McLean and Nielson." *Interchange* 15(4):74-9.

– 1985a. "A Defense of a Distinctively Christian Curriculum." *Religious Education* 80(1):37-50.

– 1985b. "Initiation, Indoctrination and Education." *Canadian Journal of Education* 10(3):229-49.

– 1985c. "Proselytizing without Intolerance." *Studies in Religion* 14(3):333-45.

– 1987a. "Educational Pluralism and Tolerance." *Journal of Educational Thought* 21(2):71-87.

– 1987b. "Two Concepts or Two Phases of Liberal Education?" *Journal of Philosophy of Education* 21(2):223-34.

– 1987c. "Three Approaches to Religious Education and the Problem of Indoctrination." *Ethics in Education* 6(3): 2-5.

– 1989. "R.S. Peters on Liberal Education – A Reconstruction." *Interchange* 20(4):1–8.

– 1990. Review of *God's Choice: The Total World of a Fundamentalist Christian School*, by Alan Peshkin. *Ethics in Education* 9(4):13-15.

– 1991a. "Christian Nurture, Indoctrination and Liberal Education." *The Christian Librarian* 34(2):40-9; *Spectrum* 23(2):105-24.

– 1991b. Review of *Secular and Spiritual Values: Grounds for Hope in Education*, by Dudley Plunkett. *Educational Studies* 22(2):167-72.

– and L.J. Roy Wilson 1979. "Curriculum in the Church-State Controversy: Are the Mennonites Justified in Rejecting the Public School Curriculum?" *Salt: Journal of the Religious Studies and Moral Education Council.* (Spring):13-27.

Toulmin, Stephen. 1990. *Cosmopolis: The Hidden Agenda of Modernity.* New York: The Free Press.

"Towards a Constitutional Definition of Religion." 1978. *Harvard Law Review* 91(5):1056-89.

Trigg, Roger. 1973. *Reason and Commitment.* London and New York: Cambridge University Press.

Vallance, Elizabeth. 1974. "Hiding the Hidden Curriculum." *Curriculum Theory Network* 4(1):5-21.

Van Brummelen, Harro. 1989. *Curriculum: Implementation in Three Christian Schools.* Grand Rapids, MI: A Calvin College Monograph.

Van Til, Cornelius. 1974. *Common Grace.* Philadelphia: Presbyterian and Reformed Publishing Company.

Vitz, Paul C. 1986. *Censorship: Evidence of Bias in our Children's Textbooks.* Ann Arbor, MI: Servant Books.

Walsh, Brian J., and J. Richard Middleton. 1984. *The Transforming Vision: Shaping a Christian World View.* Downers Grove, IL: InterVarsity Press.

Walsh, W.H. 1963. *Metaphysics.* London: Hutchinson University Library.

Ward, Keith. 1983. "Is Autonomy an Educational Ideal?" *Educational Analysis* 5(1):47-55.

Warren, Michael. 1987. "Religious Formation in the Context of Social Formation." *Religious Education* 82(4):515-28.

Watson, Brenda. 1987. *Education and Belief.* Oxford: Blackwell.

Weaver, R.M. [1948]1971. *Ideas Have Consequences.* Chicago: University of Chicago Press.

West, E.J. 1970. *Education and the State: A Study in Political Economy.* 2nd ed. London: Institute of Economic Affairs.

Westerhoff, John H. 1976. *Will Our Children Have Faith?* New York: Seabury.

– 1983. *Building God's People in a Materialistic Society.* New York: Seabury.

White, J.P. 1972a. "Indoctrination and Intentions." In *Concepts of Indoctrination: Philosophical Essays*, ed. I.A. Snook, 117-30. London: Routledge & Kegan Paul.

– 1972b. "Indoctrination without Doctrines." In *Concepts of Indoctrination*, ed. I.A. Snook, 190-210. London: Routledge & Kegan Paul.

- 1973. *Towards a Compulsory Curriculum*. London: Routledge & Kegan Paul.
- 1982. *The Aims of Education Restated*. London: Routledge & Kegan Paul.
White, P.A. 1972. "Socialization and Education." In *Education and the Development of Reason*, ed. R.F. Dearden, P.H. Hirst, and R.S. Peters, 113-31. London: Routledge & Kegan Paul.
- 1983. *Beyond Domination*. London: Routledge & Kegan Paul.
White, Ralph. 1986. "The Anatomy of a Victorian Debate: An Essay on the History of Liberal Education." *British Journal of Educational Studies* 34(1):38-65.
Whitehead, Alfred North. [1925]1967. *Science and the Modern World*. New York: The Free Press.
Wiebe, D. 1980. "Philosophical Reflections on Twentieth Century Mennonite Thought." In *Cultural and Literary Essays Dealing with Mennonite Issues*, ed. Harry Loewen, 149-64. Winnipeg: Hyperion.
Wiebe, Phillip H. 1988. *Theism in an Age of Science*. Lanham, MD: University Press of America.
Wilson, John. 1964. "Education and Indoctrination." In *Aims in Education: The Philosophic Approach*, ed. T.H.B. Hollins, 24-46. Manchester: University Press.
- 1972a. "Indoctrination and Freedom." In *Concepts of Indoctrination*, ed. I.A. Snook, 101-5. London: Routledge & Kegan Paul.
- 1972b. "Indoctrination and Rationality." In *Concepts of Indoctrination*, ed. I.A. Snook, 17-24. London: Routledge & Kegan Paul.
Wittgenstein, Ludwig. [1969]1972. *On Certainty*. ed. G.E.M. Anscombe and G.H. von Wright; trans. G.E.M. Anscombe. New York: Harper & Row.
Wolfe, David L. 1982. *Epistemology: The Justification of Belief*. Downers Grove, IL: InterVarsity Press.
Wolterstorff, N. 1976. *Reason Within the Bounds of Religion*. Grand Rapids, MI: Eerdmans.
Wood, D.J. 1980. "Cognitive Development." In *Developmental Psychiatry*, ed. M. Rutter, 230-44. Washington, DC: American Psychiatric Press.
Wringe, Colin. 1981. *Children's Rights*, London: Routledge & Kegan Paul.
Young, Michael F.D., ed. 1971. *Knowledge and Control: New Directions for the Sociology of Education*. London: Collier-MacMillan.
Young, R.E. 1984. "Teaching Equals Indoctrination: The Dominant Epistemic Practice of our Schools." *British Journal of Educational Studies*, 32(3):220-38.
- 1988. "Critical Teaching and Learning." *Educational Theory*. 38(1):47-59.
Zylberberg et al. v. Sudbury Board of Education, 29 A.O.C. 23; 65 O.R. (2d) 641, consd. (1988).

Index